Edible Medicines

Edible Medicines

An Ethnopharmacology of Food

NINA L. ETKIN

The University of Arizona Press   Tucson

The University of Arizona Press
© 2006 The Arizona Board of Regents

First paperback printing 2007
ISBN 978-0-8165-2748-9 (pbk. : alk. paper)

Library of Congress Cataloging-in-Publication Data
Etkin, Nina L. (Nina Lilian), 1948–
    Edible medicines : an ethnopharmacology of food / Nina L. Etkin.
        p. cm.
    Includes bibliographical references and index.
ISBN-13: 978-0-8165-2093-0 (hardcover : alk. paper)
ISBN-10: 0-8165-2093-3 (hardcover : alk. paper)
    1. Food habits. 2. Food preferences. 3. Ethnopharmacology.
4. Traditional medicine. 5. Alternative medicine. 6. Nutrition. I. Title.
GT2850.E874 2006
394.1'2—dc22   2005035995

Manufactured in the United States of America on acid-free, archival-quality paper
and processed chlorine free.

15   14   13   12   11   10   6   5   4   3

To my husband, Paul Ross,

for fueling this and all my other ambitions

and inspiring me in ways he cannot imagine

Contents

Illustrations and Tables

Photographs

Tables

Acknowledgments

I gratefully credit collaborations on Hausa research with Paul Ross and Malam Ibrahim Muazzamu. I acknowledge the people of Hurumi Village who taught me so much about Hausa medicine and who inspire my broader reflections on the meanings of food, medicine, and health. I thank Chris Szuter for encouragement from the time of this book's inception, too long ago, and Allyson Carter, Harrison Shaffer, and the other energetically professional staff of the University of Arizona Press.

Edible Medicines

Introduction

Let your food be your medicine, let your medicine be your food.
—Hippocrates (ca. 460–377 BCE)

HOW FOODS INFLUENCE HEALTH has customarily been studied within such disciplines as food science and nutrition, biochemistry, medicine, and agriculture. Although much has been documented regarding the protein, calorie, vitamin, and mineral values of foods, until recently little attention was accorded their "nonnutritive"[1] qualities. This discrepancy derives from the tendency in the West to divide scholarship into increasingly specialized courses of study in which curricular requirements do not leave much room for cross training. This is apparent, for example, in conventional studies that inventory medicines or foods but do not consider that an item may not be simply one or the other. In fact, virtually all societies use plants and animals in more than one way, as food, medicine, and cosmetics. Little attention has been paid to the pharmacologic potential of diet. Until the recent and rapidly escalating interest in functional foods and supplements, since the 1980s (see chapter 7), foods were regarded as virtually chemically inert, thus of no salience to disease processes.

This book is about the health implications of foods, items drawn from the cuisines (foodways) of diverse groups who invoke both cultural traditions and ongoing transformative experiences to describe the merits of particular foods and their combinations. My interest is to draw attention to the pharmacologic potential of foods in the specific cultural contexts in which they are used by peoples around the world. I take into account the complex dynamics of food choice, as well as the blurred distinctions between food and medicine. The objective is not, like so much contemporary interest in healthful foods, entrepreneurial or persuasive of some regime or other: my point is not to identify foods from which one can develop "health products." Instead, I advance a multidimensional perspective that resonates the dialectic between culture and nature and helps us to understand the health implications of people's food-centered actions in the context of real-life circumstances. I draw on an extensive literature that transects such themes as food and culture, the history of medicine, ethnopharmacology, food history, nutrition, and human evolution, and I offer as well insights from my research on the food and medicine of the Hausa of Nigeria, including previously unpublished findings.

Theoretical Frameworks: Biocultural and Coevolutionary Perspectives

This work is framed by the theoretical idioms of a human ecology that addresses the cultural constructions and social negotiations of diet as well as the physiologic implications of food and eating. This biocultural perspective views human health as affected by both the ideational elements that shape human-food interactions (e.g., the ideas and symbols that inform the identification and combination of foods) and the biological consequences of food consumption. This people-centered approach is more comprehensive than the theoretical domains of other disciplines that study food and health. The medical and biological sciences, for example, focus narrowly on the chemical composition of foods (see chapter 2). This is evident today as more and more foods, including many familiar to the Western palate, earn the imprimatur of bioscientists who report experimentally and clinically confirmable healthful actions. In some chapters, I extend discussion to issues of political economy and globalization, to emphasize that the cuisines of diverse human groups have been shaped in part by uneven access to resources and the subordination of some sociopolitical entities by others.

Another theoretical perspective that helps us to understand food pharmacology in context is coevolution, the processes by which reciprocal evolutionary changes occur in interacting species. This book is primarily about plants, which offer a significantly greater pharmacologic potential than do animal foods (see chapter 6). Intuitively we understand that plants, which lack the mobility and behavioral repertoires available to animals, would evolve various capabilities to escape predation (e.g., toxins) and aid reproduction (e.g., attractants for pollination and seed dispersal). But why would those constituents or structures benefit people as well?

That question draws attention to a suite of evolutionary adjustments that have developed among complex assemblages of plants and animals, including humans. A simple point of departure is that the world is biologically complex: no organism can be understood outside the context of its place in nature and the other organisms that share that environment.

Plant Metabolism

Secondary Metabolites or Allelochemicals

Plants assimilate simple substances such as minerals and atmospheric gases and synthesize the complex organic molecules necessary for reproduction, growth, and differentiation into specialized tissues and organs. Most plant physiology is mediated by biochemical pathways that are functionally distinguished as primary or secondary. Primary metabolism is considered essential to normal cellular function, for example, biochemical pathways involved in respiration, the oxidation of carbohydrates to provide energy, water, and carbon dioxide; photosynthesis, the use of chlorophyll and solar energy to produce carbohydrates from water and carbon dioxide; and protein synthesis, the transcription of DNA (genes) and its modification into messenger RNA, translation of messenger RNA in the ribosome, and delivery to the ribosome of transfer RNA bearing amino acids that are translocated and link in sequence to create peptide chains. Nucleic acids (RNA, DNA), L-amino acids, fatty acids, and the like are primary (or intermediary) metabolites and are similarly or identically synthesized and used throughout the biological world. For most plants as few as sixteen essential mineral nutrients provide the raw material for primary metabolic synthesis of all cellular components, including membrane and cell-wall constituents, proteins, hormones, vitamins, and other complex constituents (Table 1.1).

While secondary[2] metabolites have no known direct function in basic metabolism, they are not merely waste products, as was once argued. Earlier generations of phytochemists interpreted the role of these divergent pathways as only a mechanism to prevent accumulation of potentially toxic intermediate compounds. The idea that secondary metabolites are artifacts of metabolism without biological function has turned up recently in another form, redundancy, which refers to multiple functions

TABLE 1.1. Essential Mineral Nutrients in Plants

Essential minerals	Role in primary metabolism
Carbon, hydrogen, oxygen	structural foundation of all organic molecules
Nitrogen	part of proteins, nucleotides, chlorophyll, many other essential compounds
Molybdenum	controls nitrogen assimilation
Phosphorus	energetic bonds (ATP), membranes, nucleic acids
Sulfur	component of the essential amino acids cysteine and methionine, which are constituents of most proteins; vitamins biotin and thiamine; cell membranes; coenzyme A
Chlorine, magnesium, manganese, potassium	photosynthesis, enzyme reactions, protein synthesis
Iron	chlorophyll synthesis and respiration
Calcium	cell wall structure, stabilizes membranes, regulates many metabolic processes
Copper	photosynthesis, some hormones, enzyme cofactor
Zinc	enzyme cofactor
Boron	influences calcium metabolism

Sources: Cotton (1996); Stern (1997)

of one compound and the presence of two or more classes of phytochemi-cal in the same plant. The notion of redundancy as mere superfluity—a duplication of effort, thus inefficient—perpetuates a simplistic view of metabolism. It misunderstands the complexity of adaptations that require simultaneous or serial preparedness to compete with a variety of other plants, attract pollinators, and deter herbivores.

A perspective that better represents the reality of plants in nature casts redundancy in a positive light and interprets the diversity of phytochemi-cals through the lens of adaptation. Although the details of how com-pounds produced by one species influence other organisms may not be known, "it is increasingly evident that many organisms have highly cou-pled interactions with other organisms" (Jarvis and Miller 1996: 267).

Among contemporary theoretical and applied biologists, there is great interest in understanding how complex systems develop and function, and a growing body of evidence demonstrates that broad-spectrum biological activity, diverse and multiple functions, and synergism contribute to versatility (Harborne 1993; Romeo et al. 1996; Dyer et al. 2001; D'Ovidio et al. 2004).

Many of the more than 100,000 (Howe and Westley 1988) nonprimary metabolites that have been characterized in higher plants are biologically active in ways that are critical to plant survival. The less prejudicial term *allelochemical* replaces *secondary metabolite* and refers to signal substances of one species that influence the contemporaneous or future "growth, health, [reproduction,] behavior, or population biology of another species (excluding substances used only as food by the second species)" (Whittaker and Feeny 1971: 757). Concentrations of allelochemicals, indeed all phytochemicals, vary considerably among species, populations, and individuals and among tissues of the same individual. Much of the variability in concentration is genetically determined but can be significantly modified by environmental circumstances such as aridity, ultraviolet exposure, temperature, diurnal and seasonal cycles, soil composition, and the presence and density of other plants and animals (Björkman and Larsson 1991; Arnason et al. 2004). Allelochemicals' particular bioactivities are integral to mutualistic relationships among plants and between plants and other organisms. These natural products are allelopaths (see next section), insect and vertebrate antifeedants, defenses against pathogens and other injury, pheromones,[3] phytoalexins (antimicrobials produced in response to the entry of disease-producing entities), and signal chemicals.

The Role of Allelochemicals in Plant Defense and Reproduction

Protection of Space

Competitors for limited resources pose a fundamental threat to plants. Allelopathy is the means of assuring that a plant keeps other plants out of its space and refers generally to the effects of chemicals released from plants, including microorganisms, on other species in geographic (but not necessarily temporal) proximity. Allelochemicals may alter the amount of chlorophyll or otherwise interfere with photosynthesis in a potential competitor or infuse substances into the environment that interfere with seed germination and maturation of other plants. A plant may release volatile protective chemicals in the form of a gas through small openings in the leaf. In addition, some protective chemicals stored in the leaves or other organs of a plant leach into the soil after the organs drop and decompose. Finally, defensive chemicals exuded through the roots of one plant may be absorbed by those of another.

Protection against Herbivory

Plants have evolved a variety of defenses against herbivory by insects and vertebrates as well as by pathogenic microorganisms. Mechanical protection on plant surfaces is provided by spines that repel larger herbivores, for example, on edible cacti such as *nopales* (prickly pear, *Opuntia* spp., Cactaceae). In other plants, needlelike trichomes and glandular hairs combine physical and chemical deterrence by trapping insects, such as those on the pubescent leaves of some kidney bean cultivars (*Phaseolus vulgaris* L., Fabaceae) and potato and tomato leaves (*Solanum tuberosum* L. and *Lycopersicon esculentum* Miller, Solanaceae).

Phytochemical defenses are of two broad types: complex polymers and phytotoxins. Complex polymers deter feeding by reducing palatability and/or digestibility. Cellulose, hemicellulose, and pectin, which make up more than 85 percent of plant dry weight, are poorly digested, if at all, by carnivores and omnivores. Herbivores can digest these molecules because they have evolved structural and metabolic adaptations that depend on slow microbial fermentation of these complex sugars by symbiotic microflora. Lignins, which give shape to woody tissues and strengthen others, are themselves indigestible and further diminish digestibility by binding to carbohydrates and digestive enzymes in the gut. Tannins obstruct animal digestion by binding to food proteins and impeding the action of digestive enzymes and gut-wall proteins. Finally, inorganic silica, which is integral to carbohydrate metabolism and a common component of plant cell walls, cannot be digested by animals. Fossil evidence illustrates that these polymers and crystals have provided both structure and defense for plants for hundreds of millions of years (Howe and Westley 1988). These quantitative chemical defenses function in a generic and dose-dependent manner: the more polymers and silica present in a plant tissue, the more nutrient poor it is and the better its defense against herbivory.

Phytotoxins generally are developed selectively or stored in tissues not yet protected by lignins or silica, that is, immature leaves, buds, and fruit. They are chemically simpler than polymers, and many phytotoxins antagonize specific biochemical pathways. Except to animals that have evolved specific defenses, these qualitative toxins are poisonous when present in more than low doses. Compared to the polymers that confer generalized defense, phytotoxins are inexpensive to produce, representing less than 2 percent of plant dry weight.

Aposematic (warning) coloration (or smell, structure, and other features), a well-known defensive phenomenon in animals, has attracted little attention in plants. Like their faunal counterparts, aposematic plants sequester unpalatable or toxic substances from animals and/or plants rather than or in addition to producing their own defensive substances. Mimetic plant and animal species evolve the same organoleptic (perceived by the senses) characteristics but sequester less toxin (they merely mimic the truly toxic species). In another permutation, cryptic species do not sequester toxins but appear toxic because of color, structure, and other organoleptic characteristics (Howe and Westley 1988; Harborne 1993). Apparency (conspicuousness), unpalatability, warning coloration or structures, and mimicry and crypticry are keystones in understanding the coevolutionary relationships among species.[4]

Any given plant is likely to have several to many mechanical and chemical defenses that vary by tissue type, age, and growing conditions. Constitutive defenses offer permanent protection. These are intrinsic (preformed) compounds that are toxic, repugnant, and/or antimicrobial. Most constitutive defenses are phytochemicals but may be structural barriers or proteins as well. Induced defenses are physical or toxic deterrents that are produced after attack (herbivory) or infection. These may be localized in one or a few cells around the point of injury or systemic responses that affect the whole plant and result either in increased responsiveness to future attack or increased constitutive defenses. Many of the same phytochemicals that function in defense against herbivores are also antimicrobial. However, despite the common structural and functional features of plant defenses, studies of specific plant-herbivore and plant-pathogen relationships have not led to obvious generalizations. In any case, how a phytochemical influences human physiology may or may not be relevant to how that metabolite functions for the producing organism (Hammerschmidt and Schultz 1996).

Attracting Pollinators and Seed Dispersers

Signal chemicals attract herbivores to plants and to particular plant tissues, thus contributing to plant reproduction. Volatile compounds are released from flowering plants and, along with other stimuli, attract pollinators, especially insects. These chemicals may signal food, such as nectar, pollen, and fruit. Some plants have evolved means of deceit through visual and/or chemical mimicry (see aposematic species) to appear attractive to herbivores, who disperse seeds, although the plants do not offer nutrient value comparable to the species they mimic. Through these adaptations, plants are assisted in cross-fertilization and seed dispersal.

Basic Allelochemistry

Allelochemicals are a diverse group of phytochemicals that primarily belong to four chemical classes, as shown in Table 1.2. The following brief overview only begins to evidence the great phytochemical diversity among plants, including both medicines and foods. This genotypic and phenotypic variety is the "critical currency of ecological interactions and evolution" (Romeo et al. 1996: v).

Nitrogen Compounds

Nitrogen is a component of many primary and secondary plant compounds. Alkaloids, the largest class of allelochemicals, are chemically highly diverse and serve plants in a variety of functions. In tomato and potato, alkaloids (tomatine, demissine) act as feeding deterrents for leaf eaters such as the Colorado beetle (*Leptinotarsa decemlineata* Say, Chrysomelidae) and protect plant tissues from molds. Similarly, caffeine in coffee (*Coffea arabica* L., Rubiaceae) and kola nut (*Cola nitida* [Vent.] Schott and Endl., Sterculiaceae) is an antifeedant that kills larvae and causes sterility in some insects (see chapter 5). In humans, alkaloids commonly are associated with dramatic physiologic activities. For example, narcotic analgesics such as morphine (poppy, *Papaver somniferum* L.,

TABLE 1.2. Allelochemicals

Chemical class	Biological activity	Distribution
Nitrogen compounds		
Alkaloids	psychotropic, toxic	widespread in angiosperms
Amines	hallucinogenic, insect repellent	widespread in angiosperms
Cyanogenic glycosides	toxic	scattered in leaves and fruit
Nonprotein amino acids	toxic	widespread, especially in Fabaceae
Phenolics		
Flavonoids	antifungal	universal in vascular plants
Lignins	indigestible for animals	universal in vascular plants
Phenols	antimicrobial	universal in leaves, other tissues
Quinones	antimicrobial	widespread in vascular plants
Tannins	bind protein	widespread in plants
Sulfur compounds		
Acetyl-thiophenes	toxic	Asteraceae
Disulfides	insecticidal, antimicrobial	*Allium* spp. (onion, garlic)
Glucosinolates	insecticidal	Brassicaceae (mustard family)

Source: Cotton (1996)

Papaveraceae) relieve pain and induce sleep; central nervous system stimulants such as caffeine increase mental alertness; stachydrine (e.g., in alfalfa, *Medicago sativa* L., Fabaceae) is cardiotonic; and boldine (e.g., in sassafras, *Sassafras albidum* [Nutt.] Nees, Lauraceae) is diuretic (Hammerschmidt and Schultz 1996; Newall et al. 1996).

Phenolics

The chemically diverse phenolics also exhibit a range of biological activities, and all contain an aromatic ring in which one position (or more) is occupied by a hydroxyl group (–OH). The largest group, flavonoids, confer protection against ultraviolet light, microbial infection, and herbivory. Many food constituents that have important health implications are flavonoids. Quercetin (e.g., in aniseed, *Pimpinella anisum* L., Apiaceae; eucalyptus, *Eucalyptus globulus* Labill., Myrtaceae) is anti-inflammatory; apigenin (e.g., in fenugreek, *Trigonella foenum-graecum* L., Fabaceae; lemon verbena, *Aloysia triphylla* [L'Her.] Britton, Verbenaceae) is antispasmodic; astragalin (e.g., in hops, *Humulus lupulus* L., Moraceae) stimulates the immune system; glabrol (e.g., in licorice, *Glycyrrhiza glabra* L., Fabaceae) is bactericidal; and catechol (e.g., in onion, *Allium cepa* L., Liliaceae) is antifungal (Hammerschmidt and Schultz 1996; Newall et al. 1996; Harborne and Williams 2000).

Sulfur Compounds

Many sulfur-containing compounds are feeding deterrents. These metabolites include the disulfides of *Allium* species, including garlic (*A. sativum* L.) and onion. Allicin, for example, is antioxidant, antimicrobial, anticoagulant, and cancer protective and lowers blood sugar and cholesterol (Borek 2001; Ross et al. 2001; Aggarwal et al. 2004). In the Cruciferae (mustard family), glucosinolates are present in mustard (*Brassica nigra* [L.] Koch); rapeseed (*Brassica napus* L.); kale, collards, broccoli, and cauliflower (*Brassica oleracea* L.); radish (*Raphanus sativus* L.); and watercress (*Nasturtium officinale* R. Br.). Sinigrin in cabbage (*B. oleracea* L.) attracts aphids (Aphididae) and some butterflies but deters other insects, such as the swallowtail butterfly (*Papilio* spp., Papilionoidea) (Harborne 1993). These allelochemicals are cancer protective through inhibition of phase I enzymes that activate many carcinogens and induction of phase II enzymes that enhance excretion of carcinogens. Sulfur-containing compounds have antimicrobial properties as well (Rose et al. 2000; Tolra et al. 2000; Drewnowski et al. 2001; Fahey et al. 2001; Rouzaud et al. 2004).

Terpenoids

Botanical terpenoids are a diverse class of chemicals that have at least one isoprene unit (an unsaturated five-carbon hydrocarbon, with a branched chain). The lower terpenoids (averaging ten to fifteen carbons) are distinctively volatile, with strong pungent odors, such as the aromatic oils of basil (*Ocimum basilicum* L., Labiatae) and the mints (*Mentha* spp., Labiatae). Monoterpenoids and sesquiterpenoids are the most common constituents of flower scents and serve plants as feeding attractants that assist in pollination. Cucurbitacins B and E in squash and cucumber (*Cucurbita pepo* L. and *Cucumis sativus* L., Cucurbitaceae) are repellant to a wide range of herbivores. The terpenoid β-selinene is a defense chemical in celery (*Apium graveolens* L., Umbelliferae). Triterpenoids in watermelon (*Citrullus lanatus* [Thunb.] Matsum. & Nakai, Cucurbitaceae) attract beetles, and essential oils in fennel (*Foeniculum vulgare* Miller, Umbelliferae) attract butterflies (Harborne 1993). The active portions of saponins are water-soluble and characteristically produce foam (reducing the surface tension of water), making this subclass easily recognizable both for this feature and for bioactivity. For example, saponins in spinach (*Spinacea oleracea* L., Chenopodiaceae) and oats (*Avena sativa* L., Poaceae) increase and accelerate the absorption of some digestion-enhancing compounds such as calcium and silicon. Soybean saponins (*Glycine max* [L.] Merr., Fabaceae) are antimutagenic (Berhow et al. 2000). Another terpenoid, ursolic acid, is diuretic and anti-inflammatory and has antitumor and anti-HIV effects; it is present in *maté* (*Ilex paraguariensis* St. Hil., Aquifoliaceae; see chapter 5), almond (*Prunus dulcis* [Miller] D. Webb), and rosemary (*Rosmarinus officinalis* L., Labiatae) (Diaz et al. 2000; Hollosy et al. 2000; Kashiwada et al. 2000; Takeoka et al. 2000).

Chemical Mediation of Mutualistic Relationships

This overview of the role of allelochemicals in the life of plants is only a one-sided depiction of the complex mutualisms that characterize real ecosystems. For their part, herbivores have evolved adaptations to overcome plant defenses and outreproduce competitors. One countermeasure is the microflora of ruminant and other herbivore guts, which promotes digestibility of high-polymer and high-fiber plants. Some insects have evolved means for detoxifying the specific protective chemicals of plant species on which they regularly feed. In addition, generalized enzyme systems protect many herbivores against a wide variety of phytotoxins. Mixed-function oxidases, for example, are easily inducible after exposure and protect herbivores against a broad range of chemicals, which permits them to select foods from a wide variety of plants (Howe and Westley 1988). Some herbivores use allelochemicals for their own defense, for example, the larval stage of the cinnabar moth (*Tyria jaco-baeae* L., Arctiidae), which feeds on *Senecio* spp. (e.g., South African spinach, Asteraceae), accumulates alkaloids (e.g., senecionine) that later protect the adults against bird predators. Feeding attractants that encourage pollination provide invertebrate herbivores a safe food. More than just drawing in pollinators, flower volatiles stimulate insect behavior related to their own needs, such as feeding and mating (see chapter 6). Some plants produce chemicals that are integral to the life cycles of herbivores, such as sex pheromones and juvenile and molting hormones that regulate larval maturation and insect development. Much of the animal behavior that overlaps these signal chemicals is innate, but some aspects of plant-animal interactions are learned, as is the case in virtually all people-plant relationships.

This draws us back to coevolution, which refers to changes in the genetic makeup of a species that can be attributed specifically to the presence of another species. For example, Ehrlich and Raven (1964) described the relationship between butterfly species and the plants on which they feed, noting that toxic compounds produced by the plant influence which butterflies feed on it. There is a great deal of suggestive evidence for such animal-plant interactions. Critics caution, however, using the same example, that this does not substantiate that toxin production by a plant evolved in response to herbivory by that particular butterfly. Instead, some of these associations may have evolved together and may be better explained by a theory of plant apparency.

Feeny (1976) and Rhoades and Cates (1976) postulated that plants that are easily located by herbivores produce digestibility reducers, complex polymers or silica crystals, for defense against all herbivores. Thus, perennials tend to invest heavily in generalized protection. In contrast, plants of lower apparency, rare and short-lived species, produce qualitative toxins that are poisonous to all but specialist herbivores at lower metabolic cost. The apparency principle extends to plant structures as well. Allelochemicals and mechanical defenses tend to occur more often and in higher concentrations in structures most accessible to herbivores, for instance, external tissues such as bark and leaves. Protective chemicals are found as well in reproductive structures, for example, in immature phases and in the stone but not the edible portion of fleshy fruit. Relatively high concentrations also may exist in the vascular system, the xylem and phloem that conduct food and water through plants, which is a common mode of entry for microorganisms. Evidence does support the apparency principle, but it is not likely that a single explanation covers all patterns of plant defense; plant morphology and chemistry are subject to multiple, sometimes opposing, selection pressures.

Coevolution and its refinement by apparency provide a theoretical backdrop that helps us to understand the chemical diversity of plants. Coupling that with a biocultural perspective expands our comprehension of the bases and consequences of human plant use.

Subsistence from Evolutionary and Cross-cultural Perspectives

Subsistence strategy refers to the ways that human groups manage their physical environments, a centerpiece of which is food-getting. While subsistence is shaped in part by what kinds of plants and animals are available in a particular environment—in view of constraints imposed by temperature, climate, rainfall, topography—the physical environment is not determinative. Human population size and, most significantly, culture, also give form to food-getting design. This section reviews the range and variety of food-getting systems to suggest how health is influenced by diets that are variably positioned along these continua: proportion of plant versus animal and wild versus domesticated foods, versatility versus monotony of diet, sedentary versus migratory lifestyles, and low versus high technology inputs. The major subsistence categories, foraging, pastoralism, horticulture, agriculture, and industrial food production and globalization, are discussed here in order of complexity. This implies no necessary progression from one to the other (foragers do not necessarily become farmers), offers no insights regarding the relative merits of one economy or another in a given circumstance, and recognizes the existence of mixed subsistence economies throughout human history. To illustrate possibilities and outcomes, this short discussion necessarily simplifies the complexity of the continuum of human-plant interactions (Harris 1989; Etkin 1994a: 2–3).

Hunting and Gathering (Foraging)

Tools and Fire

Over the long course of human evolution, several major processual transformations in subsistence occurred, each associated with significant increases in population size. The first transformation resulted in a suite of biological and cultural adaptations and involved the most important "extrasomatic milestones" (James 1989) in early human evolutionary history: the production of stone tools and the management of fire. Stone tools conferred on early hominids an advantage over other animals in protection, food acquisition, and the capability to make other material objects, which further advanced adaptation to diverse environments. Control of fire played an analogous role by extending hominid range; providing warmth and light, which extended human activities and promoted sociability into the night; assisting in hunting; and, most significantly, enabling us to alter the character of foods and assure their safety and preservation.

The earliest stone artifacts in the archaeological record are associated with the late Pliocene and early Pleistocene 2.5–1.5 million years ago. Although the earliest use of fire is still debated, most researchers agree on the controlled management of fire by *Homo erectus* in the Middle Pleistocene about 0.5 million years ago (a recent study suggests 790,000 BCE), and actual hearths appeared in Neanderthal (*H. sapiens neanderthalensis*) sites of the late Middle Pleistocene, 128,000 years ago (James 1989; Goren-Inbar et al. 2004). These early food technologies relaxed the selective advantage of large masticatory structures and complex digestive systems.[5] Tools assisted in eliminating tough plant and animal tissues and in reducing the size of chewable food portions. Heating and cooking reduced profoundly the toughness and potential toxicity of foods, including food spoilage, and increased the absorbability of nutrients. Later refinements that included water-containing and other cooking vessels reduced the amount of grit and contaminants that made food chewing difficult.

Moist cooking fosters a greater diversity of flavors and recipes, and transition to this mode of food preparation would have contributed significantly to greater palatability and the diversification of individual dishes and meals and finally of cuisines.

At the end of the Pleistocene, about 14,000 years ago, the melting of glacial ice contributed to profound changes in weather and environment worldwide: sea levels rose, forests expanded into grassy steppes and Arctic tundra, and animal habitats and migration routes were modified. Humans intensified their hunting and gathering efforts, taking advantage of a wider variety of foods, including hundreds of potentially edible plants. All early foragers relied exclusively on wild plants and animals and were otherwise culturally differentiated by patterns of residence (e.g., sedentary, nomadic, seasonally nomadic), habitat (e.g., steppe, forest, island), and range (traveling in pedestrian, equestrian, or aquatic modes). Foraging both depended on and further promoted social interactions, especially cooperative ones, including the division of labor, provisioning, and food sharing. As food production became more common, about 10,000 years ago, farming and herding peoples crowded foragers from the range of fertile valley, plains, and hill environments into the marginal areas (tundra, mountain, and desert ecosystems) that most contemporary hunter-gatherers occupy today. Some foragers began to rely heavily on horticulture and subsequently returned to foraging. Today, most foragers are partly dependent on food production (primarily horticulture) or outside food producers (Kent 1996; Bates 1998).

The Diets of Contemporary Hunting-Gathering Populations

Overall, it appears that late Pleistocene peoples had diverse and plentiful diets and were healthy with low rates of infectious and chronic illness (Hole 1992). With limitations, the diets of contemporary hunting-gathering populations represent a reference standard for early humans, as well as a model for defense against diabetes, cardiovascular disease, and other so-called diseases of civilization. Research among contemporary hunter-gatherers over the last few decades has eroded the caricature of egalitarian forager societies. Instead, forager ideologies vary along an egalitarian-hierarchical continuum so that material transactions, including of foods, result in symmetries and asymmetries of exchange that influence access to nutritious and medicinal foods (Gibson 1988). From the perspective of health, two generalizations about foragers' diets are especially salient.

First, foragers' diets include a range of plant and animal resources that provide sufficient proteins, vitamins, minerals, calories, and trace elements. As species diversity tends to increase along a cold-warm gradient, the diets of tropical foragers typically include a broad range of animal and plant species. Some temperate-climate foragers also exploit a broad diversity of resources; for example, along the North Pacific coast (United States and Canada) native peoples access land, sea, and freshwater resources (wild plants and berries, sea mammals, salmon [*Oncorhynchus* spp., Salmonidae] and other fish, mountain goats [*Oreamnos* spp., Bovidae], birds).

Second, the contribution of animal products to total calorie intake in past foragers' diets—as well as whether animals were hunted and/or meat, fat, and marrow scavenged—is an issue of continued debate (Stanford and Bunn 2001), with estimates ranging from 10 percent to more than 50 percent (e.g., Cordain et al. 2000). The possibility that some hunter-gatherers consume substantial amounts of animal products has captured the imagination of many who are eager to speculate about our past, especially to reflect on what the popular media portray as hunting-centric subsistence cultures. The fact remains, however, that even where a substantial proportion of caloric intake may be derived from animals, the remainder of foods still are botanicals, through which people are exposed to significant pharmacologic potential.

Pastoral Economies

Pastoralists gain their livelihood by raising domesticated livestock in areas that are not suited to arable farming. Their lifestyle is either trans-humant, part of the group moves between specific locations at certain times of year, or nomadic, the whole group follows the irregular movements of their herds throughout the year. Pastoralists tend not to kill (many of) their own animals for food but make foods high in protein, fat, and calories by using large quantities of milk (commonly fermented; see chapter 4) and, in some East African societies, blood. When one or a few animals are sick or sacrificed for other reasons, the meat and other products are shared in patterns of reciprocity that redistribute valuable food resources among the population, creating ties of mutual obligation that are analogues to food-sharing in nonhierarchical foraging groups.

Diets of Contemporary Pastoralists

Most contemporary pastoralists either grow grains or purchase them with the profits from selling livestock or animal products. Pastoral groups along the Nile in Africa catch fish and grow grains. Exclusively milk- and meat-based diets are still common in the Asian steppes but are more rare in Africa. Among both traditional pastoralists and hunter-gatherers, the health risks of high protein, energy, and fat consumption (cardiovascular disease, elevated cholesterol, diabetes, cancers) are offset by the inclusion in the diet of less apparent, yet pharmacologically active, plants. For example, the plants that the Maasai and Batemi of East Africa and Australian Aboriginal peoples use as soup ingredients, garnishes, and masticants contain phytochemicals that have hypoglycemic, antioxidant, anticarcinogenic, and cholesterol-lowering effects (Johns and Chapman 1995; Chapman et al. 1997; Johns et al. 2000; see chapter 5). Today, many nomadic pastoralists settle near towns as a result of dependence on market economics, political instabilities, diminishing pasture lands, and loss of livestock to drought. This results in dietary shifts from high milk and mixed-species pastoralist consumption patterns to sedentary alternatives that include high fat and carbohydrates. Health and nutrition profiles worsen, especially among children, who experience anemia and other indicators of malnutrition, slowed growth, and diminished resistance to infectious disease (e.g., Shell-Duncan and Obiero 2000; Barkey et al. 2001).

Food Production: Horticulture and Agriculture

Around 10,000 years ago, when foraging was still the predominant subsistence form, people's environmental management began to shift radically. The second major transformation in subsistence occurred with the advent of food production during the Neolithic and is variably associated with sedentary lifeways, polished (rather than flaked) stone tools (e.g., axes), domesticated animals and/or plants, and pottery. This New Stone Age was a process, not a moment or revolution, of discovery that lasted thousands of years. Between 12,000 and 9000 years ago, in a few locations

and scattered across all landmasses and some islands people began to cultivate plants—in equatorial Africa, Southwest Asia, the Southeast Asian
mainland, lowland and highland South America, and Central America.
They domesticated (controlled the reproduction of) wild plants that dis-
played desirable characteristics such as flavor, fruit size, productivity,
leafiness, and ease of harvest. Animal domestication (control over food as
well as reproduction) occurred several thousand years later and centered
on the selection of such characteristics as milk production, herdability,
meat quality, suitability for traction and other work, resistance to disease,
and protection and/or companionship (Table 1.3; see chapter 6).

Domestications and the development of agriculture were not driven
simply by the pursuit of staple crops, superfoods that provide the bulk of
calories and anchor the cuisine, but also by such cultural categories as
palatability, aesthetics, and ritual function. For example, archaeological
sites that correspond to the time of incipient agriculture (at least 5000
years BCE) include evidence of domesticated flavorings, such as chile
pepper (*Capsicum annuum* L., Solanaceae) in Mexico and caper (*Cap-
paris spinosa* L., Capparidaceae) in the Mediterranean region (Farrington and Urry 1985; see chapter 3).

Even at the local level, the transformation of human foodways over
time and space has been complex, nonlinear, neither purposive nor uni-
directional, and not a "natural" and inevitable move away from what
the philosopher Thomas Hobbes characterized as a "nasty, brutish,
and short" hunter-gatherer lifestyle. All permutations along a foraging-
agriculture continuum have been possible, and some smaller number of
all possibilities is visible today among diverse peoples of the world. Contemporary foragers, for example, include groups who both deliberately
cultivate and otherwise manage small forest plots on a short- or long-term
basis (Schelhas and Greenberg 1996), and their small-scale agriculturalist
counterparts use a great variety of wild plants (Etkin 1994b; Fowler 1999;
Gollin 2001). Further, it is likely that most plants were domesticated more
than once, as experiments failed, interest in particular species was redi-
rected, and trial and error gradually reinforced the desired characteristics.

Although uncommon, domestications from wild species still occur
today in natural settings (i.e., not assisted by biotechnology). For example,
in Tlaxcala, Mexico, *Lycianthes moziniana* (Dun.) Bitt. (Solanaceae) is
an agrestic (occurring spontaneously in cultivated fields) herbaceous pe-

rennial that farmers value for its fruits but do not cultivate. This preferential treatment created an incipient phase of domestication and led to the promotion of *L. moziniana* as one with "new crop potential" (Williams 1993). Similarly, Hausa in Nigeria—in the context of what is otherwise highly intensive agriculture—foster species that technically are wild (are genetically different from cultigens) as well as semiwild species that are not deliberately cultivated but whose occurrence and form are influenced by human action. Since 1975, colleagues and I have conducted research on diet and traditional medicines, including ethnoveterinary medicine, in Hurumi (a pseudonym), a rural village on the Nigerian savanna, southeast of Kano City.[6,7] When one of our team most recently visited Hurumi, paved roads and electricity had not yet reached the village and piped water had been introduced only recently, lifestyle circumstances closer to the traditional than the cosmopolitan end of a modernity continuum. Hurumi's subsistence base is intensive, primarily nonmechanized agriculture that centers on *gero*/millets (*Pennisetum* spp., Poaceae), *dawa*/sorghum (*Sorghum* spp., Poaceae), *gyada*/peanut (*Arachis hypogaea* L., Fabaceae), and *wake*/cowpea (*Vigna unguiculata* [L.] Walpers, Fabaceae). This production is supplemented by wild plant collection, cultivation of *ganye*/leafy greens, small-scale livestock management, some cash-cropping, and trade in locally produced items such as leather goods and fiber mats and in exotic commodities such as medicinal plants and salt.

The following figures reveal the significance of wild and semiwild species in Hausa medicine and food. Of the 264 locally growing plants used as medicine, 89 percent (235) are semiwild and embody significant diversity in both species and pharmacology. Only 11 percent (29) of local medicinals are cultivated. Semiwild plants from farm borders are used across the range of locally designated uses, such as food, medicine, and cosmetics. Sixteen percent of the semiwild medicinals used locally are collected from farm borders. Another 27 percent of the semiwild medicinals are extracted from public lands. These include areas reserved for cattle grazing, as well as borders of some of the larger paths that link hamlets. These never-cultivated areas afford public access year-round to botanically diverse vegetative cover. One would have anticipated this extent of diversity in the mixed-vegetation farm borders and public lands. Paradoxically, most of the local semiwild medicinal plants (46 percent)

TABLE 1.3. Origins of Some Domesticated Plant and Animal Foods

Region	Plants	Animals
Near East, western Asia	cabbage (*Brassica oleracea* L., Cruciferae) cantaloupe (*Cucumis* sp., Cucurbitaceae) cherry (*Prunus* sp., Rosaceae) date (*Phoenix dactylifera* L., Palmae) grape (*Vitis vinifera* L., Vitaceae) lentil (*Lens culinaris* Medik., Fabaceae) oats (*Avena sativa* L., Poaceae) olive (*Olea europaea* L., Oleaceae) pea (*Pisum sativum* L., Fabaceae) rye (*Secale cereale* L., Poaceae) wheat (*Triticum* spp., Poaceae)	cow (*Bos* sp., Bovidae) dog (*Canis* sp., Canidae) goat (*Capra* sp., Bovidae) sheep (*Ovis* sp., Bovidae)
China	millet (*Pennisetum* spp., Poaceae) mulberry (*Morus* spp., Moraceae) rice (*Oryza sativa* L., Poaceae) soybean (*Glycine max* [L.] Merr., Fabaceae) tea (*Camellia sinensis* [L.] Kuntze, Theaceae) walnut (*Juglans* spp., Juglandaceae)	pig (*Sus* sp., Suidae) silkworm (*Bombyx* sp., Bombycidae)
Southeast Asia	banana (*Musa* spp., Musaceae) breadfruit (*Artocarpus atilis* [Z] Fosb., Moraceae) citrus (*Citrus* spp., Rutaceae) coconut (*Cocos nucifera* L., Palmae) sago (*Metroxylon* spp., Palmae) sugar (*Saccharum officinarum* L., Poaceae) taro (*Colocasia esculenta* [L.] Schott, Araceae)	chicken (*Gallus* sp., Phasianidae) water buffalo (*Bubalus* sp., Bovidae)
Sub-Saharan Africa	coffee (*Coffea arabica* L., Rubiaceae)	guineafowl (*Numidia* sp., Numinididae)

TABLE 1.3. *Continued*

Region	Plants	Animals
	millet (*Pennisetum* spp., Poaceae) oil palm (*Elaeis guineensis* Jacq., Palmae) sesame (*Sesamum indicum* L., Pedaliaceae) sorghum (*Sorghum* spp., Poaceae) yam (*Dioscorea* spp., Dioscoraceae)	
Central America	beans (*Phaseolus* spp., Fabaceae) maize (*Zea mays* L., Poaceae) papaya (*Carica papaya* L., Caricaceae) pumpkin (*Cucurbita* spp., Cucurbitaceae) squash (*Cucurbita* spp., Cucurbitaceae) sweet potato (*Ipomoea batatas* [L.] Lam., Convolvulaceae)	turkey (*Meleagris* sp., Meleagrididae)
South America	amaranth (*Amaranth* spp., Amaranthaceae) cassava (*Manihot esculenta* Crantz, Euphorbiaceae) peanut (*Arachis hypogaea* L., Fabaceae) pineapple (*Ananas comosus* Merr., Bromiliaceae) potato (*Solanum tuberosum* L., Solanaceae) tomato (*Lycopersicon esculentum* Miller, Solanaceae)	guinea pig (*Cavia* sp., Caviidae) llama (*Lama* sp. Camelidae)
North America	goosefoot (*Chenopodium album* L., Chenopodiaceae) squash (*Cucurbita* spp., Cucurbitaceae) sunflower (*Helianthus annuus* L., Asteraceae)	turkey (*Meleagris* sp., Meleagrididae)

Sources: Clutton-Brock (1992); Price (2002)

FIGURE 1.1. Young Hausa man planting millet at the beginning of the rainy season in Hurumi, northern Nigeria. Photo by Paul J. Ross, 1988

FIGURE 1.2. Nina Etkin and her associate, Ibrahim Muazzamu, drying medicinal and food plants in Hurumi for future ethnopharmacological research on antimalarial activity. Photo by Paul J. Ross, 1988

FIGURE 1.3. A Hausa family in Hurumi weeding what will become a mixed plot of guineacorn and beans. Some semiwild medicinal species are deliberately overlooked during the weeding as well as collected from farm boundaries, shown in the background. Photo by Paul J. Ross, 1988

are extracted from village farms. These are plants that a farmer recognizes for one or more uses; they are deliberately overlooked during weeding to ensure their availability for existing or anticipated needs (Etkin and Ross 1994).

Wherever researchers explore, we find that wild and semiwild species not only contribute significantly to diet (both macro- and micronutrients; e.g., Grivetti and Ogle 2000) but also embody substantial pharmacological potential that has, in many cases, been bred out of their cultivated counterparts (e.g., Fleuret 1986; Etkin 1994b; Johns 1996; Moreno-Black et al. 1996; Mapes et al. 1997; Cunningham 2001; Marshall 2001; Pieroni 2001; Stepp and Moerman 2001; Vieyra-Odilon and Vibrans 2001; Johnson and Grivetti 2002; Wang et al. 2003).

Once established, agricultural practices spread quickly worldwide.

This management of plants and animals for human purposes was, after fire, the "greatest harnessing of the world's natural energy" (Hole 1992: 377). As people controlled domesticates throughout their life cycles, yields increased and crops became more homogeneous. A dependable food base permitted enormous population growth, a reshaping of the family and other social units, and the division of labor and its diversion to nonsubsistence activities such as trade, art, technology, and other specialized occupations. Foods themselves were transformed from wild to domesticated, and the uses of foods were extended beyond their nutritive (and medicinal) value. Surplus could be exchanged for labor and goods; used as social and political currency, to feed animals, and to appease deities; and accumulated as reserves.

Horticulture (extensive cultivation) is low-technology food production in which people maintain mixed (intercropped) gardens, tend small domesticated animals (e.g., chickens [*Gallus* sp., Phasianidae], pigs [*Sus* sp., Suidae]), and forage for a small proportion of their subsistence. Slash-and-burn field management includes cutting natural vegetation and burning it to fertilize new crops. This practice results in rapid depletion of soil nutrients, followed by fallowing a field until natural growth restores soil nutrients and moving food production to new plots (shifting cultivation). Agriculture (intensive cultivation) involves a population subset of full-time farming specialists and is distinguished by the management of larger plots and the production of a smaller number of high-yield crops, augmented with irrigation and the use of traction animals and fertilizer. Industrial agriculture is characterized by its larger scale, the use of machinery in place of work animals, and more extensive use of irrigation, herbicides, and pesticides.

A later transformation of human food systems coincided with the era of European expansion (e.g., the Crusades) and exploration and was accompanied by population increases. Local domesticates and other plants were distributed across the globe as a consequence of trade and exploitation of cultures in Asia, Africa, and the Americas. In the modern era, continued migrations and diasporas contribute to the global circulation of foods of all kinds, thus exposing many and varied human populations to a large number of phytochemicals with diverse pharmacologic potentials (see Unique Tastes Become Transcultural Flavors: The Case of Chile in chapter 3; chapter 5).

Diet and Health of Food Producers

The diets of horticulturalists, especially those living in tropical environments, tend to be varied, as garden plots reflect the surrounding botanical diversity. As agriculturalists become dependent on a diminishing number of species, however, dietary diversity contracts significantly. Historically, the hunter-gatherer diet high in animal protein was replaced by one in which carbohydrates dominated, primarily milled and cooked seeds and tubers. Whereas pre-Neolithic populations derived about 50 percent of their food energy from vegetables and fruits from one hundred or more individual species over the course of one year, for cereal-dependent subsistence farmers plants contributed only 20 percent or less to caloric intake, and the number of species consumed by farmers was substantially smaller than one hundred (Eaton et al. 1997). Precise figures vary, but estimates cohere around figures that suggest that 7000 plants have been used for human food (3 percent of the total that exist in the world) throughout human history, 90 percent of foods are derived from twenty species, and more than 50 percent from three genera in the family Poaceae: rice (*Oryza sativa* L.), maize (*Zea mays* L.), and wheat (*Triticum* spp.). Whatever the actual numbers, this evidences significant dietary compression over time.

Dietary changes that attended the shift to agriculture have been linked to declining health. Specifically, protein-deficiency and some vitamin-deficiency diseases increased. Oral health was diminished by, for the first time in human history, a high incidence of tooth decay and gum disease. Over the longer term, the chewing of softened and otherwise refined foods contributed to third-molar irregularities and weakened jaw muscles, resulting in misaligned teeth (e.g., overbite). Reliance on a small number of cultigens and eroding knowledge of wild species increased the probability of famine resulting from the failure of just one, or a small number of, crops. Selection for palatability (see Making Sense of Sense) especially had the effect of diminishing allelochemicals, thus some pharmacological potential was sacrificed for preferred tastes. Population growth fostered crowd infections such as malaria, measles, smallpox, and other important pathologies that cannot survive in foraging and other small populations. Sedentary lifeways further encouraged the spread of communicable diseases, as well as environmental modification and contamination with infectious agents and pollutants. Finally, diet quality and health generally were compromised by the social and political asymmetries forged by labor specialization and uneven access to property and goods.

Agribusiness, Industrial Food Production, and Globalization

Over the last 200 years, food productivity has been shaped by the mechanization of agriculture and growth of the commercial food industry. In the modern era, basic foods are technologically transformed by the agrifood industries through extraction, substitution, concentration, and preservation. Worldwide, shifts in food use involve a growing delocalization of food production, processes by which food varieties and their strategies for production and consumption are dispersed throughout the world in increasingly complex networks of sociopolitical and economic interdependency. Commercial entities and global marketing shape diets in which a growing proportion of the items consumed originate in distant places. The present trend toward genetic manipulation of foods and related advances in biotechnology will continue to affect people's food productivity and dietary constructions into the future (see chapter 7). Current interest in food pharmacology is part of this latest transformation.

Diet and Health in the Modern Era

Foods and food processing in contemporary affluent populations include a vast array of commercially produced items whose natural origins are ambiguous. Despite the increased diversity of products available, those consumed in highest proportion contain high concentrations of sugar or sweeteners, salt, fats, and refined grains. A vast literature—both scientific and popular—records the complex relationships of these dietary excesses to hypertension, obesity, elevated cholesterol, cardiovascular diseases, and cancers. The quality of contemporary diets is further compromised by diminished fruit, vegetable, and fiber intake and by sedentary lifestyles. Among affluent populations in the West, and increasingly elsewhere, there is growing apprehension of these insalubrious consequences of the long-term nutrition transition. One corollary of this concern is the contemporary profusion of research on food pharmacology and so-called health-food products (see chapters 2 and 7).

Identifying the Edible and Medicinal

The Interpretation of Organoleptic Qualities

People's evaluations of foods and medicines, especially new items, are based substantially on their organoleptic characteristics (those perceived by the sense organs), which convey information about visual appearance, taste, smell, tactile sensations, satiety, temperature, and even sound. The discussion of allelochemicals earlier in this chapter provides phytochemical context here, as an item's desirability as food bears more on its secondary than its primary metabolites, which tend to be organoleptically less remarkable. Sensory experience is not merely receptive but highly interpretive as well. It is refined by the interrelations among polysensory and cognitive factors that are influenced by genetics, age, sex, diet, circumstances of health (including medication), individual and group experiences, and cultural (re)constructions of the meanings and measure of organoleptics.

Sight

The appearance of a food is typically the first attribute that we use to judge it. Immediately important appearances include color, shape, and texture. The more closely we examine items, the more we process nuances of shade, apparent ripeness, and so on. For already-known foods, appearance can heighten anticipation, such as the dusky blue of a ripe blueberry (*Vaccinium* spp., Ericaceae) or the shiny green peel of a Granny Smith apple (*Malus* spp., Rosaceae). Appearance can also discourage selection: consider the same apple with a withered, brown peel. In some cultures yellow corn never makes good tortillas, whereas white always does. Visual texture creates expectations, alerting the other senses to chemosensory, olfactory, and tactile anticipations—an observation that only begins to suggest how complex the senses are, individually and especially as they function in concert to provide the basis for a holistic appraisal of an item.

Taste

The broad definition of taste is the perception of flavor, which technically is a combination of true taste—sensations that derive from receptors on the tongue and palate—and smell. In humans, taste receptors are located in the membranes of thirty to fifty epithelial (skinlike) cells that cluster to form the taste buds contained within the bumps and grooves on the tongue surface, as well as the soft palate, tongue root, and upper throat. These taste cells communicate with sensory nerves that convey taste sensation to the brain.

Classical primary tastes are distinguished as sweet, salty, sour, and bitter. Other proposed primaries are astringent (although this is more accurately a composite of chemically generated tactile sensations); piquant or pungent, prominently in Chinese cuisines (e.g., chile pepper)[8], and *umami* (loosely from the Japanese, "delicious taste"), which is both a taste and a flavor-enhancing sensation attributed to monosodium glutamate and ribosides (alternative terms include meaty, brothy, and savory) (Bellisle 1999; Lawless and Heymann 1999; DuBois 2004). Sweet taste generally is associated with positive affect and safe foods, whereas bitter is at least initially a negative signal, often associated with toxic foods. The preference for sweet and salty foods arises early in childhood and tends to wane during late adolescence. Preference for sour taste is less well understood but may follow a similar pattern (Liem and Mennella 2003). Combinations of primary tastes create synergies, masking, and other interactions to yield a broad range of taste sensations, all of which are further modified by genetic influences, the physiology of illness and aging, and experience and learning. Thus, a continuum model of sensations better represents human sensory integration than do catalogues of discrete flavor categories (Hladik and Simmen 1996).

The Hausa verb *ci*, to eat, is a root metaphor that structures other tropes, especially those that overlap sex and reproduction, and Hausa folklore and proverbs are rich in references to eating and tasting. For example, in the story *Tatsuniya Daddawar Batso*, all the characters are tastes: *daddawar batso*, a pungent fermented soup base (see chapter 4); *gishiri*, salt; *ganyen albasa*, onion leaves; *barkono*, chile pepper; and *nari*, a peanut-based food. In the storyline and through its message, *daddawa* prevails despite her off-putting surface appearance (Ritchie 1991). In the same tone, this Hausa proverb captures the centrality of consuming and tasting as reliable means to gauge something or someone: *Gani ba ci ba*, seeing is not eating. In other Hausa proverbs the gustatory metaphors sweet (*zaki*) and bitter (*daci*) distinguish truth (*gaskiya*) and lies (*karya*), although when nuanced by irony, truth also can be bitter (*Gaskiya daci gare ta*). Other Hausa gustatory idioms that are related to chile pepper are discussed in chapter 3.

The use of tastes, including their combination, is one way in which people express the cultural identity of their foods: marking with a particular flavor is both a way to facilitate the introduction of novel staple foods (Stalberg-White and Pliner 1999) and a vehicle by which new foods are transformed into the familiar (see cuisine, below, and chapter 3, spices).

Smell

Through the sense of olfaction, we perceive the greatest diversity of flavors. When we inspire air, we inhale odor molecules that bind to receptors in the nose. Similarly, foods in or passing through the mouth are distinguished by different types of odor molecules, which stimulate various combinations of receptors to produce what we identify as discrete smells. Outside of the flavor and fragrance industry, there is no simple schema for odor terms. However, there is general agreement about these quality categories for smells: spicy, sweet (vanilla [*Vanilla planifolia* Jackson, Orchidaceae]), citrus, fruity (noncitrus), woody/nutty, green, floral, minty, and herbal/camphoraceous (Lawless and Heymann 1999: 56). The great diversity of odors and the fact that the olfactory nerves connect to portions of the brain that are closely associated with affect, emotion, and memory suggest the complex subtleties of taste and smell and the various ways in which they shade the meanings of food.

Texture

How a food feels is apprehended through rheological (geometric) and structural (surface) characteristics that are perceptible by both touch and sight. For example, the thickness (viscosity) of guacamole is conveyed by sensations in the mouth, by gauging resistance while stirring the puree with a spoon, and visually. Some textural concepts appear to be common across cultures, such as crunchy, soft, juicy, and creamy. Others, such as fluffy, springy, moist, and crisp-tender, are culture-specific or otherwise more nuanced (Booth et al. 2003). Hausa in Nigeria assign food quality in part based on distinctions between the *kauri* (thickness) and *tsinkewa* (thinness, of soups and porridges) or more general terms such as *laushi* (soft). Anderson (1988: 155) described *ts'ui* texture as "the most vital and distinctive goal of Chinese [food preparation] . . . the texture of something very fresh and at its prime, cooked just enough and no more . . . a texture offering resistance to the teeth followed by a burst of succulence," such as fresh asparagus, briefly cooked fresh fish, just-ripe fruit. These examples remind us of the holistic nature of sensory apprehension (see synaesthesia, below).

Hearing

Foods are described with reference to auditory texture as well. The crispness of breakfast cereals, a crunchy bite into an apple, the soft plop of yogurt spooned into a dish, and the fizz of carbonated and fermented beverages all have both tactile and auditory qualities. Hausa listen for the crackling sound of crushed medicinal leaves that encourage eruption of measles rash (see Making Sense of Sense) or for a solid echo from thumped calabashes that are used to hold medicines of the postpartum (when the womb resonates its emptiness). In these examples, the sound alone is not sufficient but becomes the mimetic device that embodies composite information, such as ripeness and strength, that overlaps issues of phytochemistry, which vary according to a plant's maturity and freshness.

Making Sense of Sense

Organoleptic qualities are culturally extended to enrich the meanings of foods, and there is significant cross-cultural variation in the interpretation of chemical and other stimuli (Brett and Heinrich 1998; Johns 1996). Reactions to foods range along a proximal-distal continuum. At the proximal end, foods that elicit rapid affect are readily identified as acceptable or not. Virtually all people favor sweet and reject bitter tastes and tend to form immediate impressions of specific foods with those tastes. An intermediate, delayed response, such as nausea, is less contiguous temporally and may be generalized beyond the item in question to a class of foods. This is a categorical rather than specific response. At the distal end, the timing and specificity of a food experience is more removed, and the likelihood is low that a food will be accepted or rejected on the basis of its food, medicinal, or other merits. For example, foods that do not generate a specific and rapid outcome offer more subtle clues regarding their value. These relationships are complicated by learned tastes for otherwise unpalatable qualities, such as the burn of chile pepper and the bitterness of coffee. Rozin's (1982, 1990) pioneering research on organoleptics and food selection illustrated how the strongly aversive capsaicin of chile pepper, which triggers pain receptors in the nose and mouth, becomes a valued, even cuisine-defining flavor. In the context of learned tastes, we should not be surprised that chile pepper—universally unpalatable to children and potentially troubling even for seasoned consumers—is a desired food item for many populations (see chapter 3). Here, an aversion is deliberately transformed into a liking, even a preference, and is context specific.

A common link between food plants and diseases is the taste that defines their curing properties. Tastes and smells that do not meet palatability standards for food may be selected as medicines; for example, bitter, strongly sour, astringent, and other such remarkable tastes are common selection criteria for medicines in a variety of medical traditions (Etkin 1986; Johns 1996). Consider this complex example. Hausa practitioners advise that the treatment of measles be aimed at several stages, beginning with efforts to expel disease substance from the body interior. As soon as the measles spots appear, bitter and astringent foods and medicines are sought to chase out internal sores so that the rash matures. Foods and medicines used later in the therapeutic progression are cold and aromatic because the illness "likes" those qualities. In the event that nausea and fever accompany the rash, acid and sour tastes are indicated to calm and cool. When there is evidence that all sores have been externalized (i.e., when other internal signs such as fever and lymphatic inflammation have subsided), the rash is treated with astringent and emollient medicines, no longer with medicinal foods (Etkin 1994c). In this example, taste features prominently in the selection of medicinal foods.

Finally, taste or whole-food aversions may develop out of extrafood experiences, typically foods associated with unpleasant contexts, such as illness or social disharmonies. These are learned, experiential, or acquired antipathies. Psychologists take advantage of this potential in behavior-modification therapies that treat food disorders and substance addictions. This section underscores that foods are viewed simultaneously as cultural objects and as biodynamic substances: their pharmacologic potential both transcends and contributes to their cultural meaning.

Sensational Medicines: The Therapeutic Sensorium

A growing literature on sensory ecology has documented how pervasive olfactory judgment is in the identification and assessment of medicinal and food species (Shepard 2004). This reinforces the merits of biocultural perspectives that link bioscience and traditional empirical knowledge by connecting the cultural constructions of food and medicine to physiologic properties and activity.

The Hausa sensory lexicon for medicines is substantially more elaborate than that for foods. Their assessment of the healthful qualities of foods is generally imprecise and nonspecific, referring, for example, to a food or food category that is "good for you," "makes the body strong," or "fortifies the blood." In contrast, medicinal plants are understood to neutralize internal cold, promote disease egress through the skin or mouth, dislodge phlegm, externalize rashes, and so on. This applies as well to species that are in other contexts foods, such as cosmetics, for which purposes these descriptive details are not invoked. Taste is an especially important signal for some disease categories or symptoms. Bitter species, for example, are called on for febrile and gastrointestinal disorders. Invoking bitterness may also serve a mnemonic function, marking plants that not only are bitter but also have antimicrobial actions that underlie some fevers and gastrointestinal symptoms (Etkin and Ross 1982).

Among the Ndembu of Zambia diviners are distinguished not only by extraordinary vision but also pronounced sensitivity to sound and to tactile stimuli. Gustatory and olfactory modalities play minor roles in divination (Andermann 1991).

The Kenyah Leppo'Ke of Borneo regard botanicals that have more apparent chemosensory properties to be more effective medicines, favoring astringent plants for gastrointestinal disorders and bitter ones for fevers. The novel sensory quality *nglidah*, which describes a subgroup of their foods and medicines, is phytochemically linked to highly volatile terpenoid compounds that are strongly pungent and impart to nglidah species a citruslike smell and taste (although *Citrus* spp. themselves are not part of this category). This complex sensory stimulus combines what in English would be "a rich and spicy, mildly peppery flavor with a trace of anise, clove and mint" (Gollin 2001: 305, 2004).

Matsigenka in Amazonia gauge the utility of individual plants by paying attention to a wide range of signals, such as color, shape and habit, taste, smell, and surface texture. They understand that strong and unpalatable or irritating qualities (e.g., caustic, sour, bitter, astringent) are mirrors to the plant's spirit owners and representations of the plant's healing power, which repels or reduces agents of illness. Another Amazonian group, the Yora, use spined plants to treat fever, pain, inflammation, and other disorders that are metaphorically linked to wasps (Shepard 2004).

Gustatory and olfactory signals characterize most of the medicinal plants used by Tzeltal Maya in Chiapas, Mexico; specific tastes and smells are used consistently to manage discrete illness categories (Brett 1994). Among Yucatec Maya and in Popoluca, Mexico, gustatory and olfactory signals and qualities such as astringency, bitterness, and pungency distinguish medicinal from other plants and identify illness classes for which those species are efficacious. For example, fever and pain are treated with aromatic species, and gastrointestinal disorders are treated with astringent and aromatic species (Leonti et al. 2002).

These examples stand in rather stark contrast to Western dietary and medical idioms in which the other-than-visual senses have been muted for the last few centuries. Moreover while Western languages distinguish discrete senses and discrete kinds of each sense (see Taste), in other cultures foods and medicines are synaesthetic, that is, blending tastes and smells and linking the qualities of one sense with that of another. For example, in Brazil, Desana boys' purification rituals include a tune whose odor is male, its color red, and its temperature hot; shamans select medicinal plants with primary attention to vision and secondarily to taste, smell, and temperature, which are derivative of the primary color energies (Classen 1991). Apprehension of a food, medicine, or anything else is nuanced and substantially enriched through the use of multiple senses.[9]

Metaphors and Meaning of Food and Medicine

Other ideas about food originate in the social order and bear on status, authority, identity, reciprocity, and other relationships—some aspects of which are interpreted through organoleptic qualities. Biological hunger is culturally reconfigured into appetites called *cuisines*, which represent complex cycles of pattern and social process. Foods not only nourish but also convey meaning about people's perception of the universe and their place in it: "Food presents a rich symbolic alphabet through its diversity of color, texture, smell, and taste; its ability to be elaborated and combined in infinite ways; and its immersion in norms of manners and cuisine" (Counihan and van Esterik 1997: 2). Foods' symbolic resonance is profound, and in all cultures certain items are designated for the celebration of life-cycle events, specific ages, genders, and religions; to mark emotional states and the circumstances of ill health; to identify power or mask wealth; and for consumption in the context of rites of passage.

The apprehension of bananas by Kanak peoples reinforces this point. "True" or "ancient" bananas (the subgroups Popoulou and Maoli, Pacific plantains, *Musa* spp., Musaceae) were introduced at the time of the original peopling of the New Caledonia archipelago. They are the body and animating force of ancestral spirits and are integral to Kanak religious and social relations. Different clones of these species are identified by discrete morphologies, and groups of several clones are assigned to different clans. They are cultivated in sacred places and close to domiciles and gardens, where they protect people and crops; the leaves are fashioned into incubators for newborns and are part of composite fortifying medicines. The ancestral bananas also play a central role in social and political exchanges, such as the movement of goods between fishing and horticultural communities, women between allied clans, and gifts in the celebration of life-cycle transitions. The "other" bananas (dessert bananas, subgroups Cavendish, Figue-Pomme, Mysore) were introduced much later by Europeans during the missionary and colonial eras and by groups from Asia, other parts of Oceania, and elsewhere. These are valued primarily as food and are eaten every day as a favored gathered food. Secondarily, these bananas are a cash crop that is sold both on a small scale by roadsides and through commercial networks (Kagy and Carreel 2004).

Balance

Among the abstractions that people apply in their assessment of foods are patterns of binary opposition such as heating-cooling and wet-dry. These are intrinsic qualities not related to the actual thermal or hydrous state and characterize most natural (biotic) entities, including foods and medicines, diseases, and emotions. Binary oppositions express health as a balance between certain key qualities, which can be mediated by diet and medicine (note the Hausa examples, above). The principles avoid extremes, and the selective use of opposites guides people's actions.

In China, for example, heating-cooling is perceived on five levels (cold, cool, mild, warm, hot): cooling foods such as carrot (*Daucus carota* L., Umbelliferae) and seaweed (e.g., *Rodophyta* spp., Bangiaceae) restore equilibrium in the case of rash, constipation, and other hot disorders, whereas hot foods such as adzuki bean (*Vigna angularis* [Willd.] Ohwi & Ohashi, Fabaceae) are designated for cold disorders such as difficult labor and kidney disease (Simoons 1991; Yi et al. 1999). This general kind of food therapy also characterizes the medical traditions of India, Southeast Asia, South America, the Near East, parts of Africa, and much of Europe, although the attributes ascribed to particular foods and diseases vary across and even within cultures. In China these binary oppositions intercalate with older traditions that symbolize the more cosmic yin-yang philosophy, take into account the Taoist theory of Five Phases (earth, metal, fire, wood, water), and address the concepts of *pu*, strengthening or patching up, and *qi*, intrinsic (life-force) energy. Hausa understand some illnesses as disproportions of hot (*zafi*) and cold (*sanyi*). The disorder sanyi is more common during the dry season and is caused both by environmental (morning dew, rain, wind) and social features (disjunctions, jealousies among individuals or communities). Sanyi is a particularly high risk during the early postpartum and after a boy's circumcision (see chapters 3 and 4). Similarly, the accumulation of phlegm (*majina*) may be expressed as joint pain or gastrointestinal disorders, and excesses of salt (*gishiri*) and sugar (*rake*) can eventuate in obstructions (*zaki*), including difficult childbirth (*nakuda*). Although these are only a few simple examples, they make the point that the healthful qualities of foods are manifold and are integrated in complex ways into different food cultures.

Signals

The doctrine of signatures is a generic organizing principle that understands physical characteristics as signals (signatures) of the utility of a particular item for food, medicine, and other applications. The signature resides in the shape of a plant or any of its parts (e.g., a thorn) or its color, odor, growing location (e.g., near water, at a crossroads), or aspect (e.g., quivering leaves). For example, in Taiwan, where red connotes spirit protection, red chicken eggs are eaten to assure fertility. Many medical traditions promote citrus and other yellow fruit for the treatment of liver disorders accompanied by jaundice, in which the skin and whites of the eye take on a yellowish tone. Hausa encourage pregnancy with plants that bear many flowers or fruit and with medicines made from animals that produce multiple offspring. In many European traditions, walnuts (*Juglans* spp., Juglandaceae) are associated with mental acuity based on the appearance of the brainlike kernel. Typically, these connections are not as simple as suggested here. Although appearance and other physical attributes are presented as the primary distinguishing feature of certain medicinal foods, their modes of action are complex. They are understood to interfere with disease processes in diverse ways that have to do with other characteristics that different medical cultures describe through such metaphors as strength and neutralization.

Food in Celebration

Foods and their configuration as specialized items, feasts, and signals for the end of fasts are the centerpiece of celebrations in virtually all cultures. Some mark religious and other calendrical events, evoking expectations for certain foods in specific preparations, such as Thanksgiving dinner in the northeastern United States (turkey, oyster dressing, cranberry sauce, acorn squash, pumpkin pie, apple cider); celebrations of lunar cycles in Kashmir (many and variably spiced meat dishes, lotus and other seasonal vegetables, rice, green tea); Carnaval in Brazil (rice balls, saffron chicken, rice with dried beef, nutmeg sweetbread, candied fig); New Year in China (seafood and dumplings signify good wishes, prawns invoke liveliness and happiness, raw fish salad brings good luck and prosperity, and *fai-hai* [angel hair] seaweed assures prosperity); and Ramadan in Pakistan (figs with goat cheese, potato chicken, spicy chickpeas, fig-and-lemon chicken, almond-spice starch pudding).[10] In these instances special foods are featured in abundance and commonly are highly flavored, rich (dense with sugar and fat), and involve complex preparation and presentation.

Other foods and food combinations mark life-cycle events such as births, naming ceremonies, weddings, and wakes. My research among Hausa in northern Nigeria identified these foods that mark a boy's circumcision: *kunun kanwa*, an everyday grain-based gruel (*kunu*) marked with an abundance of the not ordinarily culinary sodium carbonate salt (*kanwa*/natron); fresh *tuwo*, another everyday grain-based dish, but this one an iconic superfood; *nama*, meat of goat, chicken, cow, or sheep, all of which appear very sparingly in the diet; *kanwa* (a homonym of natron), a rich dish made with the boiled head and legs of chicken, goat, and sheep plus the compound spice *yaji* (see chapter 3); and *kayan kwadayi*, desirable foods, especially rich foods characterized by high oil or fat and sugar content. Some of these foods also overlap the category "warm foods," foods that are filling, nutritious, and healing. Interestingly, the same foods with other rules of behavior are invoked for women in the early postpartum (chapters 3 and 4). In the case of Hausa cuisine, foods identified for special occasions are not so much different from daily fare as they are "dressed up": their nutrient component is amplified and especially in the case of kanwa and yaji, the pharmacological potential is heightened.

Avoidance

Food avoidances are a negative aspect of more dynamic, comprehensive, and largely positive theories about diet and health. They range from casual, perhaps episodic, dismissal of an item to formal taboos that mark ethnic, class, and other social boundaries. Food prescriptions and proscriptions (taboos) forge group identity both by reinforcing shared values and by juxtaposing one's own group vis-à-vis others who are characterized by, among other things, different diets. Other food taboos more directly overlap health issues as proscriptions that mark phases of the life cycle, such as pregnancy, lactation, infancy, weaning, circumcision, puberty, menstruation, menopause, and old age. In Thailand, when a wound becomes infected, sour foods are denied because they are understood to encourage the accumulation and retention of pus (Golomb 1985). Similarly, for Hausa, food plants that otherwise are appreciated for the gelatinous quality they impart to soup are avoided when one has congestion from flu and in the case of certain backaches that are understood to be caused by an accumulation of phlegm within the body. These food plants include *kubewa* (okra, *Abelmoschus esculentus* [L.] Moench, Malvaceae) and *gasaya* (cat's whiskers, *Cleoma gynandra* [L.] Briq., Capparaceae). For altogether different associations, Hausa consider peanuts and other kayan kwadayi to aggravate leprosy and offset the effect of medicines for anemia. Whereas these signs, signatures, proscriptions, and prescriptions are powerful symbolic statements, they also have tangible physiologic expressions. I acknowledge the cultural presuppositions that guide food behaviors, and in this book I explore beyond to understand the physical outcomes of culturally constructed behaviors.

The Place for Place

Therapeutic landscapes are settings in which variously construed healthful circumstances promote emotional, social, and physiologic health. These environments are natural (gardens, mountain summits) or have been naturalized through interior and exterior design of constructed places. Therapeutic landscapes resonate especially for populations whose understanding of nature is contiguous with that of society and who regard people as a life form participating in a broader community whose diverse inhabitants are governed by a single set of rules of conduct (e.g., Århem 1996). Plants figure prominently in these places to emblematize health. For example, private and community gardens that are substantiated through particular species and objects (rocks, fountains, statues) and their spatial relationships may project a certain balance or ethical posture that juxtaposes a particular cosmology against, for instance, an unbalanced or otherwise different universe beyond its boundaries (e.g., Gundaker 1994; Konoshima 1994). At present, most attention is paid to the positive effects of people-plant proxemics via passive-visual and participatory-cultivating-cooking interactions (Etkin 1994d, 1996a), including horticultural therapy through gardens for children, the elderly, or immigrant communities; flowers in bereavement and religious rituals; paintings, photographs, and other reproductions of nature; and (re)connections and identity through the restoration of natural landscapes (Giesler 1992; Relf 1992; Shoemaker 2002; Cooper Marcus 2003). Some of the most poignant and scientifically compelling expressions of people-plant proxemics occur in the work of Gary Nabhan (1997). I reiterate throughout this book that the complex outcomes of coevolutionary relationships and the substance of place signifies as much for therapy as does the symbol, text, and gestalt of place; that is, what is physically constituted in plants signifies and contributes to what plants mean.

Cultural Constructions of Cuisine

The term *cuisine* denotes an integrated style of food selection, preparation, presentation, and consumption that is identified to specific geographies and/or cultural groups. There is no "national cuisine" of Indonesia
(or Thailand or Peru) but instead a suite of interdigitated regional and
microregional foodways that share some signature dishes and other common elements and otherwise diverge along geoclimatic and cultural gra-
dients. Discrete cuisines are socially rooted in place and based on locally
produced foods that are (or traditionally were) eaten by a culturally co-
herent group who share a vision of how ingredients should be combined
and prepared; what the appearance, texture, and taste of the finished dish
should be; and how foods should be sequenced in meals and other eating
events.

Each distinct cuisine embraces a series of normative customs and, like
grammars, has standards and rules of practice. The syntax of cuisine
designates oppositions (e.g., salty-sweet), exclusions, and rules of assem-
bly that instruct how individual dishes should be prepared and sequenced
into meals as well as the timing of food events, who can or cannot share
the meal, and what proper table manners are. The meaning of a food
experience issues from its role as a structured social event: sharing food in
the companionable context of a meal provides symbols for the solidarity
of families and other social groups. Snacks, meals, and other food events
that have predictable content and timing reinforce meaning and social
cohesion. Food exchange and circulation mark social connections and
foster alliances.

The cultural construction and social transaction of food and eating
has been the subject of substantial anthropological inquiry. Today, much
of the anthropological study of food centers on issues of gender, body,
identity and voice, political economy, commodification and globalization, and ethics (e.g., Howes 1996; McIntosh 1996; Mintz 1996; Beardsworth and Keil 1997; Caplan 1997; Counihan and van Esterik 1997; Counihan 1999; Plotnicov and Scaglion 1999; Probyn 2000; Atkins and Bowler
2001; Farquhar 2002; Pence 2002). Through that work, we begin to appreciate how locus and praxis—the context and social organization of
eating—extend consideration of physiological actions of foods beyond
empirical statements about pharmacologic action. Moreover, linking to

the subject of this book, the epistemological or psychological effects of foods (as elements of ceremonies, cuisines, and other cultural markers) likely have some physiologic effect, in something of the same way that context of use has been shown to affect drug action or the apprehension of music and the visual arts.

Eating Out, Ordering In

Contemporary urban lifestyles and changing family composition and residence help to erode the structure and meaning of cuisine. Fewer people come together for meals and the number of meal elements and preparation time decline; traditional snacks also have lost structure. Contemporary urban foodways now include an element of peripatetic grazing that typically involves less diversity of foods and features items of low nutrient value. In addition, the increasing use of prepared meals, eating out, and market forces that circulate once-regional foods worldwide may help to offset the declining diversity of diet. In the context of this book, the atomized nature of new food introductions is significant, as these new products are viewed as singlet items and not as part of integrated cuisines.

WHILE CONTEMPORARY BIOSCIENTIFIC IDEAS about the healthfulness of even ordinary foods is more in line with a biocultural (anthropological) perspective, it also resonates earlier biomedical paradigms. This idea is outlined in the next chapter, which gives additional theoretical perspective through overarching themes that have defined the relationships between food and medicine through the history of biomedicine. That discussion serves as foundation for the remaining chapters, each devoted to a different food category.

CHAPTER 2

Food in the History of Biomedicine

> Modern medicine is but a series of commentaries and
> elaborations on the Hippocratic writings.
> —C. Dubos, *Man Adapting*

THIS CHAPTER reviews the major paradigms that have defined the relationships between food and health through the history of biomedicine. I
examine how people understood illness—the underlying cause and processes by which a body becomes disordered—and, by extension, what
preventions and treatments were appropriate. My objective is to forge an
appreciation for how the growth of knowledge about the physical world
was disseminated in a wider sphere, where it influenced a variety of
cultural domains, including scientific ideas, representations of the body,
and authority and agency in health care. This history traces a chronology
of cognitive systems of explanation to emphasize the role that foods have
played in preventive and therapeutic medicine.

Overview

In the early history of Western biomedicine, diet figured prominently in
prevention and therapeutics, but foods gradually came to be regarded as
chemically mundane and of little consequence for disease processes. By
the 1800s biomedicine increasingly focused attention on the specificity of
both disease and treatment and, thus, maneuvered foods outside the domain of therapeutics. Today, however, the diseases that most concern us
in the West, namely cardiovascular disorders, diabetes, and cancers, are
understood to have complex etiologies and imprecise cures. Discrete
explanatory models no longer provide a universally compelling paradigm.
The plasticity of disease comprehension is illustrated by these two quotes
from Louis Pasteur: "the microbe will endure" and "the microbe is nothing: the terrain is everything." The first is emblematic of a scientist who

dedicated his professional life to advancing the theory that disease is caused by microorganisms. The second is attributed to the same Pasteur on his deathbed, purportedly acceding to his nemesis, Anton Bechamp, who emphasized that the host's resistance (determined by general health) would influence the success of an infective agent. This intellectual reconception, if real, anticipated a late-twentieth-century transformation of biomedical perspectives, in which reductionistic views shifted to more comprehensive understandings of the etiology and management of illness. Increasingly, biomedicine regards diet to be an important aspect of disease prevention and, for some conditions, treatment. In a parallel development, we see in lay comprehensions the re-emergence of earlier views of the healthy body as a dynamic equilibrium, holistic (integrative) theories of therapeutics, and a renewed interest in the health potential of foods (Etkin 1996a).

Early Greek Medicine

Hippocrates and Rational Natural Philosophy

The history of biomedicine customarily is traced to Greece and the Hippocratic *Corpus*, some sixty medical texts dating to the fifth to fourth centuries BCE that are united by a common theoretical perspective on medicine. The texts were written by different authors at different times but collectively are philosophically attributed to the physician Hippocrates (ca. 460–377 BCE), who is said to have taken Greek medicine "by the scruff of the neck, shaking out the magico-religious accretions, insisting on the observation and accurate recording of case histories, and, by comparing them, making possible the first systematic differentiation of diseases—as well as setting up standards for doctors (the Hippocratic Oath) of a kind that are still admired and accepted today" (Inglis 1965: 25).

The *Corpus* was the first systematic effort to describe diseases through mechanical and environmental causes that interact with anatomy and physiology. Hippocratic physicians explained disease as a natural process, rather than the product of occult agencies. They advanced the view that opposites cure opposites. This view eventually became allopathy, an intellectual position that directly contrasts the idea that like cures like (i.e., homeopathy), which underpinned the sympathetic-magic explanations of earlier times. Even so, in Greek antiquity this secular medicine co-existed with religious forms of healing; the two were used simultaneously and interchangeably (Siraisi 1990).

Food and the Corpus

Diet was the subject of a discrete treatise, *Nutrition and Digestion* (*Peri trophes*). Moreover, diet regulation was the most prominent element in all the Hippocratic texts, with much attention devoted to dietetics in research notes, case histories, lists of diseases and cures, musings on the scientific method, and therapeutic rationales. A key organizing principle was that all foods contain a single element that, when digested, repairs body tissues and provides energy. In other words, the way that all foods are alike has to do with their ability to mediate disease. More than curing diseases already contracted, physicians hoped to prevent illness, largely by avoiding deficiencies and other limitations of diet.

The essay "Ancient Medicine" (*Peri archaies ietrikes*) differentiated Greek medicine from both philosophy and religion, casting it as a science, a branch of knowledge. The argument was illustrated primarily by examples from dietetics and, to a lesser extent, from topics such as body temperature, configuration of the internal organs, body fluids, and humors (see below). The prominent attention accorded diet was explained by the mistrust of other therapies and by the confidence that dietary regulation is important in both healthy and ill bodies. Indeed, foods were regarded as the source of inspiration for physical medicines. The author of "Ancient Medicine" maintained that wherever medicine was practiced, it should involve some management of diet. Regulating food was complex and involved attention to the selection and proper preparation of the right foods and to issues of balance, as the blending of properties was essential to health (Inglis 1965; Levine 1971).

One historian asserted, "the nutritionist and the dietician can trace their professional ancestry to the Hippocratic Collection, no less than the physician, the nurse, and the pharmacist can" (Levine 1971: 26). A competing interpretation, using the same foundation, is that one can so trace this ancestry only because the writings are inconsistent, having been "all things to all inquirers," and that they center on diagnosis and prognosis and offer "only" palliative treatment and drugs that "would now be off-prescription" (Inglis 1965: 26, 27). This second interpretation echoes a later biomedical perspective that regarded diet as inconsequential to pre-vention and therapy and valued only those drugs over which physicians have prescriptive authority.

The *Corpus* essay "Aphorisms" (*Aphorismoi*) offered delimitations and definitions that include these general pronouncements about diet (Levine 1971): restricted diets and other extremes should be avoided for both the ill and the healthy; diets should be adapted to individual needs; the ability to fast is greatest in old age; diet should be increased in winter and spring, when sleep is longest and the alimentary tract is hottest; liquid diets are suitable for patients with fever; and during the extreme phase of illness, diet should not be altered.

"Epidemics I and III" (*Epidemiai* I and III) recorded varieties of medi-cal treatment including, for the most seriously ill, barley (*Hordeum* spp., Poaceae) soup, honey and water, or vinegar and honey. Extensive discus-sion of how each of these relieves symptoms appears in "Regimen in Acute Diseases" (*Peri diaites oxeon*). The unusual indications for which foods are withheld were carefully outlined as well.

"Regimen II" (*Peri diaites* II) catalogued many other foods, citing nu-tritive and therapeutic values. Among vegetables various brans, beans, and the seeds of cucumber were noted. Valued grains included wheat, barley, oats, and millet. Various fish (e.g., perch [Percidae] and eel [Sepiidae]) and meats (e.g., fox, and dog [*Canis* spp., Canidae]) were identified as good (Levine 1971).

Hippocrates and Humoral Theory

A nascent theory of bodily humors advanced by ancient physicians in the eighth to fifth centuries BCE was fully developed in the *Corpus* as the doctrine of the four humors. This was based in a principle of four ele-ments: earth, air, fire, and water. Their constituent humors were these respective analogues: black bile, blood, yellow bile, and phlegm. Each humor had discrete qualities and was positioned along axes of hot-cold and wet-dry: black bile/cold and dry, yellow bile/hot and dry, phlegm/cold and wet, blood/hot and wet. These humors had to be present in correct proportion to one another to minimize disease risk. Simply, dis-ease was understood as a blockage of inner vessels by a bodily humor; therapy included evacuation of the noxious fluids from "vital areas" of the body.

The maintenance or regaining of humoral balance provided a fundamental, symmetrical coherence for the most comprehensive theological, moral, and metaphorical meanings. Humoral pathology was a set of normative beliefs about health and illness embedded within a larger social configuration of values and ideas that provided order and thus helped people emotionally and cognitively to manage illness. This "model of total continuous intelligibility in the universe" (Young 1978: 4) offered a sort of universal framework in which diseases, tastes, and temperaments could be accommodated (Young 1978; Rosenberg 1997). Although this disease model does not resonate with what was formalized as twentieth-century biomedical theory, it remained the mainstay of European medicine, diet, and hygiene for more than 2000 years.

Dioscorides

In the first century, the physician and botanist Dioscorides (ca. 40–80 CE) produced the five-volume *De Materia Medica*, which catalogued 1000 natural products, primarily botanicals, with 4740 medicinal uses, compiled to identify 360 types of preventive and therapeutic actions (e.g., analgesics, purgatives, contraceptives; Riddle 1985). The scale and empiricism of *De Materia Medica* surpassed that of all earlier works. Compare, for example, Hippocrates's *Corpus*, which included only about 300 discrete drugs (Sonnedecker 1976). Although Dioscorides was not schooled in what we know as formal chemistry and pharmacy (intellectual traditions that developed in later centuries), his classification scheme was based on careful observation of how plants affect human physiology and overlaps what chemists or pharmacists likely would produce. Aptly, Dioscorides has been called the first real pharmacognosist: "He knew the preparation of lead plaster from fats and lead oxide. He mentions the processes of putrefying . . . , of making extracts by maceration followed by evaporation. . . . His remarks on the collection of drugs are excellent, his directions for storage . . . the basis for many later writers" (Sonnedecker 1976: 18).

De Materia Medica was translated into many languages and served as a guide to drugs over the next 1600 years, but it was not a comprehensive medical treatise. Because Dioscorides deliberately steered clear of medical theory, his work was not linked to any of the temporary explanatory

models that succeeded one another into the 1800s. For that reason, Dioscorides's empirical work had a timeless quality; it endured because, on
one level, it did not matter how the problem was explained, as long as the
remedy worked. Many foods were featured in *De Materia Medica*: for
example, chickpea is good for jaundice but harmful for an ulcerated
bladder; barley treats gout; and pickled olives (*Olea europaea* L. Oleaceae) are good for the upper intestinal tract (Riddle 1985).

Claudius Galen

As Hippocrates symbolizes the foundations of Greek medicine, the physician and writer Galen (ca. 130–200 CE) is credited with the apotheosis of
that tradition six centuries later: "Galen remade Hippocrates, of whom he
strongly approved, in his own image" (Siraisi 1990: 4). He synthesized the
best work of all Greek medicine that predated his time, uniting the experiential (empirical) and learned/dogmatic (book-based) schools (Wear
1992). It was essentially this Galenism that was later transmitted to Renaissance scholars in the 1500s. Hippocratic-Galenic medicine contributed to
modern biomedicine not so much a substantive foundation as the principles of naturalistic observation and empiricism.

Galenic physicians transformed humoral theory into a rigid therapeutic dogma based in Galen's testing of drugs qualitatively, with reference to
the axes hot-cold and wet-dry, and quantitatively, according to their effects on humoral balance. Foods as well as medicines were assigned a
valence along these continua and could be manipulated to restore balance and health: cold foods for hot diseases, dry foods for wet diseases, and
so on. If, for example, the affected body part was four units colder and
three units dryer than normal, the therapy had to be four units warmer
and three units wetter if the affected part was situated superficially. If it
was located more deeply, potency was adjusted to account for travel distance and time. Simples were medicines of only one quality (heat, cold,
moisture, dryness), whereas composites had a major and a minor quality.
Entities were medicines identified not by a quality but by their total
substance, which accounted for specific effects as emetics, purgatives,
and the like (Sonnedecker 1976).

Thus, Galenic therapy was based in the complementarity between disease and drug or food, and the character of the medicine was determined

relative to the human body. The medicine causes change in the body because the illness itself is some bodily change, an imbalance, not a separate entity (Temkin 1958). Nature (the environment) and the human body in various states of health are coterminous, their boundaries blurred, one phasing into the other; they are not different kinds of things. Neither is the disease detached from the patient, nor the patient from the world that he or she inhabits (nature). That humanity is inseparable from manifest nature, the "micro in the macrocosm," is more than a philosophical affirmation, it is the "essence of Greek culture" (Galdston 1969: 20), diffusing into medical theory and practice as it did into all aspects of life. The idea of humans as part of nature underpinned prevailing explanatory models of pathology and health and rationalized therapeutics well into the nineteenth century: disease continued to be viewed as a composite of an individual's interactions with the physical and social environment, not a discrete entity or physiological process.

Galen's devotion to certain texts of the *Corpus* was instrumental in the continued interest of later physicians in Hippocratic philosophy. The therapeutic merits of foods are represented in Galen's three-volume *On the Faculties of Foods*, which catalogued in careful detail the uses and effects of virtually all foods and beverages consumed at the time (Sigerist 1961; Grant 2000). A skilled diagnostician and anatomist, Galen was devoted to polypharmacy and experimented extensively to determine which combinations of foods and/or medicines were most effective for specific disorders. He had no professional misgivings about incorporating folk remedies into his writing, and he expected patients also to be knowledgeable in medicine, stressing especially the mediation of health via diet (Inglis 1965). Galen's experimentation and willingness to accept medicines from all sources reflects his perception that the action of a medicine bears on its entirety, not on individual constituents.

The Middle Ages

During the Middle Ages, secular healing was eclipsed by religion in Europe. The ascent of Christianity in late ancient times reflects the lower priority assigned to empirical investigations of nature than to belief in the supernatural and to rhetorical persuasion (Siraisi 1990: 7). Whereas the medicine of Galenic physicians was systematic and rational (although ultimately judged "wrong" by biomedical standards) and brought order to therapeutics, the period that followed was characterized by disarray. No overarching, systematic theory of etiology and therapeutics existed, and no one of equal caliber immediately succeeded Galen. Historians contend that, like other scientific subjects in late antiquity, the field of medicine experienced no important advances in the classification of diseases or knowledge of anatomy, physiology, or therapeutics (Siraisi 1990). Medical learning still flourished during the Middle Ages, however, and by the middle of the sixth century Latin translations of just a few Hippocratic and Galenic texts provided a simplified, abbreviated, and in some cases distorted version of those earlier ideas.

Secular healing increasingly was subordinated to religion. Between the seventh and eleventh centuries medicine survived in western Europe within the realm of monastic communities, while the most significant advances in medical knowledge occurred in the Middle East and Iberian Peninsula, where an amalgam was forged between Greek science and the Islamic traditions.

Influences of Arabic and Other Medical Philosophies

Arabic medicine, with Indian, Chinese, and Persian influences, significantly expanded the principles of Galenic and Dioscoridean medical practice, as it assimilated Greek philosophy into an Islamic intellectual context. From the eighth to eleventh centuries Arab physicians compiled, translated, augmented, and finally codified the classical European medical heritage. The Arabic materia medica surpassed its European counterparts—in the number of medicines, their botanical and pharmacologic characterizations, and the diversity of their sources and applications. From the ninth to thirteenth centuries Arabic medical manuscripts were produced in great abundance, including works on primarily botanical drugs and on diet therapy.

Although early-ninth-century Arabic medical treatises conformed to the Greek doctrine of humoral pathology, later works revealed a refinement of pharmacologic principles beyond the relatively simple Galenic theory of binary oppositions. Comprehensive chemical knowledge in Medieval Arabic medicine fostered the development of botany and related sciences. Prominent Arabic physicians who contributed to the medicine of western Europe include Rhazes (850–925 CE), who regarded the management of regimen (diet, rest) to be better than drugs, and the even more influential Avicenna (980–1037 CE), whose *Canon* compares in stature with the Hippocratic *Corpus* and Galen's works and ranked among standard European medical texts until the 1600s. Other important influences derived from Jewish Medieval medicine, which is epitomized in the work of the physician and scholar Maimonides (1135–1204 CE), who also stressed nutrition and digestion as mainstays of good health (Levey 1973; Rosner 1987; Siraisi 1990; Sotres 1998; Adib 2004; Brewer 2004).

By the twelfth century western Europe had witnessed something of a renaissance, when a proliferation of religious and secular healers created a demand for a larger and more sophisticated medical literature. This challenge both drove and was a by-product of the growing number of Latin translations from Greek and Arabic medical texts. The expanding Latin medical literature emphasized the systematic, theoretical, and scholarly aspects of medicine, with the eventual outcome that, even in religious communities, a specialized physical secular medicine again became popular.

The typical Medieval hospital, like its etymological root (Latin, *hospes*, guest or host), resembled more a hospice or hostel for travelers and the indigent than what a hospital later came to be, namely a locus of advanced technology, acute care, research, and instruction. Throughout the Middle Ages, recurrent epidemics of leprosy, smallpox, bubonic plague, and other infections helped to define the role of these charitable centers of community-based health care. Many were directly affiliated with monasteries and churches, and the activities of staff were more custodial than curative. Much of the care was offered by resident monks, who drew on the abundant resources of their kitchen gardens for foods and healing plants (Kealey 1981). Typically these were dried and stored in the *officina* (Latin, workshop); from this term derives *officinal*, denoting pharmaceuticals that are kept in stock, whereas *magistrals* are prepared extemporaneously following a physician's prescription.

Humoral Theory and Complexionate Therapy

Throughout the Middle Ages, humoral doctrine was still the predominant explanatory model for health and illness. The body was described in a state of illness, health, or in an intermediate phase. Illnesses were divided among three classes: congenital disorders, to which little attention was paid; trauma/injury, which became the province of surgeons in the twelfth and thirteenth centuries, when surgery emerged as an occupation discrete from medicine; and complexional imbalances, which included most internal disorders. Consequently, most medical care was preventive and centered on manipulating diet, exercise, and rest to maintain the optimum complexion. Physicians had to further adjust health regimens to accommodate the idiosyncrasies of individuals' unique complexions. Because this type of health management required substantial professional input, physicians were affordable only for the wealthy, while the general populace managed foods and medicines as best they knew how (Kealey 1981; Siraisi 1990).

Although the ultimate goal was to regain health, in complexionate therapy, healing (like illness itself) was perceived as a process, not an event. This view is shared by many contemporary non-Western medical cultures (Etkin 1988). In this schema, recovery is diffuse and poorly defined. As such, it helps to account for the structure and content of both the dietary regimen for health and the therapeutic regimen for illness. Similarly, circumstances of health and illness would have been interpreted through the inexactness that characterizes chronic diseases, malnutrition, and lingering injuries. Given this imprecision, the experience of medical specialists would indeed confirm the idea of a neutral state between health and illness (Siraisi 1990).

As specialties arose, they came to be defined more by the techniques employed than by the illnesses treated; for example, surgeons applied topical medicines and used instruments, whereas physicians prescribed internal medications. In practice, however, their actions overlapped, and surgeons and physicians also acted as their own apothecaries, compounding medicines as needed. Informed by humoral pathology, both used emetics and purgatives on the principle that humors should be evacuated or would interfere with the surgeon's craft or the physician's medicaments. In general, patients were admonished to follow healthy diets; those with wounds and simple fractures were given laxatives to keep the body soluble and were directed to consume light, liquid diets (Beier 1992).

Medieval Pharmacy

During the Middle Ages the boundary between medicines and foods remained blurred. Botanical medicines were sold not only by apothecaries and physicians but also by grocers and spice merchants. Spices and vegetables especially crossed from one category to the other. For example, lettuce was a common ingredient to foster cold complexion: its seeds cooled an aggressive libido, and its leaves treated toothache and stomach upset. Respiratory disorders were treated with licorice, figs, ginger, cumin, and butter. "The foundation of medieval European pharmacy . . . was the attribution of medicinal powers to commonly available substances, usually plants and often those that might also be used in cooking. Sharp taste, pungent aroma, and unusual texture as well as medicinal action of some kind (for example, as a laxative or opiate) were all properties that might lead to the classification of a plant as a medicinal" (Siraisi 1990: 141).

In Italy, the center of the European spice and drug trade, pharmacists and physicians were organized into a single guild that established standards for its members. Between 1297 and 1444, drug wholesalers and pharmacists outnumbered the other sixty-nine guilds. Similar pharmacy guilds developed in France and Germany. In England apothecaries functioned much like surgeons and physicians (all of them called "leeches") and were organized around 1300 as a special constituency of the grocers' guild, not gaining independent status until 1627. Drug commerce fully overlapped the spice trade, and the terms *spicer*, *pepperer*, and *apothecary* were used interchangeably (see chapter 3).

A Renaissance in Medicine

Diffusion of Hippocratic-Galenic Traditions

The Hippocratic texts had been copied, and sufficient numbers survived into Byzantine times (476–1453 CE) to be reimported into Europe during the Renaissance. The full *Corpus*, whose knowledge during the Middle Ages was incomplete, had been translated into Latin by the early 1500s, reinfusing Hippocratic ideas that included close observation, case histories, and diet therapy. The diffusion of Hippocratic-Galenic traditions was encouraged following Johannes Gutenberg's introduction of printing from movable type (1455; Wear 1992). In some scientific sectors, the pres-

FIGURE 2.1. A twenty-first-century apothecary in Xi Yuan Hospital of the China Academy of Traditional Chinese Medicine, Beijing. Photo by Paul J. Ross, 2002

tige of Hippocrates and his writings grew as physicians continued the now 1500-year-old practice of searching the *Corpus* for precedents of the medicine they were practicing themselves. Bilious fevers, for example, were understood to present a binary of elevated body heat and dryness and reflected an imbalance of blood and yellow bile. Accordingly, treatments centered on wet, cold medicines such as cucumber (Estes 1996). Moderation in the volume and richness of diet and drink (from the *Corpus*) constituted preventive medicine (Harley 1993).

For others, the so-called scientific revolution of the sixteenth and seventeenth centuries challenged the old views. For example, the first complete textbook of human anatomy (*De Humanis Corporis Fabrica*, Andreas Vesalius, 1543) and William Harvey's *The Motion of the Heart and Blood* (1628) contradicted many of Galen's teachings. A more calculating critic, Paracelsus (Theophrastus von Hohenheim, 1493–1541), literally devoted his life to refuting the humoral model of pathology, offering instead a vision of the body as a chemical laboratory. His perspective still placed the four elements (earth, air, fire, water) in the foreground, but it superimposed on them three primary principles that have these meta-phoric attributes: sulfur (combustibility), salt (permanence and fire re-sistance), and mercury (liquidity and volatility). Disease was understood to be a separation of one of the principles from the other two. This carried forward the Hippocratic understanding of illness as imbalance but lo-calized disease to a particular organ, rather than to disequilibrium of the whole body. Credited with saying that "the task of alchemy is not to make gold or silver but to prepare medicines," Paracelsus advanced a therapeu-tic paradigm based in internal medicines that had specific, hidden "heal-ing virtues," which he attempted to extract from inorganic matter. On his counsel, alcohol tinctures and extracts, essences, and pure concentrated quintessences were added to the pharmacopoeia, as were mercury, iron, lead, sulfur, copper and potassium sulfates, and opium (Galdston 1943).

According to Sonnedecker (1976: 43), Paracelsus was a "mystic as well as a revolutionary empiricist," whose medical theories were embedded in a broader religious philosophy. This is evident in his revival of the doc-trine of signatures (earlier rejected by Hippocrates), the understanding that physical attributes (e.g., color, texture) are divinely inspired signs of the utility of a substance, such as the use of red medicines for blood disorders. Nonetheless, the teachings of Paracelsus and the Paracelsians of the seventeenth century brought a new therapeutic outlook and intro-duced many chemical remedies to the pharmacopoeias of western Eu-rope (Sonnedecker 1976).

Solidar Theory of Pathology

A competing, solidar (or solidist) theory of pathology was advanced by Friedrich Hoffmann in 1695 and soon after by Hermann Boerhaave and Albrecht von Haller, who proposed that health represented a tension of the solid, constituent fibers of the body's hollow blood vessels and nerves. According to this theory, tonus was sustained by nerve fluids that kept the humors in motion. Ernst Stahl's animism (1720) understood the same tone to be under control of the soul (Latin, *anima*), which balanced all body functions through a rhythmic movement. Similarly, P. J. Barthez's vitalism (1778) imagined that tonus was sustained and restored by a vital principle or special energy. For all, therapy was directed at restoring the normal tone of the fibers. A slow pulse was a sign of weakened irritability, which required stimulant therapy, and a fast pulse, the signature of any fever, was understood to result from increased irritability and arterial tone. Accordingly, fever therapies were "sedative," "depletive," or "evacuant" and included diuretic, cathartic, narcotic, refrigerant, and emetic drugs and foods. In the early phase of treatment, depletive therapy included bleeding to reduce arterial tone and to expel foul humors. Patients were directed away from things that would feed the internal heat, such as meat, rich foods, and exercise. Diaphoretics, which promote sweating, assured the removal of internal heat. Tonic or stimulant regimens were supposed to increase arterial and heart tone so that more powerful contractions would speed the release of whatever substances had weakened the patient. Tonic therapy included cold water, drugs, and electricity (Sonnedecker 1976; Estes 1996).

Solidist physicians assigned foods to chemical categories, such as alkaline, acid, acrid, oily, spiritous, viscous, aqueous, and salty, that marked their specific medicinal application. Typically, alkaline foods included cabbage, onion, and most fish and meats. Because pus was regarded to be alkaline, meats and alkaline foods were thought to promote inflammation and fevers. Accordingly, acid foods were indicated for purulent illnesses: milk, vinegar, and especially fruits were understood to prevent both thickening of the humors and fever. Logically, acid and alkaline foods counterbalanced one another. Acrid foods flavored with aromatic spices such as garlic, pepper (*Piper nigrum* L., Piperaceae), nutmeg, and mustard were thought to increase the pulse, promoting diuresis and sweating, which concentrated and thickened the humors and led to fever. Butter, fatty meat, nuts, and other oily foods might clog glands that secrete digestive fluids but could also lubricate the tissues. Alcohol, rice, fish, and oatmeal and other viscous foods had some nutritive value but might thicken the humors and prevent their circulation. Alcohol also was regarded to be a stimulant that maintained tissue tone. Conversely, water, tea, and other aqueous foods, although nutritious, might thin the humors and diminish the tone of the solid fibers of nerves and blood vessels. Salty foods impaired nutrition but stimulated vascular fibers and diluted thickened humors (Estes 1996: 136–138).

It is important to note that, although the term *solidist* is used to distinguish these theories of pathology from humoral doctrine, the two concepts overlap, and foods and drugs were evaluated within both frame-
works. Indeed, most of the cathartics, emetics, and diuretics used in
humoral therapy were easily accommodated to evacuant and stimulant
regimens. Also, as even this brief review demonstrates, solidist theories,
like humoral pathology, were plagued by structural inconsistencies—the
assignment of foods to chemical categories and their putative effects on
disease were arbitrary and inconsistent.

Exotic Sources of Medicines and Foods

Sixteenth- and seventeenth-century European pharmacopoeias were
expanded by the inclusion of medicines and foods from other places,
especially the New World (see chapters 3 and 5). The emetic ipecac
(*Cephaelis ipecacuanha* Tussac, Rubiaceae) and the antimalarial quinine (*Cinchona* spp., Rubiaceae) came most rapidly into widespread use,
but other botanicals gained therapeutic prestige as well, including the
muscle relaxant curare (*Strychnos toxifera* Benth., Loganiaceae), the
carminative chile pepper (*Capsicum* spp., Solanaceae; see chapter 3,
Unique Tastes Become Transcultural Flavors: The Case of Chile), the
stimulants chocolate (*Theobroma cacao* L., Sterculiaceae; see chapter 5,
Chocolate/ Cacao) and tobacco (*Nicotiniana tabacum* L., Solanaceae),
the stomachic vanilla, the laxative cascara sagrada (*Rhamnus purshi-
ana* DC, Rhamnaceae), and the topical anesthetic and psychotropic
coca (*Erythroxylum coca* Lam., Erythroxylaceae). As did competing
explanatory models of pathology, the introduction of exotic botanicals
might have helped to erode confidence in Galenic medicine, as it became apparent that all the world's drug knowledge was not contained in
Dioscorides's *De Materia Medica* and other Greco-Roman and Arabic
texts.

The examples of chile pepper, chocolate, and vanilla among the
adopted medicines underscore the continued overlap of medicines and
foods, which shared a nomenclature that was generic and interchangeable (Guerra 1966; Young 1978). In the late Middle Ages and Renaissance
the expanding variety of foods and food preparations available to the
upper classes may have encouraged interest outside of medicine in the

healthfulness of foods (Siraisi 1990). Indeed, Medieval and Renaissance cookbooks combined recipes with advice about health, instructing when and how to adjust diet so that the proper balance of humors was assured, such as heating anemic and melancholy temperaments and cooling the choleric (Toussaint-Samat 1992). The overlap of food and medicine is embodied in the Medieval English statement that "a good cook is half a physician" (Simoons 1991: 52).

Shared Medical Culture among Physicians and Patients in the 1700s

By the eighteenth century, the advancing critique of the Hippocratic-Galenic tradition undermined its therapeutic authority but was not replaced by any systematic theory of pathology and therapeutics. A medical sectarianism evolved instead. Two examples from eighteenth-century England are illustrative and, more significantly, reveal the residuum of principles of balance that underlie humoral theory. William Cullen (1710–1790) argued that therapies should be either irritating or emollient to effect the convulsion or relaxation of a nervous principle that regulates all body functions. John Brown (1735–1788), a pupil of Cullen, proposed that the root cause of all illnesses was a disequilibrium between the body's state of excitability and the internal and external stimuli that affect it (Sonnedecker 1976).

There emerged in the eighteenth century, in medicine and more broadly, an ecumenical appeal for whatever was purportedly natural. Artificiality in all its guises was suspicious, including "unnatural" medicines and medical procedures. The imagery of food as medicine, still embedded in humoral physiology, resonated well in this climate. Carrying forward the Greek physiological and pathological theories, the induction of vomiting and use of enemas was a commonplace means to rid accumulations and impurities (Sigerist 1961). With exceptions (e.g., Morgagni, see below) medicine remained a hands-off practice well into the nineteenth century: physicians assessed a condition by careful examination of the patient's effluvia and his account of the illness, rather than by palpation or even superficial examination of normally clothed body parts (Estes and Goodman 1986; Nicolson 1992). The typical eighteenth- and nineteenth-century practitioners prescribed medicines liberally, although most understood that they had no way to know how much of a cure should be attributed to a natural course of events or to drugs. Skilled though they might have been in diagnosis and prognosis, practitioners' chief therapeutic strengths were advice on regimen and the comfort afforded by their presence and apparent command. However skeptical practitioners might have been—surgeon Richard Smith went so far as to claim that the London and Edinburgh pharmacopoeias were largely "useless trash"—they met the high public demand for mixtures, pills, emetics, lotions, and bleedings "for every disorder known to medicine" (Loudon 1986: 65).

The permeability between learned and popular medicine, foreshadowed by Galen, engendered a shared medical culture among physicians and patients that endured through the 1700s (Wear 1992). Popular household references from the mid-1500s and later include John Wesley's *Primitive Physick* (1547), Nicholas Culpeper's *Herbal* (*Culpeper's English Physician and Complete Herbal: Arranged for Use as a First Aid Herbal*, 1652), and John Gerard's *The Herbal or General History of Plants* (1597; see Slack 1979; Porter 1992; Estes 1996). These herbals were largely catalogues, organized not by illness categories but as botanical resources to which caretakers referred when family members fell ill. While foods clearly were perceived to be key elements of prevention and therapy and their use linked to specific disorders, there is little that documents why a particular food was beneficial in one context or another (Estes 1996); that is, the original or evolved underlying medical philosophy was not explicit in these herbals. But it was clear that the categories food and medicine blended into one another. For example, Gerard observed that since earliest times plants were "the ordinary meate of men, and have continued ever since of necessary use both for meates to maintain life, and for medicine to recover health" (quoted in Young 1978: 5). From a medicinal perspective an item might have numerous therapeutic functions, but as food all items served the same purpose.

Ingestibles were distinguished as medicines, poisons, or aliments. This last category reflects the tenacity of the Hippocratic principle that conceptualized as common to all foods a single component that, by digestion, could repair the body and provide energy. The idea that all foods serve a single universal (alimental) purpose was a conceptual barrier to understanding that illnesses can be caused by the absence of some food or other

(Young 1978). The discovery of microorganisms a century later had a similar effect (see Nutrition Science and Endocrinology, below).

In a later printed genre, the physician's knowledge base was overlapped by vernacular medical works. Some of these drew on professional texts that offered information ranging among topics such as diet, exercise, plant medicines, and the weather (Slack 1979; Fissell 1992). Continuing the tradition established in earlier texts (and distinct from the herbals), medical philosophy is explicit in these general medical books. Anyone who consulted these works was instructed which food was indicated for one disorder or other as well as general notions of what causes illness. William Smith's *Sure Guide in Sickness and Health, in the Choice of Food and Use of Medicine* (1776) explained that food is either "simple," nourishing the body and restoring its parts, or "medicinal" and capable of changing body disposition (Estes 1996). Adjusting the humors via diet and through vomiting, purging, and leech-bleeding was still the predominant effort to prevent and treat illness by adjusting the body's equilibrium.

Medicaments recommended in the vernacular texts were primarily foods, used both alone and in combination with other substances. For example, onions, hops, and carrots compounded with oyster shells were recommended to prevent bladder stones (Ramsey 1992); chicken droppings in wine was recommended for jaundice (Wilson 1992); and vinegar and rosewater treated edema in pregnancy (Ulrich 1982). Vegetarian diets were advised for fevers, a "cooling" mixture of honey and cream of tartar treated worms, and bran confected with raisins, figs, and sugar was indicated for a cold and for scurvy (Porter and Porter 1989). Beans and lentils were regarded as heavy and viscous, thus likely to cause obstructions, whereas barley and oats were described as emollient and moistening, thus restorative (Estes 1996). While these recipes for wellness are virtually identical to those of earlier centuries, there still was no shared understanding of how foods affect the course of a specific illness. Indeed some physicians argued that, whereas diet can exert general effects on the whole body, no food is a specific therapy for any specific illness. Medical discourse in the 1700s did not dwell on the relative merits of drugs proper versus medicinal foods, and physicians were as likely to prescribe one as the other (Estes 1996). As they had been in centuries earlier, drugs and foods were conceptually and substantively interchangeable.

Home Care and Layperson's Health Guides

Because home management of illness was women's terrain, its internal history is fragmented. Still, some insights into the content and context of home care are preserved in household diaries and cookbooks (e.g., Ulrich 1990; Theophano 2002) and medical manuals written by physicians for the public. Since at least the 1500s upper-class families in Europe kept diaries that included medical instructions, some taken from learned sources, alongside cooking recipes and other household accounts. These traditions endured in the United States, where women consulted herbals, Native-American and African-American neighbors, and each other; preserved medicinal plants along with their fruits and vegetables; and tended generally to the health of their families (Starr 1982). Until the nineteenth century, there was little technical distinction between what constituted domestic versus professional medical practice. Lacking a compelling body of medical theory that explained how things work, housewives, like many physicians, sought primarily to give ease through palliative care. Using tried-and-true remedies did more than relieve pain, it confirmed a fundamental order of the world, reaffirming traditions and social interrelations among caretakers and between them and their patients. In this context, familiar articles—foods—offered comfort and reassurance.

As literacy and affluence advanced, the closing decades of the eighteenth century saw an ever-wider audience that could comprehend the proper use of diet and exercise in promoting health. In Europe, Swiss physician Samuel Auguste Tissot was widely read, particularly by French speakers (e.g., *Avis au Peuple sur la Santé*, 1761; *Essai sur les Maladies des Gens du Monde*, 1770). In England, physician William Buchan's *Domestic Medicine* (1769) marked a secularizing enlightenment based in self-help and education (Emch-Dériaz 1992). Similarly, in the United States, Culpeper's *Herbal* was a domestic mainstay; John Gunn's *Domestic Medicine, Or the Poor Man's Friend* (1769) was widely consulted; and John Tennent's *Every Man His Own Doctor* (1736) was the first medical bestseller in the country. Translations of Buchan's and Tissot's works reached the United States as well, advancing naturalistic views of health and further encouraging the democratization of medical knowledge. Beginning with the publication of Henry Wilkins's *Family Medical*

Advisor (1793), another twenty U.S. physicians published domestic medical guides, rivaling those of Buchan and Tissot (Porter and Porter 1989; Gevitz 1992).

Four observations about these layperson's guides are important for the discussion that follows. First, these guides are emblematic of a social context in which health was understood to be largely an issue of personal or household responsibility. Virtually all medical care began as family/domestic medicine, also called "kitchen physic." Second, the mediation of diet, including the identification of specific foods and food combinations, continued to hold a prominent place in the prevention and treatment of illness. Third, these medical guides and kitchen physic would not have enjoyed such popularity if domesticity itself did not carry such high cachet. Finally, an analogue of medical knowledge diffusing into the popular arena and the mediation of disease with diet also characterize contemporary medicine in the West.

Nineteenth-Century Biomedicine

Humoral Theory and Systemic Illness

Informally, humoral theory still underpinned the structure of nineteenth-century European and U.S. medicine. Illnesses continued to be viewed systemically rather than discretely. In fact, regular physicians were suspicious of empiricism and regarded claims of specific therapy as quackery. Appropriately, therapies were categorized not by disease-specific efficacy but by their physiologic effects: as emetics, diuretics, sudorifics, sialagogues, and narcotics. For example, digitalis (from foxglove, *Digitalis purpurea* L., Scrophulariaceae) was identified in medical texts as a diuretic and was used to treat edema generally, whether the etiology was cardiac or some other pathology. Quinine was a tonic for a variety of conditions and when used for malaria was virtually always accompanied by a cathartic (Siraisi 1990). In this way, medicines could be assimilated to the physician's generalist cognitive framework, despite the fact that disease-specific efficacy contradicted that framework. Even when inoculation and later vaccination were proven successful against smallpox, physicians administered this with the customary dietary restructuring and the liberal use of cathartics (Rosenberg 1979). That is, physicians wrapped an anomalous procedure in layers of familiar medical culture, regulating the humors through supervision of the effluvia. According to Riely (1990: 198), "Digestion was to the 19th century what the psyche is to the twentieth—the latter day seat of the humors. . . . The digestive tract was the battleground between organic and inorganic forces—good and evil— much as, on another scale, [humans] struggled against the artificiality of modern city life."

Before the mid-nineteenth century, when pharmacologic protocols began to be used to examine the effects of drugs on living organisms, doctors in Europe, England, and the United States used an estimated 170 variably purified chemical drugs and 500 or so medicinal plant species. Any one physician used about 125 medicines (Estes 1996: 139), the makeup of which was shaped by the range of illnesses in the physician's experience and his apparent success in treating them. Lacking diagnostic tools beyond their own senses, physicians relied on these medicines and foods to mediate "intake and outgo," that is, to regulate the effluvia. The physical appearance of urine, pulse, surface eruptions, and vomitus— mutually intelligible to physician and patient—offered signs of the body's otherwise unreadable interior. To the extent that a particular substance affected the production and appearance of the effluvia, it was understood to be efficacious. A medicine might promote the desired effect, but the effect itself was an imitation of the body's "natural" response to illness (e.g., by sweating, vomiting). Thus, medicines and foods were the "legitimating elements" (Rosenberg 1979: 10) of a medical idiom shared among physicians and the public.

Erosion of Humoral Pathology and Holistic Therapy

Notions of disease specificity gradually eroded the idea of holistic therapy. We can understand this reframing of health and disease by paying attention to how science and medicine came to view normal physiologic processes and their modification during illness. In the eighteenth century a principle of anatomical discreteness was advanced by the Italian anatomist Giovanni Morgagni (1682–1771), who characterized the organs as "seats of disease." Later, the Paris School, guided by the French anatomist and physician Xavier Bichat (1771–1802), localized disease to specific tissues. The German pathologist Rudolf Virchow (1821–1902) extended the locus of illness to particular cells, which he described as the basic unit of the healthy body as well one plagued with disease. The French physiologist Claude Bernard (1813–1878) provided a theoretical synthesis for all this through his *milieu intèrieur*, a description of the body's internal environment in which (Olmsted and Olmsted 1952: 107):

> the blood contains all the elements necessary to life, which it obtains from outside. . . . [It] serves as a vehicle for all the influences which, coming from without, act upon the . . . tissues. . . . [It] comes into contact with the air and obtains from it oxygen which is subsequently carried to the whole organism. [B]y the mechanism of alimentary absorption the blood obtains from without all the liquids [that] are subsequently furnished to the organism. . . . [A]ll the products of organic decomposition are collected in the blood and circulate with it to be excreted, either in the form of gas through the skin and lungs or in the form of liquid by the kidneys.

This vision of a complex integrated body, in which blood communicates among tissues and organs, closed the intellectual door on humors.

The theoretical synthesis of disease specificity resonated early developments in the field of chemistry, especially the works of Robert Boyle, whose *Skeptical Chymist* (1661) and *Specifick Medicines* (1685) outlined a theory that specific elements (chemicals) could enter the circulation and act within the body tissues and blood. The theory could be extrapolated to foods that contain those elements and, in fact, was based in the observation that consumption of certain foods altered the color of urine and that people experienced the cathartic effects of a plant eaten by the animal whose milk they drank. Boyle even predicted that whoever would eventually explain the agent(s) responsible for fermentation would reveal the cause of disease (Galdston 1943; Pellegrino 1979; Lawrence 1992).

Germ Theory of Disease: Separating Illness from Patient

The idea of very small disease-causing entities predates their actual identification, but this notion is a more integral element of other (folk) medical traditions than of early bioscience. The construction of the first microscope in the early 1600s confirmed the existence of microorganisms, which attracted a rapidly growing interest, starting in 1676 with Antonie van Leeuwenhoek's (1632–1723) letters to the Royal Society in London. Although Dr. G. Bonomo identified the causative agent of scabies in 1687, 150 years passed before another parasite was identified. In fact, the theory of germ (microorganism) infection peaked around 1700 and then declined, while various doctrines of spontaneous generation prevailed. After 1830, advances in microscopy and laboratory techniques revealed the world of "little animals." While the idea of specific etiology was authored by no one individual, the English physician Thomas Sydenham (1624–1689) is credited with the proposal that discrete "species" of disease might be discerned. In *The Method of Curing Fevers* (1666), he outlined the idea that some illnesses occur when the body's natural defenses are overwhelmed by specific agents (Dixon 1978). Similarly, the clinician Pierre-Fidèle Bretonneau (1778–1862) is credited with recognizing that certain clinical presentations are caused by discrete agents; specifically, he discerned within the unstructured category fevers such distinct diseases as diphtheria and scarlet fever (Dubos 1980). This separation of illness from patient marks an important conceptual shift from earlier medical perspectives, which envisioned only diseased persons and systemic illnesses rather than distinct entities responsible for different constellations of symptoms.

Evidence supporting the germ theory came from concurrent research on fermentation and putrefaction, including discrete fermenting agents (see chapter 4) identified between 1857 and 1863 by the French bacteriologist and chemist Louis Pasteur. This inspired the English surgeon Joseph Lister to create antiseptic wound dressings in 1866 and to establish the foundations of aseptic surgery. In 1871 bacteriologist Carl Weigert reported that application of the same dyes that make microorganisms perceptible also reveal the damage they cause in host tissues. This microscopic evidence of parasite-caused pathology struck a final blow against notions that microorganisms were merely scavengers of debris created by some other disease process.

In 1877 Pasteur described and developed an attenuated vaccine for the anthrax bacterium. The technologically advanced work of the German bacteriologist Robert Koch was especially effective in imprinting the germ theory of disease in the biomedical psyche. His publication *The Etiology of Traumatic Infective Diseases [Wounds]* (1879) definitively established the bacterial origin of certain diseases, distinguished among diverse bacteria, and linked specific bacteria to specific effects. The principles upon which this research was conducted were based in Jacob Henle's (1809–1885) earlier work, and later were refined into Koch's postulates, the four conditions that must be met to link a particular microorganism to a specific condition.[1] Twenty-two specific infective agents were identified between 1879 and 1900. In 1895 the era of specific sero- and immunotherapy was ushered in with Emil von Behring's introduction of an antitoxin for diphtheria, with dramatic results: in London fever hospitals rates of laryngeal diphtheria dropped from 62 percent in 1894 to less than 12 percent in 1910 (Dixon 1978).

Doctrine of Specific Etiology

What emerged during the nineteenth century was an articulated doctrine of specific etiology and its corollary, specific therapy. In hindsight, this theoretical position seems destined, as the previous 300 years of biomedicine were increasingly preoccupied with morbidity and pathology. In the larger context, this shift in medical thought can be seen as a response to major changes in global ecology and the circumstances of political economy. Hippocratic-Galenic medicine resonated a relatively stable ecology that predated Hippocrates for many centuries and prevailed for the next two millennia: people experienced change as minor and transitory, and the doctrine of humoral pathology, based in balance and harmony with nature, was explanation enough. Eventually, that ecology was transformed radically: accelerating change followed contact with the New World in the fifteenth century; later the Industrial Revolution, scientific developments, urbanization, increased population size and density, and poor sanitation contributed to massive exposure to infections.[2] The frightening epidemics that plagued society in the nineteenth century required some more compelling explanatory framework with which both the medical profession and the lay public could cognitively and emotionally negotiate such phenomena.

Until the mid-1800s, the body was perceived as a "system of dynamic interactions with its environment" (Rosenberg 1979: 5), each body part was related to all others, and health or disease was a general state of the whole organism. By the late 1800s the doctrine of specific etiology interjected the notion that nature (environment), the body, and disease are not coterminous. Each is distinct from the other; the environment is a source of other, of nonself; the pathogen, thus disease, is detached from the patient. Biomedicine began a meteoric trajectory when it ceased to rely on what patients say and started to focus instead on technology-generated, increasingly lower (more specific) levels of biologic resolution.

Biomedicine charted a path into an expanding universe of the infinitely small (Vickers 1969). Rather than constellations of causal factors, diseases came to be understood as "discrete clinical entities with unique causes, courses, and pathologies" (Vogel 1979) that required individuated treatments. Increasingly these took the form of chemical and antibiotic therapies.

Institutionalization of Medical Care

Biomedicine came to be defined by its technical armamentarium, thereby banishing from the purview of medicine foods and whatever else does not resonate with specific diagnosis and treatment. What developed first as a tension between laboratory and bedside aspects of medicine (laboratory researchers typically were derisive of clinicians) evolved later as the functional interface that linked the two settings. First a matter simply of praxis and place—the transfer of methods for bacteriologic inquiry—medicine was eventually transformed ideologically as well, as the special scheme of diagnostic and therapeutic dicta of bacteriology helped to infuse medicine with such bioscientific principles as Listerian antisepsis (1870s), pathogenic specificity (1880s), and immuno- and chemotherapeutics (1890s to early 1900s) (Maulitz 1979).

A parallel development was the devaluation of whatever knowledge may have been conceived outside the laboratory, for example, in the home and especially in the kitchen: while food exemplified the gendered domain of prosaic homemaking, medicines represented a "science" that was increasingly venerated by both its practitioners and the public. The centuries-old intersecting-spheres view that defined the domestic duties of women to overlap with self help and home care gave way to male-dominated scientific medicine. As a consequence, the social context in which medical knowledge is generated was transformed.

Medical treatment was increasingly an exercise of formal knowledge and regimented technique, rather than an existential process (Vogel 1979). This shift in orientation reflects a principal dynamic in the history of biomedicine: the dialectical opposition between holism and reductionism, a juxtaposition of domestic and professional medicines (Lyng 1990). One result of this shift is that the scientific and lay sectors no longer had the same view of the physical body or of processes that determine health and disease. While domestic medicine was organized around "natural healing," professional medicine was based on the assumption that healing requires direct intervention by someone who really knows how the interior physical body works and who is thus uniquely qualified to carry out these invasive modalities that would be "unsafe and ineffective" in the hands of lay persons (Lyng 1990).

The physician-patient encounter was removed from the home to increasingly institutional and technologically complex settings, where food no longer had a therapeutic role. Foods were both too simple, because they invoke domestic imagery, and too complex, because they embody the chaos of their multiple constituents. More and more patients were directed to hospitals, as the sickest patients were consolidated in technologically dense settings in which doctors could command the assistance of professional nurses. In the United States, the first hospital-based school of nursing opened in 1873, making available what the medical profession regarded to be "women who had been especially trained to care for the sick rather than only women who cooked and cleaned but *understood little of disease or of the specific needs of their charges*" (Estes and Goodman 1986: 194–195, emphasis added). In hospitals doctors also consolidated their authority and increased medical specialization, which both made them more interdependent through cross-referrals and raised their and their patients' confidence in what they could accomplish.

The growing importance of hospital-based medicine is reflected in the following figures. In 1870 the U.S. population numbered 38,558,371 and was served by 178 institutions that provided bed care for the sick and housed about 30,000 beds. By 1910 the population had increased 2.4-fold (91,972,266) but the number of hospitals (4359) and beds (421,065) 25- and 14-fold, respectively (Galdston 1965: 157). This rapid and remarkable expansion of hospital care parallels broader social changes—fewer people stayed at home as they sought wage labor in the industrial sector—and directly reflects advances in the chemotherapy of infectious illnesses (see below).

Disjunctions between Scientific Knowledge and Actual Practice

Advances in research and theory anticipated the era of modern medicine in the mid-1800s, although practicing physicians in both Europe and the United States were largely unaffected. At best, medical knowledge cohered around a handful of theories and their permutations, and physicians were not persuaded that any one of them was more compelling than the others. The first half of the nineteenth century witnessed a large increase in the number of U.S. medical colleges, not one of which prepared its graduates in knowledge gained in European laboratories. Instead, these small, low-standard schools offered only brief courses of instruction through inadequate teaching staff who held fast to old theories and treatment modalities. Medical societies cohered around debate of practical treatments rather than theory. To wit, a resolution adopted by the Illinois State Medical Society in 1850 urged that "in consultations, theoretical discussions should be avoided, as occasioning perplexity and loss of time. For there may be much diversity of opinion concerning speculative points, with perfect agreement in those modes of practice which are founded, not on hypothesis, but on experience and observation" (Bonner 1991: 10).

In the typical physician's practice, bleeding, purging, and emetics still reigned, with remarkable inefficacy in the treatment of epidemic fevers. The limitations of these physicians, coupled with patients' dislike of heroic efforts to readjust the humors, help to explain the popularity of "irregular" (sectarian) physicians well into the twentieth century, including Thomsonians, Eclectics, homeopaths, vitapaths, and other sects. Further, the increased popularity of patent medicines (commonly of secret composition, thus, in fact, not patented) and promising miraculous cures was shaped in part by the advent of inexpensive newspapers, which made printed advertising accessible to a large public (Bonner 1991).

The early work of Pasteur and Koch was virtually lost on U.S. medicine, but by the 1880s extraordinary therapeutic efficacy in the treatment

of infectious diseases fueled the "emotional and epistemological tran-
scendence of [biomedical] science" (Rosenberg 1979). The medical profession was reinfused with an energy that it lacked during earlier decades,
which is reflected in the increased number of U.S. medical schools from
100 in 1880 (graduating 3241 students) to 160 by 1900 (5214 graduates)
(Galdston 1965: 157). Although many of these schools still had low standards and limited curricula, their proliferation is a gauge of renewed
interest.

Some, however, resisted the superscientific trend in medicine and
anticipated the limitations that would be revealed in the twentieth century when overzealous "microbe hunters" lost sight of the larger context
of disease. Although they eventually embraced both the germ theory and
the doctrine of specific etiology, critics warned that microbiology did not
hold all the answers and that "the accumulated knowledge of predispos-
ing influences and prophylactic safeguards" should not be disregarded
(Bonner 1991: 39).

The shifting focus of medical attention from treatment to etiology
marks a conceptual shift that spilled eventually from the laboratory to the
physician-patient encounter. An attitude that critics called "therapeutic nihilism" developed among physicians who lost faith in their ability
to mediate the course of disease with conventional treatments (Bonner
1991). One consequence was that medical practitioners significantly reduced the numbers and dosages of medicines administered, especially for
bleeding and other depleting treatments. This refocus on etiology accounts, in part, for the dramatic increase of medical sects in the late
nineteenth century. Patients were not satisfied simply by specific diag-
noses and palliative care. Instead they sought action, intervention, and
relief of suffering; they were inspired especially by homeopaths, for example, who provided the satisfaction of elaborate attention paid to the preparation of medicines (although the infinitesimal doses of homeopathic
medicines draw our attention to "natural" healing powers and placebo
effects). Conventional physicians, needing still to provide patients with
something intellectually and emotionally meaningful, shifted emphasis
to strengthening and stimulating, to toning the body so that illness could
"run its course." Their treatments were holistic and concentrated on diet
and regimen, including a rather strong devotion to alcohol stimulants
(Rosenberg 1979).

Impact of Pharmacological Medicine on Twentieth-Century Therapeutics

Antibiotics and the Biomedical Pharmacopoeia

Advances in chemistry, biochemistry, and microbiology revolutionized the biomedical pharmacopoeia during the first half of the nineteenth century, when the therapeutic constituents of a variety of natural products were characterized and refined, such as morphine in 1806; strychnine (*Strychnos nux-vomica* L., Loganiaceae) in 1817; quinine in 1820; atropine (*Atropa belladonna* L., Solanaceae) in 1833; and cocaine (*Erythroxylum coca*) in 1860.

Of substantially greater impact, however, was the era of antibiotics in the twentieth century. Technically, an antibiotic is a chemical substance produced by one microorganism that inhibits or destroys other microorganisms, including pathogens. Since earliest times, people had learned to use one microorganism against another. For example, treatments from diverse medical traditions include the opportunistic use of rotten wood and the deliberate spoiling of bread and other substrates and applying the resulting matter to wounds. Whereas early medics had no knowledge of the microorganisms responsible, the underlying principle was later formalized in biomedicine as bacterial antagonism. Experimentation in the 1880s and 1890s reinforced the potential of this type of therapy. For example, in 1887 Rudolf Emmerich protected rabbits against anthrax by preinfecting with the streptococcal bacterium that causes erysipelas (an acute inflammatory disease of the skin). That same year the Swiss surgeon Carl Garré described an in vitro technique to study bacterial antagonisms. This growing interest in therapy by "natural antagonism" is consistent with Darwinian perspectives that explained natural selection through survival of the fittest and with the comprehension of antibiosis as the opposite of symbiosis.

However, it was not until well into the twentieth century that true antibiotics contributed much to the control of infectious diseases. Penicillin was discovered in the late 1920s, but the first treatments with this broad-spectrum antibiotic did not occur until the 1940s. Penicillin was followed by tyrothricin, streptomycin, bacitracin, chloramphenicol, and others. Some antibiotics, like the original penicillin (*Penicillium no-*

tatum), were fortuitous discoveries (floating into Alexander Fleming's laboratory from some other researcher's experiment, an analogue of the moldy bread used by the ancients); other antibiotics were found through soil surveys; a current source of penicillin (*P. chrysogenum*) was derived from a moldy melon found in a Peoria, Illinois, market; and still another (*P. funiculosum*) was recovered from the isinglass covering a photograph of the researcher's wife (Stevenson 1958; Greenwood 1997). The thousands that have qualified for therapeutic use by now attest to the rapid development of antibiotic discovery, despite that no theoretical structure underlies how to go about finding antibiotics in nature (with the exception of some ethnopharmacology studies: Etkin 1996b, 2001; Elisabetsky and Etkin 2005).

Meanwhile, a body of knowledge that cohered around the dye industry in the early 1900s informed the development of synthetic antimicrobials. In this case, the opportunity for developing substances that have specifically targeted effects came through advances in chemotherapy, which rests on the principle that chemically similar substances will have similar therapeutic outcome. The foundations of this field are generally credited to the German bacteriologist Paul Ehrlich (1854–1915), whose objective was not therapy in the traditional sense but internal sterilization. To this end he sought "magic bullets," chemicals that targeted specific infectious agents but otherwise did no harm. Based on his experience that certain dyes stained specific cell types, his side-chain theory (1890) postulated the specific binding of drugs by molecular receptors (side chains) on the cell surface. The unique nature of the various receptors was explained by different cell types taking up different nutrients from the blood when receptors on those cells interact with some molecule(s) of that nutrient—nutrients that, fortuitously, have the same molecular configuration as some dyes and drugs. This set the intellectual climate for designing chemical agents that interact with cellular and molecular specificity.

While experimenting with the aniline dyes (derived from coal tar) used in microscopy, in 1891 Ehrlich had some success treating a case of quinine-resistant malaria with methylene blue. In 1907 he effected a more remarkable cure of trypanosomiasis in mice with the benzopurpurin dye trypan red. Over the next few decades followed the development of a suite of synthetic antimicrobials for human infections. The arsenicals salvarsan and neosalvarsan were effective against syphilis and atoxyl and tryparsamide against African sleeping sickness (trypanosomiasis), while antimony compounds treated schistosomiasis (bilharziasis). Synthetic improvements (e.g., pamaquine, aminoquinalines) on the antimalarial quinine were developed as well (Pellegrino 1979). Beginning in the 1930s sulfanilamide and other drugs of the sulfonamide family (sulfa drugs) were developed, effecting dramatic cures for scarlet fever, meningitis, bacterial pneumonia, puerperal (childbed) fever, and other infections. Finally, therapy was effective not only in resolving specific symptoms but for the first time radical in the elimination of the primary cause of disease. Medicines could be selected for specific, not generic and merely palliative, actions. Absolute cure became a realistic objective.

Remarkable Cures Reinforce the Doctrine of Specific Etiology and Therapy

The rapidity of cure undermined earlier notions of illness and therapy as process. Fast cure, especially of early, acute symptoms, seemed much more like an event than a process or even sequence of events. Whereas earlier medicine subscribed to an overarching explanatory paradigm in which efficacy was identified by some physiologic response (e.g., diuresis, emesis), by the mid-twentieth century therapeutics was distinguished by its scientific epistemology that identified efficacy as the ability to interrupt the statistically predictable natural history of the illness (Pellegrino 1979). Physicians and their patients no longer shared a knowledge base, and their encounters became increasingly multicultural: the physician's command of technical and scientific knowledge and instrumentation juxtaposed to fragmentary and inaccurate lay apprehensions of physiology and its disorders and repair. The lay-professional tension was compounded by the post-1950s trend of "medicalizing" (labeling as illness) drug abuse, crime, gambling, and other problematic behaviors whose causes and solutions are complex, nuanced by issues of political economy, and beyond the purview of specific therapeutics.

The profound effects of antimicrobial agents on health reinforced the validity of a biomedical paradigm that increasingly linked specific etiology to specific cure, at a time when infectious diseases, particularly tuberculosis and pneumonias, were the paramount health risk in industrial societies of Europe and North America. Catastrophic infections were brought under control at such an accelerated tempo that medicine and society were relatively inattentive to other developments that bear on health. In fact, the notion that antimicrobials were singly responsible is a distorted, albeit widely held, view: significant reductions in the incidence and prevalence rates of pneumonia, tuberculosis, and puerperal fever had as much to do with sanitation and other public health measures and improved standards of living that accompanied industrialization. Nonetheless, the credit was and continues to be accorded primarily to advances in clinical medicine.

In subsequent decades the doctrine of specific etiology was refined to greater powers of discrimination as researchers explored the host and tissue specificity of some microorganisms and uneven virulence among strains of the same infectious agent. The doctrine of specific etiology was reinforced as well by other branches of science and medicine: Gregor Mendel's laws of heredity and gene specificity were rediscovered in 1900 (first published in 1866), and advances in nutrition and endocrinology came prominently to the fore during the next twenty years.

Nutrition Science

Bioscience was so distracted by advances in microbiology and related disciplines that nutrition science did not chart a steady course until much later. One could argue that the discovery of essential nutrients was delayed by the insights of Koch and Pasteur, who directed attention to the presence of something that causes disease, microorganisms, rather than to deficiencies of health-sustaining substances. Although the fundamentals of digestion and metabolism had been outlined early in the nineteenth century, the term *vitamin* was not coined until 1911, most of the vitamins and essential amino acids were characterized only over the next several decades, and the Food and Nutrition Council of the U.S. National Research Council did not publish its first table of dietary standards until 1943. Specialization and fragmentation in professional medicine resulted in the autonomy of research methods and knowledge bases. The history of some vitamin-deficiency disorders instructs how the dogmatic advocacy of infectious theories stalled the exposition of vitamins, even those for which the association between diet and disease had already been recognized.

Bias in Discovering the Cause of Nutrient-Deficiency Diseases

Since the end of the Middle Ages, when navigators and merchants ventured ever further beyond western Europe, practical experience revealed that scurvy (vitamin C deficiency) could be simply prevented and treated by the inclusion of fresh fruit and vegetables in the diet. In 1739 the most celebrated figure in the history of scurvy, British naval surgeon James Lind, conducted what must have been the first controlled trial in clinical nutrition; he concluded that citrus fruit was the most effective remedy for scurvy. During the century following the Napoleonic Wars (1796–1815), on Royal instruction, ships of the British Navy were provisioned with citrus juices. But medical specialists of the later 1800s, already indoctrinated in the "new age of discovery," overlooked this knowledge to seek instead scientific (i.e., nonfood) explanations.

Over six or seven decades various etiologies were advanced, most reflecting the fashionable science of the time. The scurvy epidemic that followed the Siege of Paris in the Franco-Prussian War (1870–1871) prompted Dr. Jean-Antoine Villemin's review of the literature on scurvy. His conclusion that scurvy was a contagion was no doubt influenced by his demonstration ten years earlier that the cause of tuberculosis was an infectious agent and not, as was widely believed, the combined effects of poor diet and a debilitating environment. Villemin's idea was superceded in the 1870s by Dr. Almoth Wright's contention that diminished alkalinity explains scurvy and at the turn of the century by a ptomaine-poisoning theory. But in the first few years of the twentieth century, scurvy-as-contagion was again in ascendancy, as "the germ theory, so successful so often, must provide the ultimate model for scurvy" (Bynum 1990: 413). Some still clung stubbornly to a paradigm of contagion even after an animal model of scurvy had been established and Albert Szent-Györgyi isolated vitamin C in the 1930s (Carpenter 1986).

Similarly, signs consistent with beriberi (thiamin or vitamin B_1 deficiency) were widely reported starting in the mid-1800s, predominantly among populations subsisting on diets in which dehulled (polished) rice is the major staple. It was observed that the same diets enriched with vegetables and meats or replaced by whole grains reversed the symptoms of beriberi. That evidence notwithstanding, between 1883 and 1906, at least eighteen authors published "discoveries" of different microorganisms said to be responsible for beriberi. A noninfectious antiberiberi factor was described in 1912, and thiamin was isolated in 1926 and synthesized ten years later (Williams 1961; Combs 1992).

Vitamins as Magic Bullets

Another five water-soluble vitamins (thiamin, riboflavin, niacin, pyridoxine, and folate) and the four fat-soluble vitamins (A, D, E, and K) were isolated and synthesized by the mid-1940s. The most recent, cobalamin (water-soluble), was isolated in 1948 and synthesized only in 1973 (Guthrie and Bagby 1989). But even after dietary essentials were characterized, scientists still concentrated on how specific nutrients act as "magic bullets" for treating specific deficiency disorders as well as on how they help the immune system fight infectious disease. As further extension of the biomedical paradigm, researchers explored the evolution or exacerbation of pathogenicity of microorganisms that replicate in nutritionally deficient hosts. The conventional paradigm understands that nutritional deficiencies generically increase susceptibility to infection by suppressing host immune function, and that the presence of new and re-emergent infectious agents can be traced to such factors as global warming, environmental degradation, and disease traffic via the circulation of world travelers and their pathogens. A recent twist explains how normally avirulent Coxsackie viruses become pathogenic (through changes in the viral genome) in nutritionally deficient hosts. For example, oxidant stress of nutritional origin (due to selenium and/or vitamin E deficiency) eventuated in epidemic neuropathy in Cuba and cardiomyopathy (infection of cardiac muscle) in regions of China (Beck 2000).

"Natural Diets" Give Way to Nutrients as Specific Therapy

The lay public was amenable to considering a general role for nutrients in human health. Preoccupied with advancing technology and industrialization, in the early twentieth century Americans reinfused food folklore with "natural" foods. Food cults grew in proportion to whichever idea or proponent was most persuasive, inevitably to be replaced by some dietary configuration that appeared to be, at least temporarily, more healthful. Many of the purportedly natural diets were truncated, nutritionally unsound, and characterized by a dogmatic and stylized focus on, for example, macrobiotics, brown rice, organic foods, grapefruit (*Citrus* spp., Rutaceae), graham crackers, carrots, or cod liver oil. Advertising that linked food and health expanded in the early 1900s, centering on exaggerated claims for otherwise legitimate products. By 1930, however, advertising had been nuanced and refined to provide subtle and more compelling messages. As nutrition science advanced, advertising added the imprimatur of science to promote commercial products (Young 1978).

In time, although members of the lay public were poorly equipped to understand and distinguish among individual nutrients, they responded to product promotions that emphasized individual nutrients (e.g., "Orange Juice: Naturally High in Vitamin C") and eventually to vitamin-fortified products, such as vitamin A-fortified milk, breakfast cereals, instant noodles, margarine, fats, and oils; vitamin C-fortified fruit juices, dairy products, and cereals; vitamin D-fortified margarine, vegetable oils, and dairy products; vitamin E-fortified margarine, fats, oils, and cereals; and iron-fortified sugar, soy sauce, cookies, curry powder, and dairy products (see chapter 7). As pharmaceutical companies had done, the food industry—in the company of medical scientists and a willing public—converted "miracles" into commodities (Galdston 1965). In addition to the influence of advertising, U.S. food choices have been shaped by the regulatory actions of the U.S. Food and Drug Administration (FDA) and the advocacy actions of the American Dietetic Association, the largest group of food and nutrition professionals in the United States. Eventually, the public came to know food elements as the scientific community did—as specifics.

Endocrinology

Like advances in nutrition science, the systematization of endocrinology (which studies the physiology and pathology of internal secretions) is traced to 1902–1905, when the Canadian physiologists William Bayliss and Ernest Starling demonstrated for the first time that chemical integration occurs without influence from the nervous system. Specifically, they described release of the hormone "secretin" from duodenal mucosal cells on stimulation from acidified food and subsequent travel via the circulation to the pancreas, where secretin stimulates release of pancreatic fluid. This confirmed the nineteenth-century view (epitomized in Bernard's milieu intèrieur) that endocrine (ductless) glands secrete into the circulation (blood and lymph) agents that have regulatory activity in distant target tissues and organs. Over the next few decades many hormones were identified and structurally characterized: among the more familiar examples, insulin from the pancreas in 1921; thyroxine from the thyroid gland in 1926; estrogens and testosterone from the gonads in 1935; adrenal steroids between 1936 and 1942; prolactin (lactogenic hormone) from the pituitary in 1937; and norepinephrine from adrenal medullary tissue in 1949. By midcentury, it had been demonstrated that the adrenal cortex hormone cortisone improved biochemical indicators and clinical symptoms in rheumatoid arthritis patients (Turner and Bagnara 1976; Hadley 1992). Since then, against the backdrop of disease specificity, research continues to elucidate the structure of hormone genes and their receptors.

Just as some food-related "inborn errors of metabolism" had been specified to particular gene loci, such as gout and phenylketonuria, other diseases could be linked to disorders of specific hormones: diabetes to impaired insulin availability, goiter and growth failure to low thyroxine. Because these and many other endocrinopathies are linked to food metabolism, their early management included dietary adjustments. Increasingly, however, biomedical management of these disorders took the form of hormone replacement therapy, shifting from the early therapeutic rationale based on maintaining general balance to the twentieth-century objective to achieve specific balance, that is, to maintain normal levels of whichever hormone was secreted by those glands. In a sense, hormones, like vitamins, became analogues of Ehrlich's magic bullets.

Epidemiologic Transitions and the Biomedical Paradigm

The Changing Spectrum of Disease

At the turn of the twentieth century in the United States, pneumonia, tuberculosis, and enteritis were the major causes of death, accounting for 36.5 percent of all mortality. Heart disease was fifth among leading causes of death but represented only 6.2 percent of all mortality. Cancers ranked eighth and accounted for 3.2 percent of all deaths. By midcentury pneumonia ranked sixth among leading causes of mortality and caused only 3.4 percent of all deaths, compared to 14 percent in 1900. Similarly, in 1950 tuberculosis ranked seventh among leading causes of death and was responsible for 2.9 percent of all mortality, compared to 13.6 percent in 1900. Enteritis was no longer ranked in 1950. The maternal mortality rate, which was 850 per 100,000 live births at the turn of the century, by 1950 hovered around 200; and the infant mortality rate dropped from 36.2 per 1000 early in the century to 19.1 at midcentury (Galdston 1954; CDC 1995; Chang et al. 2003).

Accounting for less than 10 percent of all deaths in the early 1900s, cardiovascular disease and cancers were merely a backdrop to epidemic and endemic acute infections, but since 1950 these have been the leading causes of morbidity and mortality (more than 60 percent) in the West. As epidemiologists explore the multifactorial etiology of these diseases, biochemists elucidate interactions among various factors at the molecular level. For example, combined with the identification of lipids and lipoproteins as risk factors in cardiovascular disease, the metabolism of essential fatty acids has become better understood. In view of their complex etiologies, these illnesses do not submit as readily as infectious diseases once did to investigation, prevention, and treatment: whereas cortisone and insulin help us to manage rheumatoid arthritis and diabetes, they neither prevent nor cure those disorders and, significantly, have nowhere near the emotional impact of antibiotics. The penicillins, sulfa drugs, and Salk and Sabin polio vaccines set the standard for what one came to expect from biomedicine—full prevention and/or cure. In the context of today's most compelling illnesses, biomedicine no longer meets those expectations.

A New Biomedical Paradigm?

The aggregate of antibiotics, vaccination, improved nutrition, and public health measures has extended the average U.S. life span from thirty to forty years early in the twentieth century to seventy to eighty years today. Consequently, some of the goals of biomedicine have shifted from extending life to improving the quality of life in old age. A medical science once devoted to preventing and treating diseases brought from without (by bacteria, viruses) has had to turn its full attention to the interior, shifting focus from acute mortality to chronic morbidity. Preventive and curative modalities, which were clearly distinguished in the early 1900s, now approximate one another. Because specific etiology does not illuminate the medical problems of technologically advanced societies, the boundaries between nature (environment), body, and illness are blurred, as they had been in centuries past.

Since the 1970s, interest in holistic and humanistic therapeutics has emerged once again, as localization, reductionism, and discrete explanatory models no longer provide a universally compelling paradigm. In part, this trend started as a secular initiative from advocates of holistic health, who became dissatisfied with the allopathic (biomedical) health care system that serves emergency and major medical problems well but lacks personal doctors who will "bother" with minor ailments, frame their interest in health rather than in disease, and look after people "as people" (Galdston 1965: 168).

One expression of this revision of therapeutics is a renewed interest in the health potential of foods, once again blurring the distinction between food and medicine. Concern with health-promoting foods also is well established in the biomedical and nutrition sciences, as is reflected in the rapidly growing literature on functional foods and nutraceuticals (see chapter 7). Today an explosion of analytical data identifies food chemicals that have potential health benefits. Clinical studies of controlled diets demonstrate the effects of specific nutrients on biochemical and functional outcomes. Formerly mundane foods, primarily fruits and vegetables, have been scientized through reference to such healthful constituents as fiber and antioxidants. The acceptance of these molecular constituents within a holistic paradigm bears heavily on their association with natural foods.

While the rapidly growing use of nutrient and plant supplements to maintain and restore health appears to resonate a holistic essence, it has a substantial molecular basis as well. Designating common dietary components as "pharmafoods" draws attention to the chemical constituents of foods recognized for their health-promoting effects. In addition, some herbal supplements are, in fact, extracts that have specific and standardized chemical composition.

Thus, on the one hand, the reconceptualization of etiology and therapeutics represents a paradigmatic shift, a regression toward the medical idiom of earlier centuries. However, the intellectual framework of the biomedical and nutrition sciences remains intact, as particular foods command attention because of the presence of specific biochemicals that are projected onto models of cause and effect. In other words, we can locate the preventive and therapeutic potential of some foods in molecular analogues of the very drugs that are the quintessence of modern biomedicine. Consonant with the bioscientific paradigm, we now have "evidence [for] . . . the cellular and metabolic interactions between food constituents and biomarkers for disease" (Wrick 1994: 481). In the end, this perspective of specificity has significantly more impact on bioscientific research and on clinical perception and practice.

Although the biomedical model of specific etiology has lost much of its power, the public in Western countries has not lost faith in molecular models or pharmacotherapy per se. More complex phenomena are apprehended only at a lower level of resolution and so tend to be perceived through more holistic abstractions. On a general level, molecular homeostasis resonates traditional concepts of health and disease; for the public, the emerging biomedical paradigm has elements of both. If health is regarded as balance, then illness represents imbalance, and therapeutic objectives include restoring equilibrium. Foods regain some of their restorative value in this paradigm, but as molecules are incorporated into this synthetic model, specific constituents of foods and plants have recognized roles and presumed actions (Etkin and Johns 1998).

THIS SELECTIVE HISTORY centers on the relationships between food and biomedicine to set the intellectual framework for this book. The main point is that the bioscientific paradigm has both shifted and not. Although contemporary biomedicine is more holistic, emphasizing treatment of "the whole person," the tenet that links specific etiology to specific cure is still central, and foods once again hold a legitimate place in this explanatory model. This review serves as foundation for the remaining chapters, each devoted to a different food category: spices, fermented foods and beverages, social plants, animal products, and supplements and health foods.

CHAPTER 3

Spices

The Pharmacology of the Exotic

> In the dreams of all who pushed back the limits of the unknown world
> there is the same glitter of gold and precious stones, the same odor of
> far-fetched spices.
> —Sir Walter Raleigh

IN CHAPTER 2 I reviewed how, for much of the history of biomedicine, the boundary between medicines and foods was blurred. Spices in particular moved fluidly from one category to the other, sold not only by grocers and spice merchants but also by apothecaries and physicians. Interchangeable use of the terms *spicer*, *pepperer*, and *apothecary* and their European-language counterparts reflected commercial and public, as well as medical professionals', perceptions of overlap.

Western science has paid more attention to the healthful potential of spices relative to other food categories. One reason is the assumption that, because spices played a prominent role in the early history of Western medicine, these items are more likely to have significant pharmacologic action. This rationale is faulty, in view of the fact that much of biomedical practice was based in a succession of iterations on the paradigm of humors and was ineffective well through the nineteenth century. As it turns out, the premise that spices are an especially pharmocodynamic group of plants does have an empirical foundation but one that has been only relatively recently substantiated according to bioscientific standards of evidence.

Spices differ from other domesticated and commercialized plant species in at least one pharmacologically significant way: the marked organoleptic qualities that signal the presence of allelochemicals, which have been bred out of many cultivated food plants, have been retained in the domesticated spices that are valued specifically for those flavors, scents, and other redolences. In recent decades this, as well as an expanded pharmacologic potential, has been corroborated for many spices through the characterization of specific functional compounds with discrete activities. Further, I suggest that bioscience finds spices compelling because, like pharmaceuticals, they are specific (have unique and distinguishing tastes), small (in volume), and powerful (in the stimuli they emit and, in many cases, physiologic action). In this way, spices fit an allopathic model of healing: indeed, by virtue of these features, we might say that spices embody the quintessence of biomedicine.

This chapter treats spices generally, through definition and historical review, highlights chile pepper in a case study of a transglobal spice, and offers a novel approach that emphasizes evolution and context to explore the pharmacological potential of spices.

Definitions

If carbohydrate-rich superfoods anchor a cuisine (see chapter 1), spices are its sails. These botanically diverse items serve many functions. In all the world's cuisines they flavor, color, and preserve foods. Throughout history spices have served as gifts or obligations to the ruling class and as currency in commercial transactions; they are medicines (spice of life) and were included among grave goods and in embalming fluids (spice of death). As perfumes and cosmetics, spices disguise the taste and smell of unpalatable foods[1] and body odor. They mediate life-cycle ceremonies by marking individuals (e.g., monks, brides) through scent and color. Commonly they are the medium of transaction for witchcraft and sorcery and are burned as incense and fumigants for religious and funerary rites. Culturally, spices are signatures (flavor or signal prints) that distinguish the cuisines of ethnically diverse peoples and, within groups, mark social asymmetries through varied applications, combinations, and frequency and volume of consumption.

The food industry defines spices as "the dry parts of a plant, such as roots, leaves, and seeds, [that] impart to food a certain flavor and pungent stimuli" (Hirasa and Takemasa 1998: 1). Generally, the term *spice* has been used to refer to dry parts of plants of tropical or semitropical origin, whereas *culinary herb* has designated the aromatic leaves or seeds of nonwoody temperate plants. *Condiments*, which by some definitions are

TABLE 3.1. Botanical Classification of Spices[a]

Monocotyledonae

Liliiflorae	Liliaceae	chives, garlic, onion
	Iridaceae	saffron
Scitaminae	Zingiberaceae	cardamom, galangal, ginger, melegueta pepper, mioga, turmeric
Orchidales	Orchidaceae	vanilla

Dicotyledonae

Sympetale

Tubiflorae	Labiatae	basil, lavender, marjoram, mint, oregano, perilla, rosemary, sage, savory, thyme
	Solanaceae	chile, paprika
	Pedaliaceae	sesame
Campanulatae	Asteraceae	chicory, tarragon

Archichlamydeae

Piperales	Piperaceae	African cubebs, Benin pepper, black pepper, cubebs, long pepper
Ranales	Myristicaceae	mace, nutmeg
	Lauraceae	bay, cinnamon
	Illiciaceae	star anise
Rhoeadales	Brassicaceae	cress, horseradish, mustard
Rosales	Fabaceae	fenugreek, licorice, tamarind
Geraniales	Rutaceae	flower pepper, Japanese pepper
Myrtiflorae	Myrtaceae	allspice, clove
Umbelliflorae	Umbelliferae	ajwain, aniseed, caraway, celery, coriander, cumin, dill, fennel, parsley

a. Angiospermae (flowering plants); Hirasa and Takemasa (1998)

multicomponent and added to already-prepared foods, may be spices as well. These even semifixed definitions do not serve, however: the origin of some flavoring plants is not known (or of interest) outside of botany or food-science circles; places of origin do not necessarily correspond to contemporary places of production and consumption; and more than one plant part of a spice or herb may be used to flavor foods. Substantively, then, these categories overlap; the distinctions are Eurocentric, based in how people who write about food flavors came to know and use these

TABLE 3.2. Pungent Compounds in Spices

Basic structure	Spice	Pungent constituents[a]	Sensation
Acid amide group R-CO-N-R-R	chile black pepper, white pepper	capsaicin piperine, chavicine	hot ↑
Carbonyl group R-CO-R	ginger	zingerol*, shogaol*	
Thioether group R-S-R	onion	diallyl sulfide*	
Isothiocyanate group R-N-C-S	horseradish mustard	allyl-thiocyanate* allyl-thiocyanate* p-hydroxybenzyl isothiocyanate	↓ sharp

Modified from Hirasa and Takemasa (1998).
a. Volatile compounds are identified by an asterisk.

plants. Further, these are functional definitions, not botanical ones which might, for example, highlight the clustering of spice genera in certain families, such as Labiatae, Piperaceae, Umbelliferae, and Zingiberaceae (Table 3.1).

In this chapter I use the term *spice* inclusively, to designate all varieties of food flavorings, fragrances, flavor enhancers, colorings, appetite stimulants, and other stimuli from the tropics of Africa, Asia, and the Americas; the composite Mediterranean/Middle East/North Africa area; and the colder regions of northern Europe and Asia (Appendix).[2] Further, I entertain other definitions of spices that resonate simultaneously their phytochemistry, roles in traditional and transformed cuisines, and medicinal properties.

Taste

The flavor of a spice is imparted by volatile essential oils, which are primarily constituted by terpenes (carbon-oxygen-hydrogen compounds; see Table 1.2). Monoterpenes (ten-carbon compounds) typically are strongly aromatic and very volatile. Essential oils are complex compounds that vary in the relative proportions of individual chemicals of which they are comprised. The flavor characteristics of individual plants of the same spice species can vary with growth conditions (soil, hydration, temperature), collection (time of harvest, duration of drying), and the circumstances of storage and transport. The pungency of a spice, like its taste, depends on the concentration and composition of essential oils. Pungent compounds are classified with reference to the structural characteristics summarized in Table 3.2, where, in descending order of presentation, they range along a continuum of perception from hot, which diffuses through the mouth, to sharp, which stimulates the oral and nasal mucous membranes. Most sharp compounds are volatile and are identical to the flavor compounds of that spice; most hot compounds are nonvolatile, thus distinct from the flavor principles (Hirasa and Takemasa 1998).

A Cultural History of Spices

The geopolitical significance of spices is revealed in their cultural history. Aromatic and pungent plants have been used in food preparation for thousands of years. For example, as early as the third century BCE, black pepper (*Piper nigrum*) from India was an item of commerce in the Middle East, and Malukan cloves (*Syzygium aromaticum* [L.] Merr. & Perry, Myrtaceae) were traded to China. Some eastern Asian origin myths center on spices, underscoring their prominence in consolidating political power. As Arabian Muslim cultural influences moved through North Africa into the Iberian Peninsula, small quantities of rare and valuable commodities were transported, including cloves, cinnamon (*Cinnamomum zeylanicum* Blume, Lauraceae), pepper, and nutmeg (*Myristica fragrans*), as well as the more affordable saffron (*Crocus sativus*), cumin (*Cuminum cyminum* L., Umbelliferae), and coriander (*Coriandrum sativum* L., Umbelliferae). These spices were transported for consumption and trade, with care to carry seeds as well to begin production in new lands. In the West it was not until the first century CE that there was a sizeable increase in the use of spices to flavor food. Until recent times, spices were expensive and their exchange value overlapped that of precious metals and gemstones. In the early years of the spice trade, merchants generated mystery about the origin of spices, which contributed to their appeal and, as a corollary, market value. The accelerated regional circulation and eventual globalization of spices is intimately linked to European discovery of indigenous cultures and foods, colonialism, and mercantile capitalism.

Spices, especially those endemic to the tropics, have a history of substantial geopolitical significance. Mesopotamia and India were centers of spice origins and trade in the first century BCE, and ancient overland spice trade routes (e.g., the Incense Route) peppered the terrain that linked the eastern Mediterranean to Asia and Southeast Asia. Late in the first century CE, the Romans learned how to harness the wind systems (monsoons) of the Indian Ocean (which the Arabs might already have known and concealed) and built ships on a greatly increased scale, which ended the Arab monopoly of trade with India.

Much of the European voyaging of later centuries involved the search for direct trade routes to the spice-producing regions in the East. The exploration of Asia by Marco Polo (1254–1324) established Italy, specifically Venice, as the Medieval center of the European spice and drug trade. In the early 1400s Portugal initiated a systematic program of exploration and became the leader among European navigating countries. Later in that century Portuguese ships first crossed the equator, Bartholomew Díaz rounded the Cape of Good Hope (1486), Christopher Columbus reached the Americas (1492), and Vasco da Gama found a route to India's west coast (1498). In the late 1400s, Pedro Alvarez Cabral, commander of Portugal's first merchant voyage to India (1500), established two trading posts on the west coast, thus shifting the centers of commerce from Italy and Egypt to the ports of Portugal and Spain.

By the mid-1500s overland spice trade with the East had been reestablished, including the shipment of as much as a million pounds of black pepper over traditional routes through the eastern Mediterranean. But even that was less than 20 percent of the volume of spices that reached Europe via Spanish and Portuguese ports. Over the next few centuries, competition for control of spice-producing regions was the cause of much of the military conflict among European nations and great suffering among indigenous populations forced into plantation spice production for export to Europe. By the end of the 1600s the Dutch colonizers had virtually driven the Portuguese and English out of the Spice Islands (Maluku) of eastern Indonesia (the East Indies) and established monopolies not only in nutmeg, mace (*Myristica fragrans*), cloves, and cinnamon but also in pepper, ginger (*Zingiber officinale* Roscoe, Zingiberaceae), and turmeric (*Curcuma longa* L., Zingiberaceae). A century later, England was in the ascendancy, and the United States had become a major player in world spice trade. Compared with other tropical products such as sugar and tea, spices had a minor role in the economy of the British colonial empire, and the Dutch were the leading spice traders in the nineteenth and early twentieth centuries. It is safe to generalize that spice commerce was critical to many national economies, as evidenced by repeated and costly expeditions to spice-growing regions and the extension of struggles for control to political rivalries and military conflict (Toussaint-Samat 1992; Andaya 1993; Dalby 2000).

Today spice production and commerce are far less centralized than in earlier times, having expanded to include many countries in the tropics and a few in the temperate zones: for example, Brazil is a major source of black pepper, Jamaica produces allspice (*Pimenta dioica* [L.] Merr., Myrtaceae) and ginger, and the United States, Canada, and Europe are significant sources of sesame seed (*Sesamum indicum* L., Pedaliaceae), basil, parsley (*Petroselinum crispum* [Miller] A. W. Hill, Umbelliferae), and other herbs. In recent years, the United States has been the world's main spice buyer, followed by Germany, Japan, and France (Davidson 1999).

Unique Tastes Become Transcultural Flavors: The Case of Chile

New World Roots of Popular Fruits

This section highlights chile, arguably the most commonly consumed spice worldwide. *Capsicum* is the botanical and in some sectors the popular name for a plant genus that includes diverse species and cultivars: chile, pimento, pimiento, paprika, and bell (or sweet/green) peppers. A genus of the family Solanaceae, capsicums are related to the New World tomato (*L. esculentum*) and potato (*S. tuberosum*) and to the Old World eggplant (*Solanum melongena* L.) and the toxic black nightshade (*Solanum nigrum* L.).

All capsicums are New World natives. Wild chile peppers originated in present-day Bolivia to southwestern Brazil and spread throughout South and Central America via seed dispersal by birds (if nonpungent taxa are included in the genus, a second center of diversity is Meso-america). For 8000 years or so, wild chiles were an integral element in the diets of peoples of the Yucatan Peninsula and southern Mexico, where they served also as currency. Chiles featured prominently in the spiritual life of the Aztec, Maya, and Inca, who called them "bird peppers" and identified particular avian taxa as conveyors of knowledge about and propagators of the fruit (Nabhan 1997, 2004). Chiles were forbidden during fasts intended to appease the gods, and the Inca venerated the chile as a holy plant, one of the four brothers of their creation myth. Chiles were domesticated by 3000 BCE, and were cultivated in as many as thirty varieties by 500 CE, when the Aztec Empire flourished.

In 1493 Christopher Columbus returned from his quest for a western route to the East carrying a pungent spice that he found on the Caribbean island Española (Haiti/Dominican Republic). Believing he had reached the East, Columbus created some confusion by identifying the natives as Indians and calling the pungent spice *pimiento* after the Asian Indian black pepper (*pimienta*), which he so desperately sought. The indigenous Arawak of Española called the fruit *axí*, which was transliterated to the Spanish *ají*, still used today in the Dominican Republic, other parts of the Caribbean, and much of South America. Some Amerindian groups in the Andean region retain the ancient terms *uchu* and *huayca*. The Nahuatl Mexican term *chilli* was transliterated to the Spanish *chile*, both of which are regarded as variants of the *Oxford English Dictionary's* primary spelling *chilli* (Andrews 1995, 2003).

In contrast to the stammeringly slow adoption of the New World tomato, potato, and other "discovered" foods, the pungent capsicums spread east with marked speed. From Europe chile peppers rapidly diffused along established spice trade routes to Africa and Asia, where the plants adapted to the geoclimatic conditions of the tropical Old World. Even in the face of opposition from the real (black) pepper traders in Europe, chiles spread from the New World to Europe and Asia in about fifty years. On India's Malabar (southwest) Coast, three varieties of chile were developed for export along ancient trade routes to Europe through the Middle East and along the new Portuguese route around Africa to Europe. Portuguese traders introduced chiles to Japan and Southeast Asia; from there, seed dispersal by birds established chiles throughout humanly inaccessible inland areas and insular Southeast Asia. Caravan routes linking the Middle East, India, Burma, and China introduced New World foods, one artifact of which is the more prominent role of chile in the cuisines of southwestern Hunan and Szechuan, compared with other regions of China.

At the end of the fifteenth century, the Mediterranean was characterized by two discrete trading arenas: the Spanish-dominated western Mediterranean and the Ottoman Empire to the east. At the center of the European spice trade, Venice depended on goods from Asia via the Ottomans, who received commodities from Portuguese ports on the Malabar Coast and Persian Gulf. Products that reached central Europe were disseminated to other parts of Europe. Supplies from Asia and Portuguese sources in Africa, India, and Lisbon also reached Antwerp, the primary European port. Along these routes, between 1535 and 1585, chiles were introduced into the markets of Italy, Germany, England, the Balkans, and Moravia but became prominent in the cuisines only of Turkey and the Balkans. When the Napoleonic Wars interrupted European spice supplies, Balkan paprika substituted for the original American cultivars.

After chile trade and consumption had become established in the Middle East, Asia, and Europe, Spain played a more prominent role in circulating New World plants: an Acapulco-Manila trade route operated for 250 years to transfer goods between Mexico and eastern Asia. Spanish colonies in what are now New Mexico and Florida traded with the Caribbean and Mexico, receiving chiles and other goods, forty years before the introduction of the first chiles to a British colony (Virginia) in 1621 (Dewitt and Bosland 1995; Ho 1995; Dewitt 1999; Andrews 2003).

Although taxonomists and historians are clear in designating chile as native to tropical America, many contemporary world cultures understand it to be intrinsic to their own traditional cuisines and culinary identities. The apparent enthusiasm, or at least ease, with which diverse cultures embraced chiles reflects not so much an invention of tradition as it testifies to how well chiles conform to established palates. Through a syncretization of flavors, chiles were readily adopted into cuisines already marked by pungent spices such as cloves, ginger, and long (*Piper longum* L. Piperaceae), black (*P. nigrum*), flower (*Zanthoxylum zanthoxyloides* Lam., Rutaceae), and African melegueta (*Aframomum melegueta* Schumann, Zingiberaceae) peppers. They thrived in the new environments and in many areas became a spontaneous crop, growing and reseeding itself without human agency. Historians further speculate that the ready adoption of capsicums marks their confusion with black pepper, affordable then only by the wealthy. Indeed in many areas chile overshadowed or replaced the original pungents as a less expensive spice. Today India, China, and Pakistan lead the world in chile production. Familiarity with chile-flavored Szechuan dishes, Indian curries, and West African soups makes it difficult to conjure the short history of chiles in those regions.

Chile Embellishes Cuisines and Pharmacopoeias around the World

Chile pepper was widely embraced not only as a food flavoring but also as medicine. In its region of origin, Aztec peoples relieved toothache with chile juice and mixed chile with maize flour to treat sore throat, asthma, and cough; the Maya also treated respiratory disorders with chile fruit and applied its juice to infected wounds. These applications were diffused and embellished and other uses were discovered, as chile was introduced around the world. The apprehension of these medicinal uses in the context of pharmacologic actions listed in the Appendix rationalizes many indigenous pharmacopoeias (although not all preventive and therapeutic objectives overlap pharmacologic action). In contemporary Western societies, chiles are among the more commonly used botanical supplements and phytoceuticals (see chapter 7).

Hausa Cultural Construction of *Barkono*/Chile

The relatively recent introduction of chile into West Africa stands in stark contrast to its importance for populations of the region, including Hausa in northern Nigeria. In Hurumi, at least one of the three daily meals centers on a dense, bland grain porridge, *tuwo*, made from guineacorn or millet or less commonly from rice or maize. The chief ingredients of several varieties of *miya* (the companion, piquant soup) are tomato (*tumatir*), various cultivated and wild leaves (*ganye*), okra (*kubewa*), garden egg (*yalo, Solanum melongena* L., Solanaceae), pumpkin (*kabewa, Cucurbita pepo*) and/or melon (*agusi, Citrullus lanatus* [Thunb.] Mansf., Cucurbitaceae), peanut (*Arachis hypogaea*) or palm oil (*man ja, Elaeis guineensis* Jacq., Palmae) and/or butter (*man shanu*), and ideally meat or fish. The varied flavors of miya are imparted by combinations of the fermented soup base daddawa (see chapter 4) with salt, chile pepper, and the compound spice *yaji* (discussed below). Other dishes provide appropriate, if less esteemed, substitutes for tuwo da miya for the morning and midday meals. These include gruels and vegetable-leaf mixtures supplemented by peanuts, beans, rice, spices, and oils. Between-meal foods include various traditional calorie-, fat-, and/or protein-dense snacks and seasonal fruits. For contemporary villagers, the substance of cuisine, but less so its rhythm (meal and food-type sequencing), has been impacted on all levels by Hurumi's increased participation in the global economy.

Among singlet spices, *barkono*/chile is the signature of Hausa cuisine in northern Nigeria. Hausa themselves characterize their flavor repertoire as narrow and identify barkono as their primary flavor principle; outsiders (e.g., from other regions of Africa and Europe) typically characterize Hausa cuisine as remarkably hot. Hurumi residents use barkono to refer generally to chile peppers, but they further differentiate among cultivars with reference to taste, shape/size, and suitability for medicine. *Tsiduhu* is the smallest and hottest of local chiles; barkono fruit is small, and it and tsiduhu are favored medicinally because they are more powerful. The fruit of *bunsurun barkono* (goat's chile) is somewhat larger and not very hot. *Ataruhu* has a round and lobed shape; *dan kadana* is a larger, long and thin variety; and *tattasai*, the largest local chile, is drupe-shaped. These last three, milder chiles are indicated for children's medicines.

The most common Hausa medicinal uses of barkono are for intestinal disorders, including worms; abrasions and wounds; fevers; and *sabara*, a complex spirit-caused disorder, a strong disease requiring strong medicine, with internal and external phases that include one or more of these symptoms: swellings that can develop into pustular sores that may itch and fuse, fever, sloughing. For example, barkono is snorted to induce sneezing, which helps to externalize the internal phase of rash diseases such as measles and chickenpox, while medicines taken later in the therapeutic process are directed at symptom resolution. Barkono is a powerful deterrent against sorcery. For *ciwon gindi*, a type of lower back pain, chile promotes the egress of accumulated *majina* (phlegm) at the locus of soreness. In another medicinal domain, barkono is featured among proscribed foods for certain conditions, for example, *fara*, a symptom complex

FIGURE 3.1. Capsicum, okra, tomatoes, and fish sold by Maguzawa women in a local market near Hurumi. Photo by Paul J. Ross, 1987

marked chiefly by anemia, a weakened state of health for which powerful foods and medicines risk exacerbation and complications leading to *shawara*, an overlapping symptom complex that intersects hepatitis.

The cultural significance of barkono is reflected among compositional elements of *Bori*, the indigenous, pre-Islamic Hausa religion that centers on the mediation of *iskoki*/spirits who reside in the invisible city of Jangare, one of whose twelve houses is headed by Barkono.[3] In other words, ancient Hausa religious traditions were transformed some time after 1493, so that the New World barkono was added to or replaced something in the existing foundational structure of Bori. The cultural significance of chile in Hausaland is further evidenced by the metaphoric uses of barkono, as is apparent in these proverbs:

Namiji barkono ne. Sai a tauna shi a san yajinsa.
A husband is like a pepper. Not until you chew do you know how hot
  he is. [Experience reveals a man's character.]

Audu barkono ne (barkonam mutane ne).
Audu is a chile (a chile person). [Audu is irascible.]

Ta sha barkono.
She ate a chile. [She is angry.]

Political Economy, Globalization, Commodification

The transposition of the American chile to cuisines and pharmacopoeias
around the world provides an interesting, and in some ways unique,
example of the confluence of food traditions, geopolitics, and the cultural
construction and social negotiation of foods and medicines. From the
perspective of political economy, chile peppers were not simply an introduced commodity; in large part they took the place of black pepper, an
item that carried high social and cultural salience in many parts of the
world. Black pepper itself, as well as chile and other spices, and cash crops
such as tobacco (*Nicotiniana tabacum* L., Solanaceae) and coffee all are
integral to an extended history of European imperial expansion that included colonization and the appropriation of local peoples and their
products. Like other globalized commodities, chile peppers were more
than simple introductions and substitutions; they were further transformed in their cultures of destination, where they have become key
elements of highly diverse cuisines, pharmacopoeias, and languages.

Physiologic Effects of Spices

The scientific literature on spices is vast and has been expanding rapidly
in recent years. As evidence, over an arbitrarily selected recent two-
year span (2004–2005), virtually every issue of the following journals included one or more articles on the medicinal uses and pharmacology of
one or more spices: *Pharmaceutical Biology*, *Journal of Ethnopharmacology*, and *Planta Medica*. These figures from PubMed searches also reveal
scientific interest: garlic was the subject of 1984 articles, onion of 1616,

capsicum of 875, cinnamon of 513, ginger of 454, and turmeric of 360. Spices that in the last several hundred years have been incorporated into Western cuisines, as well as spices that Western scientists identify as the signature of non-Western cuisines (e.g., capsicum, ginger), are overrepresented in these scientific studies.

Because the phytochemistry of spices has been better characterized than that of any other functional or taxonomic group, more is known about their potential interactions with pharmaceuticals, foods, and other botanicals. Still, this knowledge is only emergent. Some interactions can be predicted intuitively. For example, in theory, plants that contain eugenol and other platelet inhibitors may potentiate anticoagulant drugs. However, we must seriously question whether this is clinically significant, as it applies to almost all the plants in the Appendix, whose use is widespread; also, interactions depend strongly on whether the plant and drug are consumed at or near the same time, as well as on how the plant is prepared, combined with other foods and drugs, and consumed.

Although the category spices embraces considerable botanical and phytochemical diversity, subgroups of spices can be linked through similar physiologic effects. For example, pungent compounds stimulate body heat production, influence blood pressure in the peripheral circulation, promote lipid metabolism, and affect metabolic regulation through nervous system and hormonal influences. They enhance digestion by promoting peristalsis and the secretion of digestive enzymes, stimulating the liver to produce acid-rich bile, and increasing absorption into the blood from the intestines. Antioxidant activity characterizes many spices, especially those in the Labiatae: phenolic glucosides, caffeic acid, protocatechuic acid, rosmarinic acid, and phenylpropionic acid in oregano (*Origanum vulgare* L.), and carnosol, rosmanol, epirosmanol, and isorosmanol in rosemary (*Rosmarinus officinalis* L.); combinations of antioxidant and other spices have synergistic effects (Beckstrom-Sternberg and Duke 1994; Hirasa and Takemasa 1998; Platel and Srinivasan 2004).

By way of illustration, the Appendix lists some of the constituents and isolated physiologic effects of thirty-three spices selected to represent a variety of organoleptic qualities (see chapter 1), places of origin, botanical growth form (habit), plant parts, and phytochemical spectra. This compilation resonates the bioscientific research paradigm in which natural products are reduced to their constituents and/or extracts and studied through controlled laboratory protocols that range across in vitro assays, animal studies, and human clinical contexts. The challenge is to connect these disembodied observations in an analytic framework that represents real people's experiences with spices in both medicinal and dietary contexts. The remainder of this chapter moves beyond catalogues of constituents and activities to suggest novel approaches to the ethnopharmacology of spices. This is accomplished by considering one class of activity, antimicrobial action, and addressing that from both an evolutionary and a contextualized perspective that focuses on composite spices.

Novel Approaches to Spice Pharmacology

Antimicrobial Action

Because the germ theory of disease has been the predominant paradigm in the West for the last hundred years, the antimicrobial action of spices has been a special subject of attention. Spices are prominently represented in the pharmacopoeias of contemporary indigenous groups who use these plants to treat wounds, abscesses, and systemic infections; in childbirth and early postpartum; and to improve the healthful qualities of foods. Thousands of years ago in China and India spices were used medicinally and to preserve foods. Similarly, in the West people have taken advantage of the antimicrobial attributes of spices for centuries. Ancient texts record systematic use of spices in places of their endemicity. The ancient Egyptians embalmed the dead with spices such as thyme (*Thymus vulgaris* L., Labiatae), cinnamon, and cumin. In early Greece and Rome mint was used to prevent milk from spoiling and coriander extended the shelf life of meats. Spices were consumed in such high volume in the Middle Ages that one might regard them more as foods, although they also played a specific role in treating infectious diseases such as typhus and cholera.

Starting in the 1880s and at an increasing pace through the twentieth century, biomedical research concentrated on the antimicrobial action of spices. Today, the growing problem posed by drug-resistant microorganisms accelerates bioscientific search for more effective preventions and treatments, including (again) a special interest in spices. Volatiles and pungent spices tend to have strong antimicrobial activity, as do constituents that include aldehyde (–CHO) or hydroxyl (–OH) groups. Especially when one employs the expanded definition of spice, literally tens of thousands of studies establish antimicrobial action against a taxonomically diverse range of organisms, including some of the most important pathogenic bacteria and toxin-producing microorganisms that affect humans, such as cholera, tuberculosis, dysentery, and staphylococcal infection. It is not possible to determine how important a role knowledge of such activity factors into the decisions that shape cuisines, but it would surely be wrong to suppose that it was not at all significant.

Evolutionary Implications of Spiced Cuisines

A recurrent theme in the literature on antimicrobial spices is the role they may play in food safety. Some authors invoke an evolutionary trajectory of adaptive responses, noting the antiquity and ubiquity of spice use, including during times and in places in which food preservation could not be supported by refrigeration or cognate technologies. For example, Sherman and colleagues advanced these four predictions (Billing and Sherman 1998: 4; Sherman and Flaxman 2001: 145): spices kill or inhibit food-spoilage microorganisms; spice use should be heaviest in hot climates, where (unrefrigerated) foods spoil most rapidly; spices with the most potent antimicrobial properties should be favored in areas where foods spoil most quickly; and, within a country, meat recipes should be more heavily spiced than vegetable recipes.

Their correlational study inferred (but did not measure directly) how spices affect people's health by quantifying the frequency of spice use across a range of cultures and geographies. Inclusion criteria limited the research to meat-inclusive[4] cuisines and minimally 50 (preferably more than 100) recipes from at least two traditional cookbooks. The researchers analyzed 4578 recipes from 107 cookbooks representing thirty-six countries, sixteen of the nineteen major language groups, and every continent. Additional data were compiled on the antimicrobial activities of individual spices, their botanical characterization, and temperature ranges for each country. The forty-three spices include groups that cohere around one or a small number of shared constituents, for example, "capsicum" includes all members of that genus that produce capsaicin and "onion" groups onion, garlic, leek, and other *Allium* spp.

Sherman and colleagues' findings bear out their predictions.[5] Their literature review, like the one I conducted, uncovered substantial antimicrobial activity for many spices; and all spices in their study were used medicinally in diverse indigenous therapeutic systems. Whereas the medicinal use of spices is episodic (in response to the diagnosis of specific and general symptoms) and includes consumption in relatively large volume, in cooking spices are used in small quantities and added routinely. This suggests that spiced foods may prevent food spoilage and remedy chronic problems such as micronutrient deficiencies and persistent enteric infection.

In general, the cuisines of hot-climate countries include numerous spices, which are used frequently (in more than 40 percent of recipes); cold-climate country cuisines use fewer spices and less often (in fewer than 5 percent of recipes). Significant positive correlations hold between mean annual temperature and the number of recipes that include at least one spice, mean number of spices per recipe, the proportion of frequently used spices in each country, and the mean proportion of recipes that call for each strongly inhibitory spice used in each country (at least 75 percent microbial inhibition). There is also a positive (but not significant) correlation between the proportion of microorganisms inhibited by each spice and the percentage of countries that use that spice, that is, antimicrobially more potent spices are used more broadly. Whereas there is no correspondence between mean annual temperature and the number of spice plants growing in a country, positive correlations exist between the number of countries in which each spice grows and the number that use it. Further, mean annual temperature and the proportion of spices used in the countries in which they grow are positively correlated. In other words, although people in hot countries do not have a larger selection of locally growing spices, they use a higher percentage of those that are available, especially the more potent antimicrobials. Finally, meat-based recipes from all thirty-six countries designate a significantly larger number of spices than vegetable-based recipes, an average of 3.9 and 2.4 spices, respectively; and the proportions of dishes that include more than one spice and more than one strongly antimicrobial spice are significantly higher for meat, compared to vegetable, dishes (Sherman and Hash 2001).

The methodology of these studies can be criticized on several counts. For example, only the United States and China are regarded to have regional cuisines (an artifact of the cookbooks located by the authors), and then only "northern" and "southern"; from isolated recipes one cannot know how often that dish is consumed. Still, the argument is compelling that cuisines are shaped in part by the antimicrobial action of spices.

In Sherman and colleagues' explanation, enhancing the palatability of foods is only a proximate explanation of spicing, while the ultimate reason is that spices inhibit or kill food-spoiling microorganisms. We are not served by deciding between proximate and ultimate explanations and should instead consider the multiplex and complementary nature of a suite of objectives that underlie food choice and preparation: pharmacologic action *and* aesthetics, learned tastes, and the cultural construction of cuisines (see chapter 1).

Spices in the Context of Complex Cuisines

As described above, many spices are synergists that enhance the bioavailability and potency of companion phytochemicals. Thus, we may apply a biocultural perspective that explores spice complexes in which a number of discrete flavors are blended. I selected three region-specific composite spices, with overlapping constituents, to explore the intersection of cultural constructions of cuisine and pharmacologic potential.

Ayurvedic Trikatu

The Sanskrit term for three acrids, *trikatu,* is a traditional Ayurvedic formulation that combines the fruits of long and black peppers and ginger rhizome in equal portions. Although not technically a culinary spice, trikatu has a long history as a digestive and is marketed today as a food supplement. In this way, trikatu provides a pharmacologically and culturally interesting contrast for Chinese five-spice and Hausa yaji, discussed below. Trikatu is an essential element of many, even more complex botanical mixtures that are used in the treatment of a wide variety of disorders. While some contemporary Ayurvedic practitioners dismiss the addition of trikatu as a prescription that "lacks reason" and is employed "only for the sake of rhyme," others invoke the traditional explanation that these acrids help to restore balance among the *doshas* (dynamic forces) *kapha, pitta,* and *vata.*

Occasional citations in the scientific literature note that trikatu increases the potency of medicines already clinically judged effective in their own right, as when added to the leaves of Malabar nut/*vasaka* (*Justi-cia adhatoda* L., Acanthaceae) in the treatment of asthma (Atal et al. 1981). More recent studies have determined that trikatu affects the phar-macokinetic profile of drugs; specifically, it promotes bioavailability of some (e.g., vasicine, sparteine, phenytoin, propranolol, theophylline, sul-fadiazine, and tetracycline) and reduces the bioavailability of others (e.g., the antituberculosis drugs isoniazid and rifampicin) (Johri and Zutshi 1992; Karan et al. 1999). Once it had been determined that the primary compound responsible for these effects is piperine, a major alkaloid in peppers (but not in ginger), investigations have concentrated on this phytoconstituent, rather than on the conventional three-part crude drug preparation. This approach is consistent with a biomedical research pro-tocol that narrows inquiry to discrete, isolatable units (see chapter 2). This course of study both clarifies, by identifying known or characterizable phytoconstituents, and oversimplifies, by taking out of the mix the effects of other constituents and by fragmenting the cultural integrity of this traditional spice complex. The constituents and activities of these three spices are summarized in the Appendix and suggest significant phar-macologic potential beyond synergisms.

Still, these findings have implications for polypharmacy, dose and timing of medications, and the redesign of drug administration. For exam-ple, the cost and difficulty of parenteral administration of some drugs may be mitigated by changing to oral administration accompanied by trikatu or other drug potentiators. Further, because trikatu is comprised of three culinary spices, exploration of its pharmacologic profile reinforces how consumption outside of clinical contexts may influence health.

Chinese Five-Spice

The highly aromatic Chinese five-spice is pungent, fragrant, hot, and slightly sweet all at once. It is comprised of equal amounts of star anise (*Illicium verum* Hook f., Illiciaceae), clove, cinnamon, fennel, and flower pepper. Regionally variable optional ingredients include ginger, galangal (*Alpinia officinarum* Hance, Zingiberaceae), and licorice. Although one could argue that increasing the number of components erodes the integ-rity of the five, this offers an example of how rules are created to break rules, in this case normative cuisine prescriptions. In some sectors it is referred to as the "five-spice family," underscoring both its compound

FIGURE 3.2. Preparation of a fixed-formula complex medicine, such as Chinese five-spice, in the apothecary of Xi Yuan Hospital of the China Academy of Traditional Chinese Medicine, Beijing. Photo by Paul J. Ross, 2002

nature and its structural symmetry in Chinese cosmology, which is characterized by five-part domains (see chapter 1): the universe is composed by earth, wood, fire, metal, and water, five phases that are associated with virtually everything else, so that human circumstances are understood through the integration of five colors, five large body organs, and so on. In the context of food and medicine, the five tastes include sour, salt, bitter, sweet, and piquant, and the five smells are fragrant, scorched, rancid, rotten, and putrid. Elements of the five-part domains must be carefully balanced among themselves and with parallel domains, so that the universe is harmonized by the integration of social life, cooking, medicine, and other activities. Scholars agree that throughout history the boundary between Chinese food and medicine has been especially porous (Anderson 1988).

Individually and in various permutations, these five plants figure prominently in the medical traditions of China: all are used as digestive tonics and for gastrointestinal disorders; star anise and flower pepper are diuretic, flower pepper also is carminative, cinnamon is analgesic and antiemetic and is used during the postpartum and to slow aging, and fennel is used in pain management (Simoons 1991).

This complex perspective on health and healing invites us to speculate about the pharmacologic potential of the five spices (see Appendix), for example, how the phytochemical characteristics of individual components are interpreted in the light of overarching principles of balance, judgments about the efficacy of complex versus singlet preparations for disease prevention and therapy, and how the individual as diner engages the last stage of preparation of medicinal foods by using sauces and other table items to create order out of disparate elements.

Yaji in Northern Nigeria

Based on my intimate knowledge of its cultural constructions in Hausa diet and medicine, I can speculate more productively about the pharmacologic potential of the composite spice yaji. As barkono is the singlet signature flavor of Hausa cuisine, yaji is its composite counterpart, offering nuances of taste and a complex texture. It contains barkono, as well as citta maikwaya (melegueta pepper), cittar aho (ginger), fasakwari (flower pepper), kanumfari (clove), kimba (guinea pepper), kulla (thonningia), and masoro (Benin pepper) (see Appendix). Of these, only barkono is cultivated locally. Hurumi residents purchase prepared yaji or individual constituents at markets. Some women prepare yaji in volume, powdering the ingredients together with mortar and pestle (accompanied by much sneezing throughout the compound), in anticipation of their own needs as well as for sale throughout the village.

The plants that comprise yaji all are pharmacologically dynamic. Singly and together they represent significant antimicrobial, anti-inflammatory, antioxidant, and carminative potential and are vitamin rich (see Appendix). These activities take on more meaning in the context of the specific culinary and medicinal uses of yaji, such as in the early postpartum and for male circumcision.

Haihuwa/Childbirth. Like most traditional cultures, Hausa regard pregnancy as a predominantly healthful phase for the duration of which concerns center on good nutrition, and virtually none of the circumstances of pregnancy is treated with medicines. Certainly, the potential for complications is widely understood. Gestational age, for example, can influence the baby's viability. Hausa say that a child born prematurely in the seventh month will survive, because the body lacks form, but a child born during the eighth month surely will die (see below, *kaciyar maza*). Conversely, the first forty days postpartum are regarded as a period of risk for both the new mother (*mai jego*), who risks infection and other complications of childbirth, and the baby (*jinjiri*) for whom the primary concerns are *fara* (see above) and *mayankwaniya*, another symptom complex that overlaps marasmus (protein-calorie malnutrition) and can incorporate or eventuate from *fara*.

A complex suite of medicines and behaviors address health concerns, as well as assure progress in the child's development and the mother's ability to breastfeed. Mai jego should avoid both literal and figurative exposure to *dauda*/pollution, which extends to not having sexual relations with her husband for the forty-day period. After birth the mother's body is raw and must be "cooked."[6] Medicines and foods are structured around restoring to the body the heat and blood lost during childbirth, especially to the reproductive organs. The room and bed are warmed with glowing embers; spirits are repelled by burning aromatic medicines, such as the gum of *maje* (*Daniellia oliveri* Hutch. & Dalziel, Fabaceae) and *tazargade* (*Artemisia* spp., Asteraceae), which may be embellished by adding spices. Large volumes of water are boiled to wash the mother and baby twice per day (*wankan jego, wankan jinjiri*), the water cooking their bodies, with plants (yaji and other antimicrobial species) added to the water to prevent complications and to treat any symptoms that develop. Other leafy branches are the vehicles that deliver (splash) the water, such as *darbejiya* (neem, *Azadirachta indica* A. Juss., Meliaceae) and *tsamiya* (tamarind, *Tamarindus indica* L., Fabaceae). Mai jego is encouraged to eat well: all her food must be cooked; her meals should include meat, eggs, and other nutrient-dense foods and, especially, should be liberally flavored with yaji.

In anticipation of the birth, mai jego's husband purchases (or commissions relatives' preparation of) large quantities of yaji, which she not only consumes with each meal but also gifts in small amounts to female relatives and friends who visit. Yaji also figures prominently among the

FIGURE 3.3. An itinerant medicine seller (left), who embellishes the local pharmacopoeia through sale of exotic species, Kano State, Nigeria. Photo by Paul J. Ross, 1987

visitors' gifts for the new mother. This both assures the physical health of mai jego and jinjiri and, symbolically and in fact, redistributes healthful food/medicine among a larger population. The aromatic and pungent flavor of yaji assures that the womb is properly heated and cleansed. Concern in the postpartum with the restoration of heat through fire, medicine, and food—featuring yaji—finds parallels in the rules that govern Hausa male circumcision.

Kaciyar Maza/Male Circumcision. In a structural analogue to child-birth, the Hausa barber-surgeon (*wanzami*) can circumcise boys when they are seven or nine years of age but not eight years old. An age cohort of boys may be circumcised at the same time, in a public ceremony marked by discrete stages (cutting, bleeding, washing, applying medicines) that culminate in the *dan shayi* (circumcised boys) eating a special gruel, flavored with yaji. In addition to the "seven and nine but not eight" principle and yaji that marks both haihuwa and kaciya, other structural analogues are embodied in the rules that govern cold, food, and pollution for a fifteen-day phase of partial seclusion and rest for dan shayi. Care must be taken so that *sanyi* (cold) does not penetrate the vulnerable body of the boy: fires warm the sleeping hut for the recovery period, and dan shayi eat foods similar to those for mai jego: warm foods, meat and other calorie- and fat-dense foods, all generously flavored with yaji.[7] Medicines are administered to prevent dauda, dirt or infection, also a metaphor for pollution. Menstruating women, who are *karni* (religiously polluted), should not care for or visit dan shayi, other (sexually mature) adults should stay away as well, and the boy's parents do not have sexual relations during the recovery phase.

Healthful Qualities of Yaji for Liminal Phases. The foregoing discussion briefly introduces symbolic symmetries that link the postpartum and circumcision recovery in Hausa society. Not only are these liminal phases marked in much the same way as other life-cycle transitions that have high social salience, but they also constitute periods of heightened health risk that share concerns for infection, inflammation, *kumbura* (edema), and blood/heat loss. The aromatic constituents and pungent tastes of yaji impart a physical sensation of heat, and the individual spices embody significant pharmacologic potential.

THIS CHAPTER BEGAN with a comprehensive definition for a biodynamic class of botanicals that serve diverse functions, especially as foods and medicines. The overview of the cultural history of spices overlaps issues of political economy, globalization, and commodification, as expanded in the case study of chile pepper. The general treatment of the physiologic effects of spices suggests their broad-based biopotential and connects to the next section, which offered a novel approach to the pharmacology of spices: extending conventional catalogues of activities and constituents, attention was directed to one activity class, antimicrobials, which was explored from both an evolutionary and a contextualized perspective that examined the cultural constructions and pharmacologic potential of composite spices. This chapter has focused on spices as a discrete category of culinary and medicinal products, whereas plants discussed in the next chapter cohere around a means of preparation. The fermentation of foods and medicines has important health implications from the perspectives of nutrient content and the prevention and mediation of pathologic processes.

CHAPTER 4

Fermented Foods and Beverages

> Fermentation is a miracle of transformative dimensions, a process by
> which microscopic organisms—our ancestors and allies—modify our
> biological terrain to extend the usefulness of our foods.
> —Sandor Katz, *Wild Fermentation: The Flavor, Nutrition, and
> Craft of Live-Culture Foods*

DURING THE LONG COURSE of human evolution, people have had
to contend with plants and animals that, although potentially reliable
sources of nutrients, were unpalatable, indigestible, or even poisonous.
Botanical toxins and bitter constituents are primarily allelochemicals that
evolved in wild plants as protection against pathogens, parasites, competitors, and herbivorous animals (see chapter 1). People's use of those plants
was constrained as well prior to advances in food production and preserving and other processing technology. Even later, with the advent of agriculture and plant domestication, people resisted selecting out the genes
responsible for the protective phytochemicals; an efficient strategy takes
advantage of the protective chemicals during vegetative and developmen-
tal stages, which assures higher yield, and eliminates those compounds
only after the plants have matured. Food-processing technologies from
otherwise very diverse cultures converge around the issue of food palatability and safety (Johns and Kubo 1988), so that a relatively small
number of safety processing techniques mediate the coevolutionary relationships among plants, herbivores, and pathogens.

The most profound cultural influence on the evolution and quality of
human diet is linked to the purposeful use and control of fire some time
about 500,000 years ago (see chapter 1). Heat has the potential to denature
toxins, kill parasites, improve palatability and nutrient availability, and
soften and preserve foods. For some foods people take advantage of the
ability of substances such as clay to bind (adsorb) and neutralize toxins
and other undesirable food constituents, including some microorganisms.

Foods may be soaked in mud or prepared with the addition of small amounts of clay. Toxins also can be leached from foods that are soaked or repeatedly washed in water that carries off dissolved compounds. Managing acidity/alkalinity (pH) with plant acids and lye from plant ash can both affect the solubility of toxic compounds and promote hydrolysis (breakdown). Drying removes volatile toxins, and physical processing such as grinding, macerating, mashing, and freezing breaks down plant tissues and releases more stable chemicals that are water-soluble, volatile, and/or heat labile. Food quality is further enhanced by compounding these methods: for example, the combination of heat, leaching, and maceration is more effective than each technique alone.

Within this broader context of food technology, I devote the remainder of this chapter to fermentation, which is in several ways unique among processing techniques. Its primary utility transcends food safety,[1] although that too is an objective. Fermentation alters the physical qualities of foods by affecting taste, color, texture, and smell, and fermented foods have significant nutritional, preventive, and therapeutic benefits compared to their nonfermented counterparts. Moreover, fermentation tangibly and symbolically transforms a substance from one kind of food into another: foods that fulfill one role in cuisine are literally and deliberately fashioned into an altogether different food. In the process, raw resources are transformed into value-added products.

Fermentation

Many of the plants and animals that people traditionally used for food contain sufficient water to sustain microbial growth, with the result that altered appearance, taste, and even toxicity rendered some infected foods unacceptable. At the same time, some microbial modifications came to be regarded as improvements on the original product. Worldwide, virtually all human groups learned to take advantage of some beneficial microorganisms by harnessing their metabolism for particular ends, primarily for the production of foods and beverages. Fermentation refers to the changes rendered by the enzymes of live microorganisms and yields products that range across all food categories and contribute to cuisines in a variety of physically substantive (nutritive, healthful) and otherwise meaningful (symbolic) ways (Table 4.1). Many fermentations occur

TABLE 4.1. Bacterially Transformed Foods and Beverages

Food Category	Food Items
Cereals and tubers	tortilla, gruel, poi, bread, pita, fufu
Fruits and vegetables	soy sauce, olive, sauerkraut, pickle, tempeh
Dairy products	cheese, kefir, yogurt, buttermilk
Fish sauces	anchovy, patis, ketjap-ikan
Meat products	sausages, salami, rohwurst, téliszalámi
Vinegars	apple, honey, mango, maple, peach, rice, tamarind
Alcohol beverages[a]	wine, cider, pulque, beer, kaffir, sake
Others	cocoa,[b] coffee,[b] tea,[b] *Spirulina*

a. These beverages are discussed in chapter 5.
b. Fermentation of these products is distinguished by immediate post-harvest flavor development, primarily by endogenous enzymes.

spontaneously under the right conditions; beyond that, people learned to assure the desired outcome by reserving some of the fermented product to use as an inoculum (starter culture) for future preparations.

Origins of Fermentation Techniques

Fermented foods are an important archive in the history of human food preparation. Before advances in food technology human societies, especially in the humid tropics, faced the challenge of sustaining a food reserve in environments in which drying was difficult, chilling did not occur, and food spoiled easily overnight. Those same conditions explain the paucity of artifact remains in sub-Saharan Africa, Southeast Asia, and lowland Central America compared, for example, to the cultural advances documented for the Near East. That dearth of remains obscures that early civilizations of the Old and New World tropics supported large populations, including stable city-states that were culturally diverse and socially and materially complex. This complexity is reflected in part in food technologies, which include fermentations. The botanical substrates of Old World tropical fermentations are millet, sorghum, rice, peanuts, beans (*Phaseolus* spp.), yams (*Dioscorea* spp., Dioscoraceae), and the seeds of leguminous trees (Fabaceae), palms (Palmae), and cycads (Cycadopsida). A narrower and otherwise different suite of substrates characterizes tropical New World fermentations: cassava (*Manihot esculenta* Crantz, Euphorbiaceae), maize, cocoa (see chapter 5), some palms, agave (*Agave* spp., Agavaceae; see chapter 5), and fruits not found in the Old World (Stanton 1998). In the Pacific one finds primarily fermented taro (*Colocasia esculenta* [L.] Schott, Araceae), breadfruit (*Artocarpus atilis* [Parkinson] Fosberg, Moraceae), and to a lesser extent maize, cassava, banana, and sago (*Metroxylon* spp., Palmae; Ragone 1991; Pollock 1992; Kirch 2000).[2]

The ubiquity and sophistication of techniques used in food fermentations support their antiquity. China is the postulated center of origin of the elaboration and wide-scale application of fermenting techniques, beginning at least 6000 years ago. The range and variety of Chinese fermented products is especially broad and includes pickles, relishes, sauces, fish, meat, liquors, syrups, leavening agents, and the original soy sauce. The techniques and products of fermentation were transmitted along land routes within the Chinese empire to the kingdoms of Indochina (Vietnam, Cambodia, Laos, Thailand, Malaya, and Burma). By sea and other transit routes, fermented foods were carried along the South China coasts or traversed open sea by island-hopping to the Philippines. An ancient porterage crossed South Malaya, and early Chinese also traded with small ports along the northwest coast of Borneo. From there, fermented foods reached Java, where raw materials, techniques, and nomenclature provide evidence of Chinese origins. In addition to coastal trade, there is a long tradition of overland migration into Thailand. There is evidence as well of extensive in situ development of fermentation techniques throughout Southeast Asia (Stanton 1998; Prajapati and Nair 2003). Similarly, but less extensively, the development of fermentation techniques in parts of the New World and Africa helped to provide safe, stable, and varied food supplies for early populations that ranged in size from villages to city-states.

The archaeological evidence for brewing alcohol beverages—vessels for fermentation and for drinking—is even older, dating to 5000–4000 BCE in China. In the Near/Middle East a stamp seal depicting two imbibers using traditional straws and a container is interpreted as the earliest evidence of beer drinking, dated at 4000 BCE and prominent in Sumerian and Mesopotamian art and texts in succeeding centuries. Alcohol beverages share many of the same substrates as other fermented products, but the fermentation is accomplished primarily by yeasts, not lactic acid bacteria (see next section), and the metabolic by-products, principally ethanol, have different health implications. I mention alcohol beverages in this chapter because the original beers and wines were integral elements of cuisine, and some were actually regarded and consumed as food (see chapter 5).

Lactic Acid Bacteria

The microorganisms traditionally used in food fermentations are lactic acid bacteria, a functional grouping of nonpathogenic, Gram-positive bacteria whose primary metabolic end-product is lactic acid (from the energy-yielding metabolism of sugars). Lactic acid bacteria include species of *Lactococcus, Lactobacillus, Leuconostoc, Pediococcus,* and *Streptococcus.* Which particular bacteria grow depends on substrate type and chemical composition, pH, the concentration of other constituents such as salts, and temperature. These conditions can be manipulated during fermentation to influence which microorganism predominates and to achieve a specific and reproducible succession of bacteria. Whereas Gram-negative anaerobic bacteria and yeasts typically dominate the microflora of fresh vegetables, spontaneous lactic acid fermentation commonly occurs under anaerobic conditions when substrate moisture content and temperature are adjusted to give lactic acid bacteria a competitive advantage. Gram-negative bacteria are inhibited early in the fermentation process by the addition of salt and later by the rapid production of organic (e.g., lactic, acetic, and proprionic) acids (Harris 1998).

The highly competitive character of lactic acid bacteria is reflected both in their capacity to adjust to gradual environmental changes (e.g., in pH) and in the great diversity of their natural habitats, such as plant surfaces; fish, milk, and other foods; gastrointestinal tracts of humans and other animals; and decayed plant matter. A key competitive edge over virtually all other microorganisms is that lactic acid bacteria do not require iron, neither as an essential nutrient nor for colonization (rapid growth). However, despite broad-spectrum adaptation, lactic acid bacteria (especially lactobacilli) have a relatively simple enzyme repertoire and, consequently, require multiple nutrients, including amino acids and peptides, vitamins, and nucleic acids (Harris 1998). Thus, although lactic acid bacteria are ubiquitous and fermentations can occur spontaneously, the special characteristics of lactic acid bacteria require human agency for the sustained availability of reproducible fermented foods.

Nutritional and Therapeutic Advantages of Fermented Foods

Fermentation presents several nutritional and therapeutic advantages (Etkin and Ross 2000). Specifically, fermentations destroy some undesirable elements of the raw product; improve food digestibility and constituent availability and/or solubility; enrich substrates with vitamins and amino acids; preserve foods, some for months or even years; transform vegetable protein to products that have meatlike qualities; bring forth flavors, aromas, and textures; and are relatively inexpensive preparations that salvage wastes that otherwise would not be usable as food. Because the fermented substrate is partly predigested by microorganisms, cooking time is reduced and fuel is conserved. In the developing world, fermented foods tend to be locally produced on a small scale, both in the home and by small-scale entrepreneurs, and are less expensive than imported, technology-supported products.

Diminished Toxicity

Fermentation destroys some toxic and unpalatable constituents of the raw product, including the antinutritional factors that are present in many legume seeds (Fabaceae). These factors are diverse and variably distributed and may include hemagglutinins, lectins, allergens, glycosides, and trypsin inhibitors (Stahl 1984).

Hemagglutinins and Lectins

These sugar-binding proteins agglutinate (clump together) red blood cells. In the small intestine hemagglutinins and lectins bind to receptor sites in the cellular lining with subsequent lesions and abnormal development of microvilli; they also inhibit the activity of intestinal enzymes (e.g., enterokinase) that contribute to protein digestion. Collectively these actions prevent the absorption of all nutrients and may lead to general malnutrition. Further, the polyvalent (multiple-binding) character of lectins allows them to bind to receptor sites on both the intestinal lining and on bacteria, the gluelike action promoting a pathological overgrowth of normal intestinal flora. Large doses result in death, and regular consumption of smaller quantities can cause growth interference. Toxic lectins are common among food plants of the nitrogen-fixing legume family and occur as well in potatoes and the seeds of rice, wheat, and barley. Only some lectins can be destroyed by heat (and some of those not by dry heat); grain and tuber lectins are particularly resistant to heat destruction, underscoring the importance of other detoxifying preparations, such as fermentation (Liener 1997).

Allergens

Virtually all foods can produce adverse reactions in sensitive individuals, but only a subset of foods that elicit a nontoxic intolerance are technically allergens, namely those that involve immunologic reactions, primarily those mediated by IgE antibodies. Still, the range of potentially allergenic foods is broad and includes shrimp, egg, milk, soybean, peanut, rice, rye (*Secale cereale* L., Poaceae), maize, mustard, and apple (*Malus* spp.). Most food allergies are reactions to proteins or glycoproteins. For example, allergy to cow's milk is a reaction to the B- and T-cell-reactive moieties (antigens) of the main proteins in milk: casein, α-lactalbumin, and β-lactoglobulin. During fermentation, modification of these proteins by enzyme digestion and coagulation decreases risk in sensitive individuals. Similarly, fermentative digestion of glutamine-containing wheat protein fractions diminishes reactions in people with celiac disease (see chapter 7). Fermented shrimp pastes may be only weakly allergenic, and fruit allergens are neutralized during fermentation to wines and pickles.

Glycosides

Acute glycoside poisoning causes convulsions, respiratory distress, and ultimately death. Regular low-dose exposure can cause eye problems (amblyopia, blindness) and neurological dysfunction. A large number of glycoside-containing genera are found in the rose (Rosaceae), legume, and grain (Poaceae) families, including food species, such as sorghum and other grasses, lima bean (*Phaseolus lunatus* L., Fabaceae), and sweet potato (*Ipomoea batatas* [L.] Lam., Convolvulaceae). In the context of food fermentations, important glycosides include linamarin and lotaustralin in cassava. During fermentation, low-pH enzymatic hydrolysis of these constituents releases poisonous hydrocyanic acid during the preparation phase, making cassava a safe food source. Lactic acid bacteria contribute to this hydrolysis by generating acids that force out the weakly ionized hydrogen cyanide, by producing the microorganismal enzyme linamarase, and by providing a satisfactory pH for the linamarase already present in cassava (Giraud et al. 1993; Johns 1996; Odunfa and Oyewole 1998; Lei et al. 1999).

Trypsin Inhibitors

Antienzymes suppress hydrolysis (digestion) by trypsin, with the result that proteins pass through the digestive tract without being absorbed. Over the long term this can result in loss of essential amino acids and, for children, slowed growth. Trypsin inhibitors are common, especially in high-protein plants such as the Fabaceae and in all domesticated grains. These metabolites are concentrated in the protein-rich seeds or pods, where they protect against autodigestion. Fermentation, then, improves the value of these foods by promoting protein availability.

Nutrient Bioavailability and Palatability

Fermentation further improves food quality by reducing phytic acid (myoinositol hexaphosphate) to physiologically insignificant levels, thus eliminating some of its harmful effects. Phytic acid, which makes up 1–5 percent of most cereals, nuts, legumes, and many seeds, binds divalent cations such as iron, magnesium, calcium, phosphorus, and zinc, thus reducing the bioavailability of these important nutrients. Phytates also form insoluble complexes with starches, proteins, and minerals. Negative calcium balance, anemia, low-zinc growth disturbances, and other symptoms of mineral deficiency (diminished bioavailability) have been linked to dietary phytic acid. In fermented foods, however, phytases that are released by lactobacilli hydrolyze phytic acid into lower inositol phosphates. This method of phytate reduction is more efficient than other modes of preparation. For example, in flour slurries of quinoa (*Chenopodium quinoa* Willd., Chenopodiaccae), fermentation reduces the amount of phytic acid by 82–98 percent, while cooking reduces it only by 4–8 percent, germination 35–39 percent, and soaking 61–76 percent. Enzymatic phytate reduction and the development of low-phytate hybrids also significantly improve the solubility of iron, calcium, and other nutrients (Mbugua et al. 1992; Lorri and Svanberg 1995; Oberman and Libudzisz 1998; Steinkraus 1998; Ghanem and Hussein 1999; Valencia et al. 1999; Porres et al. 2003; Hambidge et al. 2004). Of course, the health risk bears directly on whether those nutrients are delivered in the same foods and meals that contain phytic acid, as well as their relative abundance.

Further, the protective effects of phytic acid reduction may be offset, or at least are confounded, by potential beneficial effects. Phytic acid reduces the blood glucose response to carbohydrate-rich foods: consumption of phytic acid-depleted navy beans results in elevated blood glucose response, while the addition back of phytic acid flattens the response. Phytic acid also reduces plasma cholesterol and triacylglycerols, and is cancer protective. All these actions have been attributed to the same mechanism that accounts for the antinutritive effects of phytates. In the first case, phytic acid binds the enzyme amylase, which slows starch digestion. In the case of cholesterol, phytic acid-bound zinc lowers the ratio of plasma zinc to copper, which predisposes people to cardiovascular disease. The cancer-protective effect may derive from the binding of iron, which is a catalyst of lipid peroxidation and free radical generation, and/ or the binding of zinc, whose unavailability compromises DNA synthesis and cell proliferation. Anti-inflammatory, antioxidant, and antiulcer effects also have been linked to phytates (Shahidi 1997; Muraoka and Miura 2004; Sudheer Kumar et al. 2004). Again, we are reminded that the composition and metabolism of foods are complex, and that the physiologic outcomes of food behavior cannot be evaluated outside the context of food chemistry, preparation, combination, and actual consumption.

Tannins, which are ubiquitous in vascular plants, are potentially antinutritive in their capacity to bind proteins and inhibit digestive enzymes. Genetic adaptations that guard against diminished bioavailability of nutrients are apparent in specialized leaf-eaters, such as koala bears (*Phascolarctos cinereus* Goldfuss, Phascolarctidae), and animals experimentally fed high-tannin diets. Their alimentary tracts are colonized by taxonomically novel bacteria that produce tannases, which hydrolyze tannins. Recently, three *Lactobacillus* species (*L. plantarum, L. paraplantarum,*

L. pentosus) isolated from fermented foods showed tannase activity that prevented the formation of indigestible tannin-protein complexes and inhibition of digestive enzymes (Osawa et al. 2000). Mbugua et al. (1992) noted that tannin content is reduced in *uji*, a popular Kenyan fermented sorghum gruel. Similarly, Mugula and Lyimo (2001) reported that fermentation decreases tannin content by 30–94 percent in various multi-substrate Tanzanian tempehs: six sorghum cultivars blended variably with cowpea, Bambarra groundnut (*Vigna subterranea* [L.] Verdc., Fabaceae), soybean, sesame, pigeon pea (*Cajanus cajan* [L.] Huth., Fabaceae), common bean, mung bean (*Phaseolus aureus* Roxb., Fabaceae), or peanut.

Fermentations improve constituent solubility and availability, resulting in more complete use of consumed foods. Protein digestion, for example, makes available a more diverse pool of amino acids, some of them generated by the fermenting microorganisms themselves. The protein in fermented foods is already partly hydrolyzed, and the smaller size of granules (larger relative surface area) in the protein coagulum makes them more amenable to enzyme action in the gastrointestinal tract. The content of free amino acids increases two- to three-fold in fermented milks. When cereals are fermented to make gruels, protein quality and relative nutritive value improve by about 14 percent, and available lysine increases significantly, presumably produced by lactic acid bacteria. In the case of fermented milk, lactic acid modification of the protein casein enhances digestibility and promotes the secretion of salivary, stomach, and pancreatic enzymes. It also stimulates peristalsis. In raw soybean, antitrypsin factor inhibits nutrient capture by binding trypsin in insects, humans, and other potential herbivores. Antitrypsin factor is diminished to imperceptible levels during fermentation.

Fats also are more digestible after rendering by enzymes in the fermentation starter cultures, and fermented foods generally relieve constipation. Poor digestibility characterizes beans and other foods that contain oligosaccharides, condensation products of a few simple sugars such as glucose, fructose, and galactose that are not digested or absorbed from the upper intestinal tract. Their digestion by colonic flora results in gas and flatulence. However, during fermentation the content of these problematic oligosaccharides is significantly reduced and some are almost entirely degraded. The end result is increased nutrient value as well as palatability. For example, fermentation of black gram (*Vigna mungo* [L.]

Hepper, Fabaceae) and rice to make the Indian food *idli* reduces oligosac-charide content by as much as 70 percent. Similarly, oligosaccharide content reductions of greater than 80 percent have been reported for the preparation of soybean tempeh (Yukuchi et al. 1992; Naczk et al. 1997; Odunfa and Oyewole 1998; Wood 1998; Giami and Isichei 1999; Ruiz-Terán and Owens 1999).

Most of the world's population are adult lactose intolerant, meaning that the enzyme necessary for digestion of milk sugar is no longer produced, beginning at time of weaning (see chapter 7). These individuals better tolerate fermented milks, which both have lower lactose content (most of it digested by lactic acid bacteria) and introduce microorgan-ismal β-galactosidase (lactase) into the small intestine, where it contrib-utes to lactose digestion (Oberman and Libudzisz 1998). Overall nutrition is improved by virtue of both the nutrients available from milk and the curtailment of nutrient loss from other foods secondary to diarrhea and rapid intestinal emptying.

The palatability of bland cereal, tuber, and vegetable substrates is greatly enhanced through conversion to protein-dense products with meatlike flavor and texture. Among meat analogues, the versatile soybean is produced in cake or paste form, a signature of many Asian and South-east Asian cuisines, including Indonesian tempeh, Chinese *tou fu* and *sufu*, and Japanese *miso*. These are foods in their own right and are converted into a great array of other dishes by slicing, cooking, and other-wise processing and combining with other foods. In their preparation, an inedible raw seed is rendered into highly palatable foods that can be consumed in quantities sufficient to contribute significantly to protein and calorie intake. The meatlike quality of these foods is not coincidental, but a product of deliberate action that creates meat substitutes to satisfy specific culinary objectives. Chinese cuisines especially include a diverse suite of meat-imitation foods, some probably originating in Mahayana Buddhist vegetarian culinary traditions (Anderson 1988). Meat substitutes also are made from other plants, such as seeds of red sorrel (*Hibiscus sabdariffa* L., Malvaceae) and sesame, *kawal* leaves (*Cassia obtusifolia* L., Fabaceae), and onion (Dirar 1993).

During the 1970s a flurry of commercial interest in meat analogues in the United States dead-ended in several textured vegetable protein prod-ucts, which had only a passing acquaintance with palatability. Today a large variety of quality textured soy and related products are available and increasingly popular in the West. This trend is one aspect of globalization and the internationalization of cuisines that has evolved since the 1950s and, during the last few decades, a reflection of the growing interest in healthful foods, including the (re)popularization of vegetarian diets.

Vitamin Synthesis

Bacterial fermentations yield a variety of B vitamins. For sour milk, longer incubations at high temperatures result in the highest synthesis of folic acid and niacin. In the case of soybean fermentations, pyridoxine is elevated four- to fourteen-fold, biotin and pantothenate levels double, riboflavin increases two- to eight-fold, folate increases four-fold, and niacin two- to seven-fold. A thirty-three-fold increase in vitamin B_{12} is especially important, as this vitamin does not occur in vegetable foods, which dominate traditional diets. Some fermented foods, notably soybean products, have elevated levels of vitamins E and C and β-carotene (Steinkraus 1998; Wood 1998; Taranto et al. 2003).

Antioxidants, Aging, and Cholesterol Reduction

Fermented soybean foods contain significant levels of antioxidants, probably due to the release of isoflavones during fermentation and bacterial hydroxylation of the isoflavones daidzein and glycetin (Wood 1998). By whatever mechanism they are generated, antioxidants are beneficial and have been linked to enhanced immune function, as well as lower risk of cardiovascular disease, cataract, and cancers. Soy foods and soybean isoflavones have been linked to decreased calcium excretion, improved bone density, and diminished postmenopausal symptoms (Kurzer 2000; Messina and Messina 2000). Soybean isoflavones may also improve cardiovascular health through suppression of platelet activation, that is, discourage clotting (Anthony 2000). Hypotensive effects linked to the metabolic products of *Bacillus subtilis* have been reported for the Japanese fermented soybean product *natto* (Dirar 1993). Dietary supplementation with fermented milk resulted in significant decreases in systolic blood pressure in healthy adult men (Kawase et al. 2000), and some animal studies link diets high in fermented foods to increased longevity (Mizutani 1992). Because substantial evidence, at least at the cellular level, links the progression and physical infirmity of aging to oxidation (free radical reactions), it is not too far-fetched to suggest that antioxidants may contribute to what 1908 Nobel laureate Elie Metchnikoff described—and misinterpreted and exaggerated—as the "yogurt-induced longevity" of peoples living in the Caucasus Mountains (Republic of Georgia).

The effect of milk on cholesterol was first studied in the 1970s among the East African pastoral Maasai, who experience low rates of cardiovascular disease despite what would logically be construed as a high-risk atherogenic diet. In what became a classic study, Mann (1974) recorded substantial daily consumption (ca. 8 L/day) of cow milk as an enigmatic companion of low serum cholesterol. Research over the next twenty years corroborated the apparent relationship between milk and cholesterol and speculated about the significance of lower milk fat, seasonality, and the immunization of milk cows (e.g., Hepner et al. 1979; Thompson et al. 1982; Kawase et al. 2000). Finally, attention was drawn to modification of intestinal flora by milk from immunized cows, and the effects of pasteurized milk were compared to various fermented dairy products and to diets supplemented by lactic acid bacteria. On reflection, it was recalled that the Maasai consume virtually all their milk as fermented product. Review of the recent literature concludes that consumption of fermented milk results in enhanced microbial growth in the large intestine, where the bacteria ferment indigestible dietary carbohydrates. Further, fermentation decreases serum cholesterol by production of short-chain fatty acids that either redistribute cholesterol from the plasma to the liver or inhibit liver cholesterol synthesis. Increased bacteria in the intestine also enhances deconjugation of bile acids, which are excreted because they are poorly absorbed by the intestinal mucosa. Cholesterol, which is a precursor of bile acids, is then used for de novo synthesis of bile acids and does not circulate in pathologically high titers (St-Onge et al. 2000).[3]

Soybean protein also lowers blood cholesterol concentrations and inhibits atherosclerosis in nonhuman primates and other animals (Potter 1998; Anthony 2000). An antioxidant constituent from natto lowers serum cholesterol and prevents the progression of atherosclerosis by limiting oxidative modification of low-density lipoproteins (Yokota et al. 1996). Lipid-lowering effects of red yeast rice (a traditional Chinese medicine and food) were reported for a single-blind clinical trial of 446 Chinese patients with hyperlipidemia. After four weeks, treated patients who consumed 1200 mg of fermented rice per day experienced a 17.1 percent reduction of total cholesterol. The corresponding figure for control patients who took extracts of a putatively lipid-lowering medicinal plant (*Gynostemma pentaphylla* [Thunb.] Mak., Cucurbitaceae) was only 4.8 percent. Similarly, reductions of low-density lipoprotein cholesterol and serum triglycerides and increase in high-density lipoprotein were significantly better in the rice-treated group compared to the controls. Although specific cholesterol-modifying enzymes have not been characterized for lactic acid bacteria, a strain of *Lactobacillus acidophilus* has been described that metabolizes bile and takes up cholesterol under anaerobic conditions. The beneficial effect of these bacteria appears to be controlled release of cholesterol from the liver into the blood, rather than direct inhibition of cholesterol absorption. Other mechanisms of cholesterol mediation are currently under investigation. For example, cholesterol-lowering by red yeast rice is attributed to blocking cholesterol synthesis in the liver through inhibition of hydroxymethylgutaryl coenzyme reductase, isoflavones, and sterols (e.g., stigmasterol, campesterol, β-sitosterol, and related analogues; Fernandes et al. 1992; Sanders 1994; Wang et al. 1997; Li et al. 1998; Oberman and Libudzisz 1998; Farnworth 1999, 2003).

Antimicrobial Action

The medicinal uses of fermented foods are recorded in some of the world's oldest, as well as some of the most recent, written and oral texts. Fermented foods are fed to both people and livestock, especially for diarrheas and other intestinal disorders, applied to skin disorders and wounds, and given to domestic animals as an antidote to eating poisonous plants. It has been well established that lactic acid bacteria inhibit other microorganisms, including pathogenic bacteria and fungi. The relative contributions of different bacteria vary, but their shared antimicrobial action comes from the fermentative pathways they use to derive cellular energy. Wherever they grow, lactic acid bacteria produce organic acids, primarily lactic acid, which can exceed concentrations of 1 percent weight per volume (100 mM), with final pH ranging between 3.5 and 4.5. Although they occur in low concentrations, acetic, formic, proprionic, and benzoic acids will, under acidic conditions, inhibit diverse microorganisms, notably Gram-negative pathogens (Earnshaw 1992; Hosono 1992; Farnworth 1999; Ghrairi et al. 2004; Jamuna and Jeevaratnam 2004).

Hydrogen peroxide (H_2O_2) is produced by some lactic acid bacteria and inhibits several pathogenic and contaminating microorganisms (e.g., *Clostridia, Pseudomonas, Staphylococci* spp.), in some cases serving as a precursor for other potent antimicrobial compounds such as superoxide (O_2^-) and hydroxyl (OH^-) radicals. Other factors that contribute to the inhibition of competing microflora include production of carbon dioxide, diacetyl ($[CH_3CO]_2$), and ethanol; low oxidation-reduction potential; and nutrient depletion. Some lactobacilli and lactococci hydrolyze fats, producing significant concentrations of fatty acids that have antimicrobial activity. In addition, lactic acid bacteria produce bacteriocins, polypeptide antimicrobials that inhibit other bacteria across both broad and narrow inhibitory spectra. Some lactic acid bacteriocins are effective against taxa closely related to the producing organism and, thus, help to determine which strains of lactic acid bacteria dominate in a given fermentation. Others also control common food-borne and intestinal pathogens (e.g., *Clostridium perfringens, Enterococcus faecalis, Escherichia coli, Listeria monocytogenes, Salmonella typhi*). Some of these antimicrobial constituents are acidophilin, lactobacillin, lactolin, lactocydin, and lactocidine (*L. acidophilus*); deprocoxin (*Staphylococcus cremoris*); nysin (*S. lactis*); and lactobrevin (*Lactobacillus brevis*). Broad-spectrum inhibitory bacteriocins have been identified in natural vegetable fermentations, suggesting that antimicrobial proteins are integral to the ecology of traditionally fermented foods (Earnshaw 1992; Harris 1998; Oberman and Libudzisz 1998; Choi et al. 1999; Sanni et al. 1999; Jamuna and Jeevaratnam 2004).

In the last two decades several dozen clinical studies have reported the effect of diverse fermented foods and lactic acid bacteria cultures on primarily infectious, diarrheal diseases. In all cases acidity is the most important factor, and the inhibition of pathogenic microorganisms depends on reaching numbers of lactic acid bacteria sufficient to rapidly lower pH (Adams 1998). Overwhelmingly, these studies record decreased incidence, severity, and/or duration of symptoms, with specific action against *Clostridia, Staphylococci, Shigella, Escherichia coli, Salmonella paratyphi, S. typhi, Campylobacter*, and *Yersinia enterocolitica*. For example, in one study 40–70 percent of children with *Shigella* and *Salmonella* dysentery recovered after short-duration treatment with acidophilus milk, and 100 percent recovered with continued, long-term treatment. In another study, the Japanese fermented milk *yakult* was given to 500 military men with dysentery, with 100 percent recovery, while only 9 percent of the control group recovered (Gorbach 1990; Isolauri et al. 1991; Fernandes et al. 1992; Lorri and Svanberg 1994; Sanders 1994; Mensah et al. 1995; Oberman and Libudzisz 1998; Pedone et al. 2000; Agarwal and Bhasin 2002; Brown and Valiere 2004).

Anticancer Effects

Another physiologic benefit of fermented foods is the role they may play in certain cancers. Lactic acid bacteria may convert or eliminate procarcinogenic or carcinogenic compounds. For example, *Lactobacillus* strains have nitrite reductase activity and can degrade nitrites (in processed foods) in vivo, thus preventing their conversion to nitrosamines, which cause colon cancer. In vitro *L. acidophilus* inhibition of the conversion of bile salts to carcinogens may have implications for reduced cancer initiation in the intestinal tract on consumption of fermented foods. Colon cancer also has been linked to the conversion of procarcinogens to carcinogens by the fecal enzymes β-glucuronidase, nitroreductase, and azoreductase. Recent studies show that levels of these three carcinogenic enzymes are two- to four-fold lower in individuals who consume milk that contains *L. acidophilus*, compared to individuals who consume no or unfermented milk. Because these enzymes are largely of bacterial origin, the protective effect of lactic acid bacteria may be indirect, through favorable change in the composition of the intestinal flora. Similarly, a case control study in the Netherlands found an inverse relationship between breast cancers and consumption of fermented milks, which suggested that bacterial enzymes might affect the synthesis or degradation of estrogen (Fernandes et al. 1992; Sanders 1994; Oberman and Libudzisz 1998; Belicova et al. 1999; Rafter 2003; Brown and Valiere 2004).

Low incidence and mortality rates for breast and prostatic cancers have been linked in Asian countries to high dietary consumption of soybeans, including fermented products such as tofu (Lamartiniere 2000; Sonoda et al. 2004). Population studies suggest a cancer-suppressive role for phytoestrogens, primarily isoflavones such as daidzein and genistein, comparing, for example, Japan and the United States and Japanese and Finnish men (Aldercreutz et al. 1993), Shanghai and the West (Chen et al. 1999), multiethnic groups in Hawai'i and individuals consuming experimental diets designed around variable input of soy and vegetables (Kirkman et al. 1995). Soybeans naturally contain high amounts of isoflavones, the bioavailability of which is appreciably increased during fermentation (Slavin et al. 1998). While there is ample evidence linking fermented soy foods with diminished cancer risk, it has been noted that most studies have not controlled for accompanying and potentially confounding dietary factors such as increased consumption of salt and vegetables (Wu et al. 2000).

Other studies have attributed the anticancer effects of sour milk, miso, cheese, and other fermented foods to the scavenging of active radicals, the production of polysaccharides that have antitumor as well as antimutagenic effects (e.g., binding heterocyclic amines), and antimutagenic peptides generated during digestion (Hosoda et al. 1996; Rajendran and Ohta 1998; Sreekumar and Hosono 1998).

Recent studies suggest that tumor cell suppression also can be mediated through stimulation of the immune system. *Lactobacillus* spp. promote in vitro human polymorphonuclear leucocyte production of interferon, which can activate killer cells and has antiviral and antiproliferative effects. Much has been published as well on the anticancer effects of fermented foods in animal models. Treatment with fermented foods, live bacteria, or cell extracts resulted in extended animal survival, decreased mutagenicity, tumor suppression during initiation, smaller tumors, and/or improved humoral and cell-mediated immune function. These findings are very compelling, for infectious and immune system deficiency diseases as well, although their implications for humans are not yet clear (Fernandes et al. 1992; Sanders 1994; Oberman and Libudzisz 1998; Farnworth 1999, 2003; Kimoto et al. 2004).

Problem Focus: Fermented Foods in Nigeria

What shall we make of this wealth of nutritional and therapeutic potential? Should we consider in the same domain fermented foods and streamlined commercial products that contain lactic cultures? Should we be content with broad generalities about fermented foods and the wisdom of indigenous peoples? I think not. A more productive exercise would frame the question in the theoretical domain of human ecology to explore the complex nature of human-environment relationships in the context of a particular society. I return now to our research on Hausa diet and medicine.

While much attention has been paid to the fermented food plants of eastern and Southeast Asia, relatively little is known about such foods in sub-Saharan Africa. Historians of this region estimate that fermentation technology was refined between the eighth and the sixteenth centuries and became firmly established in local cuisines that continue to feature fermented main dishes, beverages, and condiments. In West Africa, fermented starchy foods include products of cassava, such as *fufu* mash, *lafun* flour, and *agbelima* dough, and grains, such as *koko*, *ogi*, and *akasa* gruels and porridges made from sorghum, millet, and maize. Fermented beverages include *burukutu* and *pito* beers and *bammi* wine. Fermented condiments based in protein-rich seeds include *ogiri* (melon, *Citrullus vulgaris* Schrad., Cucurbitaceae) and *uba* (oil bean, *Pentaclethra macrophylla* Benth, Fabaceae.). West African fermented animal products include sour milks and a few preserved fish and crustaceans, such as *bonome*, *oporo*, and *nsiko* (Uzogara et al. 1990; Odunfa and Oyewole 1998).

Fermented Foods and Medicines in Hurumi

An estimated 80 percent of Nigerians consume thirty fermented foods and beverages, representing seven food categories: grains, fruits, legumes, tubers, tree sap, meat and seafood, and milk; and many depend on them medicinally as well as economically (Uzogara et al. 1990; Iwuoha and Eke 1996; Nnanyelugo et al. 2003). Four of these fermented products are important in Hurumi: *gari*, a dry meal prepared from cassava; the grain-based gruel *koko*; *nono*, soured cow's milk; and daddawa, a soup base and condiment prepared from locust bean seeds. These products are important in both diet and medicine.

Gari

Cassava is the most abundant starch food in the tropics. In the sixteenth century the Portuguese introduced it from the New World to Africa, where today close to half the world's cassava is produced, 90 percent of that for human consumption, and almost all as fermented product. As described earlier in this chapter, cassava fermentation yields products that are more digestible and nontoxic. The most important of the fermented cassava foods is the farinaceous meal *gari*, the original technology for production of which was introduced into West Africa more than a century ago by freed slaves from Brazil who had learned to use *farinha de mandioca* (a coarse cassava flour). It is the staple of an estimated 100 million people in West Africa, and in southern Nigeria may account for as much as half of daily caloric intake for a significant proportion of the population (Odunfa and Oyewole 1998).

Women prepare gari from fresh cassava roots that are peeled, then grated and mashed, and put into baskets, cloth sacks, or other porous containers. Stones and other weights placed on top of the containers help to express fluid from the pulp, and the residual mass is allowed to ferment (*ruba*). In the first stage, lactic acid bacteria (*Lactobacillus* spp., *Corne-bacterium* spp.) hydrolyze the starch and produce organic acids that favor the growth of a yeast (*Geotrichum candidum*) that produces the various esters and aldehydes responsible for the characteristic smell and sour taste of gari. After one to three days the fermented pulp is roasted (alternating cooking and drying) for about thirty minutes. The result is a dry, granular product that swells on addition of cold water but typically is cooked in boiling water, increasing 300 percent in volume.

Hurumi residents purchase gari (local name, *kwaki*) at markets, where it is imported primarily from southern Nigeria. Gari is expensive compared to other starches and is reserved for special events such as marriage (*bikin aure*), naming ceremonies (*suna*), and Ramadan. Gari also is an important food during transitional life phases that bear on health: prominently, for mothers in the postpartum, as weaning food, and for circumcised boys (see below, Hausa Foods for Postpartum, Weaning, and Male Circumcision). Typically, gari is boiled in water (to produce the food *teba*) and consumed in the style of local porridges (tuwo) with a companion soup (miya) or with spices.

Koko

The fermented grain-based gruel koko is commonly consumed as the first of three daily meals. On any given morning, women in two or three of Hurumi's forty-six compounds (living units) sell koko that they prepare in

FIGURE 4.1. The grain emporium at a regional market in Wudil, Nigeria. Photo by Paul J. Ross, 1988

quantity as a source of income. Millets are the preferred substrate, especially late millet (*maiwa*) because its product is whiter, more bulky, and better tasting (*gardi*/nutlike). Alternatively, millet (gero) or sorghum (dawa) is used. The grain is soaked in water overnight to soften and begin fermentation, then ground to a paste consistency and filtered. The liquid is left to ferment one more day, with yeasts and lactic acid bacteria predominating among the diverse microflora. The mass (*gasara*) that coheres at the bottom of the container is mixed with a little of the fermented liquid (*tsagwaro*) on top and cooked in boiling water to gruel consistency. Like gari, prior to consumption, koko is further flavored with spices and local flavoring plants such as tamarind, a point to which I will return shortly.

Nono

Historians project the first use of animal milk in western Asia and subsequent transmission of milk-producing techniques east and west. Sheep were domesticated in the Near East about 10,000 BCE, and direct evidence of dairying is depicted in rock drawings from the Sahara region that date to approximately 6000–5000 BCE. Presumably, dairying began some time(s) between those dates (Brothwell and Brothwell 1998). Of fermented dairy products, cheese and butter probably have the longest history, as they develop spontaneously when fresh milk is left to stand, allowing collection of either the curd formed by natural fermentation or the cream that floats to the surface; fermented and coagulated milks arose from those. Milk fermentation can be initiated or accelerated as well by adding starter cultures or certain plants that contain coagulating enzymes, such as figs (*Ficus carica* L., Moraceae), pineapple (*Ananas comosus* [L.] Merr. Bromeliaceae), papaya (*Carica papaya* L., Caricaceae), sensitive plant (*Mimosa pudica* L., Fabaceae), eggplant, *naranjilla* (*Solanum quitoense* Lam., Solanaceae), and *litsusu* tree (*Wrightia calycina*, A. DC., Apocynaceae). Dairying was practiced in North Africa 2000 BCE or earlier, and fermented milk and cheese have been produced by pastoral groups of the African savanna since ancient times (Hosono 1992). Even today, in rural Africa much of the milk is processed in-village or on-farm using traditional technologies. Sour milk is the most common African fermented dairy product and is especially evident throughout sub-Saharan Africa.

Hausa agricultural lifestyle in northern Nigeria has been significantly influenced by generations of coresidence and intermarriage with Fulani, traditional nomadic cattle pastoralists from the Niger-Nigeria region. In Hurumi today, Fulani women from cattle-owning households predominate among milk vendors, even in markets (although otherwise they follow Islamic rules that confine married women to their own compounds). A few other households who own cattle produce milk for consumption within the domestic unit; others rely on purchase of this expensive food source, typically as fermented rather than fresh milk.

Milk is consumed primarily as the fermented nono prepared from fresh milk (*madara*) that has been mixed with a small amount of curdled milk (*kindirmo*) and allowed to ferment for one or two days. When fully curdled, the kindirmo is shaken in a closed calabash until butter (*man shanu*) separates from the remainder. The fermented nono can be further diluted by adding water; that diluted product, *tsala*, can also be used as a starter for fermentation. Baobab fruit pulp (*kuka*, *Adansonia digitata* L., Bombacaceae) may be added to increase volume (*auki*) and improve taste; its low pH (3.2) contributes antimicrobial action to the final product (Bankole

FIGURE 4.2. Fulani women selling fermented milk (nono) at a regional market in Wudil, Nigeria. Photo by Paul J. Ross, 1987

and Okagbue 1992). The plant *malaiduwa* (*Cissus populnea* Guill. and Perr., Vitaceae) will speed fermentation as well but may impart an undesirable slimy (*yauki*) texture. Both the curdled full-fat milk (kindirmo) and nono are consumed with porridges and other cereal-based foods.

Daddawa

The strongly pungent daddawa is a protein- and fat-dense soup base and flavor made from the dry seeds (*kalwa*) of *dorawa*, the African locust bean tree (*Parkia filicoidea* Welw. ex Oliver, Fabaceae). It is prepared by women, some of whom produce it in quantities sufficient to sell within Hurumi, but in recent years households increasingly rely on market purchase of this key food ingredient. The seeds, inedible when raw, are boiled for twelve to twenty-four hours and the testa removed. The softened cotyledons are washed and boiled for another one to two hours, then drained and spread on mats to a depth of about 10 cm. Over the next thirty-six hours the seeds ferment, primarily by the action of proteolytic spore-forming bacilli, into a sticky mass that is redolent of ammonia. A small amount of red sorrel seeds (*yakuwa*) is added as well, on the principle that these are the *namijin* or male daddawa, that is, the male necessary for daddawa reproduction, for fermentation. This solid-substrate process differs from most African food fermentations, which are based in liquids. The mass is sun-dried and shaped into 2-cm diameter disks. To help shape and impart sheen to the final product, aqueous infusions of *gwandar jeji* (*Annona senegalensis* Pers., Annonaceae) or malaiduwa are applied.

Locust bean seeds may be substituted for or stretched by several other plants. Daddawa prepared from red sorrel seeds alone is distinguished both linguistically (daddawar batso) (see chapter 1) and by the type of soup it flavors. Similarly *daddawar gurji* from wild melon (*Cucumis melo* L., Cucurbitaceae) is appreciated for its sticky (*danke*) and bitter (*daci*) qualities. Seeds of *taura*, the tallow tree (*Detarium senegalense* Gmelin, Fabaceae), are only rarely used. Fruit of *kirya* (*Prosopis africana* Taub., Fabaceae) and *loli* (*Psorospermum guineense* Hochr., Hypericaceae) were used in the past, but these trees no longer grow locally, and neither contributes to present-day daddawa production in Hurumi.

Daddawa is far and away the most important condiment in Nigeria and is widely used as well in other countries of West and central Africa. The nutty taste of this nutrient-dense product is much more palatable than the beany flavor of the starting material. For Hausa, daddawa is the foundation for all eight common varieties of soup and, depending on the circumstances of a household, may be the primary noncarbohydrate nutrient source. Liberal use of daddawa to flavor other foods provides significant amounts of vegetable protein, which is especially important in an economy in which animal protein contributes relatively little to diet.

The properties of daddawa resonate those I discussed for fermented products as a group. During the first twenty-four hours of fermentation, the levels of indigestible oligosaccharides (notably raffinose and stachyose) are significantly diminished by α- and β-galactosidase hydrolysis. Nutritional benefits include improved protein quality: *Bacillus* strains produce glutamic acid and extracellular proteinases, and protein hydrolysis increases digestibility. The nutrient value of daddawa is higher than that of unprocessed seeds, containing 18–47 percent protein and 31–43 percent fat. The fermented product also is mineral rich, especially for potassium (which doubles), calcium, iron, and phosphorus. Antinutritive and toxic constituents such as phytic and hydrocyanic acids and oxalates are removed; and protein, fat, and B vitamin (thymine, riboflavin) levels are higher than in unfermented seeds. Finally, *Bacillus* and some lactic acid bacteria in daddawa are active against pathogenic microorganisms (Campbell-Platt 1980; Eka 1980; Ikenebomeh et al. 1986; Uzogara et al. 1990; Dirar 1993; Iwuoha and Eke 1996; Odunfa and Oyewole 1998; Omafuvbe et al. 2000; Beaumont 2002; Nnam and Obiakor 2003).

Hausa Foods for Postpartum, Weaning, and Male Circumcision

What is the most productive analysis for such findings? Here are four nutrient-rich fermented foods. Are they just generically healthy or can we analyze more meaningfully when and how they affect the health of Hurumi residents? Here I further consider the issue of fermented foods by focusing on critical phases of the life cycle: the early postpartum, weaning, and male circumcision (see chapter 3).

Foods designated for the early postpartum, during weaning, and for newly circumcised boys include gari, koko, nono, and daddawa. During all these liminal phases otherwise ordinary foods are marked by choice of preferred substrate and particularly by flavoring. Daddawa is used more liberally. Nono is regarded as especially strengthening. Gari and koko are more highly flavored—especially with the pharmacologically dynamic spice yaji, which is prepared in quantity for mai jego to consume in special gruels and other foods and is used liberally in the foods prepared for circumcised boys. Both cases embody deliberate efforts to infuse the diet with nutrients and energy and to restore heat. The metaphoric and physical convergence of yaji and daddawa are represented in yajin daddawa. Yaji composed primarily of daddawa is emergency yaji made up right after birth if none has been prepared in advance; daddawa is the principal ingredient as it is the most likely to be available in quantity (ginger/cittar aho and chile pepper/barkono also are likely to be on hand and thus make up proportionately more of the total emergency yaji compared to other ingredients).

Foods designated for *yaye*/weaning overlap medicines given to prevent and treat *zawayin yaye*/weanling diarrhea. Early, abrupt, or otherwise problematic weaning may eventuate in *mayankwaniya*, *bayamma*, and/or *ayama*, a suite of worrisome complex disorders that may evolve one into the other, with the long-range consequences of growth perturbations, failure to thrive, and increased risk of comorbidities.

Fermented gruels figure prominently among Hausa medicines for infant diarrheas, a common practice in many traditional cultures. World-wide, traditional weaning foods include the fermented milks, gruels, and porridges described in this chapter. As outlined previously, there is good evidence that such foods protect children against infections. Traditional preparers of fermented foods in Hausaland and beyond remark on the need to achieve rapid fermentation. This assures the production of lactic acid bacteria in high enough numbers to rapidly lower pH, with the effect that the desired food is produced and the growth of unwanted micro-organisms inhibited. Another way that traditional preparers of fermented foods reach high starting levels of the desired fermentative organism is to use material from previous preparations. Thorough cooking of fermented products into gruels, breads, and other foods further assures food safety.

In sum, in Hurumi, fermented foods contribute to health generally as medicinal foods, and especially during the postpartum, circumcision, and weaning. They are nutrient dense, contaminant free, inexpensive, and culturally germane; and they confer antimicrobial and other therapeutic benefits. This example, like that of the Maasai mentioned earlier in this chapter, underscores the value of in-depth ethnography that uncovers the subtle features of diet and medicine that permit us to make realistic statements about how people's actions influence their health.

Weaning and Childhood Diarrheas in a Global Context

Concern for the health of children in the developing world has shaped international health policies that, in their earlier iterations, encouraged breastfeeding as a means to shield infants from contaminated food and to promote immune function through transmission of maternal anti-bodies, immunoglobulin, and other antimicrobial factors. The attention of health agencies was refocused on weaning foods when it became ap-parent that mothers may not produce sufficient breast milk or may termi-nate breastfeeding to resume work outside the home. In the shadow of these international health efforts was a pervasive formal-sector subtext that weaning foods are low in nutrients, present substantial risk of contamination and infection, and are "not fresh" (e.g., Shehu and Adesiyun 1990). This view generalizes local practices and reflects a lack of familiarity with the range, content, and preparation of weaning foods. It compounds a general bias against grain-based foods by conflating fermented products with other carbohydrate foods, and encourages technology-supported products that local people can ill afford. Moreover, this view does not reflect the experiences of people who use such foods. Many indigenous cultures recognize the value of fermented milks and gruels for fluid replacement, resolving diarrhea, stimulating lactation, and, by virtue of sour taste, enhancing appetite.

More recently, based on the growing evidence of the nutritive and antimicrobial value of traditional fermented foods, health programs are promoting these products as weaning foods and supplements, as well as for childhood and adult diarrheal diseases. Contemporary health initiatives that are conceived in-country, rather than internationally, emphasize the importance of local products that are readily available, affordable, safe, culturally appropriate, and efficacious (e.g., Olukoya et al. 1994; Lorri and Svanberg 1995; Mensah et al. 1995; Simango 1997; Adams 1998; Mugula and Lyimo 2001; Nnanyelugo et al. 2003).

In the West, fermented foods are popular as part of larger effort to promote "probiotic" (see chapter 7) foods that contain microorganisms that beneficially affect consumers through effects on the intestinal tract, primarily by improving nutrient bioavailability. These foods also reconfigure intestinal microbial balance, providing a direct antagonistic effect for enteropathogens and stimulating systemic or mucosal immunity. Most commercial probiotics in the United States and Europe are yogurts and other dairy products that contain *Bifidobacterium*, *Enterococcus*, *Lactobacillus*, and *Streptococcus* species. Freeze-dried cultures also are popular, and incorporation into vegetables and meats is predicted for a future that anticipates a range of health benefits (e.g., Marteau et al. 2001; Roberfroid 2003; Sgouras et al. 2004; Thapar and Sanderson 2004; q.v., chapter 7).

AGAIN, we are reminded that food composition and its metabolism are complex and that the physiologic outcome of food behaviors cannot be evaluated outside the context of food chemistry, preparation, combination, and actual consumption. The example of fermented foods reveals that the culturally patterned transformation of foodstuffs to achieve desired tastes, textures, and physicochemical properties transforms them into foods that are more nutritious and otherwise healthful than their unprocessed counterparts.

The next chapter reinforces issues of context and globalization by focusing on plants that mediate social relations through processes of communal consumption and exchange. While their histories show asymmetries in the sources and distribution of foods, today these items are regionally, and some globally, broadcast, with greatly expanded pharmacological potential.

CHAPTER 5

The Lives of Social Plants

The tea is ready.
—Proper invitation to a Chinese home (Simoons 1991: 444)

THIS CHAPTER is about social plants, *cordials* in the broad sense of that term.[1] Rather than foods and beverages proper, these are stand-alone items of reciprocity and communal consumption that mediate both mundane and ritual occasions. Although some of these social lubricants are used medicinally and may have become meal elements in recent times, their traditional and historical uses are grounded in other-than-nutritive features. Their context of use as vehicles of sociability and/or hospitality highlights group exposure to potentially biodynamic substances and rationalizes treating these items under the broad rubric of food pharmacology. Whatever pharmacologic merit (or detriment) these plants have is shared among the social collective. Further, sociability itself contributes to medicinal value, especially when preventive and therapeutic objectives are directed at the social fabric. The first section summarizes the origins, contexts of use, and health implications of various social plants drawn from cultures around the globe. The rest of the chapter develops more extensively the cultural history and social contexts of four of these social plants, cacao, tea, betel, and kola nut, which, although increasingly globalized in the modern era, still strike me as iconic of specific cultures or regions.

Social Plants around the World

Social plants generally are consumed in company, in environments marked by rules of inclusion/exclusion, comportment, and expected outcome. These beverages and masticatories are versatile and potent means to construct and negotiate social occasions. The circumstances of their use tend to be integrative, thus to some extent democratizing participation;

FIGURE 5.1. This cooking hearth inside a large residential compound in Hurumi regularly feeds forty-six residents and their guests. Its size and complexity embody the structural codes of cuisine, including the rotation and transformation of foods and people. Photo by Paul J. Ross, 1988

but they may be constructed around asymmetries as well, for example, imparting elevated status to the convener, supplier, preparer, or the rank order of individual consumers. The social plants described here were selected to span human cultural and ecogeographic diversities, each treated to the depth allowed by available literature on social context. Although the majority are stimulants, these species represent considerable phytochemical diversity as well.

Alcohol Beverages

Early humans might have been "awed by the phenomenon of fermentation. Here was decent grain and fruit suddenly foaming, bubbling . . . and impregnating unfermented material with the same kind of life. . . . How could people . . . escape the . . . belief that fermenting material was possessed by a spirit that penetrated drinkers . . . 'the spirit of wine,' as alcohol was first called?" (Ghalioungul 1979: 4).

Unlike other social plants treated in this chapter (with the exception of gums), alcohol beverages are made from a great many distillation and fermentation sources, such as grains (whiskey, gin, beer), potatoes (vodka, aquavit), fruit (wine, brandy), molasses and sugar cane (rum, ouzo), and honey (mead), as well as from other more regional sources such as Mexican *pulque* and *tequila* from maguey (*Agave* spp., Agavaceae), Swahili *mnanasi*/pineapple wine, Finnish *lakka*/cloudberry liqueur from *Rubus chamaemorus* L. (Rosaceae), and Russian *berëza*/birch wine from *Betula pubescens* Ehrh. (Betulaceae). Fermentation to alcohol differs from lactic acid fermentations (see chapter 4) because it involves principally yeasts that enzymatically metabolize sugars to ethanol and carbon dioxide.

Neolithic origins (7000–5000 BCE) of fermented alcohols are suggested by chemical analysis of vessel residues, hieroglyphics, pictorigraphs, and historical texts from western Asia; but it is likely that these beverages had been produced in many places and perhaps for thousands of years before (see chapter 4).[2] Techniques for distilling beverages were refined later, evolving from alchemy and perfumery, in the first millennium CE (Austin 1985; McGovern 2003).

Alcohols and Health

The individually and socially insalubrious effects of alcohol have been abundantly documented and are not addressed here. Consumed in moderation, alcohol beverages generally and in the short term diminish anxiety, tension, and fatigue and contribute to sensations associated with relaxation and well-being. Alcohol beverages are included in diverse traditional pharmacopoeias, including early biomedicine in which beers and wines mediated the Hippocratic humors and served as a vehicle for other plant medicines (see chapter 2). Positive health consequences have been suggested for tempered consumption of some alcohol beverages, but these bear on constituents of the substrate, rather than on the alcohol product. For example, wine constituents that have been linked to the prevention of cancers and cardiovascular disease (e.g., antioxidant flavonoids, resveratrol) are present in the source grapes, rather than integral to the production of that beverage (Sovak 2001; Aldini et al. 2003; Chen et al. 2004).

Many alcohol beverages were constitutive parts of diet long before they became vehicles of sociability. In traditional contexts, fermented alcohol beverages have low ethanol and high nutrient levels; traditional beers, for example, are thick brews containing 1–2 percent alcohol, some natural sugars, and ungerminated grains. Further, they are commonly produced for household consumption and special occasions; social conventions limit consumption to place, age group, and other demographics. As traditional production gave way to home cash brewing and later to industrial production and commercial distribution, these beverages came to have significantly higher ethanol content and can be acquired outside the home in large and regular enough volumes to attract the overconsumption that plagues (ab)users in historical and contemporary cultures.

Coffee

The earliest consumption of coffee (*Coffea arabica*), perhaps as long ago as the sixth century CE, was in Ethiopia, where the leaves and fruit of wild *Coffea* trees were chewed. Coffee "beans" are the seeds of coffee berries ("coffee cherries"), which ripen in bright red clusters along the branches of the tree. In addition, green or roasted ground coffee fruit was mixed with fat and consumed during hunting expeditions or other extended travel during which, presumably, caffeine mitigated hunger and fatigue. Beverage coffee appeared later, and some researchers suggest that an alcohol coffee fruit beverage predates the one made by infusing the roasted, ground seeds in water: the etymology of the word *coffee* is traced to the Turkish *kahveh*, which is derived from the Arabic *kahwah*/wine, suggesting that coffee substituted for alcohol beverages, which are proscribed by Islamic tradition. Beverage coffee reached Yemen in Medieval times, later the Mediterranean, and by the fifteenth century began its worldwide diffusion. The sociopolitical history of coffee, like that of cacao and tea (see below), resonates global commodification and economic interdependencies (Simpson and Ogorzaly 2001; Trang 2003).

Coffee and Health

The stimulant and tonic properties of coffee that have been recorded in Islamic pharmacopoeia since the eleventh century are attributed largely to the alkaloid caffeine (Tables 5.1 and 5.2; the health implications of the

TABLE 5.1. Caffeine and Theobromine Content of Popular Beverages and Masticatories[a]

Product	Caffeine (mg)	Theobromine (mg)
Coffee, 8 oz brewed	135	0
Coffee, 8 oz instant	95	0
Coffee, 8 oz decaf	3	0
Tea, 8 oz leaf or bag	50	trace
Tea, 8 oz green	30	trace
Tea, 8 oz white	15	trace
Cocoa, 8 oz	8	250
Chocolate candy, 1 oz	1–6	130
Kola nut (by weight)	2–3.5%	1%
Maté	50–100	25–150
Coca Cola, 12 oz	34	0
Jolt, 12 oz	100	0

Sources: CSPI (1997), Apgar and Tarka (1999), Mayo Clinic (2004)
a. Published figures vary, at least in part because phytochemical content can be influenced by cultivar variety, plant maturity, harvest and fermentation conditions, the blending of cultivars for commercial production, and beverage preparation.

TABLE 5.2. Strength of Physiologic Effects of Theobromine, Theophylline, and Caffeine

Organ System	Theobromine	Theophylline	Caffeine
Brain	weak	moderate	strong
Bronchia	moderate	strong	weak
Heart	moderate	strong	weak
Kidney	moderate	strong	weak
Skeletal muscle	weak	moderate	strong

Source: Apgar and Tarka (1999: 158)

methylxanthines are more fully developed in the Cacao section). The later introduction of coffee to Europe included medicinal uses to influence humoral balance and modulate temperament. Recent studies suggest inhibitory effects of beverage coffee on tumor growth and proliferation in vitro (Miura et al. 2004). Dose-dependent diminished risk of Parkinson's disease among ethnically diverse populations suggests that coffee-protective effects play some role in the complex, multifactorial etiology of this disease. High levels of antioxidants (e.g., pyrroles, furans, and maltol) in beverage and green coffees suggest pharmacologic benefit for cardiovascular and other diseases (Abbott et al. 2003; Ragonese et al. 2003; Tan et al. 2003; Daglia et al. 2004; Svilaas et al. 2004; Yanagimoto et al. 2004).

Gums and Other Masticatories

Chewing gum is commonly apprehended as a product of the modern era, a cultural icon that is commonly, and at present pejoratively, associated with U.S. culture. From the perspective of political economy, it is important to note that during most of the twentieth century when the popularity of chewing gum became emblematic of mass consumer culture in the developed world, it was primarily sourced from southeastern Mexico, mainly the Yucatan Peninsula: "Mexico's relations with the United States form the axis around which the chewing gum economy developed, and just as chewing gum represents *modernity and consumer culture* for the United States and most of the developed world, it came to represent *premodernity and resource extraction* for tens of thousands of families in the Yucatan . . . [who were subjected to] ecological and social exploitation" (Redclift 2004:3–4, 16; emphasis added). The globalization of chewing gum caricatures the geopolitics of hemispheric relationships, as the production of commercial chewing gums is based on "principles of mass consumption and popular taste that, although first developed in the United States, have come to characterize modernity at the beginning of the twenty-first century for the entire globe" (Redclift 2004: 4).

On the theme of ethnopharmacology, the practice of chewing pliable botanicals is at least 9000 years old. The earliest evidence is from archaeological excavations in Scandinavia and Germany that uncovered lumps of tar that bear human tooth impressions and chew patterns. Most of the chewed tar was from birch bark (Aveling and Heron 1999). Resin-

TABLE 5.3. Physiologic Effects of Masticatories

Plant gum	Source plant	Culture, region	Activity
Birch resins	*Betula* spp. Betulaceae	Europe	antitumor, antiviral, counterirritant; analgesic; astringent, diuretic, antimalarial, antibacterial
Chicle	*Manilkara chicle* (Pittier) Gilly Sapotaceae	Central America	antioxidant
Frankincense	*Boswellia* spp. Burseraceae	Middle East	anti-inflammatory, anticancer, common medicinal
Locust gum	*Ceratonia siliqua* L., Fabaceae	Africa, Middle East	antioxidant polyphenols, anticancer, hypoglycemic, antimicrobial, laxative
Manuka honey[a]	*Leptospermum scoparium* Forster & Forster f. Myrtaceae	New Zealand	antimicrobial, antiplaque
Mastiche gum	*Pistacia lentiscus* L. Anacardiaceae	Mediterranean	antiatherogenic, antioxidant, antifungal
Pine tars	*Pinus* spp., Pinaceae	Europe, North America	anticancer, anti-inflammatory, antioxidant, antimicrobial

Sources: Feldman et al. (1995), Aveling and Heron (1999), Rauha et al. (2000), Corsi et al. (2002), Ito et al. (2002), Kivçak et al. (2002), Kumazawa et al. (2002), Lusby et al. (2002), Nishioka et al. (2002), Andrikopoulos et al. (2003), Duru et al. (2003), Hou et al. (2003), Kordali et al. (2003), Ma et al. (2003), Zhao et al. (2003), Dedoussis et al. (2004), English et al. (2004), Erhardt et al. (2004), Reichling et al. (2004), Sime and Reeve (2004), Ziegler et al. (2004).
a. See chapter 6

producing plants grow in many of the diverse environments that humans have occupied. Because resins preserve and travel well, they have been traded worldwide for millennia. Three thousand or more years ago in the Arab world an extensive and profitable trade in incense gums, especially *Boswellia* and *Commiphora* spp. (Burseraceae), was established. Since ancient times and on all continents, Chinese-sourced ambers (fossilized resins) from Myanmar and others from the Baltic region and Central America were prized commodities for medicine, as well as adornment and architectural design (Langenheim 2003).

A generic definition of plant exudates characterizes them as solid polysaccharide mixtures made up of nonglucose sugars that absorb water or are water-soluble. The categorization of these secretions and excretions is problematic because their chemical makeup is complex, their emulsion and solubility characteristics are environmentally and anthropogenically mutable, and the terms *gum*, *latex*, *resin*, *sap*, and *tar* are not used or defined consistently in the literature. Further, the chemical characterization of the excretions or their specification to particular plant tissues does not bear on how the indigenous cultures from which these products derive interpret them. In this discussion the term *gum* is a gloss for all botanical exudates, and the tradition established by Timothy Johns et al. (2000) applies the term *gummivory* to the chewing of all these products. The plants summarized in Table 5.3 represent the range of botanical and phytochemical diversity of gums used by human groups worldwide.

Gums and Health

Whereas many botanists characterize gums as inert substances with reference to human metabolism (Simpson and Ogorzaly 2001), the natural products that are the gums of traditional consumption are pharmacologically dynamic. For example, the high tannin content and specific constituents of some gums afford antimicrobial and anti-inflammatory activities, including against caries bacteria and dental plaque (Takahashi et al. 2003; English et al. 2004). Historical records cite the use of birch bark for sore throat; and a gum from the 6500-year-old Bokeberg site in Sweden is marked with impressions from a decayed tooth, leading to speculation about medicinal chewing or cavity-packing (Aveling 1997). Since ancient times, peoples of the Mediterranean have chewed the sweet resin of the mastic tree (*Pistacia lentiscus* L., Anacardiaceae) to clean teeth and freshen breath. In South America, the South Pacific, and Malaysia gutta percha (*Palaquium* spp., Sapotaceae) is similarly used. Native Americans and later New England colonists chewed astringent and aromatic spruce (*Picea* spp., Pinaceae) gums, while Central Americans chewed sapodilla gum (*Manilkara chicle* [Pittier] Gilly, Sapotaceae), which is synonymous with the chicle of commerce (Britannica Online 2005).

TABLE 5.4. Most Commonly Chewed Maasai Tree Gums

Gum	No. of informants reporting (N = 104)	Preference index
Commiphora africana	104	0.96
Balanites aegyptica	53	0.60
Euphorbia spinescens	36	0.52
Acacia seyal, A. xanthophloea, A. tortilis, A. drepanolobium	26	0.32
Aspilia mossambicensis	14	0.51
Commiphora schimperi	12	0.66
Ficus ingens; F. spp.	12	0.63
Commiphora sp.	11	0.54
Monadenium staeploides	5	0.58
Juniperus procerus	5	0.49
Euphorbia candelabrum	4	0.44
Commiphora habessinica	3	0.40
Lamnea triphylla	3	0.57

Source: Johns et al. (2000)

The diversity of phytoconstituents and pharmacologic potential of gums suggested by Table 5.3 is given more substance by Johns's research among Maasai pastoralists in East Africa (Johns et al. 2000). That work systematically recorded the consumption of gums and other traditional masticatories (Table 5.4), which typically are ignored in conventional food surveys, and documented significant pharmacologic potential for the most commonly used species. The antioxidant, hypolipidemic, anti-microbial, anti-inflammatory, and hypoglycemic actions of some of these species is especially interesting in view of the low rate of cardiovascular disease and associated risk factors (atherosclerosis, elevated serum lipids) among Maasai, despite consumption of diets with high animal-fat content (60 percent or more of daily caloric intake). To the extent that Maasai pastoralists are a reference standard for early humans (see chapter 1) and because gummivory plays a key role in the diets of nonhuman primates, Johns's work has important evolutionary implications for the dietary composition and health of hunter-gatherers and pastoralists of the

Pliocene and Pleistocene eras. It speaks as well to contemporary health issues, including the promotion of dietary diversity and supplementation (see chapter 7).

Kava

The beverage kava is a cold-water infusion of the roots of a shrub (*Piper methysticum* Forster, Piperaceae)[3] that was probably first consumed in northern Vanuatu about 3000 years ago. Pacific Islanders subsequently transported kava with them as they colonized other island groups in the Pacific, and at the time of European contact in the eighteenth century, kava use was recorded in most of the high island chains of Polynesia. Outside observers remarked on kava's elaborate ceremonial context and communal consumption. Although kava played an important role in origin myths and other religious inspirations and as medicine, one can argue that its greatest salience for Pacific Island societies is that it fosters sociability and community identity by creating or contributing to circumstances that are apprehended as well-being, relaxation, and contentment.

Kava drinking was integral to the social, political, and religious lives of Pacific Islanders. It marked important social events such as the installation of chiefs, ratification of contracts and treaties, embarkations and voyages' end, and life-cycle transitions such as birth, circumcision, marriage, and death. The social import of kava is reflected in the Fijian term for spiritual leader, *dauvaguna*, which translates literally as "expert at drinking kava" (Denham et al. 2002). European influence in the Pacific— especially that of missionaries and to a lesser extent colonial officers— discouraged kava use generally and some ceremonial components in particular, such as the mastication of kava by children. The degree of formality associated with kava drinking varied with context, ranging from ceremonies with rigidly enforced social protocols superintended by high-ranking chiefs to informal kava-sharing by peers at day's end. In general, only adult men drank kava. However, traditionally, high-ranking women in Polynesian and Micronesian chiefdoms and (in some locations) women past menopause (Brunton 1990) were also permitted to drink kava.

Traditional kava drinking continues in much of western Oceania, and kava has become a national beverage of sorts in Vanuatu and Fiji. In eastern Polynesia, although kava consumption declined significantly on pressure from missionaries, in Hawai'i and Tahiti a resurgence of use is associated with indigenous cultural and political revitalizations. Increasingly, partaking at the "kava bar" has emerged in urban areas throughout the Pacific as a largely deracinated practice that is neither gendered nor celebratory and has few or no ritual components. Informal, ceremonially attenuated kava consumption also is commonly found in the diaspora, among Pacific Islanders who have migrated to the United States, Canada, Australia, and New Zealand. Most recently, kava has reached a global market, both as a recreational beverage and as a dietary supplement (see chapter 7) recommended for anxiety and insomnia (Brunton 1990; Lebot et al. 1997; Lindstrom 2004; Merlin and Raynor 2004).

Kava and Health

At present, kava is used in traditional Pacific Island medicines in composite preparations to treat sinus problems, earache, and bronchitis. Past medicinal applications included treating intestinal, urogenital, upper respiratory, and skin disorders and pulmonary pain and inducing abortion (Lebot et al. 1992).

The active ingredients in kava are structurally (styryl- or phenyl-substituted pyrones) and functionally grouped as the kavalactones. Varieties of kava are characterized by distinct ratios of the six major kavalactones. Further, morphotypes and chemotypes of the same cultivar grown in a homogeneous (soil and climate) environment covary with parameters such as irradiation (sunlight increases kavalactone content compared to shade-growing feral individuals under tree canopy); fertility, irrigation, and cultivated habitats also increase the amount of active ingredients.

For millennia Pacific Islanders have selected kavas for diverse uses based on observable physiological effects: some are used solely for ceremonial purposes, others as medicines, still others for drinking. The effects of kava beverage are heightened when the resinous and active components of the root are separated, which helps us to comprehend why the preparation of kava begins by chewing, grinding, or pounding the root, actions that emulsify[4] the kavalactones to produce a more potent beverage. Pacific Island peoples learned to reach the desired potency of beverage by managing this phenomenon (whether or not emulsification has any analogues in Pacific languages). The literature is equivocal whether the salivary enzyme amylase also contributes to potency; if it does, this empowers the biocultural lens by suggesting another level of human agency in influencing kava potency. Although the properties of individual kavalactones vary in important ways, the pharmacologic activity of the full kava extract is greater than any single component, suggesting that synergism among kavalactones contributes to the aggregate effect (Lebot et al. 1997, 1999; Ramzan and Tran 2004; Singh 2004a).

The principal activities of kava are sedation; analgesia and local anesthesia (slight numbing of the mouth as one drinks kava); muscle relaxation; and visual effects, including pupil dilation (Singh 2004b). Kava is also a mild diuretic and has antifungal activity (Locher et al. 1995). In the West, the sedative and relaxant properties of kava have led to its use for anxiety and insomnia.

Ethnographic studies suggest that kava drinking is not deleterious, although lassitude and reversible dermopathy (scaly skin) have been reported among chronic, high-volume kava consumers. However, while reviews of short-term clinical trials of kava extract for anxiety concluded that kava appeared safe and efficacious (Pittler and Ernst 2002; Teschke et al. 2003), concern for hepatotoxicity has been expressed. Since 1998, seventy-eight cases of hepatotoxicity have been attributed to kava, although those reports did not control for confounding variables (e.g., alcohol and other drug consumption). One consequence is that kava has been restricted in Canada and much of Europe. Subsequent reviews concluded that kava's role in hepatotoxicity is uncertain in the majority of cases, but at least some appear to implicate it unequivocally (Clouatre 2004).

Because kavalactones have themselves not been linked to hepatotoxicity, it might be caused by other constituents in commercial kava supplements—for example, the alkaloid pipermethystine, which occurs in the aboveground structures of *P. methysticum* and which may contaminate or be deliberately incorporated into commercial products. Kava might be indirectly toxic through interaction with pharmaceuticals that are themselves hepatotoxic. For example, kava is a potent inhibitor of some cytochrome P450 isoforms, several of which participate in the metabolism of some common pharmaceuticals. Kava also inhibits cyclooxygenase, which protects hepatic function (Wanwimolruk et al. 1998; Dragull et al. 2003; Anke and Ramzan 2004a, 2004b; Clouatre 2004).

Khat

Native to Ethiopia, the bitter fresh leaves and shoots of this small tree (*Catha edulis* Forsk., Celestraceae) have been chewed or infused as a beverage since at least the twelfth century CE throughout northeastern Africa and the Arabian Peninsula, and it has been cultivated since the early fourteenth century. Traditionally, khat (kat, qat) chewing was the linchpin of (especially men's) recreational and religious activities, including celebrations, business arrangements, and political meetings, across all social classes. In some locations (e.g., Somaliland) only the mystics and Sufi scholars chewed khat. In Yemeni tradition exercise regimens and the consumption of a large standardized meal preceded khat consumption. On ritual and feast occasions the meal was expanded by several special dishes. Days were structured by occupational and recreational phases in such a way that most business was concluded before the main, midday meal, which was crowned by a shared session of khat chewing. Depending on household resources, special rooms were set aside for sharing khat. Certain homes may be designated on a nonregular, rotating basis as gathering places for khat sessions. Traditionally, the gatherings were of similar-status individuals who shared political ideologies and might have been gender-segregated. Khat chewing was often accompanied by tobacco smoking, which further cemented sociability. In the contemporary era, the context of khat chewing has been transformed: it is a secular habit that transcends all demographics and serves both stimulant and sociability objectives (Kennedy 1987; Rudgley 1993).

Khat and Health

Khat is used to treat fever, headache, depression, body pain, and colds. The chemical profile of the alkaloid cathinone in fresh khat leaves is similar to that of amphetamine, imparting sensations of well-being and excitement; later, common effects include insomnia, depression, and anxiety. A second active constituent, cathine, is present in dry leaves as well. Khat chewing suppresses hunger and thirst, relieves pain, reduces swelling in the mouth, and lowers blood pressure. Hypertensive effects and elevated oxidation also have been reported and were suggested to contribute to a higher incidence of myocardial infarct reported for khat chewers. Khat chewing has been identified as a risk factor for esophageal cancer and duodenal ulcer. Limited evidence suggests that prolonged khat consumption impairs reproductive function, including reduced plasma testosterone and spermatogenesis and compromised fetal development when chewed by the mother during pregnancy. Perhaps the greatest concern with khat use in contemporary, largely urban contexts is the risk of addiction (Raja'a et al. 2001; Al-Motarreb and Broadley 2003; Carvalho 2003; Dalby 2003; Mwenda et al. 2003; Cuddy 2004).

Maté

The beverage maté (*Ilex paraguariensis*) has been used for millennia by native groups in Paraguay, Uruguay, northeastern Argentina, and southeastern Brazil. Processes for leaf preparation varied in the past as well as today. The traditional beverage is a water infusion or decoction of (sometimes blanched) roasted leaves and small stems of *yerba maté*. The foam-capped beverage is prepared in a *cuia*/gourd, which is made from the fruit of the calabash tree (*Crescentia cujete* L., Bignoniaceae) or the vine calabash (*Lagenaria* spp., Cucurbitaceae). Maté drinkers pass the cuia and share a *bombilla*, a reed, metal, or silver straw tube with a basketwork or perforated metal filter at the submerged end. Maté derives from the Quechua word *matí*, drinking cup, drawing attention to the sociability of maté drinking.

Europeans learned about maté while trying to deliver Christianity to natives of the region. During the 1500s, at the height of Jesuit missionary activity in northern Argentina, thousands of Guaraní Indians farmed yerba maté commercially to supply the mission stations. After the Jesuits were expelled and the missions declined, outsiders lost touch with maté. Locally, it remained popular: in Brazil fresh leaves were infused, in Paraguay maté was smoke-dried and drunk from the horn of a bull, and in Argentina *gauchos* (cowboys) smoke-dried it and consumed it hot from wooden cups. Variably a hot, warm, or cold beverage, maté may be flavored with citrus juice or peel, burned sugar, and milk. Most people drank maté from gourds or wooden cups, while the rich drank from silver and other ornate vessels and employed special maté preparers who were trained to the host's particular tastes. In the early 1900s the beverage regained popularity beyond the region of its origin, and today it is one of the most heavily commercialized plants in South America, with the bulk of export going to the Arabic world (Giberti 1994).

Maté and Health

Traditionally maté was used in medicine as an intestinal and digestive stimulant, tonic, diuretic, leaf poultice for wounds, and to treat headache, fatigue, and diabetes. The stimulant properties of maté are attributed to high caffeine and theobromine content (Tables 5.1 and 5.2; the health implications of the methylxanthines are more fully developed in the Cacao section). Maté contains high polyphenol, vitamin C, and tannin levels. It has antioxidant activities and contains ursolic acid, which is diuretic and anti-inflammatory and has antitumor and anti-HIV effects (see chapter 1, terpenoids). Regular and long-term consumption of maté has been linked to cancers of the head and neck (Kawakami and Kobayashi 1991; Actis-Goretta et al. 2002; Bracesco et al. 2003; Goldenberg et al. 2003; Sewram et al. 2003; Chandra and De Mejia Gonzalez 2004).

Vehicles of Sociability and Reciprocity

My objective here is not to review comprehensively the substantial literatures that have evolved for cacao, tea, betel, and kola but to contextualize them to the theoretical perspectives outlined in chapter 1, that is, to explore the intersections of culturally constructed food-related behaviors as they influence human health. These four examples also resonate a theme developed in chapter 3, where the case study of chile pepper locates particular foods and beverages in the larger context of political economy and globalization.

Chocolate/Cacao

An ardent fan of chocolate (*Theobroma cacao*), the eighteenth-century botanist Carolus Linnaeus assigned it the genus name *Theobroma*, food (*broma*) of the gods (*theo*). Seeds ("beans") of the cacao tree provide the source material for chocolate and for the beverage cocoa. It is native to the region that extends from the northern Amazon basin to southern Mexico, the most likely origin areas being the Orinoco Basin of Venezuela and Colombia, the Andean foothills of Colombia, the Amazonas region of Brazil, and Central America from southern Mexico to Guatemala (Young 1994).

Theobroma cacao was domesticated in ancient Mesoamerica, where Maya flourished in what is now Guatemala and the Yucatan during the first millennium CE. The etymology of the word *cacao* is Mixe-Zoquean (*kakaw*), suggesting influence from the Olmec culture in southern Mexico (1500–400 BCE), perhaps via the Izapans who succeeded them. The linguistic history of *chocolate* is thought to be the combination by Spaniards of the Maya *chocol*/hot and the Aztec *atl*/water, although some sources suggest origin in the Aztec *xocoatl*/bitter water. Maya cultivated *T. cacao*, mixing the seed extract with maize and chile to make a hot beverage that, prior to serving, was poured from one vessel held high above another to create a much prized froth. Other parts of Mesoamerica were not suitable for cacao cultivation, and its value increased as it became commodified as an item of exchange, serving for some time as actual currency. Political conflicts over control of cacao sources were the cornerstone of military campaigns. By late Maya times, long-distance trade had introduced cacao to western Mexico and the Aztec empire, where it became a primary source of wealth. The Aztec also drank cacao as a frothed beverage, typically cold, and developed new flavorings, such as honey (Young 1994; Coe and Coe 1996; Davidson 1999).

Cacao was a potent article of ritual and ceremony for Olmec, Maya, and Aztec, who used it to propitiate the deities, as a centerpiece of celebratory feasts, as gift exchange among nobility, and to rub on the bodies of newborns to assure their health. Images of cacao fruit were depicted on sacred walls and temples, with the pods being a symbol of life and fertility. The tree and bean were woven through origin myths: cacao was revered as the bridge between earth and heaven and featured in agricultural and sacrificial ceremonies. Bowls and other vessels to hold cacao were included among grave items buried with dignitaries and warriors, and cacao was served as a celebratory beverage at marriages, puberty rites, and other life transitions.

More to the point of this chapter is that, like tobacco smoking, cacao drinking was reserved for immediately after a meal, rather than during it (Young 1994; Davidson 1999). This identifies cacao as an integral element of cuisine whose consumption signaled sociability rather than nutriture.

Further, the social context in which cacao was consumed determined what other ingredients might be added: the most common addition for Aztec nobility was the flower of *Cymbopetalum penduliflorum* Baill. (Annonaceae); others include vanilla, flowers of *Piper amalago* L. (Piperaceae) and Mexican tarragon (*Tagetes lucida* Cav., Asteraceae), and seeds of sapote (*Pouteria sapota* [Jacq.] H. E. Moore and Stearn, Sapotaceae), *Ceiba* spp. (Bombacaceae), and annatto (*Bixa orellana* L., Bixaceae) (Coe 1997). The amount of chile added to the beverage could be adjusted to mark the significance of the occasion. The social salience of cacao is reflected in the observation that it was both gendered and marked by age and social status: consumption was reserved for adult men who represented the nobility, priesthood, military office and decorated warrior class, high government office, and victims destined for ritual sacrifice (Dillinger et al. 2000).

The Introduction of Cacao to the Old World

In 1502 Columbus returned from his last New World voyage with cacao beans. Although he witnessed their value in exchange, the Italian navigator and his crew had no knowledge of cacao beverages and generated no interest in the beans among Europeans. Almost twenty years later when Cortés and his Spanish troops invaded Yucatan, they better appreciated the economic value of the plant when they saw vast stores of cacao in Tenochtítlan, the Aztec capital. In the context of Aztec banquets, Cortés's troops came to understand the social role of cacao beverage, for which they developed a taste after initially rejecting its bitter strangeness. Emperor Motecuhzoma was served this drink in large quantities in gold goblets by women-in-attendance (who themselves did not partake). On Cortés's return to Europe bearing treasures stolen from the Aztecs, he gifted to the Spanish court three trunks of cacao beans as well as instructions for the preparation of cacao beverages (Young 1994).

Cacao's reputation preceded its availability in Europe, with the first official shipment of cacao beans traveling from Veracruz to Seville only as late as 1585. By then the Spanish royal court were preparing beverage cocoa with sugar, cinnamon, vanilla, citrus water, and other flavors. Following the lead of Mesoamerica, Europeans reserved cacao drinking, like coffee and tea consumption, for after the meal.

The Spanish imposition of authority in Mesoamerica afforded them control over agriculture and trade, establishing a world monopoly on cacao production. Despite their efforts to keep secret the cultivation of cacao and preparation of cacao beverage, within a century the culinary and medicinal uses of cacao had spread to France, Holland, and Italy and later to England. The diffusion of beans and popularity of the beverage were enhanced by the intermarriage of the Spanish royalty and their European counterparts and the inclusion of cacao among marriage properties; for example, in 1643 the engagement gifts that Spanish Princess Maria Teresa gave to Louis XIV of France included an ornate chest filled with cacao seeds.

Drinking cocoa, as the beverage came to be known in Europe, quickly became fashionable; and chocolate houses were popular frequents for the wealthy aristocracy, as well as for politicians, artists, and writers. These haunts replicated the culture of the first Near East and later European coffee houses on which they were modeled and were associated with "bourgeois masculinity, [and] serious, purposive and respectable" socializing (Goodman 1995: 132). In this way they reproduced the gendered and privileged Mesoamerican context of cacao consumption. The popularity of cocoa drove affiliate industries such as the manufacture of ornate chocolate services featuring pots, trays, and frothing whisks made from silver, porcelain, and other valuables. This and other types of beverage material culture proliferated through the 1700s as the social context of cocoa consumption (like that of coffee and tea) shifted from public to domestic. As in-home consumption became more common, the gendered nature of cocoa drinking eroded, although its connection to the wealthy class endured until inexpensive cocoa powders became available in the early 1800s.

Cacao, cocoa, and chocolate were rapidly Europeanized through colonial activities. As demand for cocoa continued to expand, the French, Dutch, English, and Germans broke the Spanish monopoly over cacao production and trade. Cacao became a pantropical crop, and its production took on the character of other colonial-driven cash crops: plantation-based, forced-labor enterprises that exploited local populations for European markets. Today the largest growers of cacao are Ivory Coast, Cameroon, Ghana, Nigeria, Brazil, Indonesia, and Malaysia. Of the three main groups within *T. cacao*, Forastero is the easiest to grow and the most common, accounting for more than 80 percent of global production.

Criollo represents the first domesticated cacaos; it is the most prized and the most scarce, and it can be made into a palatable beverage with minimal fermentation. Trinitario cacao is a cross of the other two (Marita et al. 2001). In locations where cacao grows, the sweet pulp in which the seeds develop is eaten raw or fermented into an alcohol drink.

From Olmec, Maya, and Aztec traditions, through the Spanish colonial era in Mexico, cacao was consumed in beverage form. During the early European period, water, coffee, wine, and beer were alternately used as the base for cacao beverages. The addition of sugar to cacao (and to coffee and tea) fostered a kind of fusion that was a centerpiece of mercantile capitalism and colonial expansion around the world. In the 1720s the English began to blend cacao with milk, thus creating the cocoa (hot chocolate) favored in the West today. By the end of the eighteenth century the daily issue of cocoa had become an icon of England's Royal Navy, and overseas mercantilism surpassed in-country production to the extent that consumers could rely more on the availability of cacao (and sugar, coffee, and tea) than on domestic dairy and grain products (Goodman 1995).

Cocoa/Chocolate Production

Like other foods discussed in chapter 4, in cocoa production an inedible plant is transformed into a palatable one by fermentation. Cacao fermentations differ from alcohol and lactic acid fermentations, as the former involve enzyme-driven chemical modifications of diverse compounds that contribute to complex flavors and aromas. Mature cacao pods containing an average of thirty to forty seeds are split on harvest and exposed to sun for several days. As the pulp ferments, the beans lose their bitter flavor and acquire a pleasant aroma. These are later separated from the pulp and dried before export to producers of chocolate, cocoa, cocoa butter, and related products.

Cacao-bean processing begins with roasting (which diminishes acidity and further enhances flavor), followed by removal of the outer shell and crushing and heating the inner nib to melt the cocoa butter, then grinding to a thick paste (chocolate liquor). Nibs destined to become Dutch-processed cocoa are treated with alkaline salts (sodium or potassium carbonate) so that the powder mixes more readily with both water and milk. Extracting 10–25 percent of the cocoa butter from untreated chocolate liquor leaves as residue cocoa powder or drinking chocolate (which usually has sugar added). The beverage cocoa is typically made with low-fat powder, while the richer powders are used to flavor desserts.

The expanded availability of cocoa powder not only made mixing beverages easier, it also enabled combining it with sugar and remixing with cocoa butter to create solid chocolates. By the mid-1700s cacao began to evolve beyond its beverage form. In 1828 the Dutch chocolate-maker van Houten developed inexpensive hydraulic technology to extract cocoa butter, reducing production costs and increasing the availability of both beverage and confection forms of chocolate (Bixler and Morgan 1999). Since then, the number and diversity of cacao products—as well as brand image—have grown enormously, including solid chocolate confections that have in the United States and Europe become emblematic of holidays such as Easter and St. Valentine's Day. Until recently cocoa beverage remained a more modest, less transformed cacao product, although in recent years it finds its own niche among designer commodities in the form of variably spiced, fruited, and otherwise dressed up beverages.

Cacao and Health

The medicinal uses of cacao predate its appreciation as an after-meal beverage. Olmec, Maya, and Aztec used cacao as both a primary medicine and as a medium via which other medicines were consumed. In contrast to its role as a social marker, in the context of preventive and therapeutic medicine, cacao was gender, age, and status neutral. European and Mesoamerican manuscripts from the sixteenth to early twentieth century record more than one hundred medicinal indications for cacao. Three consistent roles are: "1) to treat emaciated patients to gain weight; 2) to stimulate nervous systems of apathetic, exhausted or feeble patients; and 3) to improve digestion and elimination where . . . cacao countered the effects of stagnant or weak stomachs, stimulated kidneys and improved bowel function" (Dillinger et al. 2000: 2057S). Cacao paste was a vehicle to administer drugs and offset the taste of bitter medicines. Cacao leaves, flowers, bark, and oil (cocoa butter) also had medicinal applications.

In many of these accounts the boundary between medicine and food is blurred, as cocoa is both a medicine and a healthful food. Instructions for the preparation of cacao and its medicinal uses were transposed from the New World to the Old, where European physicians recommended cocoa for a great variety of applications ranging from general tonics to specifics for tuberculosis, typhoid, gastrointestinal disorders, and many more. In 1662 Henry Stubbe, a celebrated English physician, extolled both the nutritive and medicinal qualities of cocoa and began to include it in medical prescriptions.

As in Mesoamerica, the European medicinal uses of cacao during the sixteenth–nineteenth centuries were democratic, while the social contexts of its use remained gendered and privileged. A nineteenth-century text described cocoa as having both the "exhilarating properties of tea and the strengthening and ordinary body-supporting qualities of milk" (Johnston 1880, in Lupien 1999). Despite its medicinal importance in earlier eras, in recent years Europeans project a view more like that of U.S. consumers, who regard cocoa and chocolate as very popular but not nutritive confections.

Cacao Pharmacology The physiologic effects of the methylxanthines theobromine, theophylline, and caffeine are widely known. They inhibit drowsiness by antagonizing receptors of adenosine, an endogenous drowse-inducing chemical; all stimulate the central nervous system and heart muscle, exert diuretic effects, and relax smooth muscle, notably in the bronchial airways. But there are significant differences in the strength and locus of their actions. For example, the effect of theophylline is most intense in the kidneys, heart, and bronchia; the effects of caffeine are more pronounced in skeletal muscle and the brain (Tables 5.1 and 5.2). The vasoconstrictive activity of theobromine and caffeine may account for the efficacy of methylxanthine relief of hypertension-associated headache; but abrupt withdrawal of caffeine also causes headache through dilation of cerebral blood vessels. Caffeine stimulates the senses, shortens reaction time, increases motor activity, and diminishes fatigue.[5] High consumption (200–500 mg) can cause nervousness, headache, and irritability. Recent evidence links caffeine with antioxidant effects and in vitro protection of cells against genotoxicity. Although public impression commonly links methylxanthines with elevated blood pressure and risk of heart disease, this has not been corroborated by scientific study. Similarly, clinical studies have not supported impressions that caffeine aggravates peptic ulcer or has other adverse effects on health (Fredholm 1995; Apgar and Tarka 1999; Nawrot et al. 2003; Abraham and Stopper 2004).

Although cocoa butter contains saturated fatty acid, which generally are associated with elevated risk of coronary heart disease (due to increased thrombosis/clotting and elevated plasma lipids and lipoproteins), the predominant saturated fatty acid in cacao (stearic acid) is unusual because it does not increase blood cholesterol. A cacao cholesterol-neutralizing effect, which was suggested as early as the 1970s, has been demonstrated in humans through controlled studies with chocolate-enriched diets. In the last decade large-sample studies of dietary saturated fatty acids and cardiovascular disease risk in the United States demonstrated that cacao is not an important contributor to total saturated fatty acids or stearic acid intake. Mineral availability from cacao is generally good, in part because phytate content is reduced during fermentation; in the context of cardiovascular disease and other health risks, relatively high levels of protective minerals such as magnesium, copper, potassium, and calcium are noteworthy.

Rich stores of flavonols (catechin and epicatechin) in cacao may promote cardiovascular health through antioxidant and antiplatelet activities that improve vascular endothelial function, moderate inflammation, and delay blood clotting. On a per weight basis the flavonoid content of cacao products is higher than that found in most plant-based foods (as much as 10 percent; Steinberg et al. 2003). Cacao polyphenols are immunoregulatory; specifically, they down-regulate exaggerated immune responses. Finally, preliminary in vitro studies have linked cacao flavonols to the inhibition of human colonic cancer cells and to diminished tumor growth in other cancers (Jardine 1999; Kritchevsky 1999; Keen 2001; Carnesecchi et al. 2002; Hannum et al. 2002; Kris-Etherton and Keen 2002; Rios et al. 2003; Serafini et al. 2003; Steinberg et al. 2003). While extensive and meticulous review of the literature uncovered only this modest pharmacologic profile for cacao, quite a bit more attention has been devoted to its potential for psychoactivity.

Is Cacao Addictive? A popular argument for so-called cacao addictions is the presence of psychotropic constituents. A survey of the literature, drawing on a comprehensive review by Rogers and Smit (2000), confirms that the psychotropic actions and addictive potential of cacao have been exaggerated. This includes its reputation as an aphrodisiac, first in Mesoamerica and later in Europe and North America. Many purportedly aphrodisiac plants contain powerful stimulants such as caffeine and related methylxanthine derivatives that have similar pharmacologic properties. But the caffeine and theophylline contents of cacao are very low (Table 5.1), and its principal alkaloid, theobromine, is only a weak stimulant. Further, there is no meaningful relationship between purported chocolate craving and the preference for other foods and drinks that contain these chemicals.

Interest in the psychotropic potential of cacao was refueled in the last decade by a publication in a leading peer-reviewed scientific journal (di Tomaso et al. 1996) that identified in cacao the constituent anandamide. That this endogenous cannabinoid, which is found in the brain, is related to chemicals in marijuana (*Cannabis* spp., Cannabidaceae) generated significant public and commercial interest. However, anandamide is present in cacao in such small concentrations that for a detectable influence on mood, one would have to consume—all at once—more than one-third of one's body weight of chocolate. Other cacao constituents that have been proposed to affect mood are tyramine, phenylethylamine, magnesium, tryptophan, serotonin, and casomorphins; but these are present in higher concentrations in other beverages and foods for which preferences are not reported.

In recent decades the popularity of chocolate has taken on a persona of sufficient proportion to have generated its own vocabulary, much of it hyperbole. Reinforcing images projected by commercial interests and the media, "chocoholics" report cravings and addictions, while cacao and chocolate manufacturers appropriate the same idiom for product promotion. Both historically and today, there was/is widespread belief that cacao products elevate mood; increasingly that elevation is also linked to sensual/sexual affect with an intensity that extends beyond cacao's traditional reputation as an aphrodisiac. Scientific studies demonstrate that chocolate does influence mood, typically inducing "pleasant" feelings and reduction of "tension." Further, self-reported desire for chocolate and other foods often is linked to fatigue, depression, and other negative moods. But these observations are not sufficient to establish an addictive aspect for cacao consumption—positive mood shifts can easily be attributed to eating a particular food or just to eating.

Michener and Rozin's (1994) study of satiation in self-identified chocolate "cravers" concluded that desire for chocolate was significantly reduced on consumption of placebo or milk or white chocolate but not
cocoa capsules, which would have contained more of the purported psychotropic constituents. The logical conclusion is that whatever satisfaction ensues on consumption of chocolate, it has little if anything to do
with cacao pharmacology. This is supported by the fact that milk chocolate is more popular than dark, including among self-identified "addicts";
yet milk chocolate contains less cacao solids, thus fewer of the purportedly psychoactive constituents. Other studies of mood modulation found
that whereas "addicts" identified it as a precipitating factor in chocolate
consumption, no significant changes in depression were recorded after
chocolate was eaten (e.g., Macdiarmid and Hetherington 1995). Finally,
nothing about the pharmacology of cacao suggests that any of its constituents fosters physical dependence. Thus, it is likely that the association of
cacao with psychoactivity is iconographic, rather than phytochemical,
and these examples offer powerful testimony to how what we think about
consumables influences our apprehension of their effect on our bodies.

Cacao and Sociability

Appetite, food preference, satiation, and related phenomena are more
complex than physiological models suggest. Minimally, these are influenced by the cultural construction and social negotiation of eating (see
chapter 1). In one framework that addresses this complexity, Rogers and
Smit argue that cognitive aspects best explain so-called cravings and self-
identified food addictions. They propose that "ambivalence about certain
foods . . . leads to attempts to resist eating them and the need to provide an
explanation . . . of why this is difficult and sometimes fails" (Rogers and
Smit 2000: 6). Ambivalence about chocolate reflects that it is delicious
but not nutritive, its consumption pleasurable but decadent. The explanation by the individual of his or her failure to resist consumption takes
the form of cravings and addiction, which implies the overriding influence of biological mechanisms. This is too simplistic. I would argue that
a more compelling explanation addresses the nuances of consumption,
the complexity of context, and the role that sociability plays in fostering
shared experiences with specific foods. This is consistent with the theoretical perspective advanced in this book, apprehending issues that bear on

food and health by factoring in both the ideational elements that shape human-food interactions and the biological consequences of food consumption. In this regard, it is interesting to juxtapose the relatively modest pharmacologic profile of cacao with the number and diversity of health claims advanced by Mesoamerican and later European cultures, suggesting that cacao/chocolate means more than its physiologic activities. As it did for early Mesoamericans, for contemporary people sharing cocoa in a social context is connected with pleasure.

Tea

While the history of tea (*Camellia sinensis* [L.] Kuntze, *C.* spp., Theaceae)[6] may be more than 5000 years old in China, popular legend credits an emperor of the third century BCE (Shen Nung) with discovering the merits of the beverage when *Camellia* leaves were fortuitously blown by wind into a pot of boiled drinking water. *Camellia sinensis* has been cultivated in China for at least 2000 years. The earliest reliable written record of tea beverage is a dictionary written by the scholar Kuo Po in 350 CE (although he may have used the word in the older sense of any infused beverage). Here, *kia* (renamed *ch'a* after 725) is identified as a bitter medicinal drink made from roasted green tea leaves boiled with onion, citrus, and ginger and used in the treatment of diverse ailments ranging from lethargy and poor eyesight to stomach disorders and distemper. From the Mandarin *ch'a*, *chai* was borrowed directly into many languages, for example, Mongol, Russian, eastern European, Turkish, Swahili, and Thai. The western European *thé* (French), *tè* (Italian), *te* (Norwegian and Swedish), and *té* (Spanish), and *tea* (English) are linked etymologically to Hokkien (Min) *te* from southern China, whereas Portuguese *cha* derives from Cantonese *cha* (which is tonally distinct from the Mandarin ch'a) (Anderson 1988).

Early Szechwan tea was prepared with salt, ginger, and flour; later, flowers, fruit peel, and scents were added. Along the northern and western borders of China, pastoral groups made tea with milk or butter and salt. Tea drinking as refreshment and as a social lubricant among the upper classes and monks did not begin until the sixth century CE. After 780 CE, when Lu Yu published his three-volume tea classic, *Ch'a Ching*, tea producers learned superior methods for improving the quality of tea leaves (which Lu learned from the Buddhist monks who raised him). During the Tang Dynasty (618–907 CE) these more flavorful teas encouraged farmers to assign small plots to tea production, and a class of wholesalers emerged to purchase tea from peasants and distribute it from regional stockpiles. Tea affairs were elaborated further with the advent of tribute teas for the imperial court, where tea ceremonies proliferated.

As Buddhist monks spread tea cultivation throughout China, pressed, roasted tea leaves boiled in water with a pinch of salt became China's national beverage, a major commodity that permeated the daily lives of people of all classes. Leaf tea replaced pressed-cake tea by 850 CE; during the Sung Dynasty (960–1279 CE) dry, powdered tea leaves were whisked with bamboo sticks in hot water in ceramic bowls. The cultural renaissance of the Ming Dynasty (1368–1643) returned attention to tea and its ceremonies, for which the Chinese developed the production of green tea and introduced the steeping method to brew tea. During the Qing Dynasty (1644–1912) tea manufacturers developed the means to control fermentation and produced many varieties of tea. Beginning in its earliest days in China, tea drinking spread to the neighboring Shan States of Burma and Siam. Sustained regional trade in Chinese tea started during the Sung Dynasty, when the government permitted transborder trade into Mongolia. At the end of the 1600s, government caravans began supplying Russia with small quantities of tea. Tea trade with Europe began in the seventeenth century, all of it centered in Holland; but by the late 1800s China's market control had weakened as tea production was extended into India, Japan, Ceylon (Sri Lanka), and elsewhere. China continued to supply Russia, Mongolia, and Tibet with poor-quality brick tea.

From the perspective of political economy, the story of tea is marked by asymmetries in access to products and control of production and markets. Tea is part of the experience of British and Dutch colonial expansions in India, Ceylon, and Indonesia (Borneo, Java, Sumatra, Celebes), where considerable lands and local human resources were appropriated to sustain the tea plantations that supplied England's growing taste for the beverage. The continued tradition of small-plot cultivation of tea in China could not compete with the economies of scale offered by plantation production in India and Ceylon. Tea was also at the heart of the British opium trade and the mid-nineteenth-century Opium Wars in China: to balance their purchase of Chinese tea for export home, British merchants smuggled into China opium grown in their Indian colony, where the British had directed that vast portions of agricultural land be converted for opium-poppy production. In North America, the Revolutionary War was precipitated by British efforts to manipulate trade through the Tea Act of 1773, which directed the New World colonies to purchase tea only from the British East India Company (Simoons 1991; Weatherstone 1992; Manchester 1996; Davidson 1999).

Tea Varieties

Teas are distinguished by production processes and region of origin. For black (red) tea, wilted leaves are bruised by rolling and allowed to fully ferment by exposure for several hours to oxidation before drying to enrich the flavor. The production of green tea involves no fermentation at all, only steaming and drying immediately after harvest to prevent oxidation and to preserve the delicate flavor of young leaves. A less-known nonfermented variety is white tea, for which leaves are harvested before the leaf bud fully opens, when it is still covered by fine white hairs. Brown or oolong tea is prepared from large-leaf *Camellia* and is only partially fermented. Other tea names, such as Ceylon, Assam, and Darjeeling, identify the place where the tea is grown or originated. Today there are more than 2000 tea varieties, produced in twenty-five countries, the leaders of which are China (which itself produces more than 500 types of tea), India, Indonesia, Kenya, Malawi, and Sri Lanka.

Tea and Health

Green and later oolong teas were valued in traditional Chinese medicine as preventives and treatments for a wide range of disorders, such as tooth decay, gastrointestinal problems, lung disease, and fever. Tea also came to be a prized medicine in Europe where beverage and dry teas were offered as general tonics as well as specifics for scurvy, stomachache, and poor eyesight (Blofeld 1985; Weinberg and Bealer 2001; Lu 2002). Tea is also a cooking ingredient, used as a tenderizer and/or to impart a bitter, sweet fragrance to such classic Chinese dishes as shrimp with green tea leaves, tea-boiled eggs, and oolong-stuffed steamed fish (Simoons 1991).

Several healthful properties and constituents have been characterized in tea, including a range of flavonoid compounds that is broader than that found in other plants. Six are present at high concentrations (greater than

1 percent dry weight): catechin, gallocatechin, epicatechin, epigallocate-chin, epicatechin-3-gallate, and epigallocatechin-3-gallate. Animal stud-ies have concluded that antioxidant polyphenols in both green and black teas may protect against a variety of cancers and that green-tea consump-tion is related to diminished risk of atherosclerosis and coronary heart disease, elevated cholesterol, and high blood pressure. Epigallocatechin gallate in green tea promotes apoptosis (cell death) in cancers and pre-vents tumor growth by inhibiting the tumor-growth enzyme urokinase. Other studies have shown that tea is antiviral and antibacterial, protects against liver disease and stroke, diminishes the risk of osteoporosis, is hypoglycemic (through enhancement of insulin activity), has anti-ulcer effects, and is anti-inflammatory. The health implications of methyl-xanthines are more fully developed in the preceding section on cacao (Tables 5.1 and 5.2).

Tannins in tea (and other plants) can bind with, and thus inhibit the absorption of, iron, suggesting that excessive tea consumption with food can contribute to iron deficiency. On this same principle, tea can mediate disorders in which iron accumulates in the body and may cause organ damage and cancers. Regular tea drinking at meals can clinically de-crease iron absorption in patients with hemochromatosis (hereditary iron overload), thalassemia (an inherited anemia in which destroyed red blood cells spill iron into the circulation), and other disorders (Gomes et al. 1995; Maity et al. 1995; Halder and Bhaduri 1998; Kaltwasser et al. 1998; Hegarty et al. 2000; Mukhtar and Ahmad 2000; Anderson and Polansky 2002; Kris-Etherton and Keen 2002; McKay and Blumberg 2002; Sabu et al. 2002; Zhen 2002; Kamath et al. 2003; Siddiqui et al. 2004).

Tea and Sociability in China

With some regional variation, tea was traditionally served before meals and after but was not an integral part of the repast itself (Simoons 1991). In cities throughout Sung Dynasty China and in picturesque pastoral and garden settings, teahouses served as places where people gathered not so much to consume (although they did drink tea) as to socialize. Chinese used tea regularly to mark important occasions, during religious cere-monies and marriage exchanges, as a vehicle for business connections, and as an offering at ancestral altars. Ascending the scale from peasants to scholars and nobility, tea drinking became increasingly ritualized. Food was not served at teahouses, but fragrances were added to enhance the tea experience, such as jasmine (*Jasimum* spp., Oleaceae) for green tea and rose for black tea. Specially designated teas marked celebratory occasions, for example, *yuanbao* (gold ingot) tea laced with kumquats (*Fortunella* spp., Rutaceae) and olives (*Olea* spp., Oleaceae) was served for the lunar new year to assure prosperity (Manchester 1996). The custom expanded from the public domain of teahouses to include homes, where social status was measured by the quality of one's tea service and teas and by how much space was set aside for the entertainment of tea-drinking guests. While the merits of tea varieties were discussed in teahouses and homes, as much and more attention was devoted to music, writing, reciting poetry, and painting. Males generally outnumbered female patrons of teahouses, especially in more upscale establishments. As an even stronger statement about commensality and the gendered nature of sociability, Buddhist monks drank tea from communal bowls. Confucius (551–479 BCE) elevated the ritual etiquette of the tea ceremony into a moral imperative through which social harmony and respect were encouraged (Weinberg and Bealer 2001).

High esteem for the beverage and a prescription for "gracious, refined" etiquette (Manchester 1996: 5) characterized Chinese tea drinking for more than 200 years,[7] until the thirteenth-century invasion of China by nomadic Mongol tribes, for whom the subtleties of tea did not resonate. For the duration of Mongol rule, tea remained the national drink but was no longer held in such high esteem as during the Sung Dynasty. Earlier, largely the domain of the wealthy and learned, teahouse patronage extended to all classes by the beginning of the Ming Dynasty (1368–1644). Although they lost some of their gloss, teahouses in China remained popular until the late 1940s, when the Communist government rejected this leisurely activity (e.g., E. Anderson 1988; J. Anderson 1991; Manchester 1996).

British Tea Drinking

A discussion of British tea drinking provides contextual contrast and further reinforces the role of tea in fostering community and sociability. Although sometimes applied interchangeably, the terms *high tea* and *afternoon tea* have been used since the mid-1800s, originally to designate discrete occasions for commensality. Both are also referred to simply as *tea*. High tea is a substantial meal shaped by availability in the household of particular foods, including leftovers such as meats, salads, preserves, pickles, and breads. Although members of the household sit together at the regular high dining or kitchen table, this is not a structured meal in which a sequence of dishes is shared by the everyone in the group. Instead, each individual selects among whatever is laid out according to his or her particular appetite. The custom of afternoon tea (or *low tea*, for the small near-sofa tables on which individuals rest plates and cups) evolved from the Duchess of Bedford's (1788–1861) practice of having a midafternoon tray of tea and buttered bread served to her. Eventually she invited other women to join her for this repast, in the sitting or drawing room. As the custom became popular among the upper classes, the fare expanded to include pastries and small sandwiches (Davidson 1999).

The "eating" of tea, as well as the distinction of two forms, lends insight into English culture and society. Afternoon and high tea typically are not served on the same day. Regular consumption of afternoon tea, between a light midday lunch and a more substantial midevening dinner, reflects the ample resources and leisure that mark the upper classes. Customarily, eating high tea, often on returning home from work, is popularly (and de facto) linked to the urban or rural working class (Davidson 1999: 381). Whereas high tea was in some ways pandemographic, for example, wealthy households may adopt this less formal, earlier meal style to accommodate young children's schedules, afternoon tea is significantly gendered and classed. The fact that beverage tea is consumed for the duration of afternoon and high teas distinguishes them from regular meals, for which tea is a signature closing.

Betel

Betel nut is the seed (botanically, not a nut) of areca palm (*Areca catechu* L., Palmae) and is the foundation of a variety of masticatories that have been used for thousands of years throughout the Indo–Southeast Asian region, extending to Melanesia and Micronesia in the South Pacific. Virtually everywhere, the betel seed is wrapped in betel leaf (*Piper betle* L., Piperaceae) before chewing. Archaeologists have recovered traces of *Areca* and *Piper* from a site in northern Thailand that dates to 7000–5500 BCE (Reichart and Philipsen 1996). The earliest recorded use is a story in a Sri Lankan document dated to 504 BCE, in which a princess rewards her nurse with a betel quid. It is mentioned often in early CE Indian Sanskrit medical documents and later Hindu and Buddhist literature. Betel chewing was conveyed by Buddhist teachings to southern China and southern Tibet, where medicinal and masticatory uses overlapped. The first written record of betel chewing in China is dated to 421 CE (Chu 2001). Literary sources from the tenth century and later record widespread use of betel throughout India, China, and Southeast Asia; from there the practice was conveyed to the Arab world. Unlike other aspects of Arabic medicine that were readily adopted in Europe during the Middle Ages, medicinal betel generated little interest (Rooney 1993). Today betel is chewed by an estimated 200–400 million people, men and women, throughout Asia, Southeast Asia, and the South Pacific and among migrant communities throughout their respective diasporas.

Preparation of the Quid

With considerable transregional variation, grated or thinly sliced betel seeds are mixed with slaked lime, an acrid substance produced by heating coral (or shells or limestone) that is powdered (calcium oxide) and mixed to a paste with water (calcium hydroxide). The lime hydrolyzes (bioactivates) the betel nut alkaloids to produce the desired euphoric and stimulating effects. Betel quids may be formulated according to an individual's needs or standardized, as is typical today in ready-made packets available in urban areas and the diaspora. These mixtures are wrapped in the lime-coated *Piper* betel leaf to form a quid that is chewed and pressed with the tongue between the teeth and cheek. Some cultures favor unripe betel nuts, which are tender; the nuts may be cured before use by salting or by boiling, drying, or smoking the seeds and removing the husk. The betel leaf also is used in unripe (green) and in ripe (yellow) forms. Additional quid ingredients measure status: the larger the number and the more exotic the additives, the more socially prominent the host. Betel leaf substitutes vary regionally and have peppery and pungent tastes. Quids are flavored with some of the same ingredients that spice foods, such as black pepper, ginger, camphor (*Cinnamomum camphora* [L.] J. Presl., Lauraceae), cardamom (*Elettaria cardamomum* [L.] Maton, Zingiberaceae), nutmeg, musk (*Mimulus moschatus* Doug. ex Lind., Scrophulariaceae), clove, saffron, and coconut (*Cocos nucifera* L. Palmae) (Thierry 1969; Rooney 1993). Tobacco is a more recent but very common addition. A betel set is the equipment that stores the individual ingredients and assists in preparing the quid. Minimally this entails a cutting tool and containers. Betel paraphernalia range from simple sachets of leather, cloth, or plant fiber, with metal or bamboo cutting instruments, to the ornate silver, gold, carved-wood, and inlaid stone betel sets of the nobility.

Betel and Health

Throughout the region of traditional betel chewing, its medicinal uses include promoting oral and mucosal integrity and antihelminthic, aphrodisiac, and digestive actions. It was prescribed in Ayurvedic medicine to treat diseases attributed to the accumulation of phlegm and to remove impurities from the mouth (Rooney 1993). Contemporary users report a sense of well-being, warm body, and heightened alertness; the stimulant effect increases work capacity, suppresses hunger, sweetens breath, and promotes salivation. This suggests that betel primarily affects the autonomic and central nervous systems, and the alkaloid arecoline has significant effects on neurotransmitters (Chu 2002). Although betel is habit forming, the betel quid contains no narcotics, and no addictive constituents have been identified (Warnakulasuriya et al. 2002). The high tannin content contributes to the astringent properties of betel nut and to antibacterial activity during prolonged chewing (sixty minutes or more; de Miranda et al. 1996). Limited evidence suggests that triterpenes and β-sitosterol from *P. betle* have antiplatelet, antioxidant, and anti-inflammatory activities that might protect against cardiovascular disease; antioxidants and antimicrobial phenolics have been isolated; and hypolipidemic, glucose lowering, and anticancer effects are suggested (Saeed et al. 1993; Choudhary and Kale 2002; Ramji et al. 2002; Lei et al. 2003; Saravanan and Pugalendi 2004).

In recent years the natural products and supplements industry commercialized a large number of mass-produced, prepackaged *Areca* products that are both promoted in immigrant communities on the strength of cultural identity and generically marketed as a novelty to middle-class, "nonethnic" consumers. Various product lines are promoted for use as stimulants, breath fresheners, and antimicrobials, as well as for improved kidney and lymphatic function (e.g., Greatestherbs 2004; Himalaya 2004).

Apart from the positive affect associated with betel chewing and speculations about its pharmacologic potential, the physiologic implications of betel chewing are overwhelmingly negative. Betel chewing has been clearly established as a risk factor in liver, oral, pharynx, and esophageal carcinomas. Risk increases with duration of chewing (years of use, quids per day), the amount of betel per quid, and confounding factors such as tobacco additive (Tsai et al. 2004). The betel alkaloids arecaidine and arecoline generate carcinogenic nitrosamines. The addition of slaked lime to the quid generates cancer-promoting reactive oxygen species in the oral cavity, and safrole in *P. betle* leaf may contribute to carcinogenesis as well (Liu et al. 2000; Topcu et al. 2002; Jeng et al. 2004).

It is not clear where this fits into the analysis, but oral cancer-protective genotypes have been identified. Despite habitual betel chewing, individuals homozygous for the CYP2A6 mutation (a gene-deletion type of polymorphism) do not develop oral cancers, presumably due to the inability of these individuals to bioactivate betel-specific procarcinogens to carcinogens (the CYP2A family of enzymes catalyze nitrosamines, the deletion eliminates this ability) (Topcu et al. 2002). It may be tempting to suggest strong selective pressure for genetic adaptation in the context of a cultural practice that is the very foundation of sociability and identity. However, it is not clear that the genotype is linked directly to betel; for example, the same gene deletion protects against carcinogenesis caused by tobacco use, a much more recent introduction to this geographic region. In addition, geneticists calculate that insufficient generational time has elapsed since betel use started for such a polymorphism to have evolved.

Sociability and Betel Chewing

Throughout the region in which it occurs, betel chewing is the social denominator that connects people to one another, to their social groups, and to gods, spirits, and other extrahuman communities. Betel chewing is eminently a cultural practice that fosters identity and connection. The primary motivation for chewing betel is the affability of sharing and reciprocity, the more so because chewing betel is not intuitively or immediately pleasurable—neophytes experience the sensation of burning or constriction in the throat and may be dizzy. Rather, it is an acquired taste. Throughout Southeast Asia, betel is a central element of traditional religious offerings (to spirits and deities); calendrical celebrations; ceremonies that mark life-cycle events such as birth, death, puberty, and childbirth; and Hindu and Buddhist rites. Offering betel is a requisite of hospitality. It is a powerful metaphor for gender relationships, including sexual alliances, and since ancient times has been a customary part of courtship, marriage, and even divorce. People of rank were served by retainers devoted exclusively to tending the betel service and preparing and distributing the quid. An individual's status is marked by where he or she is situated in the ranked order of individuals receiving a betel quid at social and business encounters. The preparation and exchange of quid is an art form among the nobility throughout Asia and Southeast Asia, where in the modern era international relations are cemented when rulers gift richly ornamented betel sets to one another (Rooney 1993).

Kola Nut

Like betel, kola nut is actually a seed. Kola nut (*Cola acuminata* Schott and Endl., *C. nitida* Schott and Endl., *C.* spp., Sterculiaceae) is indigenous to Nigeria, Liberia, and Senegal in West Africa, where it has been a popular masticatory for a thousand years or more and a significant trade item since at least the fourteenth century CE through Nigeria, Benin, Togo, and Ghana. Of the more than forty kola varieties, only *C. acuminata* and *C. nitida* had significant market value. *Cola acuminata* chewing was limited to the West African forest habitats of its production, whereas *C. nitida* became the kola of long-distance trade and was exported to the northern Savanna region and eventually to North Africa, where it was not possible to cultivate kola. It became a highly prized commodity throughout the region, and in some areas substituted for cowrie-shell and other currencies (Lovejoy 1995).

The pods of kola trees contain three to twelve 1- to 2-inch diameter seeds, each of which has two (*C. nitida*) or two to five (*C. acuminata*) cotyledons. After harvest the seeds must be protected from air and drying and, because they are chewed raw, their perishability (by dehydration and microbial and insect infestation) limits trade distance to a perimeter of safe transport, a radius of about 1000 km in historic times. Although modern-era advances in refrigeration technology and transport substantially extend that radius, the range of consumption has not increased appreciably beyond West Africa. At the same time, production within the region increased during the twentieth century and extends today to the

FIGURE 5.2. Kola nuts sold in a regional market in Wudil, Nigeria. Photo by Paul J. Ross, 1988

Caribbean and Brazil, where kola-nut chewing was introduced several centuries ago by African slaves.

Kola nuts are distributed and stored in moisture-retaining containers, often wrapped in the large, tough leaves of other plants. The cotyledons are separated by hand just prior to consumption and broken into pieces and chewed; alternatively, the cotyledons are grated (especially for individuals who have lost teeth or otherwise find chewing difficult) and/or infused in water. Some explanations for the popularity of kola chewing and its integral role in social customs throughout West Africa emphasize that kola is one of few stimulants permitted for devout Muslims. Other stimulants and psychotropics also available in West Africa in the nineteenth century included coffee, cacao, and tea, whose trans-Saharan or coastal sourcing made them prohibitively expensive, and tobacco; sorghum and millet beers, palm wines, and other alcohol beverages are proscribed by Islam. Of all these, only tobacco was in common use, but its consumption was eclipsed by kola chewing. Earlier, kola chewing was restricted to the ruling elite and wealthy commoners, such as merchants, who consumed it only sparingly for official and otherwise prestigious occasions. In the twentieth century, as regional production increased and kola became more affordable, it became a commodity of mass consumption.

Kola and Health

Kola nuts were known in North Africa by the thirteenth century and had by the sixteenth century become established in Islamic medicine for the treatment of stomachache, sore throat, nausea, sexual dysfunction, headache, sore gums, and sore limbs. By the late nineteenth century, kola was consumed in Europe for tonic and therapeutic measures. For example, mixed with vanilla and sugar as "kola chocolate," it was prescribed in convalescence, to fortify, and to suppress hunger (Weinberg and Bealer 2001).

The tonic attributes of kola products eventually were transposed to carbonated and other popular beverages in Europe and the United States. Representing the commercially most successful instance, in 1869 in Atlanta, Georgia, pharmacist John Pemberton began experimenting with a "health beverage" whose ingredients included extracts of kola nut and coca leaf (*Erythroxylum coca*)[8] and started to sell Coca-Cola to the public in 1886 (marketed as "French Wine Coca").[9]

Among Hausa of northern Nigeria, kola (*goro*) is used to assuage hunger and thirst, improve work endurance, prevent and/or treat nausea and measles, and serve as a vehicle for other medicines that are chewed with it to treat the congestion of head colds and flu. Among other cultural groups in the region, kola is used medicinally for migraine, dysentery, and depression (Newall et al. 1996).

The stimulant properties of kola are attributed to caffeine, theophylline, and theobromine (Tables 5.1 and 5.2). Kola nut also contains proanthocyanidins, catechins, and other phenolics, which are antioxidants, and it exhibits astringent, diuretic, anti-inflammatory, and antioxidant properties (Daels-Rakotoarison et al. 2003).

Kola and Sociability in Northern Nigeria

Hausa mark the acerbic (astringent and bitter) and aromatic taste of goro to assign medicinal uses that are principally a mirror of the social role of kola nut: goro is a constituent of often-complex mixtures of plants prepared to cement social relations, especially romantic ones, and to assure the success of business alliances and other commercial ventures. Permutations of cotyledon size, color, shape, and perishability all signify the utility of a particular kola nut. For example, *kurman* (deaf) goro (which has no seam between the cotyledons) is a constituent of medicines that silence creditors; *farin* (white) goro is more likely than *jar* (red) and *farin jar* (pink) to be part of medicines that assure prosperity and good marriage relations. Goro also imparts strength and protects against sorcery.

Goro reached northern Nigeria from the south via ancient trade networks that extended to microregional markets. At present every village has at least one kola broker, usually several. Some goro sellers are formally recognized as regular sources, other individuals purchase surplus kola on an episodic basis to take advantage of periods of greater demand, for example, during Ramadan.

For Hausa, goro is a ubiquitous icon of sociability, the centerpiece of a series of fluid exchanges around which Hausa society coheres. Whenever it is available, in whatever quantity, goro is integral to etiquette and hospitality and is exchanged for virtually all personal, commercial, and professional encounters that range from the mundane to the ceremonial. More formalized and visible exchanges involve marriage transactions, gifting to midwives after childbirth, greeting political and Islamic religious leaders, naming ceremonies, circumcisions, deaths, marking the Friday Sabbath and Muslim holy days, recognition of drummers and praise singers, and the mediation of disputes. If goro is not available, individuals may substitute coins, which on that occasion also are called goro.

Kola exchange and chewing figured prominently in pre-Islamic Bori religious customs (see chapter 3). For example, protection offered by *sarkin ruwa* (water spirit) was mediated by kola nuts that absorbed harmful forces, and individuals demonstrated possession by the spirit *cigoro* (kola eater) by distributing goro. Goro is commonly exchanged and consumed at the end of a meal as well as for *gaisuwa* (greetings) of all kinds. Whether one's supply is one hundred or only one, the number of pieces into which kola seeds are broken is the same as the number of people present. Individuals of higher status receive first and better pieces, but everyone is included.

The red color that kola chewing imparts to teeth and lips is valued cosmetically and is interpreted as sociability written on the body. This metaphor is retold when various botanical infusions are applied to impart red color to the hand, forearm, lower leg, and feet. "He who brings goro brings life," is a popular expression in many parts of Nigeria, and was immortalized by renowned Nigerian (Igbo) author Chinua Achebe in his first novel, *Things Fall Apart*. How goro further functions metaphorically to mark Hausa values is revealed in these proverbs regarding sociability, stewardship, and generosity:

> *Karamin goro yafi babban dutse.*
> A little kola is better than a large stone.

> *Wanda ya san darajar goro, shi ya kam bidam masa huhu.*
> If one values a thing, one looks after it.

> *Wanda ya ba ka barin goro, in ya san guda ya ba ka.*
> He who gives you half a kola nut would give a whole one if he could.

> *Wanda ya ba ka barin goro, in ya san guda, ya ba ka.*
> Even a small gift shows good will.

IN THEIR PLACES OF ORIGIN social plants have served as multiplex symbols of hospitality, commensality, reciprocity, identity, and hierarchy. Beginning in the 1400s, resonating "the twin pillars of early modern economic ideology, colonialism and mercantilism" (Goodman 1995: 128–129), a suite of traditional social plants were Europeanized: their production and distribution were managed by colonial powers, and their contexts of use were attenuated and otherwise transformed from what in many cases had been rich ceremony. In the modern era some of these social plants have been appropriated as recreational drugs, first popular in the affluent West and increasingly so among the formal and urban sectors in the developing world. Social plants provide ethnopharmacologists with many interesting questions to investigate. For example, what are the social and pharmacologic implications of deracinated and transformed patterns of use? What happens when social plants become economic entities that "circulate in different regimes of value in space and time" (Appadurai 1988)? For instance, what are the social and pharmacologic implications of truncated ceremonial uses of such commodities as kava and maté? What is the connection between traditional coca-leaf chewing by natives of the Peruvian Andes and cocaine addictions in the West? What are the pharmacologic implications of converting indigenous low-ethanol, context-rich alcohols to high-volume consumption of ethanol-rich beers, wines, and spirits? Finally, what combinations of social asymmetries and political disjunctions helped to shape habituation and chemical addictions to khat, alcohol, and betel?

The next chapter begins with a coevolutionary perspective through discussion of medicinal plant use by nonhuman primates and other animals. I then review the culinary and medicinal uses of animals by cultures around the world.

CHAPTER 6

Medicinal Qualities of Animal Foods

> Catching the bugs landing near the fire-pits, only the fat beetles, not
> the moths, would do. Each crawling, alive bug was tossed into the
> hot ashes to roast. From them, a beneficial remedy for the ailing boy
> could be made.
> —T. R. Zimmermann, *June Bug: Medicinal Insect*

AS OUTLINED IN CHAPTER 1, a coevolutionary theoretical framework
helps us to understand how some of the physical characteristics of species
bear on their interrelations with other organisms. Many among the great
variety of plant allelochemicals reflect interspecific relationships, such as
plant-herbivore and plant-pollinator. Although there is more apparent
allelochemical diversity within the plant kingdom than in the animal
kingdom, it is likely that the phyto-bias of natural-products research has
exaggerated the magnitude of that difference. Indeed, a growing body of
literature evidences the pharmacologic potential of animals. Some develop protective and other allelochemicals in their own right as defensive
mechanisms against predators, competitors, and parasites; in many more
cases, defensive allelochemicals and other plant constituents are trans-
ferred and concentrated (and sequestered and transformed) up the food
chain from flora to microfauna to end-point carnivores; in still other cases,
animals deliberately self-medicate when ill.

Animals, both wild and domesticated, vertebrate and invertebrate,
have been part of human cuisines and pharmacopoeias since ancient
times. Many are foods proper, occurring as standard meal elements and
snacks, and some animal products are identified as foods that are healthful for particular conditions (e.g., chapter 2). Animal-based medicines,
originating from a wide range of taxa, are derived from organs, bones,
effluvia, bezoars, venoms, and even domiciles (e.g., cocoons and nest
linings). A review of zootherapy in the Middle East alone documented
ninety-nine medicinals of animal origin: fifty-two from the tenth to the

nineteenth century and seventy-seven for the twentieth century (Lev 2003). For no domesticated species and certainly for no wild animal does systematic documentation exist for any region on the pharmacologic potential of culinary and medicinal animals. Cultural traditions that draw on animal resources for medicine are threatened in many parts of the developing world, where governments and international entities strive to protect endangered species of macro- and megafauna, such as bans against collecting seahorse, rhinoceros horn, and sea turtle. Before I address in some depth the pharmacologic potential of animal medicines, it seems prudent to consider what animals themselves do when they are ill.

Zoopharmacognosy/Zoopharmacology: Animals Heal Themselves

Eloy Rodriguez and Richard Wrangham (1993) coined the term *zoophar-macognosy* (now used interchangeably with *zoopharmacology*) to characterize wild animals' use of pharmacologically active plants to prevent and treat illness. *Pharmacophagy* (*-phagy*: Greek, eating) refers to the deliberate act of consumption for medicinal purposes. Anecdotal evidence of self-medication by vertebrate animals has been reported in the natural-history literature for decades. Many of us empathize when our cats and dogs relieve stomach distress by eating grass (to induce vomiting). We indulge our cats with catnip, hoping to elicit the behaviors that we interpret to be playful, thus presumably pleasurable for cats. We know on some level that our dogs' actions are not idiosyncratic: our neighbors confirm that theirs do the same things, and dogs in Nigeria behave remarkably similarly. Obedience class instructors teach us to recognize and elicit other patterned behaviors. How can we generalize in a scholarly way beyond these experiences with our pets to other animals?

The pioneering efforts of Daniel Janzen (1978) to contextualize the complexity of feeding strategies beyond optimal foraging models (maximizing energy and nutrient gain for minimal energy and time expenditures) drew attention to the deliberate seeking of pharmacologically active plants by a range of vertebrates. The foregoing example is more meaningful with the knowledge that catnip has antimicrobial and insect-repellent effects, which cats presumably acquire by rolling around with it,[1] and has been used in Europe as an infused beverage and in human medicine for digestive disorders.

Isolated examples of self-medicating animals and plausible phytochemical explanations are legion. Weary donkeys and horses (*Equus* spp., Equidae) graze on stimulants such as wild tobacco (*Nicotiniana* sp., Solanaceae) and tea leaves. In India elephants (*Elephas maximus* L., Elephantidae) are attracted to the scent of ripe, fermenting fruit (with as much as 7 percent ethanol content). West African boars (*Sus scrofa* L., Suidae) dig for roots of the psychotropic iboga (*Tabernanthe iboga* Baillon, Apocynaceae). Reindeer (*Rangifer* spp., Cervidae) on the Siberian tundra forego their normal diet of lichen in favor of the psychedelic mushroom fly agaric (*Amanita muscaria* Pers., Amanitaceae), which is also used by shamans in the region. In Colombia hallucinogenic *yaje* bark (*Banisteriopsis caapi* Morton, Malpighiaceae) is chewed by jaguars (*Panthera* spp., Felidae), purportedly with the same visionary effect that humans experience upon ingestion. Many birds, especially species that reuse nests in successive years, incorporate insecticidal and antimicrobial plants into nest structures and linings. Others roll around in the nests of or rub into their plumage crushed ants, millipedes, and other insects that contain antiparasitic compounds. North American bears (*Ursus americanus* Pallas, Ursidae) seek out fungicidal, antiviral, antibacterial, and vermicidal osha (*Ligusticum porteri* Coult. and Rose, Umbelliferae) to consume and to rub on their fur.

Wild pigs, who typically carry high intestinal worm burdens, deliberately seek the roots of pomegranate (*Punica granatum* L., Punicaceae) which has antihelminthic activity, and *Boerhavia diffusa* L. (hogweed, Nyctaginaceae), an Ayurvedic antihelminthic. In India the mole rat (*Nesokia bandicota* Gray, Muridae) and desert gerbil (*Meriones hurrianae* Jerdon, Gerbillidae) consume seeds of *Citrullus vulgaris* Schrad. and *Cucurbita* species (Cucurbitaceae), which are identified as antihelminthic in diverse human pharmacopoeias; and bison (*Bison bonasus* L., Bovidae) regularly seek out the bark of kutaj (*Holarrhena antidysenterica* Wall., Apocynaceae). Eating laxative fruit may be an adaptation by carnivores against microbial exposure from carrion or intestinal and stomach contents of prey; for example, bears, dogs, and tigers (*Panthera tigris* L., Felidae) intentionally search out the fruit of species with known purging effects such as Indian blackwood (*Dalbergia latifolia* Roxb., Fabaceae) and slow match tree (*Careya arborea* Roxb., Barringtoneaceae). The high tannin content of some animal diets (e.g., nonhuman primates, rats, porcupines, rhinoceros, and deer) may suppress intestinal parasite infestations. Malay elephant consumption of large volumes of *Entada schefferi* Ridl. (Fabaceae) is always followed by long-distance travel, suggesting that this liane offers substantial energy (calories) or other sustaining properties (Janzen 1978; Siegel 1986; Lozano 1998; Nostro et al. 2001; Baranauskiene et al. 2003; Huffman 2003; Powell and Pickett 2003).

Nonhuman Primates

In recent years, increasingly systematic studies have advanced our understanding of zoopharmacognosy. This includes appreciation for the context-specific transmission of knowledge about medicine and food selection, even among animals whose behavior repertoires have been regarded to be genetically hardwired. Research on nonhuman primates has been especially fruitful and offers insights into the evolution of our own self-medicating behaviors. Except where otherwise indicated, the primate data on which my discussion is based have been summarized by Huffman (1997, 2001, 2003).

Routine consumption of pharmacologically active foods is likely to have long-term medicinal effects. For example, *Aframomum* species (Zingiberaceae), which are important food plants for many mountain and lowland forest chimpanzees (*Pan troglodytes* L., Pongidae) and gorillas (*Gorilla gorilla* Sav. & Wym., Pongidae), demonstrate broad-spectrum antibacterial and fungicidal activities. Similarly, pokeweed fruit (*Phytolacca dodecandra* L'Hérit, Phytolaccaceae), which is commonly eaten by chimpanzees in Uganda, has antimicrobial and antifertility effects. Primate plant consumption on an episodic basis, however, especially in the presence of illness, more properly constitutes zoopharmacophagy.

It has been proposed that fertility regulation—birth spacing and influencing the sex of offspring—is mediated by phytochemicals, including phytoestrogens and other plant hormones. In howler monkeys (*Alouatta palliata* Gray, Cebidae), the highly skewed sex ratios that favor (intentionally or not) either male or female offspring may reflect changes in the female reproductive organs that affect the relative viability of X- versus

Y-bearing sperm, such as medicinal or dietary phytochemicals that influence calcium, potassium, or sodium channels. Muriquis (wooly spider monkeys, *Brachyteles arachnoides* E. Geoffroy, Atelidae) appear to encourage timed and synchronous pregnancy by shifting consumption at the beginning of the rainy season to include monkey ear fruit (*Enterolobium contortisiliquum* Morong, Fabaceae), which induces progesterone-like action, and then later to concentrate primarily on leaves of *Platypodium elegans* Vogel and *Apuleia leicarpa* Macbride (Fabaceae), which contain estrogen-like constituents. Similarly, seasonal mating behaviors in vervet monkeys (*Cercopithecus aethiops* L., Cercopithecidae) are closely timed with consumption by females of *Acacia elatior* Brenan (Fabaceae) flowers, which are estrogenic. Finally, the consumption by pregnant sifakas (*Propithecus* sp., Indridae) of substantially more plants that contain tannins in the weeks before delivery may take advantage of the antiparasitic and lactagogue actions of tannins (Glander 1994).

Fur-rubbing with plants, which has been reported for a number of mammals, such as bears, has been systematically documented for non-human primates. In Costa Rica, capuchin monkeys (*Cebus capucinus* L., Cebidae) rub themselves or conspecifics with plant materials, which are applied directly or first chewed and mixed with saliva. Fruit of orange (*Citrus sinensis* Osbeck, Rutaceae), lemon (*Citrus limon* [L.] Burm. f., Rutaceae), and lime (*Citrus aurantifolia* Swingle, Rutaceae) are used most commonly, and during the dry season, exclusively. At other times citrus are mixed with other plants, such as *Clematis dioica* L. (Ranunculaceae), *Piper marginatum* Jacq. (Piperaceae), and *Sloanea teniflora* Standl. (Elaeocarpaceae). Rubbing with these astringent, aromatic plants occurs more frequently during the rainy season, perhaps because elevated temperatures and humidity increase risk of both ectoparasites and microbial infections; but fur-rubbing also mediates group scenting, grooming, and temperature regulation.

There is substantial support for the hypothesis that much of what has been reported as zoopharmacophagy in the great apes (and to a lesser extent other primates) mediates intestinal parasites and provides relief from related gastrointestinal discomfort. Whole-leaf swallowing of *Aspilia* species (Asteraceae) by chimpanzees in Tanzania and Uganda is linked to the expulsion of nematodes (*Oesophagostomum stephanostomum* Stossich, Strongyloidae) and tapeworms (*Anoplocephala gorillae* Nybelin,

Anoplocephalidae). Contrary to earlier suggestions that *Aspilia* has anti-microbial or nemocidal activity, the current interpretation is that parasite expulsion is based primarily in the physical effects of diarrhea and related rapid gut transit time. Leaf swallowing is common among African great apes, with more than thirty-five plant species identified for lowland gorilla, chimpanzee, and bonobo (*Pan paniscus*, Pongidae).

Chewing the pith of *Vernonia amygdalina* Del. and related species (Asteraceae) occurs widely in sub-Saharan African chimpanzees, most commonly during the rainy season, when risk of intestinal parasite infection is highest. Parasite and phytochemical analyses document the specific presence of illness in these chimpanzees, medicinal plant consumption by the sick individuals, and recovery. Four sesquiterpene lactones in *Vernonia* species have antihelminthic, antimicrobial, antiamoebic, antiplasmodial, and antitumor activity, which increases our confidence that we are closer to comprehending the interrelations among these primates, medicinal plants, and parasites. Further, human ethnomedical use of *Vernonia* species in or adjacent to the study areas is consistent with the consumption patterns of the nonhuman primates.[2]

A muriqui colony living in a disturbed, dense habitat, where risk of intestinal parasites is expected to be high, was observed to be relatively parasite-free compared to muriqui living in low-density, undisturbed sites. Brown howlers (*Alouatta fusca* St. Hilaire, Cebidae) sharing the disturbed habitat and many of the same plants also had low parasite burdens (Glander 1994). It is possible that primates in new (disturbed) environments adapt via zoopharmacognosy and that the medical cultures of animal species that share these habitats converge. That seems an appropriate conclusion to draw from Fedigan's (1991) observation that Japanese macaques (*Macaca fuscata* Blyth, Cercopithecidae) who were moved to a new and very different habitat learned to avoid the toxic fruit and leaves of *Karwinskia humboldtiana* Zucc. (Rhamnaceae) after eight of the colony died and others suffered neurotoxicity following consumption.

Chimpanzees, whose diets are high in sugar-rich fruit, have poor dental and oral health compared to other primates whose medicines and foods may afford antimicrobial protection, such as the phenolic compounds (anacardic acid and cardol) in cashew pedicels (*Anacardium occidentale* L., Anacardiaceae), which are consumed by primarily folivorous howler monkeys. Differences in the rates of intestinal parasites among howler and spider monkey (*Ateles geoffroyi* Kuhl, Cebidae) colonies are explained in part by the availability of fig species (*Ficus*, Moraceae), virtually all of which have antihelminthic activity (Glander 1994). *Ficus* are widely used in human pharmacopoeias for intestinal disorders, including parasites. Hausa, for example, distinguish among *Ficus* species and use several as both medicines and foods (Etkin and Ross 1982).

Sociability and experiential and reciprocal learning are important in nonhuman primate groups. Initial exposure to self-medicating behaviors occurs when individuals are young—not when they are ill, but as they observe these behaviors practiced by other group members. Huffman and colleagues observed young primates imitate consumption of certain species after experiencing mothers' self-medication; mothers reinforce learning by discouraging infants from sharing the potent medicine unless they too are ill. It is likely that zoopharmacognostic behaviors that originated in the wild during opportunistic feeding later joined the shared behavioral repertoire of primate groups (Huffman and Hirata 2004).

The list of plants consumed by primates for apparently medicinal objectives continues to expand. While little is known about the bioactivity of some species or the parts consumed, their use in traditional human pharmacopoeias suggests continuity and convergence of human and nonhuman primate medical cultures.

The Pharmacology of Medicinal Animals

Compared to their botanical counterparts and to arthropods (see below), the number of medicinal macrofauna is small. Nonetheless, isolated reports offer intriguing windows into the pharmacologic potential of animals. In recent years Brazil has been the locus of considerable interest in medicinal fauna. In the northeast, aquatic (marine and estuarine) animals are used in medicine, most commonly for wounds, respiratory disorders, and stroke. Fish predominate, but reptiles, echinoderms (e.g., urchins), and molluscs are used as well. The highest medicinal use values (reflecting both multiple-respondent reporting and multiple therapeutic applications) were recorded for queen triggerfish (*Balistes vetula* L., Balistidae), sea turtles (*Caretta caretta* L., *Chelonia mydas* L., *Eretmochelys imbricata* L., and *Lepidochelys olivacea* Esch., Cheloniidae), and toadfish (*Thalassophryne nattereri*, Batrachoididae) (Costa-Neto and Marques

2000). In southeastern Brazil lizard and chicken are the most prescribed medicinal animals: organs and other body parts are regularly cooked, dried, powdered, and conserved in anticipation of future medicinal needs. Other medicinal animals include agouti (*Agouti paca* L., Agoutidae), frog (e.g., Ranidae), howler monkey, pig, peccary (*Tayassu* sp., Dicotylidae), porcupine (*Erethizon dorsatum* L., Erethizontidae), and fish (e.g., Carangidae, Scombridae), some of the medicinal species of which are proscribed as foods (Seixas and Begossi 2001). In neighboring Bolivia, agouti gall bladder is used to treat snakebite, bone pain, and fever; tortoise (*Geochelone* spp., Testudinidae) fat treats eye infection, rheumatism, and headache; and bones of the spider monkey aid leishmania (Apaza et al. 2003).

Of pharmacologic interest among fish are analgesic, antitumor, cardiac-stimulant, anticoagulant, and antioxidant compounds. The pharmacodynamics of echinoderms is interesting as well, including antiviral (e.g., *Acanthaster planci* L., Acanthasteridae), antitumor (e.g., *Actinopyga agassizi* Sel., Holothuriidae), and anti-inflammatory (e.g., *Asterias forbesi*, Asteriidae) activities (Costa-Neto and Marques 2000). Aminosterols isolated from the dogfish shark (*Squalus acanthias* L., Squalidae) are being studied for anticancer and antimicrobial potential (Shu et al. 2002). Antimicrobial peptides have been characterized for several frogs (*Ascaphus truei* Stej., Ascaphidae; Conlon et al. 2004; *Litoria genimaculata* Horst., Hylidae; Niidome et al. 2004; *Rana esculenta* L., Ranidae; Won et al. 2004). Bile solutions from pig and bear have analgesic, anti-inflammatory, and anticonvulsive effects (Li et al. 1995).

Toxic and otherwise unpalatable chemicals are more likely to occur in the skin and feathers of vulnerable species of birds that are also conspicuous, such as woodpecker (Picidae), kingfisher (Alcedinidae), and starling (Sturnidae). The association of conspicuousness and bad taste occurs within taxonomic groups and across lineages (Wrangham 1992). For instance, both aposematic coloration and chemical defense against predation in the New Guinea pitohui bird (*Pitohui* spp., Pachycephalidae) converge with both the red/orange-and-black skin patterns and the chemical arsenal of South American poison arrow frogs (*Phyllobates aurotaenia* Boul., Dendrobatidae). The toxic steroidal alkaloid homobatrachotoxin in pitohui and batrachotoxin in arrow frogs (both sequestered from insects on which these animals feed) bind to sodium channels in excitable tissues (nerves, neuromuscular junctions, and cardiac and skeletal muscles) (Dumbacher et al. 1992). Tetrodotoxin in puffer fish (Tetraodontidae), produced by dinoflagellates or other microfauna associated with these fish, and saxitoxin, produced by planktonic algae (primarily dinoflagellates), also block sodium channels but at different sites. Consumption of sublethal amounts of these animals diffuses protective/medicinal chemicals to carnivores higher up the food chain. For example, although *fugu* (puffer fish) poisoning is a recognized risk, fugu chefs in Japan prepare the fish as a delicacy, which should contain only enough tetrodotoxin to impart a sense of euphoria and cause the lips to tingle. Efforts to link tetrodotoxin to the Haitian zombie powder used by voodoo practitioners to induce a deathlike state (e.g., Booth 1988; Davis 1988) are not convincing.

The reputed wound-healing power of sacred serpents, magical monkeys, and even our pet dogs may have an empirical basis in two recently described factors that accelerate wound healing through antimicrobial, clotting, and inflammation-mediating actions. Epidermal growth factor and secretory leukocyte protease inhibitor are endogenous components in mucosal fluids, including saliva. Animals' tendency to lick their own wounds—and those of offspring and companions, including humans—may be a way of delivering these components to the wound site (Angelov et al. 2004; Jahovic et al. 2004). Anticoagulant and anti-inflammatory agents have been identified in a variety of invertebrates as well (Arocha-Pinango et al. 1999).

Therapeutic Use of Leeches

Preventive and therapeutic bloodletting crosses all continents, with suggested origins many millennia ago and supporting archaeological evidence for ancient Hindu, Egyptian, Aztec, and Babylonian cultures. The medicinal leech, an annelid (segmented), blood-sucking worm (*Hirudo medicinalis* L., Hirudinidae), holds a prominent place among animals (and instruments) used to achieve controlled blood loss. Therapeutic and preventive bloodletting was used in early European medicine and was consistent both with etiologic models in which disease spirits are liberated when blood flows from the body and with the later Hippocratic doctrine for which bloodletting played a key role in balancing the four humors (see chapter 2). Leeches were in widespread use for such disorders as headache, obesity, kidney disease, high blood pressure, mental illness, and bleeding itself (on the theory that all surgical bleeding eventually stops). The leech jar was the physician's companion, as were a variety of accessory implements that assisted leeching in anatomically awkward areas, such as the leech glass, a hollow tube through which the worm moved toward the target tissue. Hemostatic measures after worm removal included surgical excision of the bite, direct pressure, and the application of cobwebs. By the 1830s leeching had become so popular in Europe that commercial trade in the worms developed into a major industry, importing primarily from central Europe and Asia Minor. When extinction of the medicinal leech was threatened, suppliers turned to leech farming.

As medical paradigms and materiel were transformed in the second half of the nineteenth century, leeching declined in Europe, although it was still practiced, along with cupping and other phlebotomies in other medical traditions. Chinese consider blood stasis to be the foundation of a variety of chronic disorders and have used leeching (as well as acupuncture and moxibustion) to treat joint pain, head and back trauma, body-mind imbalances, and surgeries; leeches also are consumed to treat blood stasis (e.g., for amenorrhea and endometriosis). As a complementary and alternative medicine (CAM) in the United States (see chapter 7), leeching treats hypertension, headache, and varicose veins of the lower extremities (Kerridge and Lowe 1995; Whitaker et al. 2004a, 2004b).

Following a revival of leeching during the 1980s, biomedicine now uses leech therapy after microsurgery to diminish congestion in damaged tissues in which the microvasculature is inflamed and/or blocked. Applying leeches to the affected area helps to restore blood circulation to grafted or severely injured tissue in which venous congestion (venous insufficiency due to poor drainage) is a key problem. One or more leeches are applied to the area and permitted to feed for up to several hours. As they puncture the skin, the leeches release a local anesthetic, the anticoagulant hirudin and its diffusing agent hyaluronidase, vasodilating antihistamines, and a prostaglandin. In nature, these suppress prey pain response, reduce inflammation, and promote blood flow. Leech treatment has also proved beneficial in certain otherwise refractory conditions including dermatologic and ophthalmic disorders, cardiovascular disease, osteoarthritis, and middle ear inflammation. Additional pharmacologic potential is suggested by the presence of bacteria that preserve the blood meal during its long digestion (several months) in the leech and likely contribute to the leech's effect in preventing further wound infection. Research also is under way to examine the antitumor potential of leech secretions ("saliva"), as well as to develop a mechanical analogue whose capacity for blood removal is unlimited and whose affect is more palatable than that of the leech (Michalsen et al. 2002; Worthen 2004).

Entomophagy

Most of the world does not share the repugnance with which peoples of contemporary Europe and the United States regard insects. Given the ubiquity and multitude of insects and their relatives, it is not surprising that throughout history and across the globe human groups have learned to take advantage of them as food and medicine and for clothing, dyes, and other uses.

The taxon Arthropoda (Greek: *arthro*, joint; *poda*, foot) is the most numerous phylum of living organisms in both number of species and number of individuals. Arthropods comprise an enormously diverse group, including insects (e.g., bees, beetles, moths, lice, ants), spiders, scorpions, crustaceans (e.g., crabs, lobsters), and centipedes. Arthropods have segmented bodies covered by an exoskeleton made up of the protein chitin and other chemicals; lipids, other proteins, and calcium carbonate are the lesser structural elements. At stages of many arthropods' metamorphosis, the exoskeleton is shed (molting). For many, the larva (e.g., caterpillars are butterfly and moth larvae; maggots are fly larvae) is the juvenile phase that develops from the egg. Varying by arthropod type and species, this stage is punctuated by intermolt instar phases (three to six instars in most common arthropods) and is succeeded by the pupa (which may be enclosed in a cocoon or hard chrysalis) and finally the adult. Typically the immature stages do not resemble the adult, caterpillars and butterflies being dramatic examples.

Of all arthropods, the insects have been evolutionarily most successful: 900,000 species have been named and characterized taxonomically, hundreds of new species are identified each year, and estimates for the number of species that exist range up to 30 million. In view of the preponderance of insects, in this chapter I use that term as well to refer to spiders, scorpions, and centipedes.

The paucity of research on edible insects underestimates the importance of this resource for both medicine and food in much of the tropical and subtropical world. The overlapping literatures of anthropology and ethnobiology document numerous examples of the meaning and measure of insect consumption in diverse cultures. A few systematic, scientific treatments of entomophagy have been published, notably a comprehensive review by Posey (1986) and a more recent one by DeFoliart (1999), founder and author, respectively, of the web-based *Food Insects Newsletter* (FIN 2004) and *The Human Use of Insects as a Food Resource* (DeFoliart 2004). Ramos-Elorduy's research findings, published over the last two decades, document the economic, cultural, and nutritive significance of insect consumption in Mexico (e.g., Ramos-Elorduy et al. 1996; Ramos-Elorduy 1997a, 1997b; Ramos-Elorduy and Pino Moreno 2002). Sutton's monograph (1988) catalogues food insects used by Native Americans in the Great Basin in the western United States (Idaho, Nevada, Oregon, and Utah).

Eighty percent of the world's population eat insects. Where insects are an integral part of cuisine, they contribute as much as 40 percent of animal protein to the diet. In the United States it is estimated that every adult unconsciously consumes one pound of insects each year; sources are organic and home-garden produce, poor restaurant and home hygiene, and commercial products for which the U.S. FDA permits a certain amount of insect contamination (e.g., peanut butter is marketable with 30 or fewer insect fragments per 100 g). A conservative global estimate for edible insects notes more than 1000 species. Mexico leads the list with more than 200 species, and many other countries are represented by 20–40 species (Table 6.1). These country estimates are approximations that likely conceal a great deal of regional variation. Further, only those species that had been identified to the species level were recorded,[3] meaning that the variety and number of insect species used as food and medicine has been underestimated significantly (DeFoliart 1997).

Ethnographic, historical, and archaeological data (coprolite analysis, flotation) from around the globe reveal that insects have been commonly and extensively used for millennia. Their collection is purposeful and systematic: insects are not opportunistic food resources and, rather than famine or emergency foods, are regular features of diet and medicine.

TABLE 6.1. Edible Insects from Selected Countries

Country, region	Number of each taxon consumed			
	Orders	Families	Genera	Species
Mexico	10	42	99	>200
Thailand	10	31	69	80
Native North America	10	27	53	69
Zaire	5	21	47	62
Indigenous Australia	7	22	39	49
Colombia	8	20	36	48
China	10	30	36	46
South Africa	7	16	32	36
Papua New Guinea	11	22	31	34
Zimbabwe	7	14	25	32
Congo	7	15	25	30
Japan	11	19	22	27
Indonesia	8	15	20	25
India	7	17	22	24
Vietnam	8	18	20	24
Brazil	7	14	19	23
Madagascar	7	15	22	22
Philippines	6	13	17	21
Burma	7	14	17	17

Source: DeFoliart (1997)

Insects are harvested at different stages of development (i.e., brood, larva, adult), and alone or in combination with other ingredients are consumed fresh, steamed, macerated into paste, and roasted. Although insects are consumed in all their life-cycle stages, the advantage of consuming them at an immature stage of development is that their occurrence in large aggregations makes collection easier and more productive; further, larvae are soft-bodied and digestible (whereas exoskeletons are not) and have high nutrient value. The preparation and presentation of food and medicinal insects varies within and across cultures and according to context and individual taste.

Insects and Cuisines

On the menu: birdwing butterflies in Papua New Guinea, winged termites in Ghana, Japanese cicads, *casu marzu* (cheese maggots) in the southern Mediterranean region, and, literally, thousands and thousands more.[4] Native peoples worldwide use fire and smoke to chase wasps (Vespidae) from their nests to collect adults and larvae, which are both consumed fresh at the collection site and carried home for further preparation. Fried wasps mixed with boiled rice, soy sauce, and sugar was a treasured dish for Japan's Emperor Hirohito. In Bali people use sticky twigs to capture dragonflies (*Acisoma* spp., Libellulidae) and damselflies (Coenagrionidae), which are boiled with spices or grilled. In Iran a popular confection contains the high-fructose exudate of the last instar nymph of a small lerp (sucking) insect (*Cyamophila astragalicola* Gegechkori, Psyllidae). Mexicans carry on the ancient Aztec tradition of crushing the bodies of giant water bugs (Belostomatidae) into cornhusk-wrapped patties for steaming, while the eggs are made into tortillas and tamales. Thai street vendors offer these bugs deep fried and sell the abdominal sac extract as a flavor enhancer. In Colombia, termites (Termitidae), palm grubs (Scarabaeidae), ants (Formicidae), and other insects are macerated and spread on bread. Spiders (Arachnidae) are popular among South African Bushmen, native South Americans, and Australian Aborigines. The giant tarantula (*Melopoeus* spp., Theraphosidae) embodies considerable food value both in volume and in protein and fat content: its leg span reaches 10 inches and its abdomen is the size of a tennis ball.

Australians eat roasted or fresh *Witjuti* ("witchetty") grubs, caterpillars of a large cossid moth (*Xyleutes leucomochla* Turn, Cossidae). Aborigines harvest *bogong* moths (*Agrotis infusa* Boisduval, Noctuidae) when the insects gather to hibernate, cooking them in hot ashes or grinding them into a paste to form small cakes.

In Africa termites and caterpillars are the most marketed and consumed insects, but many others are highly prized as well. In Botswana people favor larvae of the regal and silk moths, crickets (Gryllidae), palm beetles, and caterpillars of the emperor moth (Saturniidae). More than thirty-five species of caterpillar are consumed in Zaire, most commonly roasted in oil or butter. In South Africa the Mopani worm, the caterpillar of a saturniid moth (*Gonimbrasia belina* Westwood, Saturniidae), is gutted then baked or fried with peanut paste or relish. In southern Nigeria cooked termites are compressed into inch-diameter spheres that are stored as soup base. In southwestern Nigeria seasonal ataxic syndrome (neurological dysfunction resulting in poor muscle coordination) has been linked to insufficient cooking prior to consumption of African silkworm larvae (*Anaphe* spp.), which contain a potent, relatively heat-tolerant thiaminase (Adamolekun et al. 1997; Nishimune et al. 2000). In view of thiamin-deficiency related to traditional foodways, it seems plausible that the failure to adequately cook this food is an artifact of socio-economic asymmetries that have contributed over the last few decades to food and fuel shortages.

Farmers in the Philippines and Thailand flood their fields to trap mole crickets (*Gryllotalpa* spp., Gryllidae), which are boiled in vinegar and fried. In China and Korea silkworm (*Bombyx* spp., Bombycidae) cocoons that have been boiled to spin off thread are consumed as is, fried, or preserved dry. In northeastern India the pupa of the eri silkworm (*Samia* sp.) is so valued for food that the cocoon is virtually a by-product. In the Philippines June beetles (*Anomala* spp., Scarabaeidae), grasshoppers (Acridadae, Tettigoniidae), ants, mole crickets, water beetles (*Cybister* spp., Dytiscidae), katydids, locusts, and dragonfly larvae are fried, broiled, or sautéed with vegetables. Sago palms (*Metroxylon* spp.) are felled in eastern Indonesia to encourage infestation by beetles (sago grubs, *Rhynchophorus ferrungineus* Olivier, Curculionidae), which are consumed raw but more often boiled or roasted. Throughout Southeast Asia, green weaver ants (*Oecophylla* spp., Formicidae) are ground into a flavorful paste for various foods and beverages. In some Southeast Asian cuisines, the liquid of crushed ants is used interchangeably with lemon to flavor fresh vegetables.

The most significant insect resources for Native Americans in the Southwest were grasshoppers, ants, butterflies, moths, crickets, and shore flies. Indigenous groups individually coordinated mass harvests of grasshoppers (Acridadae, Tettigoniidae, including locusts and crickets) by herding them into circular pits. Their size and the great number of individuals available during swarming afforded a periodic but substantial food resource for roasting, crushing to paste, and adding to soup.

Among the ant species valued by millions of people around the world, honeypot ants (*Melophorus* spp., Formicidae) are especially prized. One of the castes of these social insects, repletes, are specialized workers that store nectar (sweet floral and some extrafloral secretions) gathered by other worker ants in their abdomens, which become distended to several times normal size, thereby immobilizing the repletes to serve as food storage for the rest of the colony. Workers also feed the repletes with honeydew, a sugary excretion of aphids and other sap-feeding insects. When stroked by the workers, the repletes regurgitate their abdominal contents. Human consumption typically involves biting off the head of the replete and swallowing the sweet remainder.

In past centuries, Europeans did consume insects, although never approximating the extent to which they are consumed in other parts of the world. For example, in ancient Greece grasshoppers (Acridadae, Tettigoniidae) were prized, larvae of the scarab beetle (Scarabaeidea) were fattened in anticipation of eating, and the larvae of the cockchafer beetle (*Melolontha melolontha* L., Scarabaeidae) were consumed in rural areas and became an important famine food in Ireland in the seventeenth century.

It has been suggested that human consumption of insects that infest plants might keep those pests in check and that cessation of traditional insect consumption may contribute to ecological shifts that overwhelm indigenous resource management strategies, including pest control (e.g., Gómez et al. 2000). In the last decade researchers have promoted insects as natural foods in the context of healthful eating and sustainable resources for both the developed and developing worlds (Paoletti and Bukkens 1997). Over the same time, a raft of popular books and Web sites have appeared to encourage insect consumption in the West: "It's an arthropod, just think of it as a small lobster." Menzel and D'Alusio (1998) provided a stunning visual backdrop to the diversity of human entomophagy, although their book is anecdotal and bears only a modicum of cultural sensitivity. Other books and Web sites urge readers to experiment with insects, offering recipes, entertaining tips, and information on sourcing and raising insects. The tone of presentation turns Westerners' repugnance to eating insects on its head by capitalizing on the cachet of the exotic and promoting this as a gourmet food experience. As for most exotic food introductions, the receptive audience for insects in the West tends to be urban, with sufficient disposable income to wrap food and eating in recreational attire. At least for the short term, it seems that insects are not likely to find an integral place in Western cuisines, but in all likelihood will continue to fill a novelty niche.

The Nutritional Value of Insects

Insects are high in calories, fat, unsaturated fatty acids, and protein, including essential amino acids that afford complementarity with other foods. Some insects also are important sources of thiamin, riboflavin, niacin, and other vitamins and minerals such as iron and zinc. For instance, the larva of the weevil *Rhynchophorus phoenicis* F. (Curculionidae) is high in riboflavin, thiamin, and zinc; the winged adult of the termite *Macrotermes subhyalinus* Rambur (Termitidae) is a rich source of copper and magnesium; and the caterpillar *Usta terpsichore* M. & W. (Saturniidae) is a valuable source of riboflavin, thiamin, copper, iron, and zinc (DeFoliart 2004). Insects range from low to high in fat content (10–30 percent fresh weight) and are relatively high in unsaturated (heart-healthy) fatty acids; for example, the fatty acid composition of housefly pupae (*Musca domestica* L., Muscidae) resembles that of fish oils. Of ninety-four edible Mexican insect species analyzed, 95 percent had a higher caloric value than wheat, rye, or teosinte (*Zea mexicana* Schrader, Poaceae); 87 percent were higher than maize; 70 percent were higher than fish, lentils, and beans; 63 percent were higher than beef; and 50 percent were higher than soybeans (Bukkens 1997; DeFoliart 2004). The fat and protein values of insects are many times higher than those of the plants on which they feed: the fat content of the agave worm (larva of the skipper butterfly, *Aegiale hesperiaris* Kirby, Hesperiidae) is as high as 58.55 percent, while that of the maguey plant on which it feeds is 3.60 percent; protein in the adult weevil (*Metamasius spinolae* Gyllenhal, Curculionidae) ranges as high as 69.05 percent, compared to 5.21 percent in the nopal cactus (*Opuntia* spp., Cactaceae) on which it feeds. Further, insects are more efficient than animals higher on the food chain in converting energy into protein: for example, the respective values for ingested food converted to protein is 5.3 percent for sheep, 10 percent for cattle, 16 percent for cutworm caterpillars (*Agrotis orthoogonia* Morrison, Noctuidae), and 44 percent for the German cockroach (*Blatella germanica* L., Blatellidae; Dunkel 1998).

Insects in Ceremony, Celebration, and Narrative

Ethnotaxonomies of Arthropoda approach the diversity of animals that comprise this taxon and offer researchers insights into the cultural constructions of both the natural and supernatural worlds. Among the Kayapó of Brazil, for example, insects are classified primarily on the basis of gross morphology, grading from ovate to elongate shape. These two forms and the relationship between them underpin Kayapó classifications as well as structural and spatial features of their way of knowing the world. Kayapó explain their own origins in the sky, where they lived with other animals and from them learned to organize themselves into stratified social groups, like those of wasps and ants. People gained ascendancy over animals through the power of social organization, and warriors acquired their power from the venomous wasp sting. Present-day Kayapó ceremonially reaffirm their humanity and power by seeking the largest nest of the most aggressive wasp (*Polistes* sp., Vespidae): warriors dance and sing beneath the nest, then climb a scaffolding to hit the nest with bare hands until the venom from repeated stings renders the warriors semiconscious. The wasp nest is a mirror of the universe, its lateral divisions representing the upper strata where Kayapó originated, the middle ground where they live today, and the lower reaches inhabited by non-Kayapó ("worthless people"). The nest also is a powerful metaphor of unity as it embodies the ovate (in cross-section) and elongate (in lateral view) shapes. Kayapó also have an affinity with ants, who, because they move and hunt on the ground, more closely resemble people than do wasps (Posey 1981). While social organization and aggressive actions of some insects contribute to Kayapó identity, they distinguish food insects by nonaggressive (stingless) behaviors. They use still other insects to control horticultural pests: nests of "smelly ants" (*Azteca* spp., Formicidae) are placed on fruit trees and in gardens to repel leaf-cutting ants (*Atta* spp., Formicidae). These protective ants also are medicines and commonly are crushed and their highly aromatic scent inhaled to decongest the sinuses.

Identity figures prominently as well in other examples of peoples' insect consumption. For Mexicans in the diaspora (e.g., in Los Angeles, Chicago, Houston) and in the transformed landscapes of resorts such as Cancun, restaurants sustain a regular clientele by offering a familiar fare that includes *insectos de la patria*. An estimated 600 kg of edible insects are exported annually from Mexico (Ramos-Elorduy and Pino Moreno 2002).

Medicinal Insects

Many insects are used medicinally. Bees, honey, and related products are used around the world (see Bees and Apitherapy, below). Bedbugs (Cimicidae) treated fever in ancient Greece; in later centuries ground cockroach was a panacea in central Europe and Spanish fly (*Lytta vesicatoria* L., Meloidae) was a popular aphrodisiac. Ticks (Ixodidae, Argasidae) were used medicinally in Europe until the 1980s. In Germany and Finland, where insects are no longer regarded as food, some species are still used medicinally, for example, for warts, rheumatism, and arthritis.

Arthropods have long been an integral part of South Korean traditional medicine and are prominently featured today in clinics in which university-trained traditional practitioners combine indigenous pharmacopoeias with pharmaceuticals. Table 6.2 itemizes fourteen products reported by twenty clinics in the order of how commonly the medicines are used. The most frequently prescribed are a fungus-infected silkworm larva, cicads, and centipedes. Most are used in combination with other insect products and pharmaceuticals. Insects have been used in traditional Chinese medicine for at least 3000 years, the number of species increasing over time, with published taxonomic revisions now totaling 143 medicinal insects representing thirteen orders and forty-eight families. Table 6.3 lists the more commonly used Chinese medicinal insects. Of interest in blister beetles is the defensive compound cantharidin, which is used routinely in China (as the demethylated norcantharidin) to treat liver cancer (Chen et al. 2003). Ants are used to treat joint pain, stimulate the circulation, and improve immune function. Silkworm pupae are consumed to relieve rheumatism, and an infusion of the frass of noctuid (*Hydrillodes morosa* Butler, Noctuidae) and pyralid (*Aglossa* sp.,

TABLE 6.2. Arthropods in Traditional Korean Medicine

Arthropod	Prescribing clinics	Medicinal uses
Fungus-infected silkworm larva (Bombycidae)	100%	cardiovascular disorders, headache, convulsions, tremor
Cicada nymph (Cicadidae)	100%	hearing disorders, cough, tetanus, rash, eye problems
Centipede (Scolopendridae)	100%	joint pain, inflammation, convulsions, tetanus, snake bite
Scorpion (Buthidae)	95%	convulsions, edema, pain, carbuncle, facial paralysis
Honeybee (Apiidae)	90%	weakness, stomachache, cough, constipation, gingivitis
Praying mantis case (Mantidae)	84%	impotence
Scarab beetle larva (Scarabaeidae)	70%	liver disease
Silk moth larva frass	55%	diabetes, joint pain, numbness, conjunctivitis
Blister beetle (Meloidae)	50%	skin infection, facial paralysis, rabies, venereal disease
Fungus-infected hepialid moth larva (Hepialidae)	45%	lung disorders, weakness
Mole cricket (Gryllidae)	40%	urinary disorders, edema, boils
Paper wasp nest (Vespidae)	30%	arthritis, rash, toothache, heart disease, worms
Silk moth adult	20%	impotence, ulcer
Horse fly adult (Tabanidae)	10%	amenorrhea, indigestion

Source: Pemberton (1999)

TABLE 6.3. Arthropods in Traditional Chinese Medicine

Arthropod	Medicinal uses
African mole cricket (Gryllotalpidae)	swelling, cleansing
Blister beetle (Meliodae)	improve circulation, amenorrhea, heart disease
Brown chafer (Scarabaeidae)	pain
Budda horse fly (Tabanidae)	pain
Cricket (Gryllidae)	swelling, fever, cleansing
German cockroach (Blatellidae)	impotence, cleansing
Giant dragonfly (Aeshnidae)	cleansing
Honeybee (Apiidae)	joint inflammation, hepatitis, sore throat
Lac insect (Coccoidea)	cough
Locust (Acrididae)	cough, pain
Mulberry longicorn (Cerambycidae)	improve circulation
Silverfish moth (Lepismatidae)	joint inflammation
Silkworm (Bombycidae)	joint pain

Source: Zimian et al. (1997)

Pyralidae) moths is a digestive aid and treats diarrhea and hemorrhoids (Chen and Akre 1994).

In Borneo the Kenyah Leppo'Ke use a cossid larva (Cossidae) as a general tonic and perhaps for malaria, favoring the more mature individuals that are identified by the intense red color that develops from their consumption of *Glochidion* sp. (Euphorbiaceae) sapwood in which they pupate (Gollin 2001). Australian Aborigines use the bush cockroach (Blattidae) as a local anesthetic; the green tree ant (Formicidae) treats cold and headache and is an antiseptic and expectorant; termitaria (termite nests) are used as an absorbent to treat diarrhea, and the rich soils that are associated with them are eaten by pregnant women. Wounds and burns are treated with a layer of crushed cockroaches, witchetty grubs, and other caterpillars (Notodontidae).

In Mexico stink bugs (Pentatomidae) treat goiter, grasshoppers (Acrididae, Tettigoniidae) are medicine for anemia, flies treat eye cysts, and the bite of a tarantula is a treatment for tumors. In northeastern Brazil a paste of macerated houseflies is applied to stimulate hair growth, and a cockroach infusion is drunk for colic. Throughout Brazil termites treat bronchitis, dog bite, goiter, measles, joint pain, cough, and sores; wasps are variably used for stomachache, burns, and spider bites; and cockroaches treat respiratory disorders and toothache. Wasp and ant infusions treat goiter and paralysis. The Kayapó make medicines of stinging ants to prepare their dogs for the hunt and adorn themselves and the dogs with sacred red paint made from annatto and empowered with ant parts. In another part of Brazil, the Pankararé collect wasp nests (*Apoica* and *Polistes* spp., Vespidae) for the treatment of asthma, stroke, and dizziness. In South America the huge mandibles of leaf-cutting ants (*Atta* spp., Formicidae) are used to suture cuts: after the ants are positioned to bite the wound margins, their bodies are snapped off. Mixtures of wasps and rhinoceros beetle (*Megasoma acaeon*, Dynastidae) are aphrodisiacs (Posey 1981; Geraldo et al. 1997; Meyer-Rochow and Changkija 1997; Costa-Neto 1998; Grami 1998; Pemberton 1999).

In Tanzania, Uganda, and Ethiopia, girls aged eight to twelve years use water beetles (Dytiscidae, Gyrinidae) for breast enlargement. The insects are held to the breast, where they bite and secrete a substance from the prothoracic defensive glands. The reported effect is immediate localized pain and swelling, which lasts about one hour, followed by gradual breast enhancement over the next six to twelve months. Of particular interest are the hormonelike steroids present in the dytiscid defensive secretions, which are also antibacterial and antifungal (Schaaf et al. 2000; Kutalek and Kassa 2005).

Hausa in Nigeria use a variety of insects in both veterinary and human medicines. The dung beetle larva, *gwazarma* (Scarabaeidae), is the most consistently and commonly named medicine for hepatitis/jaundice (shawara). This is a disease that Hausa understand to originate in disorders of the blood, which may fade into nothingness or turn weak and white. Shawara overlaps a complex of multicausality with the disorders bayamma and farin mashashara, all diagnosed as a complex that includes fatigue, anemia, and wasting. The healing potential of gwazarma finds a structural relation where the insect lives, in the dung/rubbish heap that is a locus of both decay and renewal. In a related healing metaphor, pneumonia (*ciwon hakarkari*) is treated with soil from the nests (*shuri*) of the dauber wasp (*zanzaro*, Sphecidae) and termite (*zago*), insects whose rapid progress one observes as they construct, repair, and fortify. Similarly, web-weaving spiders (*tautau*) are applied to refractory wounds and, with complex botanical mixtures, to fractured bones (*karaya*). The shuri of ants and termites are enigmatic structures with much activity at the entry, where columns of workers pass carrying unidentifiable materials but reveal nothing about the interior. Hausa accept that iskoki (spirits) reside within these large structures; families leave foods and other valuables to propitiate the spirits in advance of misfortune. Indigenous healers instruct clients to leave the wrappings and residuum of their medicines at the shuri entrance to mark recovery and thank the spirits.

Entomopharmacology

Both the biology and social and other behaviors of insects predict pharmacologic potential. In an analogue to food-chain dynamics, insect metamorphosis includes the transfer and concentration of ingested plant chemicals as well as products that the immature forms produce *sui generis*. Among the latter, venoms and defensive secretions are part of the complex systems of predation and protection that have evolved in stinging and other insects (Koehler and Oi 2003). For instance, neurotoxins of some ticks, bark scorpions, black and brown widow spiders, and Hymenoptera (wasps, ants, bees) affect the central nervous system. Vesicating venoms of millipedes, blister beetles, and some stinging caterpillars produce blisters. Tissue-destroying venoms of Hymenoptera, ground scorpions, mites, chiggers, fire ants, and brown recluse spiders are cytolytic and/or hemolytic. Anticoagulant venoms of lice, fleas, and ticks interfere with blood clotting.

Insects that inhabit soil (e.g., mole cricket, scarab larva, centipedes) produce antibacterial and antifungal compounds that protect them against soil-dwelling microbes. Similarly, antimicrobial substances are incorporated into the nests of social insects such as wasps and bees that live in large, dense groups and face considerable risk of epidemic infections. Fungus-infected hepialid moth and silkworm larvae (Table 6.2), and the predatory water beetle (*Cybister tripunctatus* Olivier, Dytiscidae) also produce antimicrobial constituents (Pemberton 1999). Cordyceps-infected silkworm larvae have antioxidant activity (Li et al. 2002); scorpion extracts lower blood pressure and are anticonvulsive (Zimian et al. 1997).

In Peru and Colombia the caterpillar (*malumbia*) of the lymantriid butterfly (*Eloria noyesi* Schs., Lymantriidae) feeds exclusively on coca and excretes cocaine in its frass (Blum et al. 1981), suggesting that this species has evolved the means to deflect the reported insecticidal properties of cocaine (Nathanson et al. 1993; see chapter 5, note 8). Extensive literature review yielded no information on human consumption of this insect in any of its life stages, whether the insect or its frass have appreciable cultural (or street) value, or how local communities understand its role in coca ecology. The only well-documented case of the widespread use of a hallucinogenic insect is the red harvester ant (*Pogonomyrmex californicus* Buckley, Formicidae) employed by native populations of south-central California to build strength and establish individual connections with the supernatural. During visionary ceremonies, live ants were swallowed in vast quantities to induce an extended loss of consciousness during which skills and knowledge were conveyed to the shaman-aspirants by spirits, some of which became life-long allies. These ants were also used in preventive and therapeutic medicine for disorders such as arthritis, pain, paralysis, and gastrointestinal symptoms (Groark 2001).

As this brief overview suggests, despite the existence of an enormous number of arthropod species and their culinary and medicinal uses by large numbers of people, very little is known of their pharmacologic potential. Among insects, maggots, bees, and bee products provide a contrast.

Medicinal Maggots

The case of medicinal maggots (fly larvae) provides an interesting parallel to leech therapy (see Therapeutic Use of Leeches): the role of maggots in wound-healing has been appreciated for millennia, and they enjoy a revival in contemporary biomedicine. (As for leeches, I did not uncover any culinary uses.) Maggot debridement therapy (MDT) is the medicinal use of larvae of the green bottle/blow fly (*Phaenicia sericata* Meigen, Calliphoridae) to clean wounds by consuming necrotic (dead) tissue, disinfecting through antimicrobial action, and stimulating healing. MDT was used by thousands of physicians until the mid-1940s, when it was replaced by antibiotics and surgical techniques refined through the experiences of two world wars. Subsequently, MDT was only occasionally used as salvage therapy for cases in which surgery, antibiotics, and other modalities failed. In the late 1980s experienced surgeons argued that if MDT was effective in refractory wounds that would have eventuated in amputations and other dire surgeries, then best practice called for MDT not as a last resort but before infection progresses. Controlled clinical trials initiated in 1990 characterized MDT as even more effective than conventional treatment in some nonhealing ulcers, and within five years the number of physicians using MDT increased to more than 2000 world-wide. The growing problem of antibiotic resistance casts into even bolder relief the significance of options such as MDT (Sherman et al. 2000; Sherman 2003). In 2004 the U.S. FDA approved the production and marketing of both maggots and leeches as "medical devices." These forms of biotherapy, or symbiotic medicines, resonate the theme of coevolution.

Bees and Apitherapy

People have been attracted to honeybees (*Apis mellifera* L., Apiidae) for millennia, arguably as much for the curiosity of their social habits as for honey, wax, and the pollinating services on which thousands of flowering plants depend. The honeybee colony or hive is a superorganism composed of functional "tissues" and "glands" (i.e., individual bees or groups of bees) whose secretions effect behavioral and physiologic changes within the organism. The most potent gland is the colony's single queen, who secretes a combination of chemicals that have hormonal effects on the only other caste in the colony, the workers. Hivemates affect one another as specialized groups of brood (eggs, larvae, and pupae), drones, and workers. The true glands of individual workers are those of the endocrine and exocrine systems, which govern internal and external secretions (Moritz and Southwick 1992).

Throughout history humans have been "functional cleptoparasites" (Moritz and Southwick 1992) of honeybees, whose products played prominent roles in folklore and mythology, served as foods and medicines, and contributed to material culture as a basis for illumination and to create sculpture, preserve artwork, and serve as currency. Honey hunting is common among a range of animals, including nonhuman primates, and has been a source of nourishment for people since earliest times. The evolution of beekeeping by diverse human cultures bears strong testimony to the plasticity of coevolutionary relationships, revealing porous boundaries and shifting dependencies between and among species.

In pre-Christian Europe beeswax was used in ceremonies for birth, circumcision, and marriage. It was used for embalming and sealing of coffins, served as a medium of purification, was sacrificed to deities, and was a currency of exchange. The Kayapó, for whom beeswax is a tangible link to the ancient world, form the wax into a ceremonial hat that represents the universe and is worn by young men who receive ceremonial names. Beeswax is burned to force out dark spirits, protect against witchcraft, and attract rains (Posey 1983). Hausa attract bees (*kudan zuma*) by placing into trees receptacles constructed from hollowed trunk segments (usually palms) or from branches and grasses, with calabash-sealed ends bored for bee entry and exit. More than thirty-five plant species representing eighteen families are used in the construction of *kwangi*, including liner species (*shafin zuma*) that are selected for both phytochemical and symbolic attributes.

Characteristics of Honeybees and Bee Products

Honeybees originated in southern Asia, probably in what is present-day Afghanistan, and today are found worldwide in habitats ranging from tropical to subarctic regions. Their broad distribution is facilitated by their organization to cache resources and by thermoregulatory capacities such as clustering to conserve heat, metabolizing honey to generate calories, and cooling by wing-fanning to evaporate water. Their colonies are perennial: at the beginning of the season each honeybee colony contains one queen, several dozen drones, thousands of foraging (nectar-gathering) workers, and about twice that number of workers that perform hive duties such as cleaning, comb construction, converting nectar into honey, temperature regulation, brood rearing, caring for the queen, and defense.

While bee behavior is genetically coded, their central nervous system is sufficiently plastic to foster learning and memory through the sight, smell, taste, touch, and distance sensory modalities that are distributed over various parts of the body. Their communication about food sources is both kinetic ("dancing") and phonetic and incorporates the taste and smell of nectar and other products with which they return to the hive. Chemical, acoustic, and other sensory signals all contribute to the complex superorganismal communications that coordinate dozens of hive behaviors, including the division of labor (between castes and by age distribution among workers) and other worker-force dynamics.

Foraging bees collect nectar and pollen and press these into comb cells. Honey is produced by workers who evaporate the water content of nectar to 15–20 percent through wing and tongue action and add a salivary enzyme that converts sucrose to the simple sugars glucose and fructose. It is the bees' primary source of carbohydrates and feeds adults or is stored in capped comb cells. Honey also contains trace amounts of vitamins, minerals, enzymes, and colloids. Pollen is transported in the pollen baskets (corbiculae) on the back legs of foraging bees from which it is unloaded by the specialized middle legs of worker bees who enzymatically digest the pollen in their midgut. The composition of pollen varies widely depending on the character and mix of source flowers, as well as seasonal and ecological parameters. Pollen is the honeybees' chief source of protein (as high as 30 percent of the dry weight). It is also rich in vitamins, particularly riboflavin, and minerals such as iron and calcium and it contains lipids and trace amounts of sterols (Linskens and Jorde 1997).[5]

Beebread is foraged pollen that is mixed with honey (about 12 percent) and worker bee secretions, packed into comb cells, and fed to most larvae and adults. The biochemical transformation into beebread includes lactic acid enrichment through fermentation (see chapter 4), which preserves the bread and increases vitamin K and protein content. The worker egg selected to be the next queen is moved into a much larger queen cell, where it is fed exclusively on large quantities of high-protein royal jelly, which is similar to beebread but contains more honey (34 percent), ten times more pantothenic acid and biopterin, and more hypopharyngeal and mandibular gland secretions (Moritz and Southwick 1992). Beeswax is a product of honey metabolism in the fat cells associated with the wax glands on the underside of the worker bee's abdomen. Workers fashion wax into brood comb and honey comb, the hexagonal cells of which are filled with honey, beebread, or a pupa, and then capped.

Propolis ("bee glue"; Greek: *pro*, in defense; *polis*, the colony) also is integral for hive architecture and is used for hive repair, to reduce the size of the hive entrance for defense or in cold weather, and to line the hive for insulation. Propolis is blended with wax to raise its melting point in hot weather, used to attach comb to the top and sides of the hive, and used to embalm intruders. Of special interest is that propolis is a product of both plants and bees and bee activity. It includes botanical exudates that bees forage and use for nest construction and protection: the gross composition is 5 percent pollen, 5–10 percent essential and volatile oils, 25–30 percent beeswax, and 55–70 percent balsams and resins that bees gnaw from bark lesions and sticky buds and transfer from mandibles to corbiculae. The aromatic fraction of propolis is a complex mixture of more than 150 compounds (Seeley 1995). In addition, bioactive bee secretions, beeswax, and bee-modified pollen are incorporated during the transport of propolis and its manipulation by worker bees for hive construction and defense. Propolis is, then, a composite of flora and fauna that has a compound pharmacologic profile as well as the discrete constituents provided by each.

The ways that diverse cultures understand and use propolis in food and medicine evoke this special, composite nature. People who use CAM in Hawaiʻi identify propolis as a general strengthener "to boost the immune system" and "for energy" (Etkin et al. 1999). Like many other CAM, propolis is valued because it is, according to our study participants, "natural" and "balanced." While most (not bee-educated) consumers cannot specify the origins and constituents of propolis, a compelling message that they take away from product promotions is the multiple-constituent and otherwise complex nature of "bee glue." The idea of an amalgam of pollens, tree barks, and bee secretions is intriguing, in part because synergy offers novel appeal. For our study participants, the idea of synergy is carried over to other products, as they use propolis as an adjuvant for other CAM and for pharmaceuticals. Several respondents explained that "it is a miracle material . . . it is made of stuff that bees collect and things they make themselves; and each time a bee makes it, it is different, has different properties." For our study participants, the liminal nature of propolis marks its general utility (immune boosting).

Propolis is further culturally marked because its specific composition is unknown and changes from one hive to another and within the same bee colony over time. This aspect has helped to propel it into a domain of products favored by a social constituency that is disfranchised from mainstream medicine. For some study participants, propolis is attractive because it does not resonate what these individuals dislike about biomedicine: propolis is ambiguous, whereas pharmaceuticals are medicines for which knowledge of substance and action is specific. For consumers of dietary supplements, propolis is a holistic and nonspecific therapy whose mode of action has not been scientized and specified by health professionals, but instead is deemed suitable for diverse complaints.

Bees and Bee Products as Medicine

Many medical cultures, including early biomedicine, have used honey as both a specific and a vehicle for other medicines. Bees and other stinging insects (e.g., wasps, ants) are used in many traditional medicines to treat arthritis. Bee-collected pollen and bee larvae and pupae are used medicinally by the Kayapó, smoke from burning beeswax being one of the most powerful medicines (Posey 1983). Hausa use *zuma* (honey) to treat the sores of chicken pox, measles, syphilis, and (in the past) smallpox; both beeswax (*kaki*) and the empty honey comb (*kakin zuma*) are used medicinally as well. Similarly, in Burkina Faso, honey is applied externally for the early phases of measles, the diagnosis confirmed if the eruptions are more pronounced the following day; additional applications include respiratory disorders, toothache, wounds, and burns (Meda et al. 2004). Some Chinese medicinal uses of honeybee products are listed in Table 6.3.

Pharmacologic studies report a range of actions. All bee products are antimicrobial across a broad spectrum of microflora. Royal jelly also demonstrates ulcer-protective, serum-lipid-reducing, and hypotensive activity and contains hormonelike steroids that enhance fertility in animals. Venom is additionally hypotensive, anti-inflammatory, antiviral, and antioxidant; and venom immunotherapy reduces the risk of systemic allergic reaction to bee sting. Honey is antioxidant and reduces the risk of periodontal disease and gingivitis. It has a long history of use in the treatment of wounds and burns: the osmolarity of honey (which promotes dehydration) has been repeatedly demonstrated as a factor in accelerating burn and wound healing. Honey also has a specific antileishmanial effect when used as dressing for ulcerated cutaneous infection. Dilute honey solutions are even more potently antimicrobial as the enzyme glucose oxidase (synthesized in the hypopharyngeal glands) catalyzes the reaction between glucose and oxygen to generate gluconic acid and the strongly antimicrobial hydrogen peroxide (Seeley 1995; Vittek 1995; Mobarok Ali and Al-Swayeh 1997; Zeina et al. 1997; Husein and Kridli 2002; English et al. 2004; Golden et al. 2004; Lee et al. 2004). Further, bee products acquire the pharmacodynamic profile of the plants on which bees feed. Honeys from particular floral sources have more potent antimicrobial activities, such as New Zealand and Australian honeys from bees that feed on *Leptospermum* species (Myrtaceae) (Lusby et al. 2002), and regional and seasonal differences in bee products may reflect different flora.

The resins that are primary constituents of propolis retain bioactivity even after collection and further manipulation by the bee, whereas pollen and nectar are microbiologically and biochemically altered as soon as bees begin collection, as microorganisms and secretions transform pollen and nectar and assure its conservation as nourishment. In resins, bees appropriate the chemical defenses of the source plant, and propolis has a broad spectrum of antimicrobial effects against bacteria, viruses, and fungi. Active constituents of resin, extracted largely from the volatile oil fraction, are primarily phenolics, including pterostilbene and caffeic and ferulic acids, and flavonoids, such as chrysin, tectochrysin, galangin, pinobanksin, pinocembrin, and sakuranetin (Seeley 1995).

The active constituents of propolis are primarily flavonoids, imparting strong antioxidant activity, including against some of the side effects of anticancer drugs. Efficacy has been reported in the treatment of periodontitis, influenza, herpes, cervical and vaginal infections, and giardiasis. Susceptible protozoa include *Toxoplasma gondii*, *Trichomonas vaginalis*, and *Trypanosoma cruzi*. Antitumor and immunostimulatory activities have been reported as well, and propolis may be an effective adjuvant to therapy in asthmatic patients (de Castro and Higashi 1995; Ivanovska et al. 1995; Isla et al. 2001; Marcucci et al. 2001; Kartal et al. 2003; Khayyal et al. 2003; Kizilay et al. 2004; Orsolic et al. 2004).

SOMETHING OF A DEPARTURE from the subject matter of other chapters, this one focused on animals, beginning with a general treatment of how animals use plants and other materials to influence their health. Because animals are generally more evocative than plants (e.g., of emotion, identity), we must be mindful of context-specific cultural constructions that influence the apprehension and use of particular species for food and medicine. The specific focus on nonhuman primates is especially instructive of coevolutionary processes and offers intriguing insights into prehominid medicinal cultures. Exploring beyond Western cuisines, we find a prominent—and both pharmacologically and nutritionally important—culinary role for insects. On a related theme, we note the revival in the West of medicinal applications for leeches and maggots. These new-old medicines lead logically to the next chapter, which concentrates on food supplements and both old and new products that span the food-medicine continuum.

CHAPTER 7

Health in the Marketplace

Complementary and Alternative Medicine,
Functional Foods, and More

"Organic" on the label conjures a whole story, even if it is the
consumer who fills in most of the details, supplying the hero
(American Family Farmer), the villain (Agribusinessman), and the
literary genre . . . "supermarket pastoral."
—Michael Pollan, "Behind the Organic-Industrial Complex"

EACH OF THE PRECEDING CHAPTERS includes a historical component
and, with the exception of chapter 2, is broadly cross-cultural. In contrast,
this final chapter locates us firmly in the present and centers on issues that
are salient primarily in the United States and western Europe, although
emergent in the developing world as well. The topics addressed bear
witness to the increasing commercialization and globalization of foods
and medicines, as well as the central role that technology plays in how we
apprehend, create, and use foods and medicines.

Complementary, Alternative, and Integrative Medicines

Over the last few decades, processes of globalization and the commodification of health and healing have cast products of complementary and
alternative medicine into bold relief. Depending on one's perspective,
CAM is a category of exclusion, preventive and therapeutic modalities
that fall outside conventional U.S. medical practice, or a category of
inclusion, a residuum of everything else, ranging widely from prayer to
acupuncture to Ayurvedic plant medicines.

The biomedical profession was first drawn to the presumed alternative
nature of CAM. Concern was expressed that products that lack formal

FDA oversight were used instead of, or delayed, biomedical treatments. As studies revealed that consumers typically use CAM simultaneously or in sequence with pharmaceuticals, the term *complementary* was added to the mix. Today, the actuality of health care in the West is an amalgam of biomedical and informal diagnosis, pharmaceutical management, and self care: in sum, a complex physician-driven and patient-augmented polypharmacy (Etkin and Ross 2002; Etkin 2004). Increasingly, health care providers try to judge how the combination of formal and self care will affect their patients' well-being. The term *integrative medicine* is the latest iteration, which more accurately (or at least optimistically) represents the direction in which health care is moving (Lewis 2002).

The National Center for Complementary and Alternative Medicine (NCCAM), a component of the National Institutes of Health, described five CAM categories (NCCAM 2004):

> alternative medical systems: integrated systems that cohere around theory and practice, such as Ayurveda, homeopathy, naturopathy, and traditional Chinese medicine;
> biologically based therapies: "natural" products such as botanicals ("herbs"); foods, including dietary supplements; and vitamins;
> energy therapies: biofield therapies manage energy fields that are understood to surround and penetrate the body via Reiki, therapeutic touch, and qi gong; bioelectromagnetic therapies employ magnetic, alternating or direct current, or pulsed fields;
> manipulative and body-based methods: body-moving modalities such as chiropractic, massage, and osteopathy;
> mind-body interventions: techniques designed to enhance the mind's capacity to influence bodily function, such as prayer, meditation, and art, music, and dance therapies.

Another effort to assemble "unconventional medicine" across a wider range of health practices created two primary taxa (Kaptchuk and Eisenberg 2001):

1. CAM that are independent of sectarian and/or bioscientific knowledge:
   professional systems—naturopathy, chiropractic, massage, acupuncture, homeopathy;

popular health reforms—megavitamins, botanicals, supplements, organic foods;

New Age healing—crystals, magnets, spirit mediums, Reiki, qi gong;

mind-body—mind cure (miracles, Deepak Chopra), cognitive-
behavioral (biofeedback);

nonnormative—chelation, cancer vaccine, iridology, hair analysis.

2. Parochial practices that are linked to limited groups:

ethnomedicine—Puerto Rican spiritism, Hmong practices, African-
American botanicals;

religious—Catholic charismatic healing, Peyote religion, Pentecostal
churches;

folk medicine—chicken soup, copper bracelet, ginger ale.

While these schemes do not include all CAM modalities, and there is
significant overlap among categories, the taxonomies suggest the range
of CAM and demonstrate how a large number can be meaningfully
grouped. However, neither these nor other proposed taxonomies (e.g.,
Furnham 2000; Koh et al. 2003) are likely to be broadly compelling to
CAM users. Most taxonomies are not organized on principles that resonate bioscientific paradigms and other special knowledge that discerns,
for example, between naturopathy and organic foods or between Puerto
Rican spiritism and religious healing. CAM users are more likely to classify diverse modalities by target disease or symptom (cancer, digestion),
general or specific activity (boosts immune system, strengthens blood),
and outcome (pain relief, lower cholesterol).

Consumers and Complementary and
Alternative Medicine

The emergence of CAM as a social phenomenon over the last few decades is complex and has been shaped by several interrelated processes: a
shifting epidemiologic landscape in which cardiovascular disease, cancers, and other chronic disorders have replaced the infectious diseases
that contributed the most to morbidity and mortality in earlier eras (see
chapter 2); more interest among the public in comprehensive ("holistic")
approaches to health care that attend to needs that transect the emotions,
religion, and different understandings of disease etiology; a growing body

of scientific evidence that links certain foods and food constituents to health benefits; a more symmetrical dynamic in the clinical encounter where patients command more agency; a perception that most CAM constitute less risk than pharmaceuticals do; the commodification of health and healing (a theme that is continued below); and three U.S. legislative acts of the 1990s that had a significant effect on the promotion of food CAM (see Functional Foods, below).

CAM is one of the most rapidly growing sectors of contemporary U.S. and European health product industries, with highest commercial volume in botanical medicines and food supplements. Like its pharmaceutical counterpart, the CAM industry maximizes profit by making available products that both fill and create niches of established or perceived need. Consumers command agency in their own health care by purchasing these products, which acquire diverse but significant cultural saliencies, and through their social transaction transform the meaning of the therapeutic experience. In the context of food ethnopharmacology, the subsets of CAM that are explicitly linked to food and diet merit additional attention.

Functional Foods

The growing lexicon for healthful foods marks increasing interest among both scientific and lay sectors, as well as the difficulty of drawing a tight conceptual boundary around these diverse products.[1] During the 1980s Japanese health authorities problematized "physiologically functional foods" to address the challenge of escalating health costs linked to a growing elderly sector, as well as to younger cohorts who consume fewer vegetables and fruit as they emulate Western diets and other lifestyle choices. The category "food for specific health use" (FOSHU) was created to subsume foods that had documented evidence of aiding specific physiologic functions beyond whatever conventional nutrients exist in the food. Today, more than 200 FOSHU products have been licensed and are distributed among categories that range from fiber to lactic acid bacteria to minerals.

The abbreviated term *functional foods* currently is applied worldwide to products that are understood to have physiologic benefit beyond basic nutritive qualities and are offered in the form of foodstuffs, including those that have been fortified or have ingredients reduced or removed and genetically modified (GM) foods. Food supplements are produced in the form of tablets, capsules, and other presentations that look more (or exactly) like pharmaceuticals than like foods. At the end of the 1980s the term *nutraceutical* was coined in the United States to designate a broadly inclusive category extending to "any substance that may be considered a food or part of a food and provides medical or health benefits, including the prevention and treatment of disease. Such products . . . range from isolated nutrients, dietary supplements and diets to . . . designer foods, . . . [botanical] products and processed foods such as cereals, soups and beverages" (DeFelice 1998: v).

Genetically Modified Foods

Discourse about GM foods illuminates the cultural constructions of food and eating, as well as the meanings with which the lay public(s) and specialists invest foods. From the perspective of political economy one can identify key variables that contribute to the highly polarized nature of the GM debates: the elaborate "web of self-interest" that characterizes the interlinked and increasingly dense agrifood industry that deals in GM foods; the enormous amount of money spent on public relations and advertising by entities that range from singlet companies to industrywide public-relations consortia; and the ability of the GM debates to give substance and shape to "a new international [social] food movement" (Rosset 2001). Further, transgenic species that constitute intellectual property are subject to international patent law that may restrict their availability in developing countries; and crops that have been modified to produce foods traditionally grown in tropical and other developing world contexts compete with those products and upset local and national economies in those locations (Nottingham 1998).

In these debates it is important to keep in mind that GM is not a unified phenomenon but one shaded by the nature of the modification— whether to influence crop production (e.g., insect-resistance, drought tolerance) or to change other characteristics of the plant (e.g., enhanced antioxidant or vitamin production). The industrialization of the food supply as agribusiness relies increasingly on technological solutions to problems identified and created by earlier generations. A key element that shapes attitudes about the relative merits of applying gene technology to food production is whether GM foods are understood as part of a continuum of means to manage food production, or a uniquely discontinuous technology. We are reminded that struggles about the nature and meaning of food are highly contextual (Teitel 2001) and contested.

Biotics

Several products that were originally designed for the livestock industry are currently under development for human consumption to promote gastrointestinal function and perhaps improve immune function and interpose some diseases. Prebiotics are nutrients and other food constituents that are indigestible for people but feed our endogenous intestinal microflora and thus stimulate their growth. Probiotics are live microbial supplements that survive gastrointestinal transit to deliver goods to the intestinal microflora. The probiotic species most often employed are *Bifidobacteria* and *Lactobacilli* (see chapter 4), which are common but not dominant constituents of the endogenous microflora of the adult human gastrointestinal tract. Synbiotics are combinations of prebiotics and probiotics. The evidence for benefits and risks of modulating the human colonic ecosystem is still emergent and includes improved immune function, lactose digestion (see below), and reduced duration of diarrhea due to rotavirus. A few studies suggest beneficial effects in some cancers and atopic dermatitis in infants (Sanders 2003; Stanton et al. 2003; Brown and Valiere 2004; Rastall 2004).

Statutory Foods and Supplements

U.S. legislation that helped foster the promotion of the functional foods concept includes the Nutritional Labeling and Education Act of 1990. This act directed the FDA to institute regulations that most foods carry a standardized label of nutrient content and to develop guidelines for claims about the content and health benefit of constituents. The Dietary Supplement Health and Education Act (DSHEA) of 1994 formally instituted a new supplements category to include products that contain one or more dietary constituents such as botanicals, amino acids, vitamins, and minerals. It also established a process through which to address issues of labeling, safety, good manufacturing practice, and health claims; encouraged scientific research on supplements; and established new government entities to reassess regulations. The FDA Modernization Act of 1997 revised the Food, Drug, and Cosmetic Act by not requiring preauthorization by the FDA for health claims based on "authoritative statements" of government entities such as the National Institutes of Health or the National Academy of Sciences.

Needless to say, the circumstances of functional food production, promotion, and evaluation are very complex. A substantial literature addresses regulatory and other policy aspects of functional foods and is not treated here (e.g., Heasman and Mellentin 2001; Hasler et al. 2004; SKLM 2004).

What Do Functional Foods Mean?

The various terms for healthful foods are metaphors that reveal the cultural constructions of health. *Pharmafood, nutraceutical, phytoceutical, phytochemical, phytonutrient, functional food, medicinal food,* and *designer food* are used interchangeably and variably to refer to whole foods or food constituents that are marketed as extracts, tablets, or other presentations not typically associated with foods. These terms resonate the emerging health paradigm in the lay sector that combines (but does not blend intellectually) elements of conventional (since the late 1800s) biomedicine—specific etiology and specific therapy—with aspects of holistic/natural healing.

This composite perspective is revealed etymologically: the affixes *-ceutical, pharma-,* and *-chemical* suggest analogues of pharmaceuticals, that is, foods and constituents with specific actions. Similarly, the "functional" benefit of these foods lies in their prevention of disease through the influence of specific "chemical constituents" (Wrick 1994: 481) on a specific "biochemical pathway" (Labuza 1994: xii). *Designer* refers to foods that have been genetically engineered to enhance some specific constituent of that product (e.g., antioxidants). *Phyto-* underscores the botanical (thus, natural) source of these foods, just as the affixes *-food* and *nutra-* evoke holistic diets. *Nutra-* suggests both specific nutrients and holistic nourishment, while the conjunction of *medicinal* and *food* explicitly embodies the composite paradigm. Parsed this way, the lay perspective is cognitively structured by two parallel streams that do not harmonize: the scientific affixes substantiate a link to the materiel of biomedicine—drugs—which still commands appreciable consumer confidence (Etkin and Ross 2002), while the other word elements disconnect from science to resonate nature.

Are Health Foods Healthy?

By now it is widely known that sulforaphane in broccoli protects against certain cancers; fish oil and gamma-amino butyric acid in tomatoes are hypotensive; and cranberry juice prevents urinary-tract infections. Catalogues like this one, which list foods and food constituents and the physiologic processes they affect, offer only an incomplete perspective on the medicinal potential of food. Much of what is reported is based on laboratory studies of purified substances and/or on animal studies using healthy subjects. Thus, although some medicine-like action may be confirmed, there is no certainty that this will be the outcome when whole foods are consumed by sick humans. One gains more insight by considering food use in its broadest physiologic and cultural contexts, taking into account the details of preparation and the incidence and quantity of consumption. For that reason, the merits of most nutraceuticals remain potential rather than established. Further, while the physiologic effects of specific foods, and even specific diets, are better understood, and one can predict with some certainty the result of changing a single dietary element, we barely begin to comprehend the consequences of several dietary and environmental factors acting in concert. Although there is apparent merit in consolidating the scientific evidence for the health benefits of foods, this engenders a false sense of clarity, because the complex circumstances of multifactorial etiology make it difficult to establish the efficacy of some particular element, dietary or otherwise.

Bioscientific and lay comprehensions of the interrelations among chronic disease, diet, and lifestyle are influenced by contradictory findings. Conclusions from feeding studies are drawn from statistical inference and in clinical contexts where it is impossible to control all variables. This is confounded by biological variability in human populations and in environmental factors. The subtext here is not that functional foods lack potential—indeed the scientific literature (phytochemistry, ethnopharmacology, pharmacognosy) suggests otherwise—but that for the real contexts in which these products are used there is much, slow work needed to resolve these discrepancies at both molecular and contextual levels.

For the most part bioscientific research on foods still resonates a reductionistic paradigm that judges foods as incremental sums of their constituents, disembodied from the whole foods that produced them, whereas whole foods are chemically very noisy and the interactions of multiple phytoconstituents are different in magnitude and nature from that of singlets. This is illustrated by the interpretation of disappointing results of clinical trials with β-carotene, which were designed on the strength of hundreds of epidemiologic and cell-culture studies that documented lower risk of premature cancer and cardiovascular deaths among people whose diets included substantial portions of β-carotene-rich vegetables and fruits. While some researchers iterate the reductionistic position by suggesting that the maximum advantage from β-carotene would derive from doses significantly lower than those used in the clinical trials or that the benefit was provided by another constituent in those same foods (e.g., lycopene) (Burri 2002), others encourage whole-food, rather than molecule-based, approaches to understanding functional foods (e.g., Gidley 2004).

The results of empirically rigorous studies should be distinguished from the popularization of nutraceuticals and supplements, which are weakly regulated and whose commercial success rests on promotional schemes that extol only vague, often sweeping claims for efficacy. Some critics argue that basic research has come to mean "basic to the commercial enterprise," rather than basic to science or to general knowledge. Aggressive marketing of both pharmaceuticals and supplements blurs the line between scientific observations and product advertisement. Products that are substantively and conceptually highly asymmetrical are presented by the industry and regarded by the public as just as likely as other supplements—and even pharmaceuticals—to be potent, disease-specific, and effective.

Some aspects of the medical sectarianism that flourished in the United States in the nineteenth and early twentieth centuries are in place again today (Gordon et al. 1998), with authority claimed by representatives of many and diverse sectors. Before the Flexner Report and professional consolidation around the American Medical Association in the early 1900s, there was little shared theory among physicians whose authority rested more on their relations with patients than on a standardized body of diagnostic and therapeutic knowledge (Hudson 1992). Similarly, today, advice outside of "orthodox" (bio)medicine is offered by naturopaths, food consultants, the nutraceuticals and supplements industry, print and electronic media, and others—the majority of whom emphasize "natural" medicines, especially foods. The various names for beneficial food products were coined to give identity to a promising area of health and food. Critics of the food products industry, however, argue that to date this identity has proven to have more to do with increasing market share than with discovery of the health potential of such products (DeFelice 1998) and of ways to assimilate them in informed ways into individual lifestyles and integrated health care.

Food by Design

The marketplace is transformed rapidly as supplements are incorporated into once pure (unmodified) food products, and plant and animal foods are genetically engineered to contain more of one thing and less of another. Molecular research on functional foods releases an endless supply of factoids—disembodied findings that are difficult to connect to the context of eating the whole foods and their combinations and sequences that are the syntax of meals and cuisines.

In recent years nutraceuticals have been developed to address general problems of food digestibility and palatability. Beano®, for example, delivers the enzyme alpha galactosidase to digest oligosaccharides in beans and other foods, to avoid intestinal distress experienced by some individuals (see chapter 1). Similarly, Prelief® is promoted as a general acid neutralizer, consumed just before or with foods to "prevent heartburn," and analogues for pets (e.g., CurTail®) assure that they will not embarrass themselves socially. While the majority of "food fixing" products are designed for the healthy general public, some are under research for clinical applications (Hauser et al. 2004). One class of these products has already offered significant benefits for individuals with celiac disease.

Eating Your Way Away from Celiac Disease

Celiac disease (CD) is a common malabsorption enteropathy characterized histologically by atrophy of the villi in the small intestine in response
to gluten, a protein fraction that occurs in some grains (the mechanism by
which the proteins become toxic is not clear). Celiac disease is mediated
by T cells of the immune system and has a strong genetic basis for susceptibility (involving both HLA and non-HLA genes). It is much more preva-
lent than previously thought, has been and is frequently underdiagnosed,
and is now identified as one of the most common life-long disorders in the
West. Clinical presentation covers a broad spectrum ranging from moderate gastrointestinal discomfort to superaccelerated intestinal transit and
diarrhea, leading to pronounced weight loss, nutrient deficiencies, and
their complications. The accepted standard of practice in U.S. pediatric
medicine is to screen infants of high-risk groups, and patients who present
with symptoms of irritable bowel syndrome (Thompson 2001; Butterworth et al. 2004; Treem 2004).

Gluten is a complex of individual proteins of two classes: prolamins,
which present the greater challenge to people with CD, and glutelins.
Prolamins exist in the starchy endosperm of wheat (gliadin), rye (seca-
linin), and barley (hordein) and elicit responses from people with CD.
Recent studies confirm that oat does not present the danger once thought,
and oat products have been reintroduced into CD diets (Hogberg et al.
2004). In the majority of cases, removal of gluten from the diet returns the
small intestine to histologically normal.

In the past, the most common food adjustments were to remove the
challenge grains and center diets on maize or rice. Today CD has caught
the attention of the functional foods industry who promote gluten-free
conventional grains and flours, as well as nontraditional ones (in the
West) such as almond (*Prunus amygdalus*), buckwheat (*Fagopyrum esculentum* Moench, Polygonaceae), quinoa (*Chenopodium quinoa*), and
sunflower seed (*Helianthus annuus* L., Asteraceae).

Nutraceuticals that have been designed and labeled for CD fill a need
voiced by a large group of individuals who understand the role that diet
modification can play in improving their quality of life. The difficulties in
adhering to gluten-free diets that CD patients expressed in the past (Butterworth et al. 2004) are addressed in part by the growing varieties of

gluten-free sources available today. CD and allergy societies actively pub-
licize these and their own lists of gluten-free foods. It is interesting to
compare the example of CD with the one that follows. Lactose intolerance intersects some of the symptoms of CD, but I argue that it has
been unnecessarily medicalized and that much of the dis-easing bears
on the nature of government regulation of a particular food group and
powerful market forces.

Lactose Intolerance

Like other mammals whose early development depends on milk, all human infants produce lactase (β-galactosidase). This enzyme is secreted by
the brush border cells (microvilli) in the epithelium of the small intestine
for the digestion of lactose, a sugar that occurs only in milk and constitutes
more than half of the solids and 40 percent of the caloric value of human
milk. Lactase cleaves lactose into its constituent simple sugars, glucose
and galactose, the latter of which is not found free in nature and whose
value in infant nutrition may lie in its contribution to brain formation
(galactose is usually a constituent of glycolipids). Lactase production,
which is governed by a regulatory gene, declines rapidly in all mammals
after weaning, the timing of which varies by species but is generally equal
to 3 percent of the lifespan. That mammals do not continue to produce
lactase when it is no longer needed is consistent with the general energy-
conservative nature of biological evolution—in this case enzyme activity is turned off when it is no longer very important to the organism's
survival.

   The maturational decline of lactase results in lactose intolerance in
most of the world's adult (human and other mammalian) populations.
This is primary adult-type lactose intolerance, which can be confirmed
genotypically and by a breath-hydrogen test or intestinal biopsy. Lactase
deficiency in full-term newborn babies also is genetically inherited but
is a rare, unrelated trait characterized by the complete suppression of
lactase production. Secondary, transient and irreversible lactase deficiencies may result from intestinal inflammation, CD, infections, and intestinal disorders such as Crohn's disease. Milk allergies, which appear to
be under some genetic control and are associated with the protein component of milk, also are not related to lactose intolerance. A general

impression among a proportion of lactose-intolerant people is that toler-ance can be forced by continuing to consume dairy products. This is a lay version of the theory of inducible enzymes, that is, lactase would continue to be produced in the presence of substrate (lactose); but researchers debated this issue through the 1990s and have concluded that lactase is not inducible (Sahi 1994a, 1994b; de Vrese et al. 2001).

When lactose-intolerant individuals consume milk and other dairy products, the undigested milk sugar moves into the large intestine, where it is fermented by microflora, resulting in diarrhea, gas, and cramping. The pattern of inheritance is simple (see below), and a causal relation-ship has been established between lactose nondigestion and symptoms of intolerance versus symptom decline with reduced consumption of lac-tose and measures to enhance lactose digestion. However, because the interrelations among the factors involved are complex, confirmed lactose intolerance does not correspond well with symptoms or with self-reported milk intolerance: eliminating lactose from the diet does not remove symp-toms from all intolerant individuals; not all individuals whose genetically inherited intolerance has been confirmed are lactose intolerant; and the decline of lactase activity occurs much earlier than the occurrence of clinical symptoms. This considerable variability in the nature and magni-tude of response to milk among intolerant individuals is not fully under-stood and may be mediated by shifting composition of the gastrointestinal microflora, rate of gastric emptying time and intestinal transit, other foods consumed at the same time, hormone and metabolic fluctuations, gen-eral and specific health status, and the individual's tolerance of discom-fort (de Vrese et al. 2001; Sibley 2004).

Dietary management of lactose intolerance avoids many dairy prod-ucts: beverage and powdered milks,[2] ice cream, and nonaged cheeses (ricotta, cream cheese, mozzarella). Attention also needs to be paid to products in which lactose is not apparent: low-fat milks may contain skim milk powder, added for body, which increases lactose content; some prod-ucts that are labeled as nondairy (e.g., powdered coffee creamer and whipped toppings) are made with milk-derived ingredients such as whey and milk solids, which include lactose; and many prescription and over-the-counter drugs are manufactured with lactose. Fermented milk products (see chapter 4) usually do not create problems for lactose-intolerant indi-viduals because microflora have already digested the lactose, and many (harder, aged) cheeses, yogurt, buttermilk, and related products are well-tolerated. The same is true for butter, which has a very low lactose profile.

In India, mothers discriminate among animal milks by invoking the binary symbolic hot-cold opposition (see chapter 1), in a sequence of diminishing heat: buffalo, cow, goat. In this case, the assignment of hotness is potently metaphoric with reference to the appropriateness of feeding/ withdrawing different milks when children experience diarrhea. This sequence also reflects lactose content/digestibility, buffalo having the highest and goat the lowest disaccharide levels (Lindenbaum 1977).

Unlike other mammals, some human babies continue to produce lactase beyond the age of weaning (two to four years) and can digest milk sugar throughout their lives. Lactase persistence, the continued production of lactase beyond infancy, is governed by a single-locus trait for a regulatory gene that turns enzyme production on and off: individuals who inherit at least one dominant allele (on chromosome 2) continue to produce lactase: homozygous dominant (LL) and heterozygous (Ll) genotypes are lactose tolerant, whereas the homozygous recessive (ll) is intolerant and is the predominant genotype worldwide.[3] While frequencies of lactase tolerance are more or less continuously distributed across populations, two patterns are readily apparent: populations among whose adults lactase production has declined and those groups among whom adult lactase production persists.

Prior to the 1960s, much (perhaps all) of the research on lactose tolerance had been conducted in countries where lactase persistence was common, reinforcing the impression that this was biologically normative. Western researchers and clinicians began to appreciate the global scale of intolerance only at the end of that decade, an era of intensified international aid in which relief efforts included the distribution of (primarily powdered and condensed) milk. Reception to such products was overwhelmingly negative. Whereas some aid workers dismissed milk rejection as stubborn traditionality, the experiences of anthropologists and others who work closely with indigenous populations is that people are generally more pragmatic than to refuse input simply because it is unfamiliar, especially in circumstances of hunger and other widely perceived need. The reality was that the milk made aid recipients sick—one need observe the results of only a few individuals developing symptoms of gastrointestinal distress before the whole community apprehends the risk. Analogue programs that distributed milk to Native American groups in the United States generated similar reactions, and where milk distribution continued despite rejection, it was put to other uses. In one example, perhaps apocryphal, but if so still a statement about cultural disjunction, milk powder was used as a foundation for whitewashing house walls and to mark baselines on baseball diamonds (Nabhan 2004).

The dry and condensed cow-milk products that were the easily transported, nonperishable part of the food distribution efforts contain as much as 50 percent and 18 percent lactose, respectively, and thus posed an even greater problem as their reconstituted forms contain 15–38 percent lactose, compared to 4–5 percent in fresh cow milk. Not only did the well-intentioned, but Eurocentric, distribution of inappropriate foodstuffs fail, it also exacerbated the existing circumstances of morbidity and hunger. The gastrointestinal distress caused by undigested milk sugar is generalized to other nutrients which, in the presence of increased transit time, also are not absorbed. Experiences such as these, as well as the acceleration of lactose-tolerance research through the 1970s, demonstrated that lactase persistence into adulthood is rare outside of Europe, the United States, the Middle East/Arabian Peninsula, and a few population isolates in sub-Saharan Africa and southern Asia (Table 7.1).

In view of the mammalian template that encodes adult lactose intolerance and especially that the overwhelming majority of the world's populations are intolerant, the occurrence of lactase persistence is intriguing. The evolutionary transition to lactose tolerance occurred in only a small number of human groups and is linked to the cultural history of the domestication of livestock and milk-based pastoralism. About 9000 years ago human groups in the Middle and Near East, and later in Africa and isolated locations in Asia, domesticated herd animals, including cow, goat, and sheep, and some time later began to consume animal milks. The necessary conditions under which lactose-tolerant genotypes would be selected in these populations include a sufficiently central role for fresh milk products in the domestic economy and diet (for at least part of the year), so that intolerant individuals would have been at a significant selective disadvantage. In evolutionary models of selection for particular phenotypes (genotypes), differences are not enough: differences that make a biological difference are required. The model is further nuanced by noting the risk of vitamin D deficiency and related impairment

TABLE 7.1. Frequency of Lactose Intolerance in Various Countries

Country, population	Lactose-intolerant adults[a]
Sweden	2%
Europeans in Australia	4%
Switzerland	10%
Euroamericans	12%
Finland	18%
Central African Tutsi	20%
West African Fulani	23%
Estonia	28%
England	32%
U.S. Latinos	52%
Maori in New Zealand	64%
Peru	70%
U.S. blacks	75%
Mexico	83%
Australian Aborigines	85%
Greece	88%
South African Bantu	89%
Philippines	90%
China	93%
Thailand	98%
West African Yoruba	99%
Native North Americans	100%

a. The figures are compiled from McCracken (1971) and Kretchmer (1972) and are intentionally dated, as they represent distributions of lactose intolerance prior to the increased population mixing of recent decades, which masks some of the heterogeneity in the lactase polymorphism.

of calcium metabolism in areas of low solar irradiation: vitamin D, which occurs naturally in very few foods, is manufactured in the skin when ultraviolet radiation stimulates conversion of 7-deydrocholesterol to vitamin D3. Because lactose absorption and digestion are slower than the metabolism of other sugars, calcium retention and absorption are enhanced, thus improving bone mineralization. This would have been important in northern Europe and other areas of low ultraviolet radiation (from sunlight) or low calcium availability. Other advantages of adult milk consumption include adding lactose to pastoralist diets, which are typically low in carbohydrates, and hydration (Simoons 2001). Further, to expand the biological model on the theme of cultural constructions of food and eating, another necessary condition for the selection of lactose tolerance is that people would have had to regard fresh milk products positively, that is, appreciated the taste and texture, found key roles for milk and fresh milk products in cuisine, and/or assigned healthful or other meaningful roles to milk.

Historically, models that link lactose tolerance to milk drinking include rapid evolution at this locus and high selection coefficients, typically 5 percent; that is, survival and reproductive success among tolerant individuals not only was significantly greater but was much greater than that of intolerant individuals. Contemporary frequencies of lactose tolerance suggest that these selective models can be expanded by including the concepts of gene flow and genetic drift followed later by selection (e.g., Cheer et al. 2000; Swallow 2003; Bersaglieri et al. 2004).

Cultural Constructions of Milk-Drinking

This description of the physiology and evolution of a polymorphism linked to lactose digestion is only part of the story. The cultural constructions and social transactions of milk drinking in the contemporary United States offer insights into interrelations among the dairy industry, the American Dairy Association (ADA), the market, and government entities.

First, bias is revealed in medical and public discourses about lactose tolerance. Whereas hypolactasia is the mammalian template and is shared by 75 percent or more of the human population, it is medicalized through reference to "lactase deficiency," "malabsorption," "insufficiency," "maldigestion," and "nonpersistence." Implicit in the language of the ADA, lactose intolerance is a "treatable condition."

Responding to this so-called problem, the functional foods industry has in the last decade developed lactose-free or lactose-reduced milks (produced by passing milk over lactase enzyme bound to an inert vehicle) and related products. In growing variety these products (e.g., Lactaid®, DairyCare®) are available in specialty and ordinary grocery stores, in pharmacies, and via Web sites and other sources of nutraceuticals. Lactase enzyme also is available commercially in liquid and chewable forms, allowing individuals to dose-regulate to match food type, quantity, and their own physiologic circumstances. The objective is to consume less than one's personal threshold level of lactose but to consume nonetheless. With some irony, although they are promoted as nondairy substitutes, analogue product lines that capitalize on the cachet of milk, such as soy, rice, and almond "milks," further reinforce the idea of milk. Still other products offer low-lactose "solutions" for our pets (e.g., Catsip®), on the logic that, like other mammals, they will become lactose intolerant after weaning. It is interesting and logical to note that after generations of coevolution with people, many European—but not Asian—cat breeds also are lactose tolerant, in all likelihood the outcome of human experiments in natural selection in which Fluffy has been caricatured as the perpetual kitten in need of the proverbial saucer of cream.

While these nutraceuticals present considerable advantage to lactose-intolerant individuals who want dairy products in their diet (here is agency writ large), the story of their perceived need illuminates the larger context of milk consumption in the United States. This includes decades-long ADA promotion of milk as "the perfect food," recommended for children from infancy through teen age, for women during pregnancy and lactation, and to prevent osteoporosis. Whether these guidelines are justified is questioned in light of evidence for good childhood growth and bone density measures in populations who consume little or no milk. Certainly in the context of lactose intolerance, milk does not necessarily "do a body good," and some critics argue that it is not even a good food for lactose-tolerant individuals. While the risk-benefit debates of milk are, like many food-health subjects, plagued by hyperbole, it merits attention that consumption of at least medium- to full-fat milk has been linked to obesity, asthma, anemia, cancers, and allergies (Swagerty et al. 2002). Since the early 1990s, the dairy industry has been the subject of growing scrutiny by both consumer and physician groups, including nudging dairy products to a less prominent position in the food pyramid. Black, Mexican, and other population-based groups in the United States argue that lessons that should have been learned from failed efforts to distribute milk to populations in Africa, Asia, and South America have not been translated adequately into industry oversight and government guidelines.

Given the high proportion of lactose intolerance among both generations-established and immigrant populations in the United States, there is no small irony in the government subsidizing the dairy industry, making milk the centerpiece in public school lunch programs and as the fortified vehicle for delivery of essential micronutrients (calcium, vitamins A and D), and continuing cultural myths about the healthful qualities of milk. The normalizing discourses that disregard biological variability in milk metabolism, or offer solutions to it, "suggest [that] milk's positive symbolism has been overdetermined . . . [and illuminate] the entrenched nature of milk in U.S. culinary culture, national identity, and agricultural economy" (Wiley 2004: 513).

The example of lactose intolerance highlights the merits of biocultural perspectives nuanced by issues of political economy. In this case, we see how culture (subsistence patterns, food choice and preparation) influenced biological evolution (selection for lactose tolerance in some populations), and how that variability has been culturally constructed in the specific context of the United States.

Consumers and Dietary Supplements

It is instructive to review examples of popular dietary supplements in the specific contexts of their promotion and use. The brief case study that follows is based in my research on CAM in Honolulu, Hawai'i, which documents widespread use of many CAM modalities, including both foods and medicines. The essential methodological refinement that separates our work from other, survey-based CAM research (e.g., Eisenberg et al. 2000; Ernst 2000; Struthers and Nichols 2004; Yussman et al. 2004) is a rigorous ethnographic inquiry that explored in depth people's reasons for using CAM, how they assessed the relative merits of different CAM and biomedicines for particular conditions, the origins of their knowledge about diverse CAM modalities, and how they judged efficacy and other outcomes of CAM use (for the details of methods and the broader results, see Etkin et al. 1999; Etkin and McMillen 2003; Etkin 2004). This depth of ethnographic knowledge affords us insights into the cultural construction and social negotiation of foods, medicines, and related products.

Noni

Among the products used by our study participants, *noni* (*Morinda citri-folia* L., Rubiaceae) stands out as a quintessential CAM: it is natural, or at least was in its early iterations; its commercial promotion reinforces existing or creates new meanings that are evocative of exotic, traditional (Polynesian) landscapes through rich images of healthy people in healthy places; and its ready availability in a variety of forms makes it highly accessible (Etkin and McMillen 2003). In other ways noni is not typical of CAM: its evolution from home production to commercialization and global distribution was explosive, unlike the more gradual trajectories of other CAM; it is advertised for an especially broad range of conditions, from general tonics and immune boosters to diabetes specifics, whereas most CAM are either generals or specifics that target a limited number of related symptoms.

Native to Southeast Asia, noni has been domesticated and cultivated for more than 1000 years by Pacific peoples who valued it for food, medicine, and articles of manufacture and commerce. Although some Pacific Islanders consumed noni fruit, including as famine food, historically it was much more important as a dye source. Throughout the Pacific and Southeast Asia, all parts of the plant were used as medicine, principally as topical applications. Like the experience of other native peoples, Hawaiian contact with Europeans included the introduction of infectious diseases (e.g., whooping cough, measles, tuberculosis) with which the local healers had no experience and for which they expanded the range of existing preventives and treatments. Prior to European contact Hawaiians used noni sparingly for internal cleansing of the blood, intestines, and otherwise. More common were topical applications for wounds, bruises, sprains, and fractures. Records from the 1930s document that noni still was used largely topically and that a few ingested noni medicines were taken infrequently to purify the blood and cleanse the body through purgation. Over the following decades a few more medicinal indications for noni evolved, including for intestinal worms, hemorrhage, obstetrical disorders, sexually transmitted diseases, and tuberculosis.

The pattern of regular, but only occasional, medicinal use of noni shifted in the early 1990s, when the number of indications for noni increased dramatically. Many households began producing their own medicinal noni. At that time the most popular preparation sealed several fruit in a large glass jar that was left to stand in the sun for hours, days, or longer. The liquid that accumulated during fermentation was consumed in variable quantities and dosing schedules, depending on the specialist or household consultant, and on the condition treated.

It is significant that, upon fermentation, much but not all of the repugnant smell and taste of the ripe noni fruit is lost. The residual acrid taste/smell, as well as the variable viscosity and color (ranging yellow to black) provided information about potency and helped to specify the efficacy of that noni for a particular condition. For example, one study participant observed that the "thickest, most malodorous, and darkest noni is reserved for serious disorders such as cancers," while noni juice with the least remarkable organoleptic qualities is "appropriate for things you treat on a daily basis such as diabetes and high cholesterol." Over time the basic fermentation was modified to include refrigeration of the jar and contents for the duration or some fraction of the fermentation and/or afterward; the addition of flavors to mask the taste; and the removal of solids by filtering the liquid prior to consumption.

Until the early 1990s home production and consumption of noni was supported by harvest from private or neighborhood trees and purchase of noni fruit in Honolulu's Chinatown shops and farmers' and other open-air markets. Within about two years, demand for noni escalated, and the cost of fruit rapidly rose from $0.99 to as much as $8.00 per pound. During the same period, quart jars of fermented liquid sold for up to $10.00 each.

Concerned with the increasingly widespread use of noni, the State of Hawai'i Department of Health issued a warning in 1992, stating that insofar as claims of efficacy for diabetes, hypertension, etcetera had not been substantiated, explicitly therapeutic promotions of noni violated FDA regulations. It is one testimony to the cultural significance of noni medications that sales of fresh fruit continued unperturbed, and by 1994 passage of the DSHEA rendered moot state concerns about monitoring noni.

In 1992 Maui massage therapist Herbert Moniz began producing noni for local markets as powdered fruit enclosed in capsules. These first-generation noni products are compact and nonperishable, can be easily stored and transported, and have a long shelf life. Noni capsules were regarded with some suspicion by vendors of conventional preparations and by some local *kahuna*, who were generally critical of the expanding celebrity of noni, never mind what form it took. His product initially banned by the FDA, in 1995 Moniz secured a patent for his drying process. In the ensuing years there proliferated a host of commercial entities devoted exclusively or in part to noni, only three of them in Hawai'i, which began to produce capsules, tablets, elixirs, fruit bark, beverages, powders, and so on. Sourcing expanded beyond Hawai'i to locations throughout the Pacific and Southeast Asia as the market for noni products globalized. Today noni products represent considerable market share among CAM.

Thus, noni has been transformed in Hawai'i from a home-based medicine (at most, a minor cottage industry) to a commercially successful global enterprise. This process embodies elements of cultural constructions and social negotiations of medicines and foods that I have stressed throughout this book. Starting in Hawai'i, the use of this traditional medicine and food by contemporary populations links them to their pasts. Noni is not just Hawaiian, it is Polynesian, and so for peoples of Hawai'i resonates a longer history and more comprehensive geocultural base.

Traditional Hawaiian uses of noni—sparingly and usually topically—have been influenced over the centuries by more recent immigrants to the islands. For example, the fermentation of noni, which was recorded as early as the 1930s, in all likelihood reflects the influence in Hawai'i of Chinese, who traditionally prepare many foods and medicines in fermentation vessels. For the five or so years when fermented noni was so popular, the ubiquity of the glass jars on roofs and *lanai* (porches, decks) was reproduced across neighborhoods throughout Oahu. Easily visible to neighbors and passersby, the large number of fermenting jars both affirmed the efficacy of noni and drew ethnically and otherwise disparate communities together. In Chinatown shops, the fermenting jars lined up along the high shelves also provided visual cues and analogues to their lanai counterparts. Some of our study participants invoked a sense of therapeutic community when they described sources and uses of noni. For example, neighbors gifted fruit from their own trees and passed along suggestions for preparation and use. One respondent noted that his "whole family use noni, we prepare several-jar batches, and drink it to-gether." Another identified noni as a traditional Hawaiian medicine, and noted that although he is Filipino, his family's multigenerational connection to Hawai'i "means that it works for [them] too."

The social transaction of noni underscores people's efforts to take part in their own health care. Nothing spoke louder to issues of agency than the observation among our study population (about 4 percent, for all products and all respondents) that although people purchase noni products and other CAM, they do not necessarily use them—ever. The purchase itself is the meaningful act. Thus, we are reminded that as much as medicines may be biodynamic substances with measurable physiologic consequences, they too are entities with social lives. Until recent decades, one could plausibly argue that pharmaceuticals have the most vigorous commodity careers and also are the "most personal of material objects, swallowed, inserted into bodies, rubbed on by anxious mothers, used to express care and intimately empower the uncertain individual" (Moerman 2002; Whyte et al. 2002: 3). Today the global spread of CAM, including to places and peoples from whose materia medica a particular product originated (e.g., noni as CAM in Polynesia), rivals the social life of drugs. This case study of noni reinforces that consumers command agency by purchasing CAM products, which acquire diverse but significant cultural saliencies, and through their social transactions transform the meaning of the therapeutic experience.

Nutraceuticals and Supplements into the Future

As discussed in chapter 2, the relationship between bioscience and social thought has been didactic: expository and clarifying, explaining through powerful vocabulary and metaphor the most intimate details of the human body in health and disease. That relationship has been emotional as well: invoking authority, the confidence of "knowing"—or that someone knows. In turn, society helps to define the scientific enterprise through support of certain institutions and research and demand for certain products. This is nowhere more true than in the case of nutraceuticals and supplements, which offer an open window on modern-era food and medicine systems (Pollan 2003):

[The food industry] has been hard at work developing a counter-counter food future . . . that borrows all that it can from the counter-cuisine and then . . . puts it in a pill. All that's really changed since the high-tech food future [projected in] the 1960s is that the laboratory materials out of which these meals will be constructed are nominally "natural"—dried apple bits, red-wine extract . . . [But] foods are more than the sum of their chemical parts, and treating them as collections of nutrients to be mixed and matched, rather than as the complex biological systems they are, simply may not work.

Conclusions

Only two decades ago the major nutrients had been deciphered, apparently definitively. Then a series of advances reinvigorated what had become a stodgy nutrition science: fermentation chemistry, lectins, antioxidants, bioflavonoids, probiotics, food-drug interactions, supplements, and more. As in much of bioscience, progress in nutritional medicine has been incremental: refined research methodologies add to a growing corpus of knowledge in stepwise fashion. I drew on many of these advances as I conducted research for this book, with the objective to offer a synthesis that invokes higher order abstractions.

The theoretical foundation of this book draws on biocultural perspectives and human ecology: the cultural construction and social transaction of all aspects of food—production, transformation, circulation, consumption—are both undergirded by, and have impact on, food culture and human physiology. One theme that emerges throughout the chapters is that foods mean more than their phytochemical profiles. The ideational elements of people-food relationships are apparent in the structure of cuisines; the characterization of some foods as medicinal but not others; the extranutritive meaning of foods that embody sociability or star in origin myths, the merely mundane aspect of others; the rapid globalization of some foods beyond their source areas (e.g., chocolate, chile) compared to the sluggish radiation of others from points of origin (e.g., tomato) and the narrow range of consumption of still others (e.g., kola and betel nuts); the role that foods play in creating and sustaining community and identity, including items that travel long distances across the diaspora of displaced peoples. At the same time, phytochemistry is important to the ways that people apprehend foods and medicines—that is, cultural meanings are in part defined by how plants look, taste, and affect our bodies. The theme of coevolution emerged as well: insofar as food beliefs influence how people produce or collect plants, ideas affect plant biology, and vice versa.

Another recurrent theme is how issues of political economy in the context of globalization inform our understanding of human-food relationships. The history of the spice trade is a series of encounters with political and economic asymmetries: mercantile capitalism, Euromonopolies, colonialism, wars. Shifting control of production and consumption of items such as tea, coffee, and chocolate are similar processes. More localized asymmetries are further revealed in food rules that govern gender, class, ethnic, or other demographic differences in access to certain food categories, and to production and preparation technologies.

As a final statement, I emphasize again that food selection and its organization into cuisines is complex, comprised by elements both ideational (symbol, metaphor, identity) and tangible (taste, medicinal properties); and that cuisines, in all their permutations, are in some way written on our bodies. This synergy of biology and culture resonates through all chapters of this book.

Appendix. Some Common Spices

English name[a]	Genus species	Family	Origin[b]	Constituents and activities[c]
Allspice tree/fruit	*Pimenta dioica* (L.) Merr.	Myrtaceae	TAm	carene, caryophyllene, curcumene, cymene, eugenol, limonene, phellandrene, pinene, thujene, thymol relieves pain, carminative, inhibits blood clots, expectorant, bactericide, fungicide
Aniseed herb/seed	*Pimpinella anisum* L.	Umbelliferae	Med	anethole, anise ketone, bergapten, methyl chavicol, estragole, flavonol, limonene, linalool, myristicin, α-pinene, rutin, scopoletin, umbelliferone antifungal, carminative, expectorant, anticonvulsant, estrogenic, lactagogue, relieves psoriasis, stimulates hepatic regeneration
Annatto shrub/fruit pulp	*Bixa orellana* L.	Bixaceae	TAm	anethole, apigenin, bixin, borneol, camphor, carotenoids, estragol, eucalyptol, eugenol, gallic acid, linalool, luteolin, pyrogallol, maslinic acid antibacterial, inhibits blood clots, estrogenic
Basil herb/leaf	*Ocimum basilicum* L.	Labiatae	TAs	anethole, borneol, cineole, methyl chavicol, methyl cinnamate, estragol, eucalyptol, eugenol, linalool, ocimeme, safrole anticancer, antibacterial, inhibits blood clots, lowers blood sugar, expectorant, carminative

English name[a]	Genus species	Family	Origin[b]	Constituents and activities[c]
Benin pepper vine/fruit	*Piper guineense* Schum. & Thonn.	Piperaceae	TAf	β-caryophyllene, cubebene, germacrene, limonene, piperine antitumor, antifungal, analgesic, carminative, anti-inflammatory, antioxidant
Black pepper, white pepper vine/fruit	*Piper nigrum* L.	Piperaceae	TAs	β-bisabolene, camphene, myristicin, phellandrene, pinene, piperidine, piperine, safrol antibacterial, antifungal, expectorant, lowers blood pressure, diuretic, carminative, anti-inflammatory, antioxidant
Caraway herb/seed	*Carum carvi* L.	Umbelliferae	NEA	carvone, carveol, limonene antibacterial, antifungal, carminative, antispasmodic, anticancer
Celery seed herb/seed	*Apium graveolens* L.	Umbelliferae	Med	apiogenin, apiin, bergapten, celereodise, delerin, glycolic acid, limonene, phthalides, β-selinene, umbelliferone bacteriostatic, antifungal, inhibits blood clots, anti-inflammatory, lowers blood pressure, carminative, antispasmodic, lowers serum glucose, diuretic, antitumor
Chile	*Capsicum annuum* L.	Solanaceae	TAm	capsaicin, capsanthin, capsicidin, capxanthin, carotene, ferredoxin, solanine, scopoletin antibacterial; lowers serum triglycerides, stimulates lipid mobilization from fat tissue; carminative; increases blood flow to skin; anti-ulcer; diminishes cluster headache; counter-irritant for rheumatism, arthritis, neuralgia, and lumbago; antioxidant, anti-inflammatory

English name[a]	Genus species	Family	Origin[b]	Constituents and activities[c]
Cinnamon tree/bark	*Cinnamomum zeylanicum* Blume	Lauraceae	TAs	cinnamaldehyde, eugenol, methyl-hydroxy chalcone, pinene, safrole, linalool, tannins antibacterial, antiviral, antifungal, antiseptic, antihelminthic, carminative, antispasmodic, antidiarrheal, inhibits blood clots, antipyretic
Clove tree/flower bud	*Syzygium aromaticum* (L.) Merr. & Perry	Myrtaceae	TAs	campestrol, eugenol, eugenin, pinene, sitosterol, stigmasterol, vanillin antibacterial, antiviral, fungistatic, antihelminthic, carminative, anti-inflammatory, inhibits blood clots, antispasmodic, anticancer, anti-emetic, trypsin potentiating, lowers blood sugar, analgesic
Fennel herb/leaf, seed	*Foeniculum vulgare* Miller	Umbelliferae	NEA	anethole, camphone, dillapianol, estragole, fenchone, limonene, pinene antimicrobial, carminative, antispasmodic, estrogenic, expectorant
Fenugreek herb/leaf, seed	*Trigonella foenum-graecum* L.	Fabaceae	Med	coumarin, disogenin, fenugreekine, tigogenin, trigonelline antiviral, lowers serum cholesterol, lowers blood pressure, anticancer, lowers blood sugar
Flower pepper shrub, tree/fruit	*Zanthoxylum zanthoxyloides* Lam., Z. spp.	Rutaceae	TAf	phenylethanoid derivative, fagaramide, fagaronine, hesperidin, zanthoxylol antisickling, antioxidant, antifungal, tumor inhibition, antibacterial
Galangal herb/rhizome	*Alpinia officinarum* Hance	Zingiberaceae	TAs	cineole, linalool, galangol, galangin, α-pinene antibacterial, antifungal, carminative, antitumor, antiulcer

English name[a]	Genus species	Family	Origin[b]	Constituents and activities[c]
Garlic herb/bulb	*Allium sativum* L.	Liliaceae	NEA	ajoene , allicin, alliin, alliinase, s-allylmercaptocysteine, citral, diallyl sulfide, geraniol, linalool, α- and β-phellandrene, prostaglandins, scordinins antibacterial, antifungal, antiviral; lowers serum cholesterol, serum triglycerides, and low density lipoproteins; increases high-density lipoproteins; blocks aortic lipid deposition; lowers blood pressure; antihepatotoxic; antineoplastic; stimulates immune system; decreases blood sugar; inhibits blood clots
Ginger herb/rhizome	*Zingiber officinale* Roscoe	Zingiberaceae	TAs	β-bisabolene, galanolactone, geraniol, gingerol, gingerdione, shogaol, zingerone, zingiberine antimicrobial, antihelminthic, carminative, antinausea, stomachic, lowers blood sugar, antiulcer, decreases serum cholesterol, inhibits blood clots, antioxidant, anti-inflammatory
Guinea pepper tree/fruit	*Xylopia aethiopica* (Dunal) A. Rich	Annonaceae	TAf	carene, linalool, imonene, myrcene, phellandrene, pinene, thujene, xylopic acid antibacterial, antimalarial
Horseradish herb/root	*Armoracia rusticana* P. Gaertner, Meyer & Scherb.	Brassicaceae	NEA	ally-thiocyanate, asparagine, gluconasturtiin, glucosinolates, peroxidase enzymes, scopoletin, sinigrin antibacterial, antispasmodic, lowers blood pressure, carcinostatic
Lemongrass herb/leaf	*Cymbopogon citratus* (Nees) Stapf.	Poaceae	TAs	citral, geraniol, limolene, pinene, perpineole antibacterial, analgesic, antipyretic, antioxidant, uterine stimulant

English name[a]	Genus species	Family	Origin[b]	Constituents and activities[c]
Licorice shrub/ rhizome, root	*Glycyrrhiza glabra* L.	Fabaceae	Med	asparagin, eugenol, glycyrin, glabrin, glabridin, glabrol, glycyrrhizin, indole, licoricone, linalool, umbelliferone antibacterial, antiviral, anti-inflammatory, antihepatotoxic, inhibits blood clots, antiulcer, antispasmodic, expectorant, laxative
Long pepper vine/fruit	*Piper longum* L.	Piperaceae	TAs	β-caryophyllene, β-bisabolene, pentadecane, piperine amoebicidal, bactericidal, anti-fungal, carminative, anti-inflammatory, antioxidant
Mace, nutmeg tree/fruit	*Myristica fragrans* Houtt.	Myristicaceae	TAs	camphene, dipentene, elincin, eugenol, geraniol, linalool, myristicin, α- and β-pinenes, safrole antimicrobial, antioxidant, antitumor, carminative, reduces cholesterol, diuretic, inhibits blood clots
Melegueta pepper herb/fruit	*Aframomum melegueta* Schumann	Zingiberaceae	TAf	caryophyllene, gingerol, humulene, paradols, shogaol, zingerone antibacterial, antifungal, anti-schistosomal
Oregano herb/leaf	*Origanum vulgare* L.	Labiatae	NEA	β-bisabolene, cavracrol, p-cymene, linalool, rosamarinic acid, thymol antibacterial, antifungal, anticancer, antioxidant, antihepatotoxic

English name[a]	Genus species	Family	Origin[b]	Constituents and activities[c]
Saffron herb/flower	*Crocus sativus* L.	Iridaceae	Med	adenosine, astragalin, crocetin, crocins, kalmferol, mangicrocin, myricetin, pinene, picrocrocin, safranal inhibits blood clots, antitumor, immunostimulatory, reduces cholesterol; bacteriostatic
Star anise tree/fruit	*Illicium verum* Hook f.	Illiciaceae	TAs	anethole, anisic acid, methyl chavicol, cineole, estragole, nerolidol, perpineol, phellandrene, safrole, salicylic acid antimicrobial, neurotropic, carminative, relieves respiratory inflammation, expectorant, estrogenic
Tamarind tree/fruit pulp	*Tamarindus indica* L.	Fabaceae	TAf	geranial, geraniol, limonene, methyl salicylate, safrole, tamarindienal, tartaric acid antioxidant, carminative, laxative, antischistosomal, antifungal, antibacterial
Thonningia parasitic herb/flower	*Thonningia sanguinea* Vahl.	Balanophoraceae	TAf	thonningianins a and b antioxidant, antibacterial, antianaphylactic, antihepatotoxic
Turmeric herb/rhizome	*Curcuma longa* L.	Zingiberaceae	TAs	curcumin, turmerin, turmerone, ukonan c, zingiberen antibacterial, antifungal, antiinflammatory, antihepatotoxic, antioxidant, antitumor, estrogenic, lowers cholesterol, antivenom, lowers blood sugar, stimulates immune system
Vanilla liane/seed pod	*Vanilla planifolia* Jackson	Orchidaceae	TAm	anisic acid, caffeic acid, catechin, guaiacol, vanillin anticariogenic, antioxidant, antibacterial, antiyeast, antimutagenic, liver protective

English name[a]	Genus species	Family	Origin[b]	Constituents and activities[c]
Wasabi herb/root, stem	*Wasabia japonica* (Miq) Matsum.	Brassicaceae	NEA	chitinase, hevein, isothicyanate antibacterial, antifungal, anti-cancer, inhibits blood clots
Wormseed herb/leaf	*Chenopodium ambrosioides* L.	Chenopodiaceae	TAm	ascaridole, p-cymene, geraniol, hydroperoxides, limonene, myrcene, methyl salicylate, pinene, spinasterol, urease antihelminthic, antifungal, trypanocidal, amoebicidal, diuretic

a. Growth form, habit/plant part is shown after the name.
b. TAs, tropical Asia; TAm, American tropics; Med, Mediterranean/Middle East/North Africa; NEA, northern/temperate Europe and Asia; TAf, tropical West Africa
c. Information is compiled from Duke (1985), Galal (1996), Newall et al. (1996), Hirasa and Takemasa (1998), Gyamfi et al. (2000), Morimitsu et al. (2000), Ohtani et al. (2000), Kwon et al. (2002), Chaaib et al. (2003), Kiba et al. (2003), Research and Editorial Staff (2003), Walton et al. (2003).

Notes

Chapter 1

1. The term *nonnutritive* (or extranutritive) denotes qualities other than those computed as conventional food values (i.e., protein, vitamins, calories). In this book, nonnutritive refers generally to pharmacologic activity or potential.

2. I use the term *secondary* here to set the theoretical stage for later discussion and to reflect the history of interest in phytochemical diversity. Otherwise, and in subsequent chapters, I use the terms *allelochemical* or *phytochemical* in order not to perpetuate the impression that such compounds are biologically less important. Indeed, one premise of this book is that these compounds are profoundly important for both producers and consumers.

3. A pheromone is a volatile chemical that serves communication within species; an allomone is its counterpart in between-species communication, although the distinction erodes when the same compound serves both functions (Harborne 1993).

4. Batesian mimicry, especially common among insects (see chapter 6), describes the similar appearance of two or more taxa, one of which (the model) is toxic and the other, which is nontoxic, survives because it resembles the model. Mullerian mimicry is the resemblance among different taxa all of which are inedible, the advantage of this being that an inedible species benefits from a predator learning from other inedible species, then avoiding all organisms that look like the one of initial contact. Technically, Mullerian mimicry might not be true mimicry: it is not obvious which species is the model and which one the mimic, and the receiver (potential predator) is not actually deceived (Howe and Westley 1988).

5. Over time, the size of the teeth and supporting bone and muscle became smaller, resulting in reduced facial volume and diminished robustness of cranial bones where chewing muscles attach. Digestive physiology changed as well, differentiating the omnivorous human gut from that of other primates who are largely herbivorous. For example, humans dedicate most gut volume to the small, rather than large, intestine; and the size of the gut relative to body mass is small (Milton 1987).

6. See Etkin and Ross (1994, 1997) and Ross et al. (1996) for details of methodology and scope of the larger study and the ethnographic context of Hurumi. Throughout this book, references to Hausa food and medicine that lack specific citations are based in our unpublished field data.

7. People have been tending the health of animals almost as long as we have medicated ourselves, but only during the last fifteen years or so have local ethnoveterinary

knowledge and praxis received much scientific attention. Much of what coheres today under the rubric ethnoveterinary medicine can be traced to the pioneering efforts of Mathias (Mathias et al. 1999; Mathias 2005) and McCorkle (McCorkle et al. 1996; see also, Pieroni 1999; Lans 2001; Martin et al. 2001).

8. Revealing the symmetries in ways of knowing the world, the five Chinese flavors/tastes find cognates in such five-kind domains as cereals, virtues, elements, cardinal points, vegetables, colors, and smells. The number five derives from the Taoist concept of five evolutions or five elements and has held a key role in Chinese cosmology since antiquity (Anderson 1988; Simoons 1991).

9. The only synaesthesia that is recognized in the West is "abnormal," a neurological condition in which the affected individual experiences gustatory or auditory visions, tactile or auditory smells, and other mixed sensations.

10. Beef (Bos sp., Bovidae), chickpea (Cicer arietinum L., Fabaceae), cranberry (Vaccinium spp., Ericaceae), fig (Ficus carica L., Moraceae), goat (Capra sp., Bovidae), lotus (Nelumbo nucifera Gaertn., Nelumbonaceae), nutmeg (Myristica fragrans Houtt., Myristicaceae), oyster (Ostreidae), prawns (Crustacea), pumpkin (Cucurbita spp., Cucurbitaceae), saffron (Crocus sativus L., Iridaceae), tea (Camellia sinensis (L.) Kuntze, Theaceae, turkey (Meleagris sp., Meleagrididae).

Chapter 2

1. Koch's four postulates are: (1) the microorganism must be present in every instance of the disease and in none other; (2) the organism can be cultivated in pure culture; (3) the disease will be reproduced when an animal is inoculated with the culture; and (4) the microorganism can be recovered from the inoculated animal and grown again in pure culture (Galdston 1943).

2. My point is that the philosophical foundation of Hippocratic-Galenic medicine was relatively static and less adequate to deal with change, although Europe was of course not at a full standstill (wars, the Renaissance, plagues). In this context medicines based in evolving religious and folk traditions afforded some of the flexibility that humoral medicine did not.

Chapter 3

1. There is some debate about the widely held belief that spices are/have been used to mask the taste of already spoiled foods. While this seems to rest on a conventional wisdom that food supplies are unsafe in the absence of modern technology, we have ample evidence for food preservation and other safety measures in both contemporary and historical low-technology populations. Further, this ignores both the health risks of ingesting spoiled food, as well as the fact that spices not only add flavor but also bring out existing flavors including, presumably, the taste of putrefaction.

2. The seasonings salt and sugar seem obvious inclusions but are not treated in this chapter because each has an extensive literature of its own documenting complex social,

medicinal, and culinary histories (e.g., Mintz 1985, 1996; Lovejoy 1986; Attwood 1992; Montanari 1994; Laszlo 2001; Kurlansky 2002; Woloson 2002). These ubiquitous and low-cost seasonings of the modern era were expensive commodities in their early histories, salt itself (and to a lesser extent sugar) serving as currency at various times and places. Like the other spices discussed in this chapter, salt and sugar have interesting clinical applications, and their global patterns of production and consumption offer insight into the political economy of food sourcing, globalization, and commodification.

3. Although formerly condemned by Islamic clerics in the jihad of the early nineteenth century, Bori continues to exist in regionally variable, attenuated forms (in part because the iskoki find parallels in the Islamic *jinn*/spirits). It follows an idiom of affliction to which people are drawn to resolve physical, psychological, and social problems. Integral to Bori are musicians, noninitiates who preserve the oral traditions through song; *yam Bori*, the adepts ("horses"); and divine spirits who reside in the invisible city Jangare and deliver to their victims, in turn, illness and misfortune then resolution. Cure is effected as the adepts are first drawn into trance and dancing then "mounted" by the spirit; in the end, they serve as a medium for that spirit's voice through mimetic representation of its appearance and actions. Jangare social organization finds parallels in Hausa society: it is governed by *Sarkan Aljan* (Chief of Spirits), with or without a royal court; authority is further divided among twelve *zauruka* (houses, sing. *zaure*) that are distinguished by ethnicity, occupation, and descent: for example, *Zauren Turawa*, house of North African spirits, whose head is *Barkono*/chile pepper; *Zauren Kutare*, house of the lepers, headed by *Kuturu* the leper (Besmer 1983).

4. The authors focused on meat-inclusive recipes because the spoilage rate of animal products is greater and associated with more instances of food-borne illness than are vegetables: dead plants, compared to animal flesh, are better protected from microorganisms due to the presence of antimicrobial phytochemicals, difficult-to-digest lignin and cellulose, pH lower than what supports most bacteria, and low fat content. A recipe is qualified as "meat-based . . . [if] at least one-third of its total weight or volume consists of red meat, poultry, pork, veal or seafood" (Billing and Sherman 1998: 6).

5. The examples of lemon, lime, and black and white peppers at first seem to contradict the hypothesis. Although they number among the "five most commonly used spices and appear in the meat-based cuisine of every country in [the] sample, they are among the least effective" antimicrobials, and their use does not correlate with temperatures (Billing and Sherman 1998: 17). However, these spices act synergistically with other spices and foods and could, arguably, play an adjuvant role in the collective antimicrobial action. The issue of spice blends is treated in the section Spices in the Context of Complex Cuisines.

6. One of the most instructive of Hausa symbolic representations links human reproduction and alimentation. The fundamental metaphor of this allegory likens eating with intercourse, both expressed in the homonym verb *ci*. Elaborations of the *ci* allegory include the homonym *sanwa* for both semen and cooking water; describing the vagina as the locus of consumption; surgical excision during the naming ceremony of the *beli* (uvula) and the *tantani* (hymen), appendages that are understood to block consumption; and in rude vernacular reference to divorced women as *bazawara* (leftover, partially consumed food).

Further elaborations are apparent in the rules that govern birth and the early postpartum, as well as in songs, proverbs, and epithets. Corollary symbolic expressions that link gestation to food production include the representation of the penis and vagina as, respectively, the pestle and mortar (based on structure/function) and the penis and testicles as the *murhu* (three-stoned cooking hearth). Similarly, the developing fetus rests on a murhu while developing in the *mahaifa* (womb). Reproductive development finds an analogue in the fire that is alimentation: the cooking, forming, and transforming from raw to cooked (see also Darrah 1980).

7. Hausa food rules for circumcision are developed in more detail in chapter 1, Food in Celebration.

Chapter 4

1. This conclusion is based on my interpretation of Johns and Kubo's (1988) comprehensive survey of traditional methods that are used deliberately to detoxify and/or reduce bitterness in plant foods: fermentation, heating, solution, adsorption, drying, grating/chopping, pH modification, and combinations of those. Of the 216 species (representing sixty-five families) of vascular plants, algae, fungi, and lichens for which one or more method was reported, only eighteen species (8 percent, representing twelve families) were fermented. That aesthetics compels the fermentative processing of foods is suggested by the examples of traditional cuisines (e.g., Fiji and Tikopia) for which as many as eight starches may be fermented at the same time to assure the availability not only of food but of different tastes and textures as well (Pollock 1992).

2. The relatively uncertain nature of food supply in (especially small) island ecosystems, as well as the voyaging traditions of Pacific Island cultures, reinforced the significance of fermentation, which assured availability during shortage and famine as well as safety during transit.

3. In the case of the Maasai, the salubrious effects of fermented milk are amplified by plants that are added to the milk and to soups and by tree gums that are regularly chewed (see chapter 5). The most widely used plants have the highest content of antioxidant phenolics, for example, *Acacia nilotica* (L.) Del. (Fabaceae; *babul*) and *Euclea divinorum* Hiern. (Ebenaceae; *msanganetu*). Several other species contain high amounts of saponins that may lower serum cholesterol by emulsifying fats, such as *Myrsine africana* L. (Myrsinaceae; *nghasi*). The most commonly chewed gum, a type of myrrh (*Commiphora africana* [A. Rich] Engl., Burseraceae), contains steroids with potential hypolipidemic action (Johns et al. 1999, 2000; see chapter 5). Researchers preoccupied with what they regard to be inordinately high milk consumption have overlooked Maasai use of plants as food and medicine. Similarly, the preparation and storage of fermented milks by other East African groups likely impact the pharmacodynamics of the finished product: for example, the addition of charcoals from particular trees to flavor and/or influence the appearance of the milk; the addition of plants that impart medicinal qualities to the milk; and the use of gourds of designated species for storage and transport of fermented milk (Mureithi et al.

2000). The use of these wild and otherwise less apparent plants in food has likely been overlooked in other populations as well (Etkin 1994b).

Chapter 5

1. More precisely, a cordial is a liqueur, a strong, highly flavored, sweet alcohol beverage that is usually drunk just before or after a meal.

2. First proposed more than 125 years ago, the idea periodically resurfaces (without any compelling evidence) that beer provided a more important incentive for the domestication of grains than did the discovery of flour-based breads and gruels (e.g., Braidwood et al. 1953; Katz and Voigt 1986). Given the virtual ubiquity of porridges as staple foods and that porridge is a foundation phase in both bread and beer production, it is more logical that experimentation with grains for food preceded production of beer on a sizeable scale (Kavanagh 1994), although this does not preclude early peoples' appreciation of the diversity of grain products, including alcohol beverages.

3. This discussion of kava draws appreciably on an early draft of Jonathan D. Baker's Ph.D. dissertation (in preparation).

4. An emulsion is a system of two immiscible liquids in which one, the internal phase, is dispersed as very small globules throughout the external phase. Maceration transforms the root mass into small particles, releasing from the cell tissues kavalactone-containing resins that are poorly soluble in water.

5. Within plants, caffeine (and perhaps other methylxanthines) affords protection against bacteria and fungi, reduces the reproductive capacity of some insects, and, by permeating the surrounding soil, acts as an allelochemical to inhibit the growth of competing plants (see chapter 1; Weinberg and Bealer 2001).

6. The term *herbal tea* currently is applied to a great variety of beverages not even remotely related to *Camellia* tea. This is a statement about signature and the meaning of foods and beverages, an artifact of the prominence of *Camellia* among hot drinks made from infused plants. Infusions of rose hip (*Rosa* spp., Rosaceae) and mint leaf, for instance, are best called *tisanes*.

7. Tea customs that developed later in Japan were even more formal and ritualized and in the fifteenth century were codified into *chado*, the tea ceremony. This is a Buddhist art form in which tea conveys philosophic ideals: a multitude of prescriptions and proscriptions govern the issuing of invitations, selection and brewing of tea, implements used, location, gestures, and much more (e.g., Anderson 1988; Anderson 1991; Manchester 1996).

8. Leaves of the social plant coca, which has an extensive literature of its own and is not treated individually in this chapter, have been chewed in the South American Andes for millennia. It is the centerpiece of social transactions and identity and is integral to many aspects of daily life, including religion, medicine, and mythology. Coca leaves have relatively high protein and vitamin contents, and chewing them increases energy and mental alertness, diminishes hunger and thirst, and enhances capacity for physical labor. A primary obstacle to understanding the history, cultural construction, and pharmacodynamics of

coca chewing has been the tendency by Westerners to functionally equate coca with cocaine. Although this alkaloid is produced by the coca plant (and is insecticidal; Nathanson et al. 1993), very little cocaine is absorbed with (even habitual) chewing (Weil 1986; Sanabria 2004). Today the social transactions of coca and cocaine are inextricably linked to geopolitical processes in countries in which coca is produced and distributed (Young 2004).

9. Within a few years of Pemberton's creation, another pharmacist in North Carolina, Caleb Brabham, created Coca-Cola's chief competitor: Brad's Drink, later named Pepsi-Cola for the ingredients pepsin and kola, experienced a similar commodification trajectory. By the 1890s Coca-Cola was one of the most popular fountain drinks in the United States and still carried the reputation of medical elixir and brain tonic. The beverage was registered in the U.S. Patent Office in 1893, and by 1900 syrup sales had increased more than 4000 percent. Botanical coca and kola extracts remained ingredients of Coca-Cola until 1905. By 1917, sales were 3 million Cokes per day. Today Coca-Cola operates in more than 200 countries and is the largest manufacturer and distributor of nonalcohol beverage concentrates and syrups (Prendergrast 2000).

Chapter 6

1. Sensitivity to catnip (*Nepeta cataria* L., Labitae) in cats, who range from the familiar domestics to large wild felines, is governed by an autosomal dominant gene, one copy of which (genotypes CC or Cc) is sufficient to code for the animated response to the nepeta-lactone constituents (genotype cc does not respond).

2. Among Hausa in Nigeria, for example, *Vernonia amygdalina* (*shiwaka*) is a bitter medicine, which (among other reasons) signals its utility in both human and veterinary medicines for stomach disorders. As for many Hausa medicines, one therapeutic objective is disease egress, as evidenced by the expulsion of intestinal parasites, diarrhea, color change of effluvia, and so on. A leaf infusion of shiwaka is drunk three times daily for three days. In the context of cuisine, more and regular exposure to shiwaka occurs as the bitter leaves are added to vegetable dishes (e.g., *fatefate*) and soups (miya); for culinary purposes some of the rough leaf surface is reduced. These leaves and foods are most often consumed during the rainy months, when fresh plants are more abundant and when leaf-based dishes replace those organized around grains, stores of which have diminished since the last harvest. Further, year-round, small branches of shiwaka are fashioned into chewing sticks, which are held in the mouth for hours, during which intermittent teeth-cleaning and stick-chewing assure oral health and further extend individuals' exposure to *Vernonia* phyto-constituents. Hausa use the related species *Vernonia kotscyhyana* Sch. Bip. (*domashi*) and *Vernonia colorata* Drake (*farin shuwaka*) for stomach and intestinal disorders that are compounded by more severe symptomology (e.g., anemia, wasting, blockage), as well as for spirit-mediated preventions (Etkin and Ross 1982).

3. For example, the forty-six species recorded for China include one species in each of the three families (Apiidae, Vespidae, and Scoliidae), while other researchers reported five species for each of those families; and the thirty-two Zimbabwe species include six caterpil-

lar species, although as many as fifteen Shone (local vernacular) names have been reported by different investigators.

4. Permutations of preparation and presentation for these and other insect foods appear in popular and professional sources. Except where otherwise indicated, discussion in this section draws on overviews by DeFoliart (2004) and FIN (2004).

5. Pollen that has not been collected or transformed by bees has its own history as food and medicine and is commonly promoted today by the same commercial entities that sell bee products. Pollen is consumed incidentally with flowers that have medicinal or culinary uses, and it is also harvested on its own. For example, Native North Americans used pollen extensively, commonly kneading, sun drying, and then grinding it into a powder used to thicken soups, make beverages, garnish grain dishes, and bake into breadlike products. Pollen also played an important role in Native North and South American religious ceremonies and medicine (Linskens and Jorde 1997).

Chapter 7

1. The terms for healthful food products have met different degrees of acceptance in various sectors (e.g., the food industry, clinical medicine, popular media); *functional food* and *nutraceutical*, the most common terms, are used interchangeably in this chapter.

2. Full-cream products may be tolerated better than low-fat milks because as fat slows gastrointestinal transit, lactose leaves the stomach and small intestine more gradually.

3. This characterization of lactase inheritance suffices for purposes of the present discussion but oversimplifies. In fact, four common variants of the lactase haplotype (an alternative form of the genotype of a gene complex; not simply an allele) have been identified. One, which is most common in northern Europe, decreases across southern Europe and India, where two other variants are common; a fourth variant occurs among most other populations except Indo-European groups (Bersaglieri et al. 2004). Further, the age at which lactase production declines varies among human groups, ranging from two (for most) to twenty years, with longer duration of lactase production among intolerant members of largely lactose-tolerant populations (Sahi 1994b).

References

Abbott, R. D., G. W. Ross, L. R. White, W. T. Sanderson, C. M. Burchfiel, M. Kashon, D. S. Sharp, K. H. Masaki, J. D. Curb, and H. Petrovitch. 2003. Environmental, lifestyle, and physical precursors of clinical Parkinson's disease: recent findings from the Honolulu-Asia aging study. *Journal of Neurology* 250(Suppl. 3): 30–39.

Abraham, S. K., and H. Stopper. 2004. Anti-genotoxicity of coffee against N-methyl-N-nitrosoguanidine in mouse lymphoma cells. *Mutation Research* 561(1/2): 23–33.

Actis-Goretta, L., G. G. Mackenzie, P. I. Oteiza, and C. G. Fraga. 2002. Comparative study on the antioxidant capacity of wines and other plant-derived beverages. *Annals of the New York Academy of Sciences* 957: 279–283.

Adamolekun, B., D. W. McCandless, and R. F. Butterworth. 1997. Epidemic of seasonal ataxia in Nigeria following ingestion of the African silkworm *Anaphe venata*: role of thiamine deficiency. *Metabolic Brain Disease* 12(4): 251–258.

Adams, M. R. 1998. Fermented weaning foods. In *Microbiology of Fermented Foods*. 2nd ed. B. J. B. Wood, ed. Pp. 790–811. Blackie Academic, London.

Adib, Salim M. 2004. From the biomedical model to the Islamic alternative: a brief overview of medical practices in the contemporary Arab world. *Social Science and Medicine* 58(4): 697–702.

Agarwal, K. N., and S. K. Bhasin. 2002. Feasibility studies to control acute diarrhoea in children by feeding fermented milk preparations Actimel and Indian Dahi. *European Journal of Clinical Nutrition* 56(Suppl. 4): 56S–59S.

Aggarwal, B. B., Y. Takada, and O. V. Oommen. 2004. From chemoprevention to chemotherapy: common targets and common goals. *Expert Opinion on Investigational Drugs* 13(10): 1327–1338.

Aldercreutz, Herman, Helene Markkanen, and Shaw Watanabe. 1993. Plasma concentrations of phyto-oestrogens in Japanese men. *Lancet* 342: 1209–1210.

Aldini, G., M. Carini, A. Piccoli, G. Rossoni, and R. M. Facino. 2003. Procyanidins from grape seeds protect endothelial cells from peroxynitrite damage and enhance endothelium-dependent relaxation in human artery: new evidences for cardioprotection. *Life Sciences* 73(22): 2883–2898.

Al-Motarreb, A. L., and K. J. Broadley. 2003. Coronary and aortic vasoconstriction by cathinone, the active constituent of khat. *Autonomic and Autacoid Pharmacology* 23(5/6): 319–326.

Andaya, Leonard Y. 1993. *The World of Maluku: Eastern Indonesia in the Early Modern Period*. University of Hawai'i Press, Honolulu.

Andermann, Lisa. 1991. 'To render visible': making sense among the Ndembu. In *The Varieties of Sensory Experience*. D. Howes, ed. Pp. 203–209. University of Toronto Press, Toronto.

Anderson, E. N. 1988. *The Food of China*. Yale University Press, New Haven, Conn.

Anderson, Jennifer L. 1991. *An Introduction to Japanese Tea Ritual*. State University of New York Press, Albany.

Anderson, R. A., and M. M. Polansky. 2002. Tea enhances insulin activity. *Journal of Agriculture and Food Chemistry* 50(24): 7182–7186.

Andrews, Jean. 1995. *Peppers: The Domesticated Capsicums*. Rev. ed. University of Texas Press, Austin.

Andrews, Jean. 2003. Chili peppers. In *Encyclopedia of Food and Culture*. S. H. Katz, ed. Pp. 368–378. Charles Scribner, New York.

Andrikopoulos, N. K., A. C. Kaliora, A. N. Assimopoulou, and V. P. Papapeorgiou. 2003. Biological activity of some naturally occurring resins, gums and pigments against in vitro LDL oxidation. *Phytotherapy Research* 17(5): 501–507.

Angelov, N., N. Moutsopoulos, M. J. Jeong, S. Nares, G. Ashcroft, and S. M. Wahl. 2004. Aberrant mucosal wound repair in the absence of secretory leukocyte protease inhibitor. *Thrombosis and Haemostasis* 92(2): 288–297.

Anke, J., and I. Ramzan. 2004a. Pharmacokinetic and pharmacodynamic drug interactions with kava (*Piper methysticum* Forst. f.). *Journal of Ethnopharmacology* 93: 153–160.

Anke, J., and I. Ramzan. 2004b. Kava hepatotoxicity: Are we any closer to the truth? *Planta Medica* 70(3): 193–196.

Anthony, Mary S. 2000. Soy and cardiovascular disease: cholesterol lowering and beyond. *Journal of Nutrition* 130: 662S–663S.

Apaza, Lilian, Ricardo Godoy, David Wilkie, Elizabeth Byron, Tomás Huanca, William R. Leonard, Eddy Peréz, Victoria Reyes-García, and Vincent Vadez. 2003. Markets and the use of wild animals for traditional medicine: a case study among the Tsimane' Amerindians of the Bolivian rain forest. *Journal of Ethnobiology* 23(1): 47–64.

Apgar, Joan L., and Stanley M. Tarka. 1999. Methylxanthines. In *Chocolate and Cocoa: Health and Nutrition*. I. Knight, ed. Pp. 153–173. Blackwell Science, Oxford.

Appadurai, Arjun. 1988. *The Social Life of Things: Commodities in Cultural Perspective*. Cambridge University Press, Cambridge.

Århem, Kaj. 1996. The cosmic food web: human-nature relatedness in the northwest Amazon. In *Nature and Society*. P. Descola and G. Pálson, eds. Pp. 185–204. Routledge, London.

Arnason, John T., Gabriel Guillet, and Tony Durst. 2004. Phytochemical diversity of insect defenses in tropical and temperate plant families. In *Advances in Insect Chemical Ecology*. R. T. Cardé and J. G. Millar, eds. Pp. 1–20. Cambridge University Press, Cambridge.

Arocha-Pinango, C. L., R. Marchi, Z. Carvajal, and B. Guerrero. 1999. Invertebrate compounds acting on the hemostatic mechanism. *Blood Coagulation and Fibrinolysis* 10(2): 43–68.

Atal, C. K., U. Zutshi, and P. G. Rao. 1981. Scientific evidence on the role of Ayurvedic herbals in bioavailability of drugs. *Journal of Ethnopharmacology* 4(2): 229–232.

Atkins, Peter, and Ian Bowler. 2001. *Food in Society: Economy, Culture, Geography.* Oxford University Press, New York.

Attwood, Donald A. 1992. *Raising Cane: The Political Economy of Sugar in Western India.* Westview Press, Boulder, Colo.

Austin, Gregory A. 1985. *Alcohol in Western Society from Antiquity to 1800: A Chronological History.* ABC-CLIO Information Services, Santa Barbara, Calif.

Aveling, Elizabeth M. 1997. Ancient chewing gum. *British Archaeology* 21(Feb.). http://www.britarch.ac.uk/ba/ba21, 1 March 2005.

Aveling, Elizabeth M., and C. Heron. 1999. Chewing tar in the early Holocene: an archaeological and ethnographic evaluation. *Antiquity* 73: 579–584.

Baker, Jonathan D. [In Preparation] Kava Tradition and Toxicity: Local and Global Discourses about the Safety of an Indigenous Ceremonial and Medicinal Plant. Ph.D. diss., Department of Anthropology, University of Hawai'i.

Bankole, Mobolaji O., and Richard N. Okagbue. 1992. Properties of "nono," a Nigerian fermented milk food. *Ecology of Food and Nutrition* 27: 145–149.

Baranauskiene, R., R. P. Venskutonis, and J. C. Demyttenaere. 2003. Sensory and instrumental evaluation of catnip (*Nepeta cataria* L.) aroma. *Journal of Agricultural and Food Chemistry* 51(13): 3840–3848.

Barkey, N. L., B. C. Campbell, and P. W. Leslie. 2001. A comparison of health complaints of settled and nomadic Turkana men. *Medical Anthropology Quarterly* 15(3): 391–408.

Bates, Daniel. 1998. *Human Adaptive Strategies: Ecology, Culture, and Politics.* Allyn and Bacon, Boston.

Beardsworth, Alan, and Teresa Keil. 1997. *Sociology on the Menu: An Invitation to the Study of Food and Society.* Routledge, New York.

Beaumont, M. 2002. Flavouring composition prepared by fermentation with *Bacillus*. *International Journal of Food Microbiology* 75(3): 189–196.

Beck, Melinda. 2000. Nutritionally induced oxidative stress: effect on viral disease. *American Journal of Clinical Nutrition* 71: 1676S–1679S.

Beckstrom-Sternberg, S. M., and James A. Duke. 1994. Potential for synergistic action of phytochemicals in spices. In *Spices, Herbs, and Edible Fungi.* G. Charalambous, ed. Pp. 201–223. Elsevier, Amsterdam.

Beier, Lucinda McCray. 1992. Seventeenth-century English surgery: the casebook of Joseph Binns. In *Medical Theory, Surgical Practice: Studies in the History of Surgery.* C. Lawrence, ed. Pp. 48–84. Routledge, New York.

Belicova, A., J. Krajcovic, J. Dobias, and L. Ebringer. 1999. Antimutagenicity of milk fermented by *Enterococcus faecium*. *Folia Microbiologia* 44: 513–518.

Bellisle, F. 1999. Glutamate and the UMAMI taste: sensory, metabolic, nutritional and behavioural considerations: a review of the literature published in the last 10 years. *Neuroscience and Biobehavioral Reviews* 23(3): 423–438.

Berhow, M. A., E. D. Wagner, S. F. Vaughn, and M. J. Plewa. 2000. Characterization and antimutagenic activity of soybean saponins. *Mutation Research* 448: 11–22.

Bersaglieri, T., P. C. Sabeti, N. Patterson, T. Vanderploeg, S. F. Schaffner, J. A. Drake, M. Rhodes, D. E. Reich, and J. N. Hirschhorn. 2004. Genetic signatures of strong recent positive selection at the lactase gene. *American Journal of Human Genetics* 74(6): 1111–1120.

Besmer, Fremont E. 1983. *Horses, Musicians, and Gods: The Hausa Cult of Possession-Trance*. Bergin and Garvey, South Hadley, Mass.

Billing, Jennifer, and Paul W. Sherman. 1998. Antimicrobial functions of spices: why some like it hot. *Quarterly Review of Biology* 73(1): 3–49.

Bixler, Ronald G., and Jeffrey N. Morgan. 1999. Cacao bean and chocolate processing. In *Chocolate and Cocoa: Health and Nutrition*. I. Knight, ed. Pp. 43–60. Blackwell Science, Oxford.

Björkman, Christer, and Stig Larsson. 1991. Pine sawfly defense and variation in host plant resin acids: a trade-off with growth. *Ecological Entomology* 16: 283–289.

Blofeld, John. 1985. *The Chinese Art of Tea*. Allen and Unwin, London.

Blum, M., L. Rivier, and T. Plowman. 1981. Fate of cocaine in the lymantriid *Eloria noyesi*, a predator of *Erythroxylon coca*. *Phytochemistry* 11: 2499–2500.

Bonner, Thomas N. 1991. *Medicine in Chicago, 1850–1950: A Chapter in the Social and Scientific Development of a City*. 2nd ed. University of Illinois Press, Urbana.

Booth, D. A., T. Earl, and S. Mobini. 2003. Perceptual channels for the texture of a food. *Appetite* 40(1): 69–76.

Booth, W. 1988. Voodoo science. *Science* 240: 274–277.

Borek, C. 2001. Antioxidant health effects of aged garlic extract. *Journal of Nutrition* 131: 1010S–1015S.

Bracesco, N., M. Dell, S. Behtash, T. Menini, A. Gugliucci, and E. Nunes. 2003. Antioxidant activity of a botanical extract preparation of *Ilex paraguariensis*. *Journal of Alternative and Complementary Medicine* 9: 379–387.

Braidwood, Robert J., Jonathan D. Sauer, Hans Helbaek, Paul C. Mangelsdorf, Hugh C. Cutler, Carleton Coon, Ralph Linton, Julian Steward, and A. Leo Oppenheim. 1953. Did man once live by beer alone? *American Anthropologist* 55: 515–526.

Brett, John A. 1994. Medicinal Plant Selection Criteria among the Tzeltal Maya of Highland Chiapas, Mexico. Ph.D. diss., Department of Anthropology, University of California, San Francisco.

Brett, John A., and Michael Heinrich. 1998. Culture, perception and the environment: the role of chemosensory perception. *Angewandte Botanik* 72: 67–69.

Brewer, H. 2004. Historical perspectives on health: early Arabic medicine. *Journal of the Royal Society for the Promotion of Health* 124(4): 184–187.

Britannica Online. 2005. Chewing gum. *Britannica Encyclopedia*. http://www.britannica.com, 26 February.

Brothwell, Don, and Patricia Brothwell. 1998. *Food in Antiquity: A Survey of the Diet of Early Peoples*. Expanded ed. Johns Hopkins University Press, Baltimore, Md.

Brown, Amy C., and A. Valiere. 2004. Probiotics and medical nutritional therapy. *Nutrition in Clinical Care* 7(2): 56–58.

Brunton, Ron. 1990. *The Abandoned Narcotic: Kava and Cultural Instability in Melanesia.* Cambridge University Press, Cambridge.

Bukkens, Sandra G. F. 1997. The nutritional value of edible insects. *Ecology of Food and Nutrition* 36(2–4): 287–319.

Burri, Betty J. 2002. Lycopene and human health. In *Phytochemicals in Nutrition and Health.* M. S. Meskin, W. R. Bidlack, A. J. Davies, and S. T. Omaye, eds. Pp. 157–172. CRC Press, Boca Raton, Fla.

Butterworth, Jeffrey R., Luke M. Banfield, Tariq H. Iqbal, and Brian T. Cooper. 2004. Factors relating to compliance with a gluten-free diet in patients with coeliac disease: comparison of white Caucasian and South Asian patients. *Clinical Nutrition* 23(5): 1127–1134.

Bynum, W. F. 1990. "*C'est un malade*": animal models and concepts of human diseases. *Journal of the History of Medicine and Allied Sciences* 45: 397–413.

Campbell-Platt, Geoffrey. 1980. African locust bean (*Parkia* species) and its West African fermented food product, dawadawa. *Ecology of Food and Nutrition* 9: 123–132.

Caplan, Pat, ed. 1997. *Food, Health, and Identity: Approaches from the Social Sciences.* Routledge, New York.

Carnesecchi, S., Y. Schneider, S. A. Lazarus, D. Coehlo, F. Gosse, and F. Raul. 2002. Flavonols and procyanidins of cocoa and chocolate inhibit growth and polyamine biosynthesis of human colonic cancer. *Cancer Letters* 175(2): 147–155.

Carpenter, Kenneth J. 1986. *The History of Scurvy and Vitamin C.* Cambridge University Press, Cambridge.

Carvalho, Félix. 2003. The toxicological potential of khat. *Journal of Ethnopharmacology* 87(1): 1–2.

CDC (Centers for Disease Control and Prevention). 1995. Differences in maternal mortality among black and white women: United States, 1990. *CDC Morbidity and Mortality Weekly Report* 44: 6–7, 13–14.

Chaaib, F., E. F. Queiroz, K. Ndjoko, D. Diallo, and K. Hostettmann. 2003. Antifungal and antioxidant compounds from the root bark of *Fagara zanthoxyloides. Planta Medica* 69(4): 316–20.

Chandra, S., and E. De Mejia Gonzalez. 2004. Polyphenolic compounds, antioxidant capacity, and quinone reductase activity of an aqueous extract of *Ardisia compressa* in comparison to mate (*Ilex paraguarensis*) and green (*Camellia sinensis*) teas. *Journal of Agricultural and Food Chemistry* 52(11): 3583–3589.

Chang, Jeani, Laurie D. Elam-Evans, Cynthia J. Berg, Joy Herndon, Lisa Flowers, Kristi A. Seed, and Carla J. Syverson. 2003. Pregnancy-related mortality surveillance: United States, 1991–1999. *CDC Morbidity and Mortality Weekly Report* 52(SS02): 1–8.

Chapman, Laurie, T. Johns, and R. L. A. Mahunnah. 1997. Saponin-like in vitro characteristics of extracts from selected non-nutrient wild plant food additives used by Maasai in meat and milk based soups. *Ecology of Food and Nutrition* 36: 1–22.

Cheer, Susan M., John S. Allen, and Judith Huntsman. 2000. Lactose digestion capacity in Tokelauans: a case for the role of gene flow and genetic drift in establishing the lactose absorption allele in a Polynesian population. *American Journal of Physical Anthropology* 113: 119–127.

Chen, Y., S. H. Tseng, H. S. Lai, and W. J. Chen. 2004. Resveratrol-induced cellular apoptosis and cell cycle arrest in neuroblastoma cells and antitumor effects on neuroblastoma in mice. *Surgery* 136(1): 57–66.

Chen, Y. N., and R. D. Akre. 1994. Ants used as food and medicine in China. *Food Insects Newsletter* 7(2): 1–8.

Chen, Y. N., C. C. Cheng, J. C. Chen, W. Tsauer, and S. L. Hsu. 2003. Norcantharidin-induced apoptosis is via the extracellular signal-regulated kinase and c-Jun-NH$_2$-terminal kinase signaling pathways in human hepatoma HepG2 cells. *British Journal of Pharmacology* 140(3): 461–470.

Chen, Z., W. Zheng, L. J. Custer, Q. Dai, X. O. Shu, F. Jin, and A. A. Franke. 1999. Usual dietary consumption of soy foods and its correlation with the excretion rate of isoflavonoids in overnight urine samples among Chinese women in Shanghai. *Nutrition and Cancer* 33: 82–87.

Choi, H.-J., H.-S. Lee, S. Her, D.-H. Oh, and S.-S. Yoon. 1999. Partial characterization and cloning of leuconocin J, a bacteriocin produced by *Leuconostoc* sp. J2 isolated from the Korean fermented vegetable kimchi. *Journal of Applied Microbiology* 86: 175–181.

Choudhary, D., and R. K. Kale. 2002. Antioxidant and non-toxic properties of *Piper betle* leaf extract: in vitro and in vivo studies. *Phytotherapy Research* 16(5): 461–466.

Chu, Nai-Shin. 2001. Effects of betel chewing on the central and autonomic nervous systems. *Journal of Biomedical Science* 8: 229–236.

Chu, Nai-Shin. 2002. Neurological aspects of areca and betel chewing. *Addiction Biology* 7(1): 111–114.

Classen, Constance. 1991. Creation by sound/creation by light: a sensory analysis of two South American cosmologies. In *The Varieties of Sensory Experience*. D. Howes, ed. Pp. 239–255. University of Toronto Press, Toronto.

Clouatre, D. L. 2004. Kava kava: new reports of toxicity. *Toxicology Letters* 150: 85–96.

Clutton-Brock, Juliet. 1992. Domestication of animals. In *The Cambridge Encyclopedia of Human Evolution*. S. Jones, R. Martin, and D. Pilbeam, eds. Pp. 380–385. Cambridge University Press, Cambridge.

Coe, Sophie D. 1997. Cacao: gift of the New World. In *Chocolate: Food of the Gods*. A. Szogyi, ed. Pp. 147–153. Greenwood Press, Westport, Conn.

Coe, Sophie D., and Michael D. Coe. 1996. *The True History of Chocolate*. Thames and Hudson, London.

Combs, Gerald F. 1992. *The Vitamins: Fundamental Aspects in Nutrition and Health*. Academic Press, San Diego, Calif.

Conlon, J. Michael, Agnes Sonnevend, Carlos Davidson, D. David Smith, and Per F. Nielsen. 2004. The ascaphins: a family of antimicrobial peptides from the skin secretions of the most primitive extant frog, *Ascaphus truei*. *Biochemical and Biophysical Research Communications* 320(1): 170–175.

Cooper Marcus, Clare. 2003. Healing havens. *Landscape Architecture* 93(8): 85–91, 107–109.

Cordain, Loren, Janette B. Miller, S. Boyd Eaton, Neil Mann, Susanne H. A. Holt, and John D. Speth. 2000. Plant-animal subsistence ratios and macronutrient energy estimations in worldwide hunter-gatherer diets. *American Journal of Clinical Nutrition* 71: 682–692.

Corsi, L., R. Avallone, F. Cosenza, F. Farina, C. Baraldi, and M. Baraldi. 2002. Antiproliferative effects of *Ceratonia siliqua* L. on mouse hepatocellular carcinoma cell line. *Fitoterapia* 73(708): 674–684.

Costa-Neto, Eraldo M. 1998. Folk taxonomy and cultural significance of "abeia" (Insecta, Hymenoptera) to the Pankararé, northeastern Bahia State, Brazil. *Journal of Ethnopharmacology* 18(1): 1–13.

Costa-Neto, Eraldo M., and José G. W. Marques. 2000. Faunistic resources used as medicines by artisanal fishermen from Siribinha Beach, State of Bahia, Brazil. *Journal of Ethnobiology* 20(1): 93–109.

Cotton, C. M. 1996. *Ethnobotany: Principles and Applications*. Wiley, New York.

Counihan, Carole M. 1999. *The Anthropology of Food and Body: Gender, Meaning, and Power*. Routledge, New York.

Counihan, Carole, and Penny van Esterik, eds. 1997. *Food and Culture: A Reader*. Routledge, New York.

CSPI (Center for Science in the Public Interest). 1997. Caffeine content of foods and drugs. http://www.scpinet.org/new/cafchart.htm, 21 May 2004.

Cuddy, M. L. 2004. Common drugs of abuse. Part II. *Journal of Practical Nursing* 54(1): 5–8, 25–31.

Cunningham, Anthony B. 2001. *Applied Ethnobotany: People, Wild Plant Use, and Conservation*. Earthscan Publications, London.

Daels-Rakotoarison, Dominique, Gisèle Kouakou, Bernard Gressier, Thierry Dine, Claude Brunet, Michel Luyckx, François Bailleul, and Francis Trotin. 2003. Effects of a caffeine-free *Cola nitida* nut extract on elastase/alpha-1-proteinase inhibitor balance. *Journal of Ethnopharmacology* 89: 143–150.

Daglia, M., M. Racchi, A. Papetti, C. Lanni, S. Govoni, and G. Gazzani. 2004. In vitro and ex vivo antihydroxyl radical activity of green and roasted coffee. *Journal of Agricultural and Food Chemistry* 52(6): 1700–1704.

Dalby, Andrew. 2000. *Dangerous Tastes: The Story of Spices*. University of California Press, Berkeley.

Dalby, Andrew. 2003. Stimulants. In *The Encyclopedia of Food and Culture*. S. H. Katz, ed. Pp. 344–348. Charles Scribner's Sons, New York.

Darrah, Alan C. 1980. A Hermeneutic Approach to Hausa Therapeutics: The Allegory of the Living Fire. Ph.D. diss., Department of Anthropology, Northwestern University.

Davidson, Alan. 1999. *The Oxford Companion to Food*. Oxford University Press, Oxford.

Davis, Wade. 1988. *Passage of Darkness: The Ethnobiology of the Haitian Zombie*. University of North Carolina Press, Chapel Hill.

de Castro, S. L., and K. O. Higashi. 1995. Effect of different formulations of propolis on mice infected with *Trypanosoma cruzi*. *Journal of Ethnopharmacology* 46: 55–58.

Dedoussis, G. V., A. C. Kaliora, S. Psarras, A. Chiou, A. Mylona, N. G. Papadopoulos, and

N. K. Andrikopoulos. 2004. Antiatherogenic effect of *Pistacia lentiscus* via GSH restoration and downregulation of CD36 mRNA expression. *Atherosclerosis* 174(2): 293–303.

DeFelice, Stephen L. 1998. Preface. In *Nutraceuticals: Developing, Claiming, and Marketing Medical Foods*. S. L. DeFelice, ed. Pp. v–viii. Marcel Dekker, New York.

DeFoliart, Gene R. 1997. An overview of the role of edible insects in preserving biodiversity. *Ecology of Food and Nutrition* 36(2–4): 109–132.

DeFoliart, Gene R. 1999. Insects as food: why the Western attitude is important. *Annual Review of Entomology* 44: 21–50.

DeFoliart, Gene R. 2004. *The Human Use of Insects as a Food Resource*. http://www.food-insects.com/book, 21 August.

de Miranda, C. M., C. W. van Wyk, P. Van der Biji, and N. J. Basson. 1996. The effect of areca nut on salivary and selected oral microorganisms. *International Dental Journal* 46(4): 350–356.

Denham, Alison, Michael McIntyre, and Julie Whitehouse. 2002. Kava—the unfolding story: report on a work-in-progress. *Journal of Alternative and Complementary Medicine* 8(3): 237–263.

de Vrese, Michael, Anna Stegelmann, Bernd Richter, Susanne Fenselau, Christiane Laue, and Jürgen Schrezenmeir. 2001. Probiotics: compensation for lactase insufficiency. *American Journal of Clinical Nutrition* 73(2): 421S–429S.

Dewitt, Dave. 1999. *The Chile Pepper Encyclopedia*. William Morrow, New York.

Dewitt, Dave, and Paul W. Bosland. 1995. *The Pepper Garden*. Ten Speed Press, Berkeley, Calif.

Diaz, A. M., M. J. Abad, L. Fernandez, C. Recuero, L. Villaescusa, A. M. Silvan, and P. Bermejo. 2000. In vitro anti-inflammatory activity of iridoids and triterpenoid compounds isolated from *Phillyrea latifolia* L. *Biological Pharmacology Bulletin* 23: 1307–1313.

Dillinger, Teresa L., Patricia Barriga, Sylvia Escárcega, Martha Jimenez, Diana Salazar Lowe, and Louis E. Grivetti. 2000. Food of the gods: Cure for humanity? A cultural history of the medicinal and ritual use of chocolate. *Journal of Nutrition* 130: 2057S–2072S.

Dirar, Haid A. 1993. *Indigenous Fermented Foods of the Sudan: A Study in African Food and Nutrition*. CAB International, Wallingford, England.

di Tomaso, E., M. Beltramo, and D. Piomelli. 1996. Brain cannabinoids in chocolate. *Nature* 382: 677–678.

Dixon, Bernard. 1978. *Beyond the Magic Bullet*. Harper and Row, New York.

D'Ovidio, R., A. Taiola, C. Capodicasa, A. Devoto, D. Pontiggia, S. Roberti, R. Galletti, E. Conti, D. O'Sullivan, and G. De Lorenzo. 2004. Characterization of the complex locus of bean encoding polygalacturonase-inhibiting proteins reveals subfunctionalization for defense against fungi and insects. *Plant Physiology* 135(4): 2424–2435.

Dragull, K., W. Y. Yoshida, and C.-S. Tang. 2003. Piperidine alkaloids from *Piper methysticum*. *Phytochemistry* 63: 193–198.

Drewnowski, Adam, Susan A. Henderson, and Anne Barratt-Fornell. 2001. Genetic taste markers and food preferences. *Drug Metabolism and Disposition* 29: 535–538.

DuBois, Grant E. 2004. Unraveling the biochemistry of sweet and umami tastes. *Proceedings of the National Academy of Sciences USA* 101(39): 13972–13973.

Dubos, René. 1980. *Man Adapting.* Enlarged ed. Yale University Press, New Haven, Conn.

Duke, James A. 1985. *Handbook of Medicinal Herbs.* CRC Press, Boca Raton, Fla.

Dumbacher, John P., Bruce M. Beehler, Thomas F. Spande, H. Martin Garraffo, and John W. Daly. 1992. Homobatrachotoxin in the genus *Pitohui*: Chemical defense in birds? *Science* 258: 799–801.

Dunkel, F. 1998. Information on the efficiency of traditional livestock and minilivestock. *Food Insects Newsletter* 11(1): 9.

Duru, M. E., A. Cakir, S. Kordali, H. Zengin, M. Harmandar, S. Izumi, and T. Hirat. 2003. Chemical composition and antifungal properties of essential oils of three *Pistacia* species. *Fitoterapia* 74(1/2): 170–176.

Dyer, L. A., C. D. Dodson, J. Beihoffer, and D. K. Letourneau. 2001. Trade-offs in antiherbivore defenses in *Piper cenocladum*: ant mutualists versus plant secondary metabolites. *Journal of Chemical Ecology* 27(3): 581–592.

Earnshaw, Richard G. 1992. Natural food preservation systems. In *The Lactic Acid Bacteria in Health and Disease.* B. J. B. Wood, ed. Pp. 211–232. Elsevier Science, Essex, England.

Eaton, S. B., S. B. Eaton III, and M. J. Konner. 1997. Paleolithic nutrition revisited: a twelve-year retrospective on its nature and implications. *European Journal of Clinical Nutrition* 51: 207–216.

Ehrlich, Paul R., and Peter H. Raven. 1964. Butterflies and plants: a study in coevolution. *Evolution* 18: 586–608.

Eisenberg, David M., Ronald C. Kessler, Maria I. Van Rompay, Ted J. Kaptchuk, Sonja Wilkey, Scott Appel, and Roger B. Davis. 2000. Perceptions about complementary therapies relative to conventional therapies among adults who use both: results from a national survey. *Annals of Internal Medicine* 135(5): 344–351.

Eka, O. U. 1980. Effect of fermentation on the nutrient status of locust beans. *Food Chemistry* 5: 303–308.

Elisabetsky, Elaine, and Nina L. Etkin, eds. 2005. UNESCO On-line Encyclopedia: Global Sustainable Development, Water, Energy, Environment, Food and Agriculture, Knowledge Foundations. UNESCO/EOLSS, Oxford. http://www.eolss.net.

Emch-Dériaz, Antoinette. 1992. The non-naturals made easy. In *The Popularization of Medicine, 1650–1850.* R. Potter, ed. Pp. 134–159. Routledge, New York.

English, H. K., A. R. Pack, and P. C. Molan. 2004. The effects of manuka honey on plaque and gingivitis: a pilot study. *Journal of the International Academy of Periodontology* 6(2): 63–67.

Erhardt, H., S. Fulda, M. Fuhrer, K. M. Debatin, and L. Jeremias. 2004. Betulinic acid-induced apoptosis in leukemia cells. *Leukemia* 18(8): 1406–1412.

Ernst, E. 2000. Prevalence of use of complementary/alternative medicine: a systematic review. *Bulletin of the World Health Organization* 78(2): 252–257.

Estes, J. Worth. 1996. The medical properties of food in the eighteenth century. *Journal of the History of Medicine and Allied Sciences* 51: 127–154.

Estes, J. Worth, and David M. Goodman. 1986. *The Changing Humors of Portsmouth: The Medical Biography of an American Town, 1623–1983*. Francis A. Countway Library of Medicine, Boston.

Etkin, Nina L., ed. 1986. *Plants in Indigenous Medicine and Diet: Biobehavioral Approaches*. Taylor and Francis (Redgrave), New York.

Etkin, Nina L. 1988. Cultural constructions of efficacy. In *The Context of Medicines in Developing Countries*. S. van der Geest and S. R. Whyte, eds. Pp. 299–326. Kluwer Publishers, Dordrecht, The Netherlands.

Etkin, Nina L. 1994a. The cull of the wild. In *Eating on the Wild Side: The Pharmacologic, Ecologic, and Social Implications of Using Noncultigens*. N. L. Etkin, ed. Pp. 1–21. University of Arizona Press, Tucson.

Etkin, Nina L., ed. 1994b. *Eating on the Wild Side: The Pharmacologic, Ecologic, and Social Implications of Using Noncultigens*. University of Arizona Press, Tucson.

Etkin, Nina L. 1994c. The negotiation of "side" effects in Hausa (northern Nigeria) therapeutics. In *Medicines: Meanings and Contexts*. N. L. Etkin and M. L. Tan, eds. Pp. 17–32. Medical Anthropology Unit, University of Amsterdam, Amsterdam.

Etkin, Nina L. 1994d. Consuming a therapeutic landscape: a multicontextual framework for assessing the health significance of human-plant interactions. *Journal of Home and Consumer Horticulture* 1(2/3): 61–81.

Etkin, Nina L. 1996a. Medicinal cuisines: diet and ethnopharmacology. *International Journal of Pharmacognosy* 34(5): 313–326.

Etkin, Nina L. 1996b. Ethnopharmacology: the conjunction of medical ethnography and the biology of therapeutic action. In *Medical Anthropology: Contemporary Theory and Method*. Rev. ed. C. F. Sargent and T. M. Johnson, eds. Pp. 151–164. Praeger, New York.

Etkin, Nina L. 2001. Perspectives in ethnopharmacology: forging a closer link between bioscience and traditional empirical knowledge. *Journal of Ethnopharmacology* 76: 177–182.

Etkin, Nina L. 2004. Polypharmacy, complementary and alternative medicines (CAM), and cancer. *Hawai'i Medical Journal* 63: 349–350.

Etkin, Nina L., and Timothy Johns. 1998. "Pharmafoods" and "nutraceuticals": paradigm shifts in biotherapeutics. In *Plants for Food and Medicine*. H. D. V. Prendergast, N. L. Etkin, D. R. Harris, and P. J. Houghton, eds. Pp. 3–16. Royal Botanic Gardens, Kew, England.

Etkin, Nina L., and Heather L. McMillen. 2003. The ethnobotany of noni (*Morinda citrifolia* L., Rubiaceae): dwelling in the land between la'au lapa'au and testiNONIals. In *Proceedings of the 2002 Hawai'i Noni Conference*. S. C. Nelson, ed. Pp. 11–16. College of Tropical Agriculture and Human Resources, University of Hawai'i, Honolulu.

Etkin, Nina L., and Paul J. Ross. 1982. Food as medicine and medicine as food: an adaptive framework for the interpretation of plant utilization among the Hausa of northern Nigeria. *Social Science and Medicine* 16: 1559–1573.

Etkin, Nina L., and Paul J. Ross. 1994. Pharmacologic implications of "wild" plants in Hausa diet. In *Eating on the Wild Side: The Pharmacologic, Ecologic, and Social*

Implications of Using Noncultigens. N. L. Etkin, ed. Pp. 85–101. University of Arizona Press, Tucson.

Etkin, Nina L., and Paul J. Ross. 1997. Malaria, medicine, and meals: a biobehavioral perspective. In *The Anthropology of Medicine.* 3rd ed. L. Romanucci-Ross, D. E. Moerman, and L. R. Tancredi, eds. Pp. 169–209. Praeger, New York.

Etkin, Nina L., and Paul J. Ross. 2000. The ethnopharmacology of fermented medicinal foods. In *Proceedings of the International Symposium on Ethnobotany.* R. Chaves, ed. Universidad Para La Paz, San José, Costa Rica. CD-ROM.

Etkin, Nina L., and Paul J. Ross. 2002. Polypharmacy and the elderly cancer patient: rethinking "noncompliance." In *Living in Old Age: The Western World and Modernization.* A. Guerci, and S. Consigliere, eds. Pp. 21–32. Erga Edizioni, Genoa, Italy.

Etkin, Nina L., Anna R. Dixon, Patricia W. Nishimoto, and Paul J. Ross. 1999. Medicinal foods in multiethnic Honolulu, Hawai'i. In *Cultural Food.* A. Guerci, ed. Pp. 12–26. Erga Edizioni, Genoa, Italy.

Fahey, J. W., A. T. Zalcmann, and P. Talalay. 2001. The chemical diversity and distribution of glucosinolates and isothiocyanates among plants. *Phytochemistry* 56: 5–51.

Farnworth, Edward R. 1999. Kefir: from folklore to regulatory approval. *Journal of Nutraceuticals, Functional and Medical Foods* 1: 57–68.

Farnworth, Edward R., ed. 2003. *Handbook of Fermented Functional Foods.* CRC Press, Boca Raton, Fla.

Farquhar, Judith. 2002. *Appetites: Food and Sex in Post-Socialist China.* Duke University Press, Durham, N.C.

Farrington, I. S., and James Urry. 1985. Food and the early history of cultivation. *Journal of Ethnobiology* 5(2): 143–157.

Fedigan, Linda M. 1991. History of the Arashiyama west Japanese macaques in Texas. In *The Monkeys of Arashiyama: Thirty-Five Years of Research in Japan and the West.* L. M. Fedigan and P. J. Asquith, eds. Pp. 54–73. State University of New York Press, Albany.

Feeny, P. 1976. Plant apparency and chemical defence. *Recent Advances in Phytochemistry* 10: 1–40.

Feldman, N., C. Norenberg, H. Boet, E. Manor, Y. Berner, and Z. Madar. 1995. Enrichment of an Israeli ethnic food with fibres and their effects on the glycaemic and insulinaemic responses in subjects with non-insulin-dependent diabetes mellitus. *British Journal of Nutrition* 74(5): 681–688.

Fernandes, Custy F., R. C. Chandan, and K. M. Shahani. 1992. Fermented dairy products and health. In *The Lactic Acid Bacteria in Health and Disease.* B. J. B. Wood, ed. Pp. 297–339. Elsevier Science, Essex, England.

FIN. 2004. *Food Insects Newsletter.* http://www.food-insects.com.

Fissell, Mary E. 1992. Readers, texts, and contexts: vernacular medical works in early modern England. In *The Popularization of Medicine, 1650–1850.* R. Potter, ed. Pp. 72–96. Routledge, New York.

Fleuret, Anne. 1986. Dietary and therapeutic uses of fruit in three Taita communities. In *Plants in Indigenous Medicine and Diet: Biobehavioral Approaches.* N. L. Etkin, ed. Pp. 151–170. Taylor and Francis (Redgrave), New York.

Fowler, Cynthia T. 1999. The Creolization of Natives and Exotics: The Changing Symbolic and Functional Character of Culture and Agriculture in Kodi, West Sumba (Indonesia). Ph.D. diss., Department of Anthropology, University of Hawai'i.

Fredholm, B. B. 1995. Astra Award lecture: adenosine, adenosine receptors and the actions of caffeine. *Pharmacology and Toxicology* 76(2): 93–101.

Furnham, A. 2000. How the public classify complementary medicine: a factor analytic study. *Complementary Therapies in Medicine* 8: 82–87.

Galal, Ahmed M. 1996. Antimicrobial activity of 6-paradol and related compounds. *International Journal of Pharmacognosy* 34(1): 64–69.

Galdston, Iago. 1943. *Behind the Sulfa Drugs: A Short History of Chemotherapy*. Appleton, New York.

Galdston, Iago. 1954. *The Meaning of Social Medicine*. Harvard University Press, Cambridge, Mass.

Galdston, Iago. 1965. *Medicine in Transition*. University of Chicago Press, Chicago.

Galdston, Iago. 1969. Medicine and culture. In *Medicine and Culture*. F. N. L. Poynter, ed. Pp. 15–25. Wellcome Institute of the History of Medicine, London.

Geraldo, J., W. Marques, and E. M. Costa-Neto. 1997. Insects as folk medicines in the state of Algoas, Brazil. *Food Insects Newsletter* 10(1): 7–8.

Gevitz, Norman. 1992. "But all those authors are foreigners": American literary nationalism and domestic medical guides. In *The Popularization of Medicine, 1650–1850*. R. Potter, ed. Pp. 232–251. Routledge, New York.

Ghalioungul, P. 1979. Fermented beverages in antiquity. In *Fermented Food Beverages in Nutrition*. C. F. Gastineau, W. J. Darby, and T. B. Turner, eds. Pp. 3–19. Academic Press, New York.

Ghanem, K. Z., and L. Hussein. 1999. Calcium bioavailability of selected Egyptian foods with emphasis on the impact of fermentation and germination. *International Journal of Food Science and Nutrition* 50: 351–356.

Ghrairi, T., M. Manai, J. M. Berjeaud, and J. Frere. 2004. Antilisterial activity of lactic acid bacteria isolated from rigouta, a traditional Tunisian cheese. *Journal of Applied Microbiology* 97(3): 621–628.

Giami, S. Y., and I. Isichei. 1999. Preparation and properties of flours and protein concentrates from raw, fermented and germinated fluted pumpkin (*Telfairia occidentalis* Hook) seeds. *Plant Foods and Human Nutrition* 54: 67–77.

Giberti, G. C. 1994. Maté (*Ilex paraguariensis*). In *Neglected Crops: 1492 from a Different Perspective*. J. E. Hernándo Bermejo and J. León, eds. Pp. 245–252. FAO, Rome, Italy.

Gibson, Thomas. 1988. Meat sharing as a political ritual: forms of transaction versus modes of subsistence. In *Hunters and Gatherers*. Vol. 2. *Property, Power, and Ideology*. T. Ingold, D. Riches, and J. Woodburn, eds. Pp. 165–179. Berg, Oxford.

Gidley, M. J. 2004. Naturally functional foods: challenges and opportunities. *Asia Pacific Journal of Clinical Nutrition* 13(Suppl.): 31S.

Giesler, Wilbert M. 1992. Therapeutic landscapes: medical issues in light of the new cultural geography. *Social Science and Medicine* 34(7): 735–746.

Giraud, Eric, Laurent Gosselin, and M. Raimbault. 1993. Production of a *Lactobacillus plantarum* starter with linamarase and amylase activities for cassava fermentation. *Journal of the Science of Food and Agriculture* 62: 77–82.

Glander, Kenneth E. 1994. Nonhuman primate self-medication with wild plant foods. In *Eating on the Wild Side: The Pharmacologic, Ecologic, and Social Implications of Using Noncultigens*. N. L. Etkin, ed. Pp. 227–239. University of Arizona Press, Tucson.

Golden, D. B., A. Kagey-Sobotka, P. S. Norman, R. G. Hamilton, and L. M. Lichtenstein. 2004. Outcomes of allergy to insect stings in children, with and without venom immunotherapy. *New England Journal of Medicine* 351(7): 668–674.

Goldenberg, D., A. Golz, and H. Z. Joachims. 2003. The beverage maté: a risk factor for cancer of the head and neck. *Head and Neck* 25(7): 595–601.

Gollin, Lisa. 2001. The Taste and Smell of Taban Kenyah (Kenyah Medicine): An Exploration of Chemosensory Selection Criteria for Medicinal Plants among the Kenyah Leppo'Ke of East Kalimantan, Borneo, Indonesia. Ph.D. diss., Department of Anthropology, University of Hawai'i.

Gollin, Lisa. 2004. Subtle and profound sensory attributes of medicinal plants among the Kenyah Leppo' Ke of East Kalimantan, Borneo. *Journal of Ethnobiology* 24(2): 173–201.

Golomb, Louis. 1985. *An Anthropology of Curing in Multiethnic Thailand*. University of Illinois Press, Urbana.

Gomes, A., J. R. Vedasiromoni, M. Das, R. M. Sharma, and D. K. Ganguly. 1995. Antihyperglycemic effect of black tea (*Camellia sinensis*) in rat. *Journal of Ethnopharmacology* 45: 223–226.

Gómez, Benigno, Adriana Castro, Christiane Junghans, Lorena R. Montoya, and Francisco J. Villalobos. 2000. Ethnoecology of white grubs (Coleoptera: Melolonthidae) among the Tzeltal Maya of Chiapas. *Journal of Ethnobiology* 20(1): 43–59.

Goodman, Jordan. 1995. Excitantia: how Enlightenment Europe took to soft drugs. In *Consuming Habits*. J. Goodman, P. E. Lovejoy, and A. Sherratt, eds. Pp. 126–147. Routledge, London.

Gorbach, S. I. 1990. Lactic acid bacteria and human health. *Annals of Medicine* 22: 37–41.

Gordon, Rena J., Barbara Cable Nienstedt, and Wilbert M. Gesler. 1998. *Alternative Therapies: Expanding Options in Health Care*. Springer, New York.

Goren-Inbar, N., N. Alperson, M. E. Kislev, O. Simchoni, Y. Melamed, A. Ben-Nun, and E. Werker. 2004. Evidence of hominid control of fire at Gesher Benot Ya'aqov, Israel. *Science* 304(5671): 725–727.

Grami, Bahram. 1998. Gaz of Khunsar: the manna of Persia. *Economic Botany* 52(2): 83–191.

Grant, Mark. 2000. *Galen on Food and Diet*. Routledge, London.

Greatestherbs. 2004. Nature's Sunshine Products Chinese Kidney Activator. http://www.greatestherbsonearth.com, 28 May.

Greenwood, D. 1997. Historical introduction. In *Antibiotic and Chemotherapy: Anti-Infective Agents and Their Use in Therapy*. 7th ed. F. O'Grady, H. P. Lambert, R. G. Finch, and D. Greenwood, eds. Pp. 2–9. Churchill Livingstone, New York.

Grivetti, Louis, and Britta M. Ogle. 2000. Value of traditional foods in meeting macro-

and micronutrient needs: the wild plant connection. *Nutrition Research Reviews* 13(1): 31–46.

Groark, Kevin P. 2001. Taxonomic identity of "hallucinogenic" harvester ant (*Pogonomyrmex californicus*) confirmed. *Journal of Ethnobiology* 21(2): 133–144.

Guerra, F. 1966. Drugs from the Indies and the political economy of the sixteenth century. In *Materia Medica of the XVIth Century*. M. Florkin, ed. Pp. 29–30. Permagon, Oxford.

Gundaker, Grey. 1994. African-American history, cosmology, and the moral universe of Edward Houston's yard. *Journal of Garden History* 14(4): 179–205.

Guthrie, Helen A., and Robin S. Bagby. 1989. *Introductory Nutrition*. Mosby, St. Louis, Mo.

Gyamfi, M. A., N. Hokama, K. Oppong-Boachie, and Y. Aniya. 2000. Inhibitory effects of the medicinal herb, *Thonningia sanguinea*, on liver drug metabolizing enzymes of rats. *Human Experimental Toxicology* 19(11): 623–631.

Hadley, Mac E. 1992. *Endocrinology*. 3rd ed. Prentice Hall, Englewood Cliffs, N.J.

Halder, J., and A. N. Bhaduri. 1998. Protective role of black tea against oxidative damage of human red blood cells. *Biochemical and Biophysical Research Communications* 244(3): 903–907.

Hambidge, K. Michael, John W. Huffer, Victor Raboy, Gary K. Grunwald, Jamie L. Westcott, Lei Sian, Leland V. Miller, John A. Dorsch, and Nancy F. Krebs. 2004. Zinc absorption from low-phytate hybrids of maize and their wild-type isohybrids. *American Journal of Clinical Nutrition* 79(6): 1053–1059.

Hammerschmidt, Ray, and Jack C. Schultz. 1996. Multiple defenses and signals in plant defense against pathogens and herbivores. In *Phytochemical Diversity and Redundancy in Ecological Interactions*. J. T. Romeo, J. A. Saunders, and P. Barbosa, eds. Pp. 121–154. Plenum Press, New York.

Hannum, S. M., H. H. Schmitz, and C. L. Keen. 2002. Chocolate: a heart-healthy food? Show me the science. *Nutrition Today* 37: 103–109.

Harborne, Jeffrey B. 1993. *Introduction to Ecological Biochemistry*. 4th ed. Academic Press, London.

Harborne, J. B., and C. A. Williams. 2000. Advances in flavonoid research. *Phytochemistry* 55: 481–504.

Harley, David N. 1993. Medical metaphors in English moral theology, 1560–1660. *Journal of the History of Medicine and Allied Sciences* 48: 396–435.

Harris, David R. 1989. An evolutionary continuum of people-plant interaction. In *Foraging and Farming: The Evolution of Plant Exploitation*. D. R. Harris and G. C. Hillman, eds. Pp. 11–26. Unwin Hyman, London.

Harris, Linda J. 1998. The microbiology of vegetable fermentations. In *Microbiology of Fermented Foods*. 2nd ed. B. J. B. Wood, ed. Pp. 45–72. Blackie Academic, London.

Hasler, C. M., A. S. Bloch, C. A. Thomson, E. Enrione, and C. Manning. 2004. Position of the American Dietetic Association: functional foods. *Journal of the American Dietetic Association* 104(5): 814–826.

Hauser, A. C., M. Lorenz, and G. Sunder-Plassmann. 2004. The expanding clinical spectrum of Anderson-Fabry disease: a challenge to diagnosis in the novel era of enzyme replacement therapy. *Journal of Internal Medicine* 255(6): 629–636.

Heasman, Michael, and Julian Mellentin. 2001. *The Functional Foods Revolution: Healthy People, Healthy Profits?* Earthscan Publications, London.

Hegarty, Verona M., Helen M. May, and Kay-Tee Khaw. 2000. Tea drinking and bone mineral density in older women. *American Journal of Clinical Nutrition* 71(4): 1003–1007.

Hepner, G., R. Fried, S. St. Jeor, L. Fusetti, and R. Morin. 1979. Hypocholesterolemic effect of yogurt and milk. *American Journal of Clinical Nutrition* 32: 19–24.

Himalaya. 2004. Herbal monograph *Areca catechu.* http://www.himalayahealthcare.com, 28 May.

Hirasa, Kenji, and Mitsuo Takemasa. 1998. *Spice Science and Technology.* Marcel Dekker, New York.

Hladik, C. M., and B. Simmen. 1996. Taste perception and feeding behavior in nonhuman primates and human populations. *Evolutionary Anthropology* 5: 58–71.

Ho, P. T. 1995. The introduction of American food plants into China. *American Anthropologist* 55: 191–201.

Hogberg, L., P. Laurin, K. Falth-Magnusson, C. Grant, E. Grodzinsky, G. Jansson, H. Ascher, L. Browaldh, J. A. Hammersjo, E. Lindberg, U. Myrdal, and L. Stenhammar. 2004. Oats to children with newly diagnosed coeliac disease: a random double blind study. *Gut* 53(5): 649–654.

Hole, Frank. 1992. Origins of agriculture. In *The Cambridge Encyclopedia of Human Evolution.* S. Jones, R. Martin, and D. Pilbeam, eds. Pp. 373–379. Cambridge University Press, Cambridge.

Hollosy, F., G. Meszaros, G. Bokonyi, M. Idei, A. Seprodi, B. Szende, and G. Keri. 2000. Cytostatic, cytotoxic and protein tyrosine kinase inhibitory activity of ursolic acid in A431 human tumor cells. *Anticancer Research* 20: 4563–4570.

Hosoda, M., H. Hashimoto, F. He, H. Morita, and A. Hosono. 1996. Effect of administration of fecal mutagenicity and microflora in the human intestine. *Journal of Dairy Science* 69: 2237–2242.

Hosono, Akiyoshi (B. W. Howells, trans.). 1992. Fermented milk in the Orient. In *Functions of Fermented Milk: Challenges for the Health Sciences.* Y. Nakazawa and A. Hosono, eds. Pp. 61–78. Elsevier Science, Essex, England.

Hou, W. C., R. D. Lin, K. T. Cheng, Y. T. Hung, C. H. Cho, C. H. Chen, S. Y. Hwang, and M. H. Lee. 2003. Free radical-scavenging activity of Taiwanese native plants. *Phytomedicine* 10(2/3): 170–175.

Howe, Henry F., and Lynn C. Westley. 1988. *Ecological Relationships of Plants and Animals.* Oxford University Press, New York.

Howes, David, ed. 1996. *Cross-Cultural Consumption: Global Markets, Local Realities.* Routledge, New York.

Hudson, Robert P. 1992. Abraham Flexner in historical perspective. In *Beyond Flexner: Medical Education in the Twentieth Century.* B. Brazansky and N. Gevitz, eds. Pp. 1–18. Greenwood, Westport, Conn.

Huffman, Michael A. 1997. Current evidence for self-medication in primates: a multidisciplinary perspective. *Yearbook of Physical Anthropology* 49: 171–200.

Huffman, Michael A. 2001. Self-medicative behavior in the African great apes: an evolutionary perspective into the origins of human traditional medicine. *BioScience* 51(8): 651–661.

Huffman, Michael A. 2003. Animal self-medication and ethno-medicine: exploration and exploitation of the medicinal properties of plants. *Proceedings of the Nutrition Society* 62: 371–381.

Huffman, Michael A., and Satoshi Hirata. 2004. An experimental study of leaf swallowing in captive chimpanzees: insights into the origin of a self-medicative behavior and the role of social learning. *Primates* 45(2): 113–118.

Husein, M. Q., and R. T. Kridli. 2002. Reproductive responses following royal jelly treatment administered orally or intramuscularly into progesterone-treated Awassi ewes. *Animal Reproduction Science* 74(1): 45–53.

Ikenebomeh, Marcel J., Robert Kok, and Jordan M. Ingram. 1986. Processing and fermentation of the African locust bean (*Parkia filicoidea* Welw) to produce dawadawa. *Journal of the Science of Food and Agriculture* 37: 273–282.

Inglis, Brian. 1965. *A History of Medicine*. World Publishing Company, Cleveland, Ohio.

Isla, M. I., M. I. Nieva Moreno, A. R. Sampietro, and M. A. Vattuone. 2001. Antioxidant activity of Argentine propolis extracts. *Journal of Ethnopharmacology* 76: 165–170.

Isolauri, E., M. Juntunen, T. Rautanen, P. Sillanaukee, and T. Koivula. 1991. A human *Lactobacillus* strain (*Lactobacillus casei* sp. strain GG) promotes recovery from acute diarrhea in children. *Pediatrics* 88: 90–97.

Ito, H., E. Kobayashi, S. H. Li, T. Hatano, D. Sugita, N. Kubo, S. Shimura, Y. Itoh, H. Tokuda, H. Nishino, and T. Yoshida. 2002. Antitumor activity of compounds isolated from leaves of *Eriobotrya japonica*. *Journal of Agricultural and Food Chemistry* 50(8): 2400–2403.

Ivanovska, N. D., V. B. Dimov, V. S. Bankova, and S. S. Popov. 1995. Immunomodulatory action of propolis. VI. Influence of a water-soluble derivative on complement activity in vivo. *Journal of Ethnopharmacology* 47: 145–147.

Iwuoha, C. I., and O. S. Eke. 1996. Nigerian indigenous fermented foods: their traditional process operation, inherent problems, improvements and current status. *Food Research International* 29: 527–540.

Jahovic, Nermina, Esra Güzel, Serap Arbak, and Berrak Ç. Yeğen. 2004. The healing-promoting effect of saliva on skin burn is mediated by epidermal growth factor (EGF): role of the neutrophils. *Burns* 30(6): 531–538.

James, Steven R. 1989. Hominid use of fire in the Lower and Middle Pleistocene. *Current Anthropology* 30: 1–26.

Jamuna, M., and K. Jeevaratnam. 2004. Isolation and characterization of lactobacilli from some traditional fermented foods and evaluation of the bacteriocins. *Journal of General and Applied Microbiology* 50(2): 79–90.

Janzen, D. H. 1978. Complications in interpreting the chemical defenses of trees against tropical arboreal plant-eating vertebrates. In *The Ecology of Arboreal Folivores*. G. G. Montgomery, ed. Pp. 73–84. Smithsonian Institution Press, Washington, D.C.

Jardine, Nicholas. 1999. Phytochemicals and phenolics. In *Chocolate and Cocoa: Health and Nutrition*. I. Knight, ed. Pp. 119–142. Blackwell Science, Oxford.

Jarvis, Bruce B., and J. David Miller. 1996. Natural products, complexity, and evolution. In *Phytochemical Diversity and Redundancy in Ecological Interactions*. J. T. Romeo, J. A. Saunders, and P. Barbosa, eds. Pp. 265–293. Plenum Press, New York.

Jeng, J. H., Y. J. Wang, W. H. Chang, H. L. Wu, C. H. Li, B. J. Uang, J. J. Kang, J. J. Lee, L. J. Hahn, B. R. Lin, and M. C. Chang. 2004. Reactive oxygen species are crucial for hydroxychavicol toxicity toward KB epithelial cells. *Cellular and Molecular Life Sciences* 61(1): 83–96.

Johns, Timothy. 1996. *The Origins of Human Diet and Medicine*. University of Arizona Press, Tucson.

Johns, Timothy, and Laurie Chapman. 1995. Phytochemicals ingested in traditional diets and medicines as modulators of energy metabolism. In *Phytochemistry of Medicinal Plants*. J. T. Arnason, R. Mata, and J. T. Romeo, eds. Pp. 161–188. Plenum Press, New York.

Johns, Timothy, and Isao Kubo. 1988. A survey of traditional methods employed for the detoxification of plant foods. *Journal of Ethnobiology* 8: 81–129.

Johns, T., R. L. A. Mahunnah, P. Sanaya, L. Chapman, and T. Ticktin. 1999. Saponins and phenolic content in plant dietary additives of a traditional subsistence community, the Batemi of Ngorongoro District, Tanzania. *Journal of Ethnopharmacology* 66: 1–10.

Johns, Timothy, Mythili Nagarajan, Moringe L. Parkipuny, and Peter J. H. Jones. 2000. Maasai gummivory: implications for paleolithic diets and contemporary health. *Current Anthropology* 41(3): 454–459.

Johnson, N., and L. E. Grivetti. 2002. Gathering practices of Karen women: questionable contribution to beta-carotene intake. *International Journal of Food Science and Nutrition* 53(6): 489–501.

Johri, R. K., and U. Zutshi. 1992. An Ayurvedic formulation: 'trikatu' and its constituents. *Journal of Ethnopharmacology* 37: 85–91.

Kagy, Valérie, and Françoise Carreel. 2004. Bananas in New Caledonian Kanak society: their sociocultural value in relation with their origins. *Ethnobotany Research and Applications* 2: 29–35.

Kaltwasser, J. P., E. Werner, K. Schalk, C. Hansen, R. Gottschalk, and C. Seidl. 1998. Clinical trial on the effect of regular tea drinking on iron accumulation in genetic haemochromatosis. *Gut* 43: 699–704.

Kamath, Arati B., Lisheng Wang, Hiranmoy Das, Lin Li, Vernon N. Reinhold, and Jack F. Bukowski. 2003. Antigens in tea-beverage prime human V gamma 2V delta 2T cells in vitro and in vivo for memory and nonmemory antibacterial cytokine responses. *Proceedings of the National Academy of Sciences USA* 100(10): 6009–6014.

Kaptchuk, Ted J., and David M. Eisenberg. 2001. Varieties of healing. 2. A taxonomy of unconventional healing practices. *Annals of Internal Medicine* 135(3): 196–204.

Karan, R. S., V. K. Bhargava, and S. K. Garg. 1999. Effect of trikatu, an Ayurvedic prescription, on the pharmacokinetic profile of rifampicin in rabbits. *Journal of Ethnopharmacology* 64: 259–264.

Kartal, Murat, Sulhiyi Yildiz, Serdar Kaya, Semra Kurucu, and Gülaçti Topçu. 2003. Antimicrobial activity of propolis samples from two different regions of Anatolia. *Journal of Ethnopharmacology* 86: 69–73.

Kashiwada, Y., T. Nagao, A. Hashimoto, Y. Ikeshiro, H. Okabe, L. M. Cosentino, and K. H. Lee. 2000. Anti-AIDS agents. 38. Anti-HIV activity of 3-O-acyl ursolic acid derivatives. *Journal of Natural Products* 63: 1619–1622.

Katz, Solomon H., and Mary M. Voigt. 1986. Bread and beer: the early uses of cereals in the human diet. *Expedition* 28(2): 23–34.

Kavanagh, Thomas W. 1994. Archaeological parameters for the beginnings of beer. http://www.brewingtechniques.com, 15 July 2004.

Kawakami, M., and A. Kobayashi. 1991. Volatile constituents of green mate and roasted mate. *Journal of Agricultural and Food Chemistry* 39: 1275–1277.

Kawase, M., H. Hashimoto, M. Hosoda, H. Morita, and A. Hosono. 2000. Effect of administration of fermented milk containing whey protein concentrate to rats and healthy men on serum lipids and blood pressure. *Journal of Dairy Science* 83: 255–263.

Kealey, Edward J. 1981. *Medieval Medicus*. Johns Hopkins University Press, Baltimore, Md.

Keen, Carl L. 2001. Chocolate: food as medicine/medicine as food. *Journal of the American College of Nutrition* 20: 436S–439S.

Kennedy, John G. 1987. *The Flower of Paradise: The Institutionalized Use of the Drug Qat in North Yemen*. Reidel, Dordrecht, The Netherlands.

Kent, Susan, ed. 1996. *Cultural Diversity among Twentieth-Century Foragers: An African Perspective*. Cambridge University Press, New York.

Kerridge, I. H., and M. Lowe. 1995. Bloodletting: the story of a therapeutic technique. *Medical Journal of Australia* 163: 631–633.

Khayyal, M. T., M. A. el-Ghazaly, A. S. el-Khatib, A. M. Hatem, P. J. de Vries, S. el-Shafei, and M. M. Khattab. 2003. A clinical pharmacological study of the potential beneficial effects of a propolis food product as an adjuvant in asthmatic patients. *Fundamental and Clinical Pharmacology* 17(1): 93–102.

Kiba, A., H. Saitoh, M. Nishihara, K. Omiya, and S. Yamamura. 2003. C-terminal domain of a hevein-like protein from *Wasabia japonica* has potent antimicrobial activity. *Plant and Cell Physiology* 44(3): 296–303.

Kimoto, H., K. Mizumachi, T. Okamoto, and J. Kurisaki. 2004. New lactococcus strain with immunomodulatory activity: enhancement of Th1-type immune response. *Microbiology and Immunology* 48(2): 75–82.

Kirch, Patrick V. 2000. *On the Road of the Winds: An Archaeological History of the Pacific Islands before European Contact*. University of California Press, Berkeley.

Kirkman, L. M., J. W. Lampe, D. R. Campbell, M. C. Martini, and J. L. Slavin. 1995. Urinary lignan and isoflavonoid excretion in men and women consuming vegetable and soy diets. *Nutrition and Cancer* 24: 1–12.

Kivçak, Bijen, Tuba Mert, and H. Tansel Öztürk. 2002. Antimicrobial and cytotoxic activities of *Ceratonia siliqua* L. extracts. *Turkish Journal of Biology* 26: 197–200.

Kizilay, A., M. T. Kalcioglu, E. Ozerol, M. Iraz, M. Gulec, O. Akyol, and O. Ozturan. 2004. Caffeic acid phenethyl ester ameliorated ototoxicity induced by cisplatin in rats. *Journal of Chemotherapy* 16(4): 381–387.

Koehler, P. G., and F. M. Oi. 2003. Stinging or venomous insects and related pests. Florida Cooperative Extension Service, Institute of Food and Agricultural Sciences, University of Florida. http://edis.ifas.ufl.edu, 23 August 2004.

Koh, Hwee-Ling, Hsiao-Huei Teo, and Hui-Ling Ng. 2003. Pharmacists' patterns of use, knowledge, and attitudes toward complementary and alternative medicine. *Journal of Alternative and Complementary Medicine* 9(1): 51–63.

Konoshima, Haruo. 1994. The first community garden in Japan. *Japanese Journal of Agricultural Education* 25(2): 101–108.

Kordali, S., A. Cakir, H. Zengin, and M. E. Duru. 2003. Antifungal activities of the leaves of three *Pistacia* species grown in Turkey. *Fitoterapia* 74(1/2): 164–167.

Kretchmer, Norman. 1972. Lactose and lactase. *Scientific American* 227(4): 70–78.

Kris-Etherton, P. M., and C. L. Keen. 2002. Evidence that the antioxidant flavonoids in tea and cocoa are beneficial for cardiovascular health. *Current Opinion in Lipidology* 13(1): 41–49.

Kritchevsky, David. 1999. Cocoa butter and constituent fatty acids. In *Chocolate and Cocoa: Health and Nutrition*. I. Knight, ed. Pp. 79–88. Blackwell Science, Oxford.

Kumazawa, S., M. Taniguchi, Y. Suzuki, M. Shimura, M. S. Kwon, and T. Nakayama. 2002. Antioxidant activity of polyphenols in carob plants. *Journal of Agricultural and Food Chemistry* 50(2): 373–377.

Kurlansky, Mark. 2002. *Salt: A World History*. Walker and Company, New York.

Kurzer, Mindy S. 2000. Hormonal effects of soy isoflavones: studies in premenopausal and postmenopausal women. *Journal of Nutrition* 130: 660S–661S.

Kutalek, Ruth, and Afework Kassa. 2005. The use of gyrinids and dytiscids for stimulating breast growth in East Africa. *Journal of Ethnobiology* 25(1): 115–128.

Kwon, Y. S., W. G. Choi, W. J. Kim, W. K. Kim, M. J. Kim, W. H. Kang, and C. M. Kim. 2002. Antimicrobial constituents of *Foeniculum vulgare*. *Archives of Pharmacal Research* 25(2): 154–157.

Labuza, Theodore P. 1994. Foreword. In *Functional Foods: Designer Foods, Pharmafoods, Nutraceuticals*. I. Goldberg, ed. Pp. xi–xiii. Chapman and Hall, New York.

Lamartiniere, Coral A. 2000. Protection against breast cancer with genistein: a component of soy. *American Journal of Clinical Nutrition* 71: 1705S–1707S.

Langenheim, Jean H. 2003. *Plant Resins: Chemistry, Evolution, Ecology, and Ethnobotany*. Timber Press, Portland, Ore.

Lans, Cheryl. 2001. Creole Remedies: Case Studies of Ethnoveterinary Medicine in Trinidad and Tobago. Ph.D. diss., Group Technology and Agrarian Development, Wageningen University, The Netherlands.

Laszlo, Pierre (Mary Beth Mader, trans.). 2001. *Salt: Grain of Life*. Columbia University Press, New York.

Lawless, Harry T., and Hildegarde Heymann. 1999. *Sensory Evaluation of Food: Principles and Practices*. Aspen Publishers, Gaithersburg, Md.

Lawrence, Christopher. 1992. Democratic, divine, and heroic: the history and historiography of surgery. In *Medical Theory, Surgical Practice: Studies in the History of Surgery.* C. Lawrence, ed. Pp. 1–47. Routledge, New York.

Lebot, Vincent, Mark Merlin, and Lamont Lindstrom. 1992. *Kava: The Pacific Drug.* Yale University Press, New Haven, Conn.

Lebot, Vincent, Mark Merlin, and Lamont Lindstrom. 1997. *Kava: The Pacific Elixir.* Healing Arts Press, Rochester, Vt.

Lebot, Vincent, Ed Johnston, Qun Yi Zheng, Doug McKern, and Dennis J. McKenna. 1999. Morphological, phytochemical, and genetic variation in Hawaiian cultivars of ʻawa (kava, *Piper methysticum,* Piperaceae). *Economic Botany* 53(4): 407–418.

Lee, J. D., S. Y. Kim, T. W. Kim, S. H. Lee, H. I. Yang, D. I. Lee, and Y. H. Lee. 2004. Anti-inflammatory effect of bee venom on type II collagen-induced arthritis. *American Journal of Chinese Medicine* 32(3): 361–367.

Lei, D., C. P. Chan, Y. J. Wang, T. M. Wang, B. R. Lin, C. H. Huang, J. J. Lee, H. M. Chen, H. J. Jeng, and M. C. Chang. 2003. Antioxidative and antiplatelet effects of aqueous inflorescence of *Piper betle* extract. *Journal of Agricultural and Food Chemistry* 51(7): 2083–2088.

Lei, V., W. K. Amoa-Awua, and L. Brimer. 1999. Degradation of cyanogenic glycosides by *Lactobacillus plantarum* strains from spontaneous cassava fermentation and other microorganisms. *International Journal of Food Microbiology* 53: 169–184.

Leonti, Marco, Otto Sticher, and Michael Heinrich. 2002. Medicinal plants of Popoluca, México: organoleptic properties as indigenous selection criteria. *Journal of Ethnopharmacology* 81: 307–315.

Lev, Efraim. 2003. Traditional healing with animals (zootherapy): medieval to present-day Levantine practice. *Journal of Ethnopharmacology* 85: 107–118.

Levey, Martin. 1973. *Early Arabic Pharmacology.* E. J. Brill, Leiden, The Netherlands.

Levine, Edwin B., ed. 1971. *Hippocrates.* Twayne Publishers, New York.

Lewis, Penny, ed. 2002. *Integrative Holistic Health, Healing, and Transformation: A Guide for Practitioners, Consultants, and Administrators.* Charles C. Thomas, Springfield, Ill.

Li, Changling, Yan Zhu, Yinye Wnat, Jia-Shi Zhu, Joseph Chang, and David Kritchevsky. 1998. *Monascus purpureus*–fermented rice (red yeast rice): a natural food product that lowers blood cholesterol in animal models of hypercholesterolemia. *Nutrition Research* 18: 71–81.

Li, S. P., Z. R. Su, T. T. Dong, and K. W. Tsim. 2002. The fruiting body and its caterpillar host of *Cordyceps sinensis* show close resemblance in main constituents and antioxidation activity. *Phytomedicine* 9(4): 319–324.

Li, Ya-Wei, Xiu-Yuan Zhu, Paul P.-H. Butt, and Hin-Wing Yeung. 1995. Ethnopharmacology of bear gall bladder. *Journal of Ethnopharmacology* 47: 27–31.

Liem, D. G., and J. A. Mennella. 2003. Heightened sour preferences during childhood. *Chemical Senses* 28(2): 173–180.

Liener, I. E. 1997. Plant lectins: properties, nutritional significance, and function. In *Antinutrients and Phytochemicals in Food.* F. Shahidi, ed. Pp. 31–43. American Chemical Society, Washington, D.C.

Lindenbaum, S. 1977. The "last course": nutrition and anthropology in Asia. In *Nutrition and Anthropology in Action*. T. K. Fitzgerald, ed. Pp. 141–155. Van Gorcum, Assen, The Netherlands.

Lindstrom, L. 2004. History, folklore, traditional and current uses of kava. In *Kava: From Ethnology to Pharmacology*. Y. N. Singh, ed. Pp. 10–28. CRC Press, Boca Raton, Fla.

Linskens, H. F., and W. Jorde. 1997. Pollen as food and medicine: a review. *Economic Botany* 51(1): 78–87.

Liu, Chung-Ji, Chiu-Lan Chen, Kuo-Wei Chang, Cheng-Hsin Chu, and Tsung-Yun Liu. 2000. Safrole in betel quid may be a risk factor for hepatocellular carcinoma: a case report. *Canadian Medical Association Journal* 162(3): 359–360.

Locher, C. P., M. T. Burch, H. F. Mower, J. Berestecky, H. Davis, B. Van Poel, A. Lasure, D. A. Vanden Berghe, and A. J. Vlietinck. 1995. Anti-microbial activity and anti-complement activity of extracts obtained from selected Hawaiian medicinal plants. *Journal of Ethnopharmacology* 49: 23–32.

Lorri, W., and U. Svanberg. 1994. Lower prevalence of diarrhoea in young children fed lactic acid-fermented cereal gruels. *Food and Nutrition Bulletin* 15: 57–63.

Lorri, Wilbald, and Ulf Svanberg. 1995. An overview of the use of fermented foods for child weaning in Tanzania. *Ecology of Food and Nutrition* 34: 65–81.

Loudon, Irvine. 1986. *Medical Care and the General Practitioner, 1750–1850*. Clarendon Press, Oxford.

Lovejoy, Paul E. 1986. *Salt of the Desert Sun: A History of Salt Production and Trade in the Central Sudan*. Cambridge University Press, Cambridge.

Lovejoy, Paul E. 1995. Kola nuts: the 'coffee' of the central Sudan. In *Consuming Habits*. J. Goodman, P. E. Lovejoy, and A. Sherratt, eds. Pp. 103–125. Routledge, London.

Lozano, G. A. 1998. Parasitic stress and self-medication in wild animals. In *Advances in the Study of Behavior*. A. P. Møller, M. Milinski, and P. J. B. Slater, eds. Pp. 291–317. Academic Press, London.

Lu, Wei-Bo. 2002. Therapeutic uses of tea in traditional Chinese medicine. In *Tea: Bioactivity and Therapeutic Potential*. Y.-S. Zhen, ed. Pp. 231–241. Taylor and Francis, London.

Lupien, John R. 1999. Overview of the nutritional benefits of cocoa and chocolate. In *Chocolate and Cocoa: Health and Nutrition*. I. Knight, ed. Pp. 3–8. Blackwell Science, Oxford.

Lusby, P. E., A. Coombes, and J. M. Wilkinson. 2002. Honey: a potent agent for wound healing? *Journal of Wound, Ostomy, and Continence Nursing* 29(6): 273–274.

Lyng, Stephen. 1990. *Holistic Health and Biomedical Science: A Countersystem Analysis*. State University of New York Press, Albany.

Ma, J., X. D. Luo, P. Protiva, H. Yang, C. Ma, M. J. Basile, I. B. Weinstein, and E. J. Kennelly. 2003. Bioactive novel polyphenols from the fruit of *Manilkara zapota* (Sapodilla). *Journal of Natural Products* 66(7): 983–986.

Macdiarmid, H. I., and M. M. Hetherington. 1995. Mood modulation by food: an exploration of affect and cravings in "chocolate addicts." *British Journal of Clinical Psychology* 34(1): 129–138.

Maity, S., J. R. Vedasiromoni, and D. K. Ganguly. 1995. Anti-ulcer effect of the hot water extract of black tea (*Camellia sinensis*). *Journal of Ethnopharmacology* 46: 167–174.

Manchester, Carole. 1996. *Tea in the East*. Hearst Books, New York.

Mann, G. V. 1974. Studies of a surfactant and cholesteremia in the Maasai. *American Journal of Clinical Nutrition* 27: 464–469.

Mapes, Cristina, Francisco Basurto, and Robert Bye. 1997. Ethnobotany of quintonil: knowledge, use, and management of edible greens, *Amaranthus* spp. (Amaranthaceae) in the Sierra Norte de Puebla, Mexico. *Economic Botany* 51(3): 293–306.

Marcucci, M. C., F. Ferreres, C. García-Viguera, V. S. Bankova, S. L. de Castro, A. P. Dantas, P. H. M. Valente, and N. Paulino. 2001. Phenolic compounds from Brazilian propolis with pharmacological activities. *Journal of Ethnopharmacology* 74: 105–112.

Marita, J. M., J. Nienhuis, J. L. Pires, and W. M. Aitken. 2001. Analysis of genetic diversity in *Theobroma cacao* with emphasis on witches' broom disease resistance. *Crop Science* 41: 1305–1316.

Marshall, Fiona. 2001. Agriculture and use of wild and weedy greens by the Piik Ap Oom Okiek of Kenya. *Economic Botany* 55(1): 32–46.

Marteau, P. R., M. de Vrese, C. J. Cellier, and J. Schrezenmeir. 2001. Protection from gastrointestinal diseases with the use of probiotics. *American Journal of Clinical Nutrition* 73: 430S–436S.

Martin, Marina, Evelyn Mathias, and Constance M. McCorkle. 2001. *Ethnoveterinary Medicine: An Annotated Bibliography of Community Animal Healthcare*. ITDG Publishing, London.

Mathias, Evelyn. 2005. Ethnoveterinary medicine: a resource for development. *New Agriculturalist Online*. http://www.new-agri.co.uk, 3 March.

Mathias, Evelyn, D. V. Rangnekar, and Constance M. McCorkle, eds. 1999. *Ethnoveterinary Medicine: Alternatives for Livestock Development*. BAIF Development Research Foundation, Pune, India.

Maulitz, Russell C. 1979. Physician versus bacteriologist: the ideology of science in clinical medicine. In *The Therapeutic Revolution*. M. J. Vogel, ed. Pp. 91–107. University of Pennsylvania Press, Philadelphia.

Mayo Clinic. 2004. Caffeine content in beverages. http://MayoClinic.com, 8 July.

Mbugua, S. K., R. A. Ahrens, H. N. Kigutha, and V. Subramanian. 1992. Effect of fermentation, malted flour treatment and drum drying on nutritional quality of uji. *Ecology of Food and Nutrition* 28: 271–277.

McCorkle, Constance M., Evelyn Mathias, and Tjaart W. Schillhorn van Veen, eds. 1996. *Ethnoveterinary Research and Development*. Intermediate Technology Publications, London.

McCracken, Robert D. 1971. Lactase deficiency: an example of dietary evolution [followed by commentary]. *Current Anthropology* 12(4/5): 479–517.

McGovern, Patrick E. 2003. *Ancient Wine: The Search for the Origins of Viniculture*. Princeton University Press, Princeton, N.J.

McIntosh, William Alex. 1996. *Sociologies of Food and Nutrition*. Plenum, New York.

McKay, Diane L., and Jeffrey B. Blumberg. 2002. The role of tea in human health: an update. *Journal of the American College of Nutrition* 21(1): 1–13.

Meda, Aline, Charles E. Lamien, Jeanne Millogo, Marco Romito, and Odile G. Nacoulma. 2004. Therapeutic uses of honey and honeybee larvae in central Burkina Faso. *Journal of Ethnopharmacology* 95: 103–107.

Mensah, P., C. I. Ndiokwelu, A. Uwaegbute, A. Ablordey, A.M. van Boxtel, C. Brinkman, M. J. Nout, and P. O. Ngoddy. 1995. Feeding of lactic acid–fermented high nutrient density weaning formula in paediatric settings in Ghana and Nigeria: acceptance by mother and infant and performance during recovery from acute diarrhoea. *International Journal of Food Sciences and Nutrition* 46: 353–362.

Menzel, Peter, and Faith D'Alusio. 1998. *Man Eating Bugs: The Art and Science of Eating Insects*. Ten Speed Press, Berkeley, Calif.

Merlin, M., and W. Raynor. 2004. Modern use and environmental impact of the kava plant in remote Oceania. In *Dangerous Harvest: Drug Plants and the Transformation of Indigenous Landscapes*. M. K. Steinberg, J. J. Hobbs, and K. Mathewson, eds. Pp. 274–293, Oxford University Press, Oxford.

Messina, M., and V. Messina. 2000. Soyfoods, soybean isoflavones, and bone health: a brief overview. *Journal of Renal Nutrition* 10: 63–68.

Meyer-Rochow, V. B., and S. Changkija. 1997. Uses of insects as human food in Papua New Guinea, Australia, and northeast India: cross-cultural considerations and cautious conclusions. *Ecology of Food and Nutrition* 36(2–4): 159–185.

Michalsen, A., S. Moebus, G. Spahn, T. Esch, J. Langhorst, and G. J. Dobos. 2002. Leech therapy for symptomatic treatment of knee osteoarthritis: results and implications of a pilot study. *Alternative Therapies in Health and Medicine* 8(5): 84–88.

Michener, Willa, and Paul Rozin. 1994. Pharmacological versus sensory factors in the satiation of chocolate craving. *Physiology and Behavior* 56: 419–422.

Milton, Katharine. 1987. Primate diets and gut morphology: implications for hominid evolution. In *Food and Evolution: Toward a Theory of Food Habits*. M. Harris and E. B. Ross, eds. Pp. 93–115. Temple University Press, Philadelphia.

Mintz, Sidney W. 1985. *Sweetness and Power: The Place of Sugar in Modern History*. Penguin Books, New York.

Mintz, Sidney W. 1996. *Tasting Food, Tasting Freedom: Excursions into Eating, Culture, and the Past*. Beacon Press, Boston.

Miura, Y., K. Ono, R. Okauchi, and K. Yagasaki. 2004. Inhibitory effect of coffee on hepatoma proliferation and invasion in culture and on tumor growth, metastasis and abnormal lipoprotein profiles in hepatoma-bearing rats. *Journal of Nutritional Science and Vitaminology* 50(1): 38–44.

Mizutani, Takeo. 1992. The relationship between microorganisms and the physiology of aging. In *Functions of Fermented Milk: Challenges for the Health Sciences*. B. W. Howells (trans.), Y. Nakazawa and A. Hosono, eds. Pp. 305–324. Elsevier Science, Essex, England.

Mobarok Ali, A. T. M., and O. A. Al-Swayeh. 1997. Natural honey prevents ethanol-induced increased vascular permeability changes in the rat stomach. *Journal of Ethno-pharmacology* 55: 231–238.

Moerman, Daniel. 2002. *Meaning, Medicine and the 'Placebo Effect'*. Cambridge University Press, Cambridge.

Montanari, Massimo (Carl Ipsen, trans.). 1994. *The Culture of Food*. Blackwell, Oxford.

Moreno-Black, Geraldine, Watana Akanan, Prapimporn Somnasang, Sompong Thamathawan, and Paul Brozvosky. 1996. Non-domesticated food resources in the marketplace and marketing system of northeastern Thailand. *Journal of Ethnobiology* 16(1): 99–117.

Morimitsu, Y., K. Hayashi, Y. Nakagawa, F. Horio, K. Uchida, and T. Osawa. 2000. Antiplatelet and anticancer isiothiocyanates in Japanese domestic horseradish, wasabi. *Biofactors* 13: 271–276.

Moritz, R. F. A., and E. E. Southwick. 1992. *Bees as Superorganisms: An Evolutionary Reality*. Springer Verlag, Berlin.

Mugula, J. K., and M. Lyimo. 2001. Evaluation of nutritional quality and acceptability of sorghum-based tempe as potential weaning foods in Tanzania. *International Journal of Food Sciences and Nutrition* 51: 269–277.

Mukhtar, Hasan, and Nihal Ahmad. 2000. Tea polyphenols: prevention of cancer and optimizing health. *American Journal of Clinical Nutrition* 71(6): 1698S–1702S.

Muraoka, S., and T. Miura. 2004. Inhibition of xanthine oxidase by phytic acid and its antioxidative action. *Life Sciences* 74(13): 1691–1700.

Mureithi, William, Christoffel den Biggelaar, Edward W. Wesakania, Kuria Kamau, and Catherine Gatundu. 2000. Management of trees used in *mursik* (fermented milk) production in Trans-Nzoia District, Kenya. *Journal of Ethnobiology* 20(1): 75–91.

Mwenda, J. M., M. M. Arimi, M. C. Kyama, and D. K. Langat. 2003. Effects of khat (*Catha edulis*) consumption on reproductive functions: a review. *East African Medical Journal* 80(6): 318–323.

Nabhan, Gary. 1997. *Cultures of Habitat: On Nature, Culture, and Story*. Counterpoint Press, Washington, D.C.

Nabhan, Gary. 2004. *Why Some Like It Hot*. Island Press, Washington, D.C.

Naczk, M., R. Amarowicz, and F. Shahidi. 1997. Alpha-galactosides of sucrose in foods: composition, flatulence-causing effects, and removal. In *Antinutrients and Phytochemicals in Food*. F. Shahidi, ed. Pp. 127–151. American Chemical Society, Washington, D.C.

Nathanson, James A., Edward J. Hunnicutt, Lakshmi Kantham, and Cristoforo Scavone. 1993. Cocaine as a naturally occurring insecticide. *Proceedings of the National Academy of Sciences USA* 90: 9645–9648.

Nawrot, P., S. Jordan, J. Eastwood, J. Rotstein, A. Hugenholtz, and M. Feeley. 2003. Effects of caffeine on human health. *Food Additives and Contaminants* 20(1): 1–30.

NCCAM (National Center for Complementary and Alternative Medicine). 2004. What is complementary and alternative medicine (CAM)? http://nccam.nih.gov/health, 17 March.

Newall, Carol A., Linda A. Anderson, and J. David Phillipson. 1996. *Herbal Medicines: A Guide for Health Care Professionals*. Pharmaceutical Press, London.

Nicolson, Malcolm. 1992. Giovanni Battista Morgagni and eighteenth-century physical examination. In *Medical Theory, Surgical Practice: Studies in the History of Surgery*. C. Lawrence, ed. Pp. 101–134. Routledge, New York.

Niidome, T., K. Kobayashi, H. Arakawa, T. Hatakeyama, and H. Aoyagi. 2004. Structure-activity relationship of an antibacterial peptide, maculatin 1.1, from the skin glands of the tree frog, *Litoria genimaculata*. *Journal of Peptide Science* 10(7): 414–422.

Nishimune, Takahiro, Yoshihiro Watanabe, Hideki Okazaki, and Hiromu Akai. 2000. Thiamin is decomposed due to *Anaphe* spp. entomophagy in seasonal ataxia patients in Nigeria. *Journal of Nutrition* 130: 1625–1628.

Nishioka, Y., S. Yoshioka, M. Kusunose, T. Cui, A. Hamada, M. Ono, M. Miyamura, and S. Kyotani. 2002. Effects of extract derived from *Eriobotrya japonica* on liver function improvement in rats. *Biological and Pharmaceutical Bulletin* 25(8): 1053–1057.

Nnam, N. M., and P. N. Obiakor. 2003. Effect of fermentation on the nutrient and anti-nutrient composition of baobab (*Adansonia digitata*) seeds and rice (*Oryza sativa*) grains. *Ecology of Food and Nutrition* 42(4/5): 265–277.

Nnanyelugo, D. C., E. C. Okeke, and V. Ibeanu. 2003. Knowledge, attitude and usage patterns of fermented and germinated complementary foods in Nigeria. *Plant Foods and Human Nutrition* 58(1): 41–51.

Nostro, A., M. A. Cannatelli, G. Crisafi, and V. Alonzo. 2001. The effect of *Nepeta cataria* extract on adherence and enzyme production of *Staphylococcus aureus*. *International Journal of Antimicrobial Agents* 18(6): 583–585.

Nottingham, Stephen. 1998. *Eat Your Genes: How Genetically Modified Food Is Entering Our Diet*. University of Cape Town Press, Rondebosch, South Africa.

Oberman, H., and Z. Libudzisz. 1998. Fermented milks. In *Microbiology of Fermented Foods*. 2nd ed. B. J. B. Wood, ed. Pp. 308–350. Blackie Academic, London.

Odunfa, S. A., and O. B. Oyewole. 1998. African fermented foods. In *Microbiology of Fermented Foods*. 2nd ed. B. J. B. Wood, ed. Pp. 713–752. Blackie Academic, London.

Ohtani, I. N. Gotoh, J. Tanaka, T. Higa, M. A. Gyamfi, and Y. Aniya. 2000. Thonnin-gianins A and B, new antioxidants from the African medicinal herb *Thonningia san-guinea*. *Journal of Natural Products* 63(5): 676–679.

Olmsted, James M. D., and E. Harris Olmsted. 1952. *Claude Bernard and the Experimental Method in Medicine*. Henry Schuman Publishers, New York.

Olukoya, D. K., S. I. Ebigwei, N. A. Olasupo, and A. A. Ogunjimi. 1994. Production of *dogik*, an improved *ogi* (Nigerian fermented weaning food) with potentials for use in diarrhea control. *Journal of Tropical Pediatrics* 40: 108–113.

Omafuvbe, B. O., O. O. Shonukan, and S. H. Abiose. 2000. Microbiological and bio-chemical changes in the traditional fermentation of soybean for 'soy-daddawa', Ni-gerian food condiment. *Food Microbiology* 17: 469–474.

Orsolic, Nada, Anica Horvat Knezevic, Lidija Sver, Svjetlana Terzic, and Ivan Basic. 2004. Immunomodulatory and antimetastatic action of propolis and related polyphenolic compounds. *Journal of Ethnopharmacology* 94(2/3): 307–315.

Osawa, Ro, Keiko Kuroiso, Satoshi Goto, and Akira Shimizu. 2000. Isolation of tannin-degrading lactobacilli from humans and fermented foods. *Applied and Environmental Microbiology* 66: 3093–3097.

Paoletti, Maurizio G., and Sandra G. F. Bukkens, eds. 1997. Special Issue: Minilivestock. *Ecology of Food and Nutrition* 36(2–4).

Pedone, C. A., C. C. Arnaud, E. R. Postaire, C. F. Bouley, and P. Reinert. 2000. Multicentric study of the effect of milk fermented by *Lactobacillus casei* on the incidence of diarrhoea. *International Journal of Clinical Practice* 54: 568–571.

Pellegrino, Edmund D. 1979. The sociocultural impact of twentieth-century therapeutics. In *The Therapeutic Revolution*. M. J. Vogel, ed. Pp. 245–266. University of Pennsylvania Press, Philadelphia.

Pemberton, Robert W. 1999. Insects and other arthropods used as drugs in Korean traditional medicine. *Journal of Ethnopharmacology* 65: 207–216.

Pence, Gregory E., ed. 2002. *The Ethics of Food: A Reader for the Twenty-first Century*. Rowman and Littlefield, Lanham, Md.

Pieroni, Andrea, ed. 1999. *Herbs, Humans and Animals: Proceedings of the International Seminar, Creglia (Tuscany), Italy*. eXperiences Verlag, Koln, Germany.

Pieroni, Andrea. 2001. Evaluation of the cultural significance of wild food botanicals traditionally consumed in northwestern Tuscany, Italy. *Journal of Ethnobiology* 21(1): 89–104.

Pittler, M. H., and E. Ernst. 2002. Kava extract for treating anxiety. *Cochrane Database Systematic Review* 2:CD003383

Platel, Kalpana, and K. Srinivasan. 2004. Digestive stimulant action of spices: A myth or reality? *Indian Journal of Medical Research* 119: 167–179.

Plotnicov, Leonard, and Richard Scaglion. 1999. *The Globalization of Food*. Waveland Press, Prospect Heights, Ill.

Pollan, Michael. 2001. Behind the organic-industrial complex. *New York Times*, 13 May.

Pollan, Michael. 2003. The futures of foods. *New York Times Magazine*, 4 May.

Pollock, Nancy J. 1992. *These Roots Remain: Food Habits in Islands of the Central and Eastern Pacific since Western Contact*. Institute for Polynesian Studies, Laie, Hawai'i.

Porres, J. M., P. Aranda, M. Lopez-Jurado, and G. Urbano. 2003. Effect of natural and controlled fermentation on chemical composition and nutrient dialyzability from beans (*Phaseolus vulgaris* L.). *Journal of Agricultural and Food Chemistry* 51(17): 5144–5149.

Porter, Dorothy, and Roy Porter. 1989. *Patient's Progress: Doctors and Doctoring in the Eighteenth Century*. Stanford University Press, Stanford, Calif.

Porter, Roy. 1992. Introduction. In *The Popularization of Medicine, 1650–1850*. R. Potter, ed. Pp. 1–16. Routledge, New York.

Posey, Darrell A. 1981. Wasps, warriors and fearless men: ethnoentomology of the Kayapó Indians of central Brazil. *Journal of Ethnobiology* 1(1): 165–174.

Posey, Darrell A. 1983. Keeping of stingless bees by the Kayapó of Brazil. *Journal of Ethnobiology* 3(1): 63–73.

Posey, Darrell A. 1986. Topics and issues in ethnoentomology with some suggestions for the development of hypothesis-generation and testing in ethnobiology. *Journal of Ethnobiology* 6(1): 99–120.

Potter, S. M. 1998. Soy protein and cardiovascular disease: the impact of bioactive components in soy. *Nutrition Reviews* 56: 231–235.

Powell, Wilf, and John A. Pickett. 2003. Manipulation of parasitoids for aphid pest management: progress and prospects. *Pest Management Science* 59(2): 149–155.

Prajapati, Jashbhai B., and Baboo M. Nair. 2003. The history of fermented foods. In *Handbook of Fermented Functional Foods*. E. R. Farnworth, ed. Pp. 1–25. CRC Press, Boca Raton, Fla.

Prendergrast, Mark. 2000. *For God, Country, and Coca-Cola: The Definitive History of the Great American Soft Drink and the Company That Makes It*. 2nd ed. Basic Books, New York.

Price, Edward O. 2002. *Animal Domestication and Behavior*. CABI Publishing, New York.

Probyn, Elspeth. 2000. *Carnal Appetites: Food, Sex, Identities*. Routledge, London.

Rafter, J. 2003. Probiotics and colon cancer. *Best Practice and Research: Clinical Gastroenterology* 17(5): 849–859.

Ragone, Diane. 1991. Ethnobotany of breadfruit in Polynesia. In *Islands, Plants, and Polynesians: An Introduction to Polynesian Ethnobotany*. P. A. Cox and S. A. Banack, eds. Pp. 203–220. Dioscorides Press, Portland, Ore.

Ragonese, P., G. Salemi, L. Morgante, P. Aridon, A. Epifanio, D. Buffa, F. Scoppa, and G. Savettieri. 2003. A case-control study on cigarette, alcohol, and coffee consumption preceding Parkinson's disease. *Neuroepidemiology* 22(5): 297–304.

Raja'a, Y. A., T. A. Norman, A. K. al Warafi, N. A. as Mashraki, and A. M. al Yosofi. 2001. Khat chewing is a risk factor of duodenal ulcer. *East Mediterranean Health Journal* 7(3): 568–570.

Rajendran, Rajam, and Yoshiyuki Ohta. 1998. Binding of heterocyclic amines by lactic acid bacteria from miso, a fermented Japanese food. *Canadian Journal of Microbiology* 44: 109–115.

Ramji, Niranjan, Nivedita Ramji, Ritu Iyer, and S. Chandrasekaran. 2002. Phenolic antibacterials from *Piper betle* in the prevention of halitosis. *Journal of Ethnopharmacology* 83: 149–152.

Ramos-Elorduy, Julieta. 1997a. Insects: A sustainable source of food? *Ecology of Food and Nutrition* 36(2–4): 247–276.

Ramos-Elorduy, Julieta. 1997b. The importance of edible insects in the nutrition and economy of people of the rural areas of Mexico. *Ecology of Food and Nutrition* 36(5): 347–366.

Ramos-Elorduy, Julieta, and Jose M. Pino Moreno. 2002. Edible insects of Chiapas, Mexico. *Ecology of Food and Nutrition* 41(4): 271–299.

Ramos-Elorduy, J., E. Motte-Florac, J. M. Pino, and C. Andary. 1996. Les insectes utilisés en médecine traditionnelle au Mexique: perspectives. Presented to the European Colloquium on Ethnopharmacology and the International Conference on Anthropology and the History of Health and Disease, Genoa, Italy, 29 May–2 June.

Ramsey, Matthew. 1992. The popularization of medicine in France, 1650–1900. In *The Popularization of Medicine, 1650–1850*. R. Potter, ed. Pp. 97–133. Routledge, New York.

Ramzan, I., and V. H. Tran. 2004. Chemistry of kava and kavalactones. In *Kava: From Ethnology to Pharmacology*. Y. N. Singh, ed. Pp. 76–103. CRC Press, Boca Raton, Fla.

Rastall, R. A. 2004. Bacteria in the gut: friends and foes and how to alter the balance. *Journal of Nutrition* 134(Suppl.): 2022S–2026S.

Rauha, J. P., S. Remes, M. Heinonen, A. Hopia, M. Kahkonen, T. Kujala, K. Pihlaja, H. Vuorela, and P. Vuorela. 2000. Antimicrobial effects of Finnish plant extracts containing flavonoids and other phenolic compounds. *International Journal of Food Microbiology* 56(1): 3–12.

Redclift, Michael. 2004. *Chewing Gum: The Fortunes of Taste*. Routledge, New York.

Reichart, Peter A., and Hans P. Philipsen. 1996. *Betel and Miang*. White Lotus Press, Bangkok, Thailand.

Reichling, J., H. Schmokel, J. Fitzi, S. Bucher, and R. Saller. 2004. Dietary support with *Boswellia* resin in canine inflammatory joint and spinal disease. *Schweizer Archiv für Tierheilkunde* 146(2): 71–79.

Relf, Diane, ed. 1992. *The Role of Horticulture in Human Well-Being and Social Development*. Timber Press, Portland, Ore.

Research and Editorial Staff of the Pharmacists' Letter and Prescribers' Letter. 2003. *Natural Medicines Comprehensive Database*. 5th ed. Therapeutic Research Faculty, Stockton, Calif.

Rhoades, D. F., and R. G. Cates. 1976. Toward a general theory of plant antiherbivore chemistry. *Recent Advances in Phytochemistry* 19: 168–213.

Riddle, John M. 1985. *Dioscorides on Pharmacy and Medicine*. University of Texas Press, Austin.

Riely, E. 1990. Sylvester Graham and the origins of the breakfast cereal industry. In *Oxford Symposium on Food and Cookery*. H. Walker, ed. Pp. 198–201. Prospect Books, London.

Rios, L. Y., M. P. Gonthier, C. Remesy, I. Mila, C. Lapierre, S. A. Lazarus, G. Williamson, and A. Scalbert. 2003. Chocolate intake increases urinary excretion of polyphenol-derived phenolic acids in healthy human subjects. *American Journal of Clinical Nutrition* 77(4): 912–918.

Ritchie, Ian. 1991. Fusion of the faculties: a study of the language of the senses in Hausaland. In *The Varieties of Sensory Experience*. D. Howes, ed. Pp. 193–202. University of Toronto Press, Toronto.

Roberfroid, M. 2003. Probiotics and prebiotics: Why should the medical community pay attention? *Drug Discovery Today* 8(24): 1107–1108.

Rodriguez, Eloy, and Richard W. Wrangham. 1993. Zoopharmacognosy: the use of medicinal plants by animals. In *Recent Advances in Phytochemistry*. K. R. Downum, J. T. Romeo, and H. Stafford, eds. Pp. 89–105. Plenum Press, New York.

Rogers, Peter J., and Hendrik J. Smit. 2000. Food craving and food "addiction": a critical review of the evidence from a biopsychosocial perspective. *Pharmacology, Biochemistry, and Behavior* 66(1): 3–14.

Romeo, John T., James A. Saunders, and Pedro Barbosa, eds. 1996. *Phytochemical Diversity and Redundancy in Ecological Interactions*. Plenum Press, New York.

Rooney, Dawn F. 1993. *Betel Chewing Traditions in South-East Asia*. Oxford University Press, Oxford.

Rose, Peter, Kathy Faulkner, Gary Williamson, and Richard Mithen. 2000. 7-Methyl-sulfinylheptyl and 8-methylsulfinyloctyl isothiocyanates from watercress are potent inducers of phase II enzymes. *Carcinogenesis* 21: 1983–1988.

Rosenberg, Charles E. 1979. The therapeutic revolution. In *The Therapeutic Revolution*. M. J. Vogel, ed. Pp. 3–25. University of Pennsylvania Press, Philadelphia.

Rosenberg, Charles E. 1997. *No Other Gods: On Science and American Social Thought*. Rev. ed. Johns Hopkins University Press, Baltimore, Md.

Rosner, Fred. 1987. The medical writings of Moses Maimonides. *New York State Journal of Medicine* 87: 656–661.

Ross, Paul J., Nina L. Etkin, and Ibrahim Muazzamu. 1996. A changing Hausa diet. *Medical Anthropology* 17: 143–163.

Ross, Z. M., E. A. O'Gara, D. J. Hill, H. V. Sleightholme, and D. J. Maslin. 2001. Antimicrobial properties of garlic oil against human enteric bacteria: evaluation of methodologies and comparisons with garlic oil sulfides and garlic powder. *Applied Environmental Microbiology* 67: 475–480.

Rosset, Peter M. 2001. Toward a political economy of opinion formation on genetically modified foods. *Medical Anthropology* 15(1): 22–25.

Rouzaud, Gabrielle, Sheila A. Young, and Alan J. Duncan. 2004. Hydrolysis of glucosinolates to isothiocyanates after ingestion of raw of microwaved cabbage by human volunteers. *Cancer Epidemiology, Biomarkers and Prevention* 13(1): 125–131.

Rozin, Paul. 1982. Human food selection: the interaction of biology, culture, and individual experiences. In *The Psychobiology of Human Food Selection*. L. M. Barker, ed. Pp. 225–254. AVI Publishing, Westport, Conn.

Rozin, Paul. 1990. Getting to like the burn of chili pepper: biological, psychological and cultural perspectives. In *Chemical Senses*. Vol. 2. B. G. Green, J. R. Mason, and M. R. Kare, eds. Pp. 231–269. Marcel Dekker, New York.

Rudgley, Richard. 1993. *Essential Substances: A Cultural History of Intoxicants*. Kodansha America, New York.

Ruiz-Terán, Francisco, and J. David Owens. 1999. Fate of oligosaccharides during production of soya bean tempe. *Journal of the Science of Food and Agriculture* 79: 249–252.

Sabu, M. C., K. Smitha, and Ramadasan Kuttan. 2002. Anti-diabetic activity of green tea polyphenols and their role in reducing oxidative stress in experimental diabetes. *Journal of Ethnopharmacology* 83: 109–116.

Saeed, S. A., S. Farnaz, R. U. Simjee, and A. Malik. 1993. Triterpenes and β-sitosterol from *Piper betle*: isolation, antiplatelet and anti-inflammatory effects. *Biochemical Society Transactions* 21(4): 462S.

Sahi, Timo. 1994a. Hypolactasia and lactase persistence: historical review and terminology. *Scandinavian Journal of Gastroenterology* 29(Suppl. 202): 7–20.

Sahi, Timo. 1994b. Genetics and epidemiology of adult-type hypolactasia. *Scandinavian Journal of Gastroenterology* 29(Suppl. 202): 1–6.

Sanabria, Harry. 2004. The state and the ongoing struggle over coca in Bolivia: legitimacy, hegemony, and the exercise of power. In *Dangerous Harvest: Drug Plants and the Transformation of Indigenous Landscapes.* M. K. Steinberg, J. J. Hobbs, and K. Mathewson, eds. Pp. 153–166, Oxford University Press, New York.

Sanders, Mary Ellen. 1994. Lactic acid bacteria as promoters of human health. In *Functional Foods: Designer Foods, Pharmafoods, Nutraceuticals.* I. Goldberg, ed. Pp. 294–322. Chapman and Hall, New York.

Sanders, M. E. 2003. Probiotics: considerations for human health. *Nutrition Reviews* 61(3): 91–99.

Sanni, A. I., A. A. Onilude, S. T. Ogunbanwo, and S. I. Smith. 1999. Antagonistic activity of bacteriocin produced by *Lactobacillus* species from ogi, an indigenous fermented food. *Journal of Basic Microbiology* 39: 189–195.

Saravanan, R., and K. V. Pugalendi. 2004. Effect of *Piper betle* on blood glucose and lipid profiles in rats after chronic ethanol administration. *Pharmaceutical Biology* 42(4/5): 323–327.

Schaaf, O., J. Baumgarten, and K. Dettner. 2000. Identification and function of prothoracic exocrine gland steroids of the dytiscid beetles *Graphoderus cinereus* and *Lacophilus minutus. Journal of Chemical Ecology* 26: 2291–2305.

Schelhas, John, and Russell Greenberg, eds. 1996. *Forest Patches in Tropical Landscapes.* Island Press, Washington, D.C.

Seeley, Thomas D. 1995. *The Wisdom of the Hive: The Social Physiology of Honey Bee Colonies.* Harvard University Press, Cambridge, Mass.

Seixas, Cristiana S., and Alpina Begossi. 2001. Ethnozoology of fishing communities from Ilha Grande (Atlantic Forest Coast, Brazil). *Journal of Ethnobiology* 21(1): 107–135.

Serafini, M., R. Bugianesi, G. Maiani, S. Valtuena, S. De Santis, and A. Crozier. 2003. Plasma antioxidants from chocolate. *Nature* 424: 1013.

Sewram, V., E. De Stefani, P. Brennan, and P. Boffetta. 2003. Maté consumption and the risk of squamous cell esophageal cancer in Uruguay. *Cancer Epidemiology, Biomarkers and Prevention* 12(6): 508–513.

Sgouras, D., P. Maragkoudakis, K. Petraki, B. Martinez-Gonzalez, E. Eriotou, S. Michopoulos, G. Kalantzopoulos, E. Tsakalidou, and A. Mentis. 2004. In vitro and in vivo inhibition of *Helicobacter pylori* by lactobacillus strain Shirota. *Applied and Environmental Microbiology* 70(1): 518–526.

Shahidi, F. 1997. Beneficial health effects and drawbacks of antinutrients and phytochemicals in food. In *Antinutrients and Phytochemicals in Food.* F. Shahidi, ed. Pp. 1–9. American Chemical Society, Washington, D.C.

Shehu, Ladan M., and Abiodun A. Adesiyun. 1990. Characteristics of strains of *Escherichia coli* isolated from locally fermented milk ("nono") in Zaria, Nigeria. *Journal of Food Production* 53: 574–577.

Shell-Duncan, B., and W. O. Obiero. 2000. Child nutrition in the transition from nomadic pastoralism to settled lifestyles: individual, household, and community-level factors. *American Journal of Physical Anthropology* 113(2): 183–200.

Shepard, Glenn H. 2004. A sensory ecology of medicinal plant therapy in two Amazonian societies. *American Anthropologist* 106(2): 252–266.

Sherman, Paul W., and Samuel M. Flaxman. 2001. Protecting ourselves from food. *American Scientist* 89: 142–151.

Sherman, Paul W., and Geoffrey A. Hash. 2001. Why vegetable recipes are not very spicy. *Evolution and Human Behavior* 22(3): 147–163.

Sherman, R. A. 2003. Maggot therapy for treating diabetic foot ulcers unresponsive to conventional therapy. *Diabetes Care* 26(2): 446–451.

Sherman, R. A., M. J. R. Hall, and S. Thomas. 2000. Medicinal maggots: an ancient remedy for some contemporary afflictions. *Annual Review of Entomology* 45: 55–81.

Shoemaker, Candice A., ed. 2002. *Interaction by Design: Bringing People and Plants Together for Health and Well-Being.* Iowa State University Press, Ames.

Shu, Y., S. R. Jones, W. A. Kinney, and B. S. Selinsky. 2002. The synthesis of spermine analogs of the shark aminosterol squalamine. *Steroids* 67(3/4): 291–304.

Sibley, E. 2004. Genetic variation and lactose intolerance: detection methods and clinical implications. *American Journal of Pharmacogenomics* 4(4): 239–245.

Siddiqui, I. A., F. Afaq, V. M. Adhami, and H. Mukhtar. 2004. Antioxidants of the beverage tea in promotion of human health. *Antioxidants and Redox Signalling* 6(3): 571–582.

Siegel, Ronald L. 1986. Jungle revelers. *Omni* 8(6): 70–72, 74, 100.

Sigerist, Henry E. 1961. *A History of Medicine.* Oxford University Press, Oxford.

Simango, Clifford. 1997. Potential use of traditional fermented foods for weaning in Zimbabwe. *Social Science and Medicine* 44: 1065–1068.

Sime, S., and V. E. Reeve. 2004. Protection from inflammation, immunosuppression and carcinogenesis induced by UV radiation in mice by topical Pycnogenol. *Photochemistry and Photobiology* 79(2): 193–198.

Simoons, Frederick J. 1991. *Food in China: A Cultural and Historical Inquiry.* CRC Press, Boca Raton, Fla.

Simoons, Frederick J. 2001. Persistence of lactase activity among northern Europeans: a weighing of evidence for the calcium absorption hypothesis. *Ecology of Food and Nutrition* 40(5): 397–469.

Simpson, Beryl B., and Molly C. Ogorzaly. 2001. *Economic Botany: Plants in Our World.* 3rd ed. McGraw-Hill, New York.

Singh, Y. N. 2004a. Pharmacology and toxicology of kava and kavalactones. In *Kava: From Ethnology to Pharmacology.* Y. N. Singh, ed. Pp. 104–139. CRC Press, Boca Raton, Fla.

Singh, Y. N., ed. 2004b. *Kava: From Ethnology to Pharmacology.* CRC Press, Boca Raton, Fla.

Siraisi, Nancy G. 1990. *Medieval and Early Renaissance Medicine: An Introduction to Knowledge and Practice.* University of Chicago Press, Chicago.

SKLM (Senate Committee on Food Safety, Germany), ed. 2004. *Functional Food: Safety Aspects.* Wiley VCH, Weinheim, Germany.

Slack, Paul. 1979. Mirrors of health and treasures of poor men: the uses of vernacular medical literature of Tudor England. In *Health, Medicine and Mortality in the Sixteenth Century*. C. Webster, ed. Pp. 237–273. Cambridge University Press, Cambridge.

Slavin, J. J., S. C. Karr, A. M. Hutchins, and J. W. Lampe. 1998. Influence of soybean processing, habitual diet, and soy dose on urinary isoflavonoid excretion. *American Journal of Clinical Nutrition* 68(Suppl. 6): 1492S–1499S.

Sonnedecker, Glenn. 1976. *Kremer's and Urdang's History of Pharmacy*. 4th ed. American Institute of the History of Pharmacy, Madison, WI.

Sonoda, T., Y. Nagata, M. Mori, N. Miyanaga, N. Takashima, K. Okumura, K. Goto, S. Naito, K. Fujimoto, Y. Hirao, A. Takahashi, T. Tsukamoto, T. Fujioka, and H. Akaza. 2004. A case-control study of diet and prostate cancer in Japan: possible protective effect of traditional Japanese diet. *Cancer Science* 95(3): 238–242.

Sotres, Pedro Gil. 1998. The regimes of health. In *Western Medical Thought from Antiquity to the Middle Ages*. M. D. Grmek, ed. Pp. 291–318. Harvard University Press, Cambridge, Mass.

Sovak, M. 2001. Grape extract, resveratrol, and its analogs: a review. *Journal of Medicinal Food* 4(2): 93–105.

Sreekumar, O., and A. Hosono. 1998. The antimutagenic properties of a polysaccharide produced by *Bifidobacterium longum* and its cultured milk against some heterocyclic amines. *Canadian Journal of Microbiology* 44: 1029–1036.

Stahl, Ann Brower. 1984. Hominid dietary selection before fire. *Current Anthropology* 25: 151–168.

Stalberg-White, C., and P. Pliner. 1999. The effect of flavor principles on willingness to taste novel foods. *Appetite* 33(2): 209–221.

Stanford, Craig B., and Henry T. Bunn, eds. 2001. *Meat-eating and Human Evolution*. Oxford University Press, Oxford.

Stanton, Catherine, Colette Desmond, Mairead Coakley, J. Kevin Collins, Gerald Fitzgerald, and R. Paul Ross. 2003. Challenges facing development of probiotic-containing functional foods. In *Handbook of Fermented Functional Foods*. E. R. Farnworth, ed. Pp. 27–58. CRC Press, Boca Raton, Fla.

Stanton, W. R. 1998. Food fermentation in the tropics. In *Microbiology of Fermented Foods*. 2nd ed. B. J. B. Wood, ed. Pp. 696–712. Blackie Academic, London.

Starr, Paul. 1982. *The Social Transformation of American Medicine*. Basic Books, New York.

Steinberg, Francene, Monica M. Bearden, and Carl L. Keen. 2003. Cocoa and chocolate flavonoids: implications for cardiovascular health. *Journal of the American Dietetic Association* 103(2): 215–223.

Steinkraus, K. H. 1998. Bio-enrichment: production of vitamins in fermented foods. In *Microbiology of Fermented Foods*. 2nd ed. B. J. B. Wood, ed. Pp. 603–621. Blackie Academic, London.

Stepp, John R., and Daniel E. Moerman. 2001. The importance of weeds in ethnopharmacology. *Journal of Ethnopharmacology* 75(1): 19–23.

Stern, Kingsley R. 1997. *Introductory Plant Biology*. W. C. Brown, Dubuque, Iowa.

Stevenson, Lloyd. 1958. Antibacterial and antibiotic concepts in early bacteriological stud-
    ies and in Ehrlich's chemotherapy. In *The Impact of the Antibiotics on Medicine and
    Society*. I. Galdston, ed. Pp. 38–57. International Universities Press, New York.
St-Onge, Marie-Pierre, Edward R. Farnworth, and Peter J. H. Jones. 2000. Consumption of
    fermented and nonfermented dairy products: effects on cholesterol concentrations and
    metabolism. *American Journal of Clinical Nutrition* 71: 674–681.
Struthers, R., and L. A. Nichols. 2004. Utilization of complementary and alternative medi-
    cine among racial and ethnic minority populations: implications for reducing health
    disparities. *Annual Review of Nursing Research* 22: 285–313.
Sudheer Kumar, M., B. Sridhar Reddy, S. Kiran Babu, P. M. Bhilegaonkar, A. Shirwaikar,
    and M. K. Unikrishnan. 2004. Antiinflammatory and antiulcer activities of phytic acid
    in rats. *Indian Journal of Experimental Biology* 42(2): 179–185.
Sutton, Mark Q. 1988. *Insects as Food: Aboriginal Entomophagy in the Great Basin*. Ballena
    Press, Novato, Calif.
Svilaas, A., A. K. Sakhi, L. F. Andersen, T. Svilaas, E. C. Strom, D. R. Jacobs, L. Ose, and R.
    Blomhoff. 2004. Intakes of antioxidants in coffee, wine, and vegetables are correlated
    with plasma carotenoids in humans. *Journal of Nutrition* 134(3): 562–567.
Swagerty, Daniel L., Anne D. Walling, and Robert M. Klein. 2002. Lactose intolerance.
    American Family Physician 65: 1845–1850, 1855–1856.
Swallow, Dallas M. 2003. Genetics of lactase persistence and lactose intolerance. *Annual
    Review of Genetics* 37: 197–219.
Takahashi, K., M. Fukazawa, H. Motohira, K. Ochiai, H. Nishikawa, and T. Miyata. 2003.
    A pilot study on antiplaque effects of mastic chewing gum in the oral cavity. *Journal of
    Periodontology* 74(4): 501–505.
Takeoka, G., L. Dao, R. Teranishi, R. Wong, S. Flessa, L. Harden, and R. Edwards. 2000.
    Identification of three triterpenoids in almond hulls. *Journal of Agriculture and Food
    Chemistry* 48: 3437–3439.
Tan, E. K., C. Tan, S. M. Fook-Chong, S. Y. Lum, A. Chai, H. Chung, H. Shen, Y. Zhao,
    M. L. Teoh, Y. Yih, R. Pavanni, V. R. Chandran, and M. C. Wong. 2003. Dose-
    dependent protective effect of coffee, tea, and smoking in Parkinson's disease: a study
    in ethnic Chinese. *Journal of the Neurological Sciences* 216(1): 163–167.
Taranto, María P., José L. Vera, Jeroen Hugenholtz, Gradiela F. De Valdez, and Fernando
    Sesma. 2003. *Lactobacillus reuteri* CRL1098 produces cobalamin. *Journal of Bacteriol-
    ogy* 185(18): 5643–5647.
Teitel, Martin. 2001. Public beliefs about GM foods. *Medical Anthropology* 15(1): 20–21.
Temkin, Owsei. 1958. Galenicals and Galenism in the history of medicine. In *The Impact of
    the Antibiotics on Medicine and Society*. I. Galdston, ed. Pp. 18–37. International
    Universities Press, New York.
Teschke, R., W. Gaus, and D. Loew. 2003. Kava extracts: safety and risks including rare
    hepatotoxicity. *Phytomedicine* 10: 440–446.
Thapar, N., and I. R. Sanderson. 2004. Diarrhoea in children: an interface between de-
    veloping and developed countries. *Lancet* 363: 641–653.

Theophano, Janet. 2002. *Eat My Words*. Palgrave, New York.

Thierry, Solange. 1969. *Le Bétel. I. Inde et Asie du Sud-Est*. Centre National de la Recherche Scientifique, Paris.

Thompson, L. U., D. J. Jenkins, M. A. Amer, R. Reicher, A. Jenkins, and J. Kamulsky. 1982. The effect of fermented and unfermented milks on serum cholesterol. *American Journal of Clinical Nutrition* 36: 1106–1111.

Thompson, T. 2001. Wheat starch, gliadin, and the gluten-free diet. *Journal of the American Dietetic Association* 101(12): 1456–1459.

Tolra, R. P., R. Alonso, C. Poschenrieder, D. Barcelo, and J. Barcelo. 2000. Determination of glucosinolates in rapeseed and *Thlaspi caerulescens* plants by liquid chromatography-atmospheric pressure chemical ionization mass spectrometry. *Journal of Chromatography* 889: 75–81.

Topcu, Zeki, Itsuo Chiba, Masaki Fujieda, Toshiyuki Shibata, Noritaka Ariyoshi, Hiroshi Yamazaki, Figen Sevgican, Malsantha Muthumala, Hiroshi Kobayashi, and Tetsuya Kamataki. 2002. CYP2A6 gene deletion reduces oral cancer risk in betel quid chewers in Sri Lanka. *Carcinogenesis* 23(4): 595–598.

Toussaint-Samat, Maguelonne (Anthea Bell, trans.). 1992. *History of Food*. Blackwell, Oxford.

Trang, Corinne. 2003. Coffee. In *The Encyclopedia of Food and Culture*. S. H. Katz, ed. Pp. 429–434. Charles Scribner, New York.

Treem, William R. 2004. Emerging concepts in celiac disease. *Current Opinion in Pediatrics* 16(5): 552–559.

Tsai, J. F., J. E. Jeng, L. Y. Chuang, M. S. Ho, Y. C. Ko, Z. Y. Lin, M. Y. Hsieh, S. C. Chen, W. L. Chuang, L. Y. Wang, M. L. Yu, and C. Y. Dai. 2004. Habitual betel quid chewing and risk for hepatocellular carcinoma complicating cirrhosis. *Medicine* 83(3): 176–187.

Turner, C. Donnell, and Joseph T. Bagnara. 1976. *General Endocrinology*. 6th ed. W. B. Saunders, Philadelphia.

Ulrich, Laurel Thatcher. 1982. *Good Wives: Image and Reality in the Lives of Women in Northern New England, 1650–1750*. Alfred Knopf, New York.

Ulrich, Laurel Thatcher. 1990. *A Midwife's Tale: The Life of Martha Ballard, Based on Her Diary, 1785–1812*. Alfred Knopf, New York.

Uzogara, S. G., L. N. Agu, and E. O. Uzogara. 1990. A review of traditional fermented foods, condiments and beverages in Nigeria: their benefits and possible problems. *Ecology of Food and Nutrition* 24: 267–288.

Valencia, S., U. Svanberg, A. S. Sandberg, and J. Ruales. 1999. Processing of quinoa (*Chenopodium quinoa* Willd): effects on in vitro iron availability and phytate hydrolysis. *International Journal of Food Science and Nutrition* 50: 203–211.

Vickers, Geoffrey. 1969. Medicine's contribution to culture. In *Medicine and Culture*. F. N. L. Poynter, ed. Pp. 5–14. Wellcome Institute of the History of Medicine, London.

Vieyra-Odilon, Leticia, and Heike Vibrans. 2001. Weeds as crops: the value of maize field weeds in the valley of Toluca, Mexico. *Economic Botany* 55(3): 426–443.

Vittek, J. 1995. Effect of royal jelly on serum lipids in experimental animals and humans with atherosclerosis. *Experientia* 51(9/10): 927–935.

Vogel, Morris J. 1979. Introduction. In *The Therapeutic Revolution: Essays in the Social History of American Medicine*. M. J. Vogel and C. E. Rosenberg, eds. Pp. vii–xiii. University of Pennsylvania Press, Philadelphia.

Walton, Nicholas J., Melinda J. Mayer, and Arjan Narbad. 2003. Vanillin. *Phytochemistry* 63(5): 505–515.

Wang, J., L. Zongliang, and J. Chi. 1997. Multicenter clinical trial of the serum lipid-lowering effects of a *Monascus purpureus* (red yeast) rice preparation from traditional Chinese medicine. *Current Therapeutic Research* 58(12): 964–978.

Wang, S. Y., H. N. Chang, K. T. Lin, C. P. Lo, N. S. Yang, and L. F. Shyur. 2003. Antioxidant properties and phytochemical characteristics of extracts from *Lactuca indica*. *Journal of Agriculture and Food Chemistry* 51(5): 1506–1512.

Wanwimolruk, S., S. Bhawan, P. F. Coville, and S. C. W. Chalcroft. 1998. Genetic polymorphism of debrisoquine (CYP2D6) and proguanil (CYP2C19) in South Pacific Polynesian populations. *European Journal of Clinical Pharmacology* 54: 431–435.

Warnakulasuriya, Saman, Chetan Trivedy, and Timothy J. Peters. 2002. Areca nut use: an independent risk factor for oral cancer. *British Medical Journal* 324: 799–800.

Wear, Andrew. 1992. The popularization of medicine in early modern England. In *The Popularization of Medicine, 1650–1850*. R. Potter, ed. Pp. 17–41. Routledge, New York.

Weatherstone, J. 1992. Historical introduction. In *Tea: Cultivation to Consumption*. K. C. Willson and M. N. Clifford, eds. Pp. 1–23. Chapman and Hall, London.

Weil, Jim. 1986. Beyond the mystique of cocaine: coca in Andean cultural perspective. In *Plants in Indigenous Medicine and Diet: Biobehavioral Approaches*. N. L. Etkin, ed. Pp. 306–328. Taylor and Francis (Redgrave), New York.

Weinberg, Bennett A., and Bonnie K. Bealer. 2001. *The World of Caffeine: The Science and Culture of the World's Most Popular Drug*. Routledge, New York.

Whitaker, I. S., J. Rao, D. Izadi, and P. E. Butler. 2004a. *Hirudo medicinalis*: ancient origins of, and trends in the use of, medicinal leeches throughout history. *British Journal of Oral and Maxillofacial Surgery* 42(2): 133–137.

Whitaker, I. S., D. Izadi, D. W. Oliver, G. Monteath, and P. E. Butler. 2004b. *Hirudo medicinalis* and the plastic surgeon. *British Journal of Plastic Surgery* 57(4): 348–353.

Whittaker, Robert H., and Paul P. Feeny. 1971. Allelochemicals: chemical interactions between species. *Science* 171: 757–770.

Whyte, Susan Reynolds, Sjaak van der Geest, and Anita Hardon. 2002. *Social Lives of Medicines*. Cambridge University Press, Cambridge.

Wiley, Andrea S. 2004. "Drink milk for fitness": the cultural politics of human biological variation and milk consumption in the United States. *American Anthropologist* 106(3): 506–517.

Williams, David E. 1993. *Lycianthes moziniana* (Solanaceae): an underutilized Mexican food plant with "new" crop potential. *Economic Botany* 47: 387–400.

Williams, Robert R. 1961. *Toward the Conquest of Beriberi*. Harvard University Press, Cambridge, Mass.

Wilson, Philip K. 1992. Acquiring surgical know-how: occupational and lay instruction in early eighteenth-century London. In *The Popularization of Medicine, 1650–1850*. R. Potter, ed. Pp. 42–71. Routledge, New York.

Woloson, Wendy A. 2002. *Refined Tastes: Sugar, Confectionery, and Consumers in Nineteenth-Century America*. Johns Hopkins University Press, Baltimore, Md.

Won, H. S., S. S. Kim, S. J. Jung, W. S. Son, B. Lee, and B. J. Lee. 2004. Structure-activity relationships of antimicrobial peptides from the skin of *Rana esculenta* in Korea. *Molecules and Cells* 17(3): 469–476.

Wood, B. J. B. 1998. Protein-rich foods based on fermented vegetables. In *Microbiology of Fermented Foods*. 2nd ed. B. J. B. Wood, ed. Pp. 484–504. Blackie Academic, London.

Worthen, D. B. 2004. Pharmacy through the ages: medicinal leeches. *Journal of the American Pharmaceutical Association* 44(1): 51.

Wrangham, Richard. 1992. The taste of birds: *pitohui*! *Science* 258: 1867.

Wrick, Kathie L. 1994. The potential role of functional foods in medicine and public health. In *Functional Foods: Designer Foods, Pharmafoods, Nutraceuticals*. I. Goldberg, ed. Pp. 480–494. Chapman and Hall, New York.

Wu, A. H., D. Yang, and M. C. Pike. 2000. A meta-analysis of soyfoods and risk of stomach cancer: the problem of potential confounders. *Cancer Epidemiology, Biomarkers and Prevention* 10: 1051–1058.

Yanagimoto, K., H. Ochi, K. G. Lee, and T. Shibamoto. 2004. Antioxidative activities of fractions obtained from brewed coffee. *Journal of Agricultural and Food Chemistry* 52(3): 592–596.

Yi, Dang, Peng Yong, and Li Wenkui. 1999. *Chinese Functional Food*. New World Press, Beijing, China.

Yokota, T., T. Hattori, H. Ohishi, K. Hasegawa, and K. Watanabe. 1996. The effect of antioxidant-containing fraction from fermented soybean food on atherosclerosis development in cholesterol-fed rabbits. *Lebensmittel-Wissenschaft und Technologie/Food Science and Technology* 29: 751–755.

Young, Allen M. 1994. *The Chocolate Tree*. Smithsonian Institution Press, Washington, D.C.

Young, James H. 1978. The agile role of food: some historical reflections. In *Nutrition and Drug Interrelations*. J. N. Hancock and J. Coon, eds. Pp. 1–18. Academic Press, New York.

Young, Kenneth R. 2004. Environmental consequences of coca/cocaine in Peru: policy alternatives and a research agenda. In *Dangerous Harvest: Drug Plants and the Transformation of Indigenous Landscapes*. M. K. Steinberg, J. J. Hobbs, and Kent Mathewson, eds. Pp. 249–273. Oxford University Press, New York.

Yukuchi, Hiroya, Tsutomu Goto, and Shigeo Okonogi. 1992. The nutritional and physiological value of fermented milks and lactic milk drinks. In *Functions of Fermented Milk: Challenges for the Health Sciences*. B. W. Howells (trans.), Y. Nakazawa and A. Hosono, eds. Pp. 217–245. Elsevier Science, Essex, England.

Yussman, S. M., S. A. Ryan, P. Auinger, and M. Weitzman. 2004. Visits to complementary and alternative medicine providers by children and adolescents in the United States. *Ambulatory Pediatrics* 4(5): 429–435.

Zeina, Baasam, Ben I. Zohra, and Saada Al-Assad. 1997. The effects of honey on leishmania parasites: an in vitro study. *Tropical Doctor* 27(Suppl. 1): 36–38.

Zhao, W., F. Entschladen, H. Liu, B. Niggemann, Q. Fang, K. S. Zaenker, and R. Han. 2003. Boswellic acid acetate induces differentiation and apoptosis in highly metastatic melanoma and fibrosarcoma cells. *Cancer Detection and Prevention* 27(1): 67–75.

Zhen, Yong-Su, ed. 2002. *Tea: Bioactivity and Therapeutic Potential*. Taylor and Francis, London.

Ziegler, H. L., H. Franzyk, M. Sairafianpour, M. Tabatabai, M. D. Tehrani, K. Bagherzadeh, H. Hagerstrand, D. Staerk, and J. W. Jaroszewski. 2004. Erythrocyte membrane modifying agents and the inhibition of *Plasmodium falciparum* growth. *Bioorganic and Medicinal Chemistry* 12(1): 119–127.

Zimian, Ding, Zhao Yonghua, and Gao Xiwu. 1997. Medicinal insects in China. *Ecology of Food and Nutrition* 36(2–4): 209–220.

General Index

Horse, 175
Horseradish, 85t, 86t
Horticulture, 15, 17, 27–28, 37, 41
Hospital, 52, 69
Hospitality. *See* Sociability
Human ecology, 4, 124, 227
Humoral pathology and therapy, 46–49,
  51–53, 56–59, 61, 63–64, 136, 139, 181;
  erosion of, 64–65, 67, 70, 83,
  238n2(chap. 2). *See also* Binary
  opposition

Iboga, 175
Identity, 32, 36, 40–42, 84, 91, 202, 222, 225–
  228; and insects, 190–191; and social
  plants, 143, 165–166, 171, 241n8
Immune function disorders and therapies,
  12, 118, 123, 131–132, 155, 191, 200, 202,
  206, 209, 223; celiac, 214; lymph, 165
Infectious diseases and therapies, 19, 67,
  70–75, 80, 121, 123, 131–132, 206, 215;
  anthrax, 66, 72; antiamoebic, 178; antibacterial, 140t, 161, 165, 175–176, 194–195,
  241n5; antibiotic, 72–74, 80, 196–197;
  antimicrobial, 7, 9, 12, 35, 73–75, 97–100,
  103, 120–122, 127, 130–131, 141–142, 174,
  181, 202, 239n4–5; antiparasitic, 175, 177;
  antiseptic, 66, 68, 193; antiviral, 123, 140t,
  161, 175, 180, 201; chicken pox, 93, 201;
  cholera, 97–98; diphtheria, 66–67; distemper, 158; dysentery, 98, 122, 170;
  erysipelas, 72; fungicide, 11t, 140t, 145,
  175–176, 194–195, 241n5; giardiasis, 202;
  leishmania, 180, 201; leprosy, 41, 52;
  malaria, 28, 58, 63, 73–74, 140t, 178, 193;
  measles, 28, 34, 93, 170, 194, 201, 223;
  meningitis, 74; nemocide, 178; plague,
  52; polio, 80; puerperal fever, 74–75, 191;
  rabies, 192t; scarlet fever, 66, 74; schistosomiasis, 74; sleeping sickness, 74; smallpox, 28, 52, 63, 201; staphylococcal, 98,
  121; streptococcal, 72; tetanus, 192t; tuberculosis, 74–76, 79–80, 98, 154, 223;

typhoid, 154; typhus, 97; vaccination, 63,
  66, 80; whooping cough, 223
Inflammation and therapies, 36, 57, 106,
  182, 192t, 193t, 215; anti-inflammatory,
  12–13, 103, 115, 140t, 141–142, 148, 155, 161,
  165, 170, 180–181, 201; edema, 61, 63, 106,
  192t
Insects: edible, 184–190; medicinal, 190–
  202
Integrative medicine, 205. *See also* Holism
Ipecac, 58

Jaguar, 175
Jasmine, 162

Kale, 12
Kava, 143–145, 172
Kayapó, 190, 194, 198, 201
Khat, 146–147, 172
Koala bear, 115
Koch, Robert, 66, 70, 75, 238n1(chap. 2);
  *The Etiology of Traumatic Infective Dis-
  eases*, 66–67
Kola, 10, 138t, 167–171, 227, 242n9; Coca
  Cola, 138t, 169; Pepsi Cola, 242n9
Korean traditional medicine, 191, 192t
Kumquat, 162
Kutaj, 175

Lac insect, 193t
Lactation, 40, 104, 177, 221; and weaning,
  40, 130–132. *See also* Life cycle transitions; Reproductive disorders
Lactic acid bacteria, 111–112, 114, 116, 119–
  122, 125, 130–131; as commodity, 207
Lactose intolerance. *See under* Milk
Larvae, 183, 185–189, 192t, 193–196; agave
  worm, 189; cossid, 193; cutworm, 190; eri
  silkworm, 187; hepialid moth, 195; Mopani worm, 186; palm grub, 186; sago
  grub, 187; scarab, 195; silkworm, 22t, 187,
  191, 192t, 195; witchetty grub, 186, 193.
  See also Maggots

Scientific Index

About the Author

Nina Etkin (deceased) was a professor of anthropology and was the graduate chair at the University of Hawai'i , where she coordinated the medical anthropology concentration. She was also appointed to the Department of Ecology and Health of the University of Hawai'i Medical School. She earned a BA in zoology from Indiana University and an MA and PhD in anthropology from Washington University–St. Louis.

Etkin was best known for her pioneering work on the pharmacologic implications of plant use, especially the interrelations among foods and medicines. Her research addressed both cultural and pharmagologic aspects of botanicals and human cultures, including polypharmacy and the role of complementary and alternative medicines in integrative medicine in the United States. She had field experience in northern Nigeria; in Maluku, eastern Indonesia; and in Hawai'i. Etkin combined in-depth ethnography with laboratory studies through an interdisciplinary perspective that linked physiology, culture, and society to understand the dialectics of nature and culture in diverse ecologic and ethnographic settings.

Etkin was one of the two recipients of the 2009 Distinguished Economic Botanist Award from the Society for Economic Botany, and she was awarded the prestigious Hawai'i Regents' Medal for Excellence in Research. Her extensive list of publications includes *Foods of Association: Biocultural Perspectives on Foods and Beverages that Mediate Sociability* and *Eating on the Wild Side: The Pharmacologic, Ecologic, and Social Implications of Using Noncultigens*, both published by the University of Arizona Press.

CPSIA information can be obtained at www.ICGtesting.com
Printed in the USA
LVOW060306110213

319488LV00004B/6/P